# National Audubon Society Field Guide to North American Birds

A Chanticleer Press Edition

# National Audubon Society Field Guide to North American Birds

*Eastern Region*

Revised Edition

John Bull and John Farrand, Jr.
Revised by John Farrand, Jr.

Visual Key by Amanda Wilson
and Lori Hogan

Alfred A. Knopf, New York

This is a Borzoi Book
Published by Alfred A. Knopf, Inc.

 Published in the United States by Alfred A. Knopf, Inc., New York, and simultaneously in Canada by Random House of Canada Limited, Toronto. Distributed by Random House, Inc., New York. Originally published in the United States in somewhat different form by Alfred A. Knopf, Inc., New York, in 1977.

Prepared and produced by Chanticleer Press, Inc., New York.

Printed and bound in Japan.

Published July, 1977.
Second edition, fully revised, August, 1994.

Library of Congress Cataloging-in-Publication Number: 94-7768
ISBN: 0-679-42852-6

# CONTENTS

# NATIONAL AUDUBON SOCIETY

*The mission of the* NATIONAL AUDUBON SOCIETY *is to conserve and restore natural ecosystems, focusing on birds and other wildlife for the benefit of humanity and the Earth's biological diversity.*

We have 500,000 members and an extensive chapter network, plus a staff of scientists, lobbyists, lawyers, policy analysts, and educators. Through our sanctuaries we manage 150,000 acres of critical habitat.

Our award-winning *Audubon* magazine, sent to all members, carries outstanding articles and color photography on wildlife, nature, and the environment. We also publish *American Birds,* an ornithological journal, *Audubon Activist,* a newsjournal, and *Audubon Adventures,* a newsletter reaching 600,000 elementary school students. Our *World of Audubon* television shows air on TBS and public television.

For information about how you can become a member, please write or call the Membership Department at:

## ACKNOWLEDGMENTS

The revisor is very grateful to Wayne R. Petersen, of the Massachusetts Audubon Society, for his critical reading of the entire text and his comments on the illustrations. His scrutiny has improved the accuracy of the book, but any remaining errors are the responsibility of the revisor.

This revision has been made possible by the creative and enthusiastic contributions of Andrew Stewart and his staff at Chanticleer Press: Edie Locke, Lori Hogan, Amanda Wilson, Deirdre Duggan Ventry, and Kelly Beekman.

Paul Steiner, the founding publisher of Chanticleer Press, and Milton Rugoff, Gudrun Buettner, Susan Rayfield, Mary Suffudy, Kathy Ritchell, Helga Lose, and Carol Nehring all made highly valuable contributions to the first edition of this field guide.

This revision has benefited greatly from the editorial skills of Patricia Fogarty.

The revised edition follows the effective and workable design created by Massimo Vignelli for the first edition.

The original range maps were researched by David Ewert, John Dunn, and Kimball Garrett, and were coordinated by Jill Farmer. The range maps themselves, including recent revisions, have been skillfully rendered by Paul Singer.

# THE AUTHORS

*John Bull,* a leading authority on birds of the Northeast, has been on the staff of the Ornithology Department of the American Museum of Natural History since 1962. He is the author of two classics on Eastern birds, *Birds of the New York City Area* (1964) and *Birds of New York State* (1974); author of a four-volume set of books on herons, ducks, owls, and swallows (Communications Ventures, 1975, 1976); editor of *Guide to Birds of the World* (Simon & Schuster, 1981); co-author of the *Macmillan Field Guides to Birds of North America,* Eastern and Western Regions (1985, 1989); and a contributor of articles on birds to various books and magazines. He has also served as a nature guide on tours around the world, including Africa, South America, the United States, the Caribbean, and Australia. He has been a delegate to many meetings of the International Ornithological Congress and received a National Science Foundation grant in 1973. He has given courses in ornithology for Cornell's Adult University and for the New School for Social Research in New York City.

*John Farrand, Jr.,* has authored several field guides, including the *National Audubon Society Handbooks* (McGraw-

Hill, 1988) and several volumes in the *National Audubon Society Pocket Guide* series (Knopf). He was the general editor of the *National Audubon Society Master Guide to Birding* (Knopf, 1983). He is a past president of the Linnaean Society of New York, a Life Elective Member of the American Ornithologists' Union, and a Life Member of the Wilson Ornithological Society. Before becoming a free-lance nature writer, he served in the Division of Birds at the Smithsonian Institution and the Ornithology Department of the American Museum of Natural History. He has watched birds in most parts of North America, as well as in Central America, South America, Europe, Turkey, and East Africa.

# INTRODUCTION

Each year thousands of people take up the absorbing hobby of bird-watching, or birding. Regardless of their motives, their first goal is learning to identify the hundreds of species in their own area. This book has been prepared with the intention of making that step as simple and pleasurable as possible. The book's pocket size and its format make it easy to carry into the field and consult on the spot. Take it with you. And welcome to the hobby, or sport, or science, of birding.

**Geographical Scope**

A number of American bird guides divide North America into eastern and western regions at the 100th meridian. This is an arbitrary line that bears no relationship to natural habitats. We have chosen a line (see map) that follows the eastern front of the Rocky Mountains, a natural barrier in the range of many eastern and western birds. Of course, many birds can and do pass over this barrier in both directions. People who live near the dividing line may need to own both this guide and its western companion, the *National Audubon Society Field Guide to North American Birds (Western Region).* Slowly but surely, the number of species found on both sides is increasing. Indeed, an ornithologist long ago predicted that by the year 2000 all the species in the

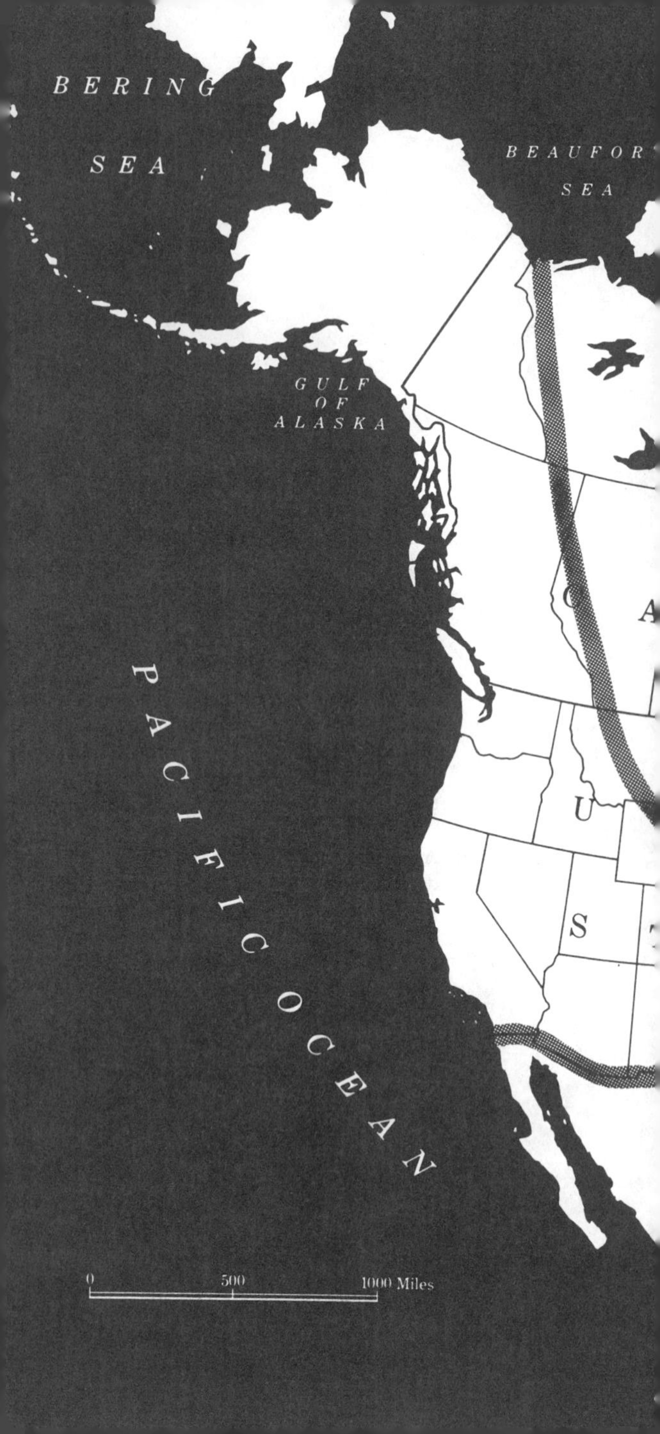
BERING
SEA
BEAUFOR
SEA
GULF
OF
ALASKA
C
A
U
S
PACIFIC OCEAN
0
500
1000 Miles

GREENLAND
BAFFIN BAY
HUDSON BAY
N A D A
I T E D
A T E S
ATLANTIC OCEAN
GULF OF MEXICO
CUBA
XICO
CARIBBEAN SEA

United States will have reached California. This prophecy has not yet been fulfilled, but the century is not yet over.

### Photographs as a Visual Guide

There are two major ways of illustrating bird guides, each with its advantages and disadvantages: One is the traditional way, by means of paintings, and the other is a newer way, by means of photographs. In these guides we have chosen to use color photographs because it has become possible in recent years to obtain superb photographic portraits of almost every bird seen regularly in North America. In using the work of America's leading bird photographers, we believe we have added an exciting dimension to what generally appears in guides illustrated by an artist. Every artist's rendering of a bird is his own interpretation, whereas a good photograph captures the natural color and stance of birds as one usually sees them. In most instances it also shows birds in their usual habitat or in a typical natural setting, making identification that much easier. Finally there is the beauty of pictures made by outstanding photographers: This guide is meant to be a delight to look at as well as use.

### How the Guide Works

In most field guides the birds are arranged according to scientific classification, which is based on anatomic or even biochemical differences. These features can be subtle or even invisible in a living bird. What a birder first notes when he or she glimpses a bird is its size, shape, and color. But if he then consults a standard field guide, organized by families, he must already know what family the bird belongs to—whether it is a warbler, a vireo, a finch—in order to locate it in the guide. What he generally ends up doing is thumbing laboriously through the book until he happens on an illustration that resembles the bird he has seen. By the time he finds what he is looking for, the bird may have disappeared. A new birder must go through this trial-and-error procedure each time he tries to identify a bird. To avoid this hit-or-miss approach, the photographs in this guide have been organized on visual principles, that is, by what you see. The 646 photographs (in the first half of the book) are arranged according to a bird's shape and, in most cases, its color or pattern. Captions under each pictured species include the plate number (which refers to the photograph), the size of the bird, and the number of the page on which the species is described in the text. If the photograph is not of a breeding male—or an adult if the sexes are alike—that is also indicated. Since you may be afforded only a brief glimpse of a bird, you must learn to note essential details quickly. Such essentials include the following:

**Field Marks** When you see a new bird, make note of such points as the size and shape of the bill (whether long or short, slender or stout, curved or straight), the tail (long or short, rounded, squared, wedge-shaped, notched, or forked), and the wings (long or short, rounded or pointed). Note any distinctive features such as a crest, eye rings, or wing bars, or a flashing white patch in the wings, in the tail, or on the rump. Many species have color patterns that identify them at a glance; by studying the pictures in this book in advance, you may be able to identify many species at first sight.

**Relative Size** It is useful to keep in mind the sizes of a few common species like the House Sparrow, Blue Jay, American Robin, and American Crow so that you can quickly estimate the relative size of an unfamiliar bird.

**Behavior** Note what the bird is doing. Is it alone, or in a flock? Is it walking like a starling, or hopping like a sparrow? Is it foraging in foliage, like a warbler or a vireo? Is it foraging on the ground like a thrasher or a sparrow? Is it creeping about on the trunk of a tree? If so, is it hitching up the tree like a woodpecker or a creeper, or is it working its way headfirst down the trunk like a nuthatch? If the bird is in flight, is it flapping or soaring? If it is soaring, are the wings held horizontally, as with gulls and most hawks, or in a shallow V or dihedral, as with the Turkey Vulture, Rough-legged Hawk, and Northern Harrier? If the bird is in the water, is it feeding at the surface or diving? Make note also of the bird's song or calls.

**What the Photographs Show** Most of the photographs show adult males, or adults when the sexes are alike, since the plumages of these are characteristic of a species, but pictures of females (♀), immatures (imm.), juveniles (juv.), color phases, and birds in winter plumage are also included when they differ significantly from the typical breeding male or adult.
The photographs are grouped according to (*a*) obvious similarities in appearance, such as "Long-legged Waders" or "Duck-like Birds," or (*b*) a visible similarity in behavior or habitat, as in "Tree-clinging Birds." Sometimes (*a*) and (*b*) coincide, as in "Chicken-like Marsh Birds," many of which not only look alike but have much the same lifestyle and live in the same habitat.

**Groups** The photographs are grouped as follows:

Long-legged Waders
Gull-like Birds
Upright-perching Water Birds
Duck-like Birds
Sandpiper-like Birds
Chicken-like Marsh Birds
Upland Ground Birds

Owls
Hawk-like Birds
Pigeon-like Birds
Swallow-like Birds
Tree-clinging Birds
Perching Birds:
- Brown
- Red
- Orange
- Yellow
- Olive
- Green
- Blue
- Gray
- Black

These broad categories are of course not foolproof and are intended to serve only as a starting point.
Within each major category, the birds are grouped according to other similarities. Thus, among the "Duck-like Birds" the photographs of the Canvasback and Redhead, or of the Common Goldeneye and Barrow's Goldeneye, are shown together so that they can be compared at a glance. Similarly, among the "Tree-clinging Birds" all the woodpeckers with barred backs are placed together for easy comparison.

**Silhouette and Thumbprint Guides**

Preceding the photographs is a section showing silhouettes of birds typical of each group. For example, the "Long-legged Waders" are represented by a silhouette of an ibis; and each type of bird within this group, such as herons, bitterns, and cranes, is also represented by a typical silhouette. To make it easy to locate each group, a silhouette typical of the group has been inset as a "thumbprint" on the left of all the picture spreads in that section.

**Perching Birds: Grouped by Color**

The perching birds are by far the largest category, but that term is now technically restricted to the songbirds that make up the group known as the passerines. We have included additional species that we thought belonged best in this section, such as cuckoos, kingfishers, and hummingbirds. Because songbirds are so numerous, these birds are arranged according to their most prominent color (either an overall color or only a distinctive patch) in the following nine groups: Brown, Red, Orange, Yellow, Olive, Green, Blue, Gray, and Black.

This arrangement of the perching birds by color depends, of course, on such factors as the light in which a bird is seen or even on individual judgment as to color. A few birds, such as the multicolored male Painted Bunting, do not fit easily into any single color category. We have placed each species in the color category where it seemed to fit best. Since most birds the average birder will see are perching birds, this color key will help you make a more rapid initial identification.

Finally, following this Introduction, under the title "How to Use This Guide" are samples of how to use this book to identify a particular bird.

**Species Accounts: Arranged by Family**

In the species accounts, which follow the color plates, birds have been grouped according to their formal classification, as given in the 1983 edition of the American Ornithologists' Union's *Check-list of North American Birds* and as revised in *Check-list* supplements published through 1994. Bird species are grouped into families. At the beginning of each family's section in the text, a short essay provides general information about the birds in the family, emphasizing features its members share. The scientific classification can help in the identification process: Even if you pick the wrong photograph you will be referred to a species account within a family of similar birds. Reading about the various members of the family may allow you to identify the bird you saw.

The number to the left of the bird's English name is that of the photograph of the bird.

**English and Scientific Names** The English or "common" names of birds are those accepted in the American Ornithologists' Union's *Check-list of North American Birds,* as revised through 1994. When a bird has recently had a different but widely used English name, we have included this name in quotation marks.

Every bird has a scientific name consisting of two Greek or Latin words. The first word is the genus and the second is the species. The genus, which is always capitalized, may include a number of species. Thus, the scientific name of the Mallard, *Anas platyrhynchos,* tells us that it is a member of the genus *Anas,* which includes most of the surface-feeding or dabbling ducks in North America and elsewhere. The species name, *platyrhynchos,* refers specifically to the Mallard. The scientific name of the Green-winged Teal, *Anas crecca,* tells us at once that this is another species of dabbling duck, closely related to the Mallard. Since common names vary not only from country to country but even from region to region within North America, the scientific names identify birds everywhere and provide ornithologists with an international language.

**Species Descriptions** The first paragraph of each species account describes the physical characteristics of that bird—its size, color, distinguishing marks or features—often with reference to another related or similar bird. The description of each species covers all or almost all of the following:

**Size** Measurements of average overall length (from tip of bill to tip of tail) of each species are given in inches, along with the metric equivalent. Since

measurements of either living birds or museum specimens depend on the way they are measured as well as the individual bird, these measurements are only approximate and are useful mainly for comparison.
Wingspread measurement (W.) is given for many of the larger birds.

Color and Plumage

The opening paragraph of each species account covers physical characteristics and plumage. In general, the most striking or distinctive features or field marks are italicized. While species such as the Blue Jay and the American Crow look much the same throughout the year and at every age, in many birds the plumage varies with age, sex, or season. In the European Starling, for example, adults of both sexes look much alike, but juveniles, instead of being glossy black like the adults, are dull gray; adults have white spots in winter and, except in late fall and early winter, a yellow bill. The breeding plumage is usually the brightest plumage in both sexes and is generally worn in spring and summer.
The young of some species, such as the Herring Gull, pass through a number of distinct plumages before they acquire their final adult plumage. In many species the male and female differ in appearance, but the young bird looks like the female; in the Northern Cardinal, for example, the adult male is bright red, while the female and young are duller and browner. Many species show seasonal variation: Male Scarlet Tanagers are bright red during the breeding season but in the fall acquire an olive green plumage not unlike that of the female. These variations in plumage may be puzzling at first, but one soon learns to recognize the major variations in each species.
For several species that resemble each other closely, we have described the features that distinguish them. Certain

birds, such as some of the hawks, ducks, gulls, and swallows, are likely to be glimpsed in flight. To help in recognizing them on the wing, many drawings of birds in flight have been provided.

Voice Most species have characteristic songs and calls. A few birds, among them some of the dull-colored flycatchers, are more readily identified by their songs and calls than by appearance. The song, generally more complex than any of the calls, is given to advertise ownership of a nesting or feeding territory, and in most species is sung only by males. Calls are usually shorter and simpler, and generally express some emotion, such as alarm or anger. A brief description or a simple phonetic transcription is given for all species. Although one can now obtain recordings of voices of many species, a knowledge of calls is best gained by experience with birds in the field.

Habitat We next describe the habitat or habitats that each species prefers—beaches, lakes, deciduous forests, grasslands, city parks, suburban areas—as well as the type of area preferred within the habitat. When a species has a different habitat during the winter from that occupied during the breeding season, this, too, is indicated.

Nesting The eggs and nests of each species are briefly described. The number of eggs given is the range normally found in a nest; sometimes a larger clutch may be found, perhaps due to the fact that a second female has laid eggs in a nest.

Range The geographic range in North America is given for all species, even when the bird is one whose range extends beyond this continent. The breeding range is described first, followed by detailed information on the North American portion of the winter range. Following common practice, we have generally

given the range of each species from west to east and from north to south. We have tried to name enough localities for the reader to be able to draw a clear line between the various points. Thus, when we say that the Yellow-throated Warbler breeds from Illinois, Ohio, and New Jersey south to Missouri, Texas, the Gulf Coast, and northern Florida, a line connecting the first three localities defines the northern limits of the species' breeding range and another line, drawn through the last four localities, gives the southern limits.
The term "local" is used when birds occur at widely scattered localities, usually because of very specific habitat requirements.

**Range Maps** In addition to a statement of the geographic range, a range map is provided for species of more than irregular or casual occurrence within the area covered by this book. No range maps are provided for exclusively oceanic species or for species that appear only occasionally and in unpredictable places. On these maps the following designations are used:

Breeding range

Winter range

Areas in which a species occurs in both winter and summer are indicated by cross-hatching:

Permanent range

**Notes** At the end of each species account are notes on such subjects as behavior and feeding habits, population status, and lore.

**How to Find Birds** Although it is almost impossible to go outdoors without seeing at least a few birds, some advance planning will enable you to increase the number of species you see on a field trip. Many birds tend to confine their activity to one particular habitat, so you should plan to visit as many different habitats as possible during a day of birding. A good system is to begin your field trip at dawn, going first to a freshwater marsh. Rails, bitterns, and other marsh birds are most active and vocal at that hour, and a few minutes in a marsh at sunrise can be more productive than several hours later in the day. From the marsh you can go on to woodlands, fields, or thickets. Until the middle of the morning most songbirds are busily searching for food and singing and are relatively easy to see. From mid-morning until late in the afternoon land birds are quiet, while the birds of the beaches, lakes, and other aquatic or marine habitats are active all day. The middle of the day, then, is the time to search for herons, cormorants, ducks, and sandpipers. Late in the day land birds start singing and foraging again, so you can return to woods and other inland habitats to find species you may have missed in the morning. To round out a full day of birding, make an after-dark visit to a forest or wooded swamp to listen for owls.

The greatest variety of birds can be seen during the migration seasons. It is therefore a good idea to plan several field trips during the spring and fall. In spring the best time to search is during the latter half of April and the first half of May, when most songbirds migrate north through eastern North America. Most migrating birds fly at night, breaking their journey during the day, when they rest and feed. They tend to gather in quiet places where food is easy to find. In a light woodland along a stream, where there are newly opened leaves and an abundance of small insects, it is possible to see as many as two dozen species of warblers in a single spring morning. Migrating songbirds also concentrate in isolated groves of trees along the coast or on the prairie, and in well-planted city parks. When the land bird migration tapers off in late May, sandpipers and plovers are still flying through. Then is the time to visit beaches, lakes, and marshes. The fall migration is under way by August, when the first of the sandpipers and plovers reappear. In September and October most of the songbirds pass through. The migration of ducks, geese, and other water birds continues into November; visits to lakes and bays will pay dividends then. While many species are rather tame, others are shy or secretive. Learn to move slowly and quietly and avoid wearing brightly colored or black clothing. Some of these elusive birds can be lured into view by an imitation of the sound of a bird in distress, or by a whistled imitation of an Eastern Screech-Owl. Rails and certain other secretive species can be attracted by playing tape recordings of their calls.

# PARTS OF A BIRD

The generalized drawing of a bird on the following two pages shows the external parts of a bird that are mentioned frequently in the species accounts in this book. Definitions of terms that are not in everyday use (such as "gorget" or "mantle") will also be found in the Glossary on pp. 765–770.

Crown

Eye stripe / Forehead

Nares

Auriculars / Upper mandible / Lower mandible

Nape

Chin

Side of neck

Throat

Mantle

Back

Breast

Scapulars / Bend of wing

Shoulder

Wing coverts

Side

Secondaries

Rump

Flank

Abdomen or Belly

Upper tail coverts

Primaries

Under tail coverts

Tail feathers or Rectrices

Tarsus

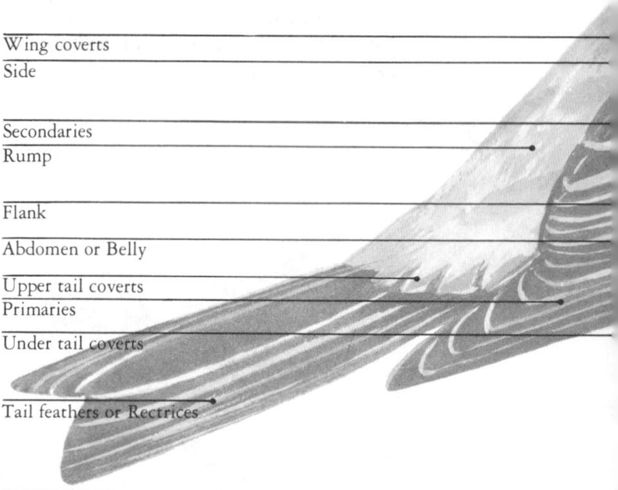

Example: A Bird Clinging to a Tree Trunk

You have seen a sparrow-sized bird with a longish bill creeping down the trunk of a maple or other deciduous tree. It was grayish blue above, with a white face, black cap, and white breast.

1. To make sure it was one of the Tree-clinging Birds, check the typical silhouettes preceding the entire color section.
2. Turn to the photographs in the section labeled Tree-clinging Birds.
3. Among the 20 photographs in this section, all showing birds clinging to the trunks of trees, some have red on the cap or body, several have black, and one is brown. Only two, the White-breasted Nuthatch and the Red-breasted Nuthatch, have grayish-blue backs and a black cap.
4. Under the photographs you find the numbers of the pages on which the nuthatches are described. The Red-breasted and White-breasted nuthatches both have grayish-blue upperparts. The Red-breasted Nuthatch has rusty underparts and a prominent white eyebrow, and is usually found in conifers, while the White-breasted Nuthatch has a white face and underparts, no distinct eyebrow, and is usually seen in deciduous trees. Although both of these nuthatches

habitually creep downward on tree trunks, your bird is obviously a White-breasted Nuthatch.

Example: Birds Flying Over a Beach

You have seen several birds flying overhead. They had white bodies with gray backs, white tails, yellow legs and feet, and bills that were yellow and black.

1. You turn to the bird silhouettes at the opening of the color section and find that your birds look most like the gulls found on Plates 31–55.
2. After glancing at the color plates, you find that the Herring Gull, Ring-billed Gull, and Glaucous Gull all resemble the birds you saw. But the Glaucous Gull has no black on its wing tips or bill, and the Herring Gull has pinkish feet and no black on its bill. Only the Ring-billed Gull seems to fit.
3. In the captions under the plates you find the page numbers on which these three birds are described. The descriptions confirm that the birds you saw were Ring-billed Gulls.

# Part I
# Color Key

## Keys to the Color Plates

The color plates in the following pages are divided into thirteen groups:

Long-legged Waders
Gull-like Birds
Upright-perching Water Birds
Duck-like Birds
Sandpiper-like Birds
Chicken-like Marsh Birds
Upland Ground Birds
Owls
Hawk-like Birds
Pigeon-like Birds
Swallow-like Birds
Tree-clinging Birds
Perching Birds

**Thumb Prints** To make it easy to locate a group, a typical outline of a bird from that group is inset as a thumb print at the left edge of each double-page of plates. Thus you can find the Long-legged Waders by flipping through the color pages until you come to a series of thumb prints showing the outline of a typical wading bird.

**Silhouettes of the Families in Each Group** To help you recognize birds by their general shape, the color plates are preceded by pages showing you silhouettes of the families in each group. If the bird you saw looks like one of these silhouettes, you will find the bird in that group.

**Captions** The caption under each photograph gives the common name of the bird, its size, and the page number on which it is described. The color plate number is repeated in front of each description as a cross reference.
Most of the photographs show birds in typical breeding plumage. Certain birds, as indicated in the caption, are also shown in distinctive immmature, juvenile or winter plumage.

| Symbol | Category |
| --- | --- |
|  | Long-legged Waders |

| Family Symbols | | Plate Numbers |
|---|---|---|
|  | herons, egrets | 1–9, 13–20, 28 |
|  | storks | 10 |
|  | spoonbills | 29 |
|  | flamingos | 30 |
|  | bitterns | 25–26 |
|  | limpkins | 21 |
|  | ibises | 12, 22–24 |
|  | cranes | 11, 27 |

| Symbol | Category |
| --- | --- |
|  | Gull-like Birds |

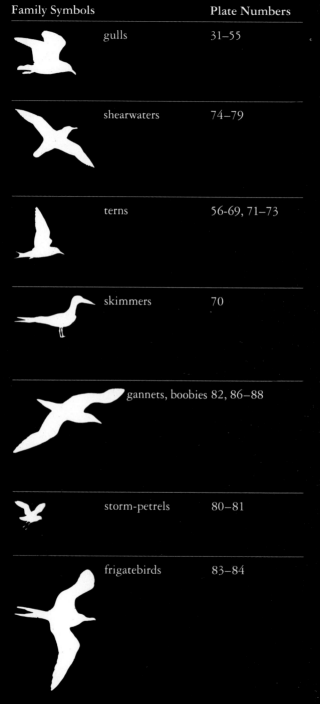

| Family Symbols | | Plate Numbers |
|---|---|---|
|  | gulls | 31–55 |
|  | shearwaters | 74–79 |
|  | terns | 56-69, 71–73 |
|  | skimmers | 70 |
|  | gannets, boobies | 82, 86–88 |
|  | storm-petrels | 80–81 |
|  | frigatebirds | 83–84 |

| Symbol | Category |
| --- | --- |
|  | Gull-like Birds |
|  | Upright-perching Water Birds |
|  | Duck-like Birds |

| Family Symbols | | Plate Numbers |
|---|---|---|
|  | skuas, jaegers | 89–93 |
|  | tropicbirds | 85 |
|  | auks, murres, puffins | 100–107 |
|  | cormorants | 95–96, 98–99 |
|  | anhingas | 94, 97 |
|  | surface-feeding ducks | 111–112, 114 116–119, 134, 149, 156–165, 168 |
|  | diving ducks | 108–110, 113, 115, 120–126, 130–131, 135–155, 166–167 |

| Symbol | Category |
|---|---|
|  | Duck-like Birds |

| Family Symbols | | Plate Numbers |
|---|---|---|
|  | stiff-tailed ducks | 133, 151 |
|  | mergansers | 128–129, 132, 169–171 |
|  | coots | 127 |
|  | whistling-ducks | 172–173 |
|  | geese | 174–179 |
|  | swans | 180–181 |
|  | pelicans | 182–183 |
|  | grebes | 184–187 193–199 |
|  | loons | 188–192 |

| Symbol | Category |
| --- | --- |
| 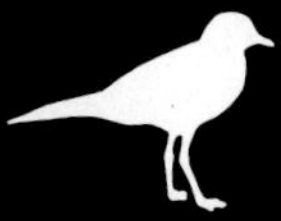 | Sandpiper-like Birds |
|  | Chicken-like Marsh Birds |

| Family Symbols | | Plate Numbers |
|---|---|---|
|  | sandpipers | 200–212, 214–215, 217–238 |
| 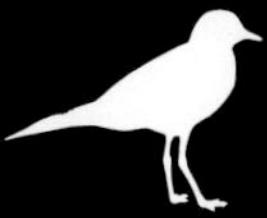 | plovers, turnstones | 213, 216, 250–258 |
|  | phalaropes | 243, 245–249 |
| 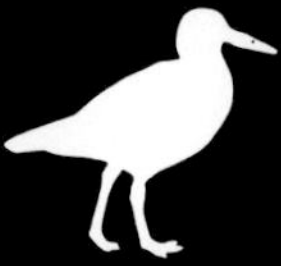 | oystercatchers | 244 |
|  | avocets, stilts | 239–241 |
|  | rails, gallinules | 259–266 |
|  | jacanas | 267 |

| Symbol | Category |
| --- | --- |
|  | Upland Ground Birds |
|  | Owls |

| Family Symbols | | Plate Numbers |
|---|---|---|
|  | snipes, woodcocks | 242, 288 |
|  | quails, partridges, pheasants | 269–271, 274, 286–287 |
|  | grouse | 272–273, 275–283 |
|  | turkeys | 284–285 |
|  | roadrunners | 289 |
|  | chachalacas | 268 |
|  | nightjars | 290–296 |
|  | true owls | 297–309 |
|  | barn owls | 310 |

| Symbol | Category |
| --- | --- |
|  | Hawk-like Birds |

| Family Symbols | | Plate Numbers |
|---|---|---|
|  | hawks | 324, 327–336, 338 |
|  | kites | 315–320 |
|  | eagles | 321–323 |
|  | ospreys | 313 |
|  | harriers | 325–326 |
|  | caracaras | 314 |
|  | falcons | 337, 339–343 |
|  | vultures | 311–312 |

| Symbol | Category |
| --- | --- |
|  | Pigeon-like Birds |
|  | Swallow-like Birds |
|  | Tree-clinging Birds |
|  | Perching Birds |

| Family Symbols | | Plate Numbers |
|---|---|---|
|  | pigeons, doves | 344–352 |
|  | swallows | 353–361 |
|  | swifts | 362 |
|  | woodpeckers | 363–378 |
|  | nuthatches | 379–381 |
|  | creepers | 382 |
|  | wood warblers | 439–440, 446, 459–461, 500, 504–517, 519–538, 543–544, 574, 600–601, 610, 618–619, 629 |
|  | vireos | 547, 566–573 |

| Symbol | Category |
| --- | --- |
|  | Perching Birds |

| Family Symbols | | Plate Numbers |
| --- | --- | --- |
|  | titmice | 518, 616–617, 621–623 |
|  | cardinals, grosbeaks | 383, 4[redacted]57, 482, 4[redacted]01, 592, 608–609, 624 |
|  | buntings, finches, sparrows | 384, 38[redacted]90–395, 397[redacted]98, 400–420, 422, 426–430, 462–464, 474, 481, 483–484, 486–487, 503, 539, 548, 578, 584, 593–594, 602–603, 613, 620, 626 |
|  | orioles, blackbirds | 386–387, 425, 431–434, 477–480, 491–494, 497, 502, 545–546, 628[redacted]30–632, 634[redacted]39 |
|  | tanagers | 488–489, 495–496, 549–550, 595 |
|  | flycatchers | 389, 47[redacted]490, 540–54[redacted]551–565, 604 |
|  | meadowlarks | 498–499 |
|  | thrushes | 385, 435–438, 445, 458, 598–599 |

| Symbol | Category |
| --- | --- |
|  | Perching Birds |

| Family Symbols | | Plate Numbers |
|---|---|---|
|  | mockingbirds, thrashers | 441–444, 611–612 |
|  | shrikes | 614–615 |
|  | jays, magpies | 475, 586, 596–597, 605, 627 |
|  | becards | 575 |
|  | kingfishers | 590–591 |
|  | gnatcatchers, kinglets | 576–577, 607 |
|  | hummingbirds | 579–583 |
|  | parrots | 585, 587–589 |

| Symbol | Category |
|---|---|
|  | Perching Birds |

| Family Symbols | | Plate Numbers |
|---|---|---|
|  | wrens | 465–473 |
|  | waxwings | 450–451 |
|  | bulbuls | 625 |
|  | cuckoos | 447–449, 640–641 |
|  | weaver finches | 396, 399, 421 |
|  | pipits | 423–424 |
|  | larks | 452 |
|  | starlings | 606, 633 |
|  | crows | 642–646 |

The color plates on the following pages are numbered to correspond with the number preceding each species description in the text. Most of the birds shown are adults or adult males, but also shown are some distinctive females, immatures, and juveniles, as well as a few instances of seasonal changes in plumage.

## Long-legged Waders

These are medium to large-sized water birds with long legs adapted for wading in fresh or salt water. Most of these species, such as herons, egrets, cranes, ibises, spoonbills, and flamingos, are conspicuously patterned, and many are entirely white. Others are pink, but some have concealing colors that make them difficult to detect.

1 Cattle Egret, 20″, p. 372

2 Cattle Egret nonbreeding plumage, 20″, p. 372

3 Little Blue Heron imm., 25–30″, p. 370

4 "Great White Heron", 39–52″, p. 367

5 Snowy Egret nonbreeding plumage, 20–27″, p. 369

6 Snowy Egret, 20–27″, p. 369

7 Great Egret nonbreeding plumage, 35–41″, p. 368

8 Great Egret, 35–41″, p. 368

9 Reddish Egret white phase, 30″, p. 371

10 Wood Stork, 40–44″, p. 379

11 Whooping Crane, 45–50″, p. 463

12 White Ibis, 23–27″, p. 376

13 Black-crowned Night-Heron, 23–28″, p. 374

14 Black-crowned Night-Heron imm., 23–28″, p. 374

15 Yellow-crowned Night-Heron, 22–27″, p. 374

16 Yellow-crowned Night-Heron imm., 22–27″, p. 374

17 Little Blue Heron, 25–30″, p. 370

18 Tricolored Heron, 25–30″, p. 370

19 Great Blue Heron, 39–52″, p. 367

20 Reddish Egret dark phase, 30″, p. 371

21 Limpkin, 25–28″, p. 461

22 Glossy Ibis, 22–25″, p. 376

23 White-faced Ibis, 22–25″, p. 377

24 White Ibis imm., 23–27″, p. 376

25 American Bittern, 23–34″, p. 365

26 Least Bittern, 11–14″, p. 366

27 Sandhill Crane, 34–48″, p. 462

28 Green Heron, 16–22″, p. 373

29 Roseate Spoonbill, 30–32″, p. 378

30 Greater Flamingo, 48″, p. 380

## Gull-like Birds

These water birds spend much of their time in flight. All have long, pointed wings. Gulls, terns, gannets, and boobies are predominantly white, while frigatebirds are black. Most of these birds occur along seacoasts or on the ocean, but some of the gulls and terns are found on inland waters.

31 Laughing Gull, 15–17″, p. 503

32 Franklin's Gull, 13–15″, p. 504

33 Common Black-headed Gull, 15″, p. 505

34 Bonaparte's Gull, 12–14″, p. 506

35 Sabine's Gull, 13–14″, p. 514

36 Great Black-backed Gull, 30″, p. 512

37 Thayer's Gull, 24″, p. 509

38 Lesser Black-backed Gull winter plumage, p. 510

39 Glaucous Gull, 28″, p. 511

40 Iceland Gull, 23″, p. 509

41 Ring-billed Gull, 18–20″, p. 507

42 Herring Gull, 23–26″, p. 508

43 Ross' Gull, 12–14″, p. 513

44 Ivory Gull imm., 17″, p. 515

45 Little Gull winter plumage, 11″, p. 504

46 Little Gull imm., 11″, p. 504

47 Iceland Gull imm., 23″, p. 509

48 Ring-billed Gull imm., 18–20″, p. 507

49 Great Black-backed Gull imm., 30″, p. 512

50 Glaucous Gull first winter, 28″, p. 511

51 Herring Gull juv., 23–26″, p. 508

52 Laughing Gull imm., 15–17″, p. 503

53 Bonaparte's Gull winter plumage, 12–14″, p. 506

54 Black-legged Kittiwake, 16–18″, p. 512

56 Common Tern winter plumage, 13–16″, p. 519

57 Forster's Tern winter plumage, 14–15″, p. 521

58 Gull-billed Tern, 13–15″, p. 515

59 Forster's Tern, 14–15″, p. 521

60 Roseate Tern, 14–17″, p. 518

61 Common Tern, 13–16″, p. 519

62 Royal Tern, 18–21″, p. 517

63 Caspian Tern, 19–23″, p. 516

64 Arctic Tern, 14–17″, p. 520

65 Brown Noddy, 15″, p. 525

66 Black Noddy, 12″, p. 525

67 Bridled Tern, 14–15″, p. 522

68 Black Tern, 9–10″, p. 524

69 Sooty Tern, 16″, p. 523

70 Black Skimmer, 18″, p. 526

71 Least Tern, 8–10″, p. 522

72 Sandwich Tern, 16″, p. 518

73 Sandwich Tern winter plumage, 16″, p. 518

74 Audubon's Shearwater, 11–12″, p. 350

75 Cory's Shearwater, 20–22″, p. 347

76 Manx Shearwater, 12½–15″, p. 350

77 Sooty Shearwater, 16–18″, p. 349

78 Greater Shearwater, 18–20″, p. 348

79 Northern Fulmar, 18″, p. 346

80 Wilson's Storm-Petrel, 7″, p. 352

81 Leach's Storm-Petrel, 8–9″, p. 352

82 Northern Gannet imm., 35–40″, p. 356

83 Magnificent Frigatebird, 38–40″, p. 364

84 Magnificent Frigatebird ♀, 38–40″, p. 364

85 White-tailed Tropicbird, 32″, p. 354

86 Northern Gannet, 35–40″, p. 356

87 Masked Booby, 32″, p. 355

88 Brown Booby, 30″, p. 355

89 Great Skua, 23″, p. 502

90 South Polar Skua, 21″, p. 502

91 Long-tailed Jaeger, 21″, p. 501

92 Parasitic Jaeger, 21″, p. 500

93 Pomarine Jaeger, 22″, p. 499

## Upright-perching Water Birds

These birds are usually seen perching on rocks or trees at the edge of the water. In most cases, their feet are located far back on the body, which gives the birds a distinctive upright posture when perching. The murres and puffins are patterned in black and white, while the cormorants and anhingas are largely or entirely black.

94 Anhinga, 34–36″, p. 363

95 Neotropic Cormorant, 25″, p. 362

96 Great Cormorant, 35–40″, p. 360

97 Anhinga ♀, 34–36″, p. 363

98 Double-crested Cormorant, 30–35″, p. 361

99 Double-crested Cormorant imm., 30–35″, p. 361

100 Common Murre, 17″, p. 528

101 Thick-billed Murre, 18″, p. 529

102 Razorbill, 17″, p. 529

103 Dovekie, 8″, p. 527

104 Atlantic Puffin, 12″, p. 531

105 Black Guillemot, 13″, p. 530

106 Common Murre winter plumage, 17″, p. 528

107 Thick-billed Murre winter plumage, 18″, p. 529

## Duck-like Birds

Included here are the many ducks, geese, and swans, as well as other birds that, like the ducks, are usually seen swimming. Many of the male ducks, and breeding-plumaged loons and grebes, are boldly patterned, while female ducks and winter-plumaged loons and grebes are clad in modest browns and grays.

108 Eurasian Wigeon, 18–20″, p. 397

109 Canvasback, 19–24″, p. 398

110 Redhead, 18–22″, p. 399

111 Cinnamon Teal, 14–17″, p. 395

112 [redacted]orthern Pintail, 25–29″, p. 393

113 Masked Duck, 12–14″, p. 415

114 Green-winged Teal, 12–16″, p. 390

115 Bufflehead, 13–15″, p. 411

116 Wood Duck, 17–20″, p. 389

117 American Wigeon, 18–23″, p. 398

118 Northern Shoveler, 17–20″, p. 395

119 Mallard, 18–27″, p. 392

120 Lesser Scaup, 15–18″, p. 402

121 Greater Scaup, 15–20″, p. 401

122 Tufted Duck, 17″, p. 401

123 Ring-necked Duck, 14–18″, p. 400

124 White-winged Scoter, 19–24″, p. 409

125 Black Scoter, 17–21″, p. 407

126 Surf Scoter, 17–21″, p. 408

127 American Coot, 15″, p. 460

128 Common Merganser, 22–27″, p. 413

129 Red-breasted Merganser, 19–26″, p. 414

130 Barrow's Goldeneye, 16½–20″, p. 410

131 Common Goldeneye, 16–20″, p. 409

132 Hooded Merganser, 16–19″, p. 412

133 Ruddy Duck, 14–16″, p. 414

134 Blue-winged Teal, 14–16″, p. 394

135 Harlequin Duck, 14–20″, p. 405

136 King Eider, 18–25″, p. 404

137 Common Eider, 23–27″, p. 403

138 Oldsquaw winter plumage, 19–22″, p. 406

139 Oldsquaw breeding plumage, 19–22″, p. 406

140 Greater Scaup ♀, 15–20″, p. 401

141 Lesser Scaup ♀, 15–18″, p. 402

142 Barrow's Goldeneye ♀, 16½–20″, p. 410

143 Common Goldeneye ♀, 16–20″, p. 409

144 Bufflehead ♀, 13–15″, p. 411

145 Surf Scoter ♀, 17–21″, p. 408

146 Black Scoter ♀, 17–21″, p. 407

147 White-winged Scoter ♀, 19–24″, p. 409

148 Tufted Duck ♀, 17″, p. 401

149 Wood Duck ♀, 17–20″, p. 389

150 Ring-necked Duck ♀, 14–18″, p. 400

151 Ruddy Duck ♀, 14–16″, p. 414

152 Oldsquaw ♀, 15–17″, p. 406

153 Harlequin Duck ♀, 14–20″, p. 405

154 King Eider ♀, 18–25″, p. 404

155 Common Eider ♀, 23–27″, p. 403

156 Gadwall, 18–21″, p. 396

157 Gadwall ♀, 18–21″, p. 396

158 Mallard ♀, 18–27″, p. 392

159 Northern Shoveler ♀, 17–20″, p. 395

160 Green-winged Teal ♀, 12–16″, p. 390

161 Mottled Duck, 21″, p. 391

162 Blue-winged Teal ♀, 14–16″, p. 394

163 Cinnamon Teal ♀, 14–17″, p. 395

164 American Black Duck, 19–22″, p. 390

165 American Wigeon ♀, 18–23″, p. 398

166 Redhead ♀, 18–22″, p. 399

167 Canvasback ♀, 19–24″, p. 398

168 Northern Pintail ♀, 21–23″, p. 393

169 Red-breasted Merganser ♀, 19–26″, p. 414

170 Hooded Merganser ♀, 16–19″, p. 412

171 Common Merganser ♀, 22–27″, p. 413

172 Black-bellied Whistling-Duck, 20–22″, p. 382

173 Fulvous Whistling-Duck, 18–21″, p. 381

174 Brant, 22–30″, p. 387

175 Greater White-fronted Goose, 27–30″, p. 384

176 Ross' Goose, 24″, p. 386

177 Snow Goose, 25–31″, p. 385

178 Snow Goose blue phase, 25–31″, p. 385

179 Canada Goose, 22–45″, p. 388

180 Mute Swan, 58–60″, p. 383

181 Tundra Swan, 48–55″, p. 383

182 American White Pelican, 55–70″, p. 358

183 Brown Pelican, 45–54″, p. 359

184 Red-necked Grebe winter plumage, p. 342

185 Pied-billed Grebe winter plumage, 12–15″, p. 341

186 Horned Grebe winter plumage, 12–15″, p. 341

187 Eared Grebe winter plumage, 12–14″, p. 343

188 Common Loon winter plumage, 28–36″, p. 339

189 Red-throated Loon winter plumage, p. 337

190 Common Loon, 28–36″, p. 339

191 Red-throated Loon, 24–27″, p. 337

192 Pacific Loon, 24″, p. 338

193 Least Grebe, 8–10″, p. 340

194 Red-necked Grebe, 18–20″, p. 342

195 Pied-billed Grebe, 12–15″, p. 341

196 Clark's Grebe, 22–29″, p. 345

197 Western Grebe, 22–29″, p. 344

198 Eared Grebe, 12–14″, p. 343

199 Horned Grebe, 12–15″, p. 341

## Sandpiper-like Birds

This is a large group of small to medium-sized birds that have long legs and slender bills and are usually seen foraging on the beach or along the margins of lakes, ponds, marshes, or streams. Although these birds are collectively called "shorebirds," a few, such as the Killdeer, are often found on bare ground, far from water. Many of these birds are cryptically colored, but some, like the American Oystercatcher and the avocets and stilts, are boldly patterned in black and white.

200 Semipalmated Sandpiper, 5½–6¾″, p. 484

201 Least Sandpiper, 6″, p. 485

202 Western Sandpiper, 6½″, p. 485

203 White-rumped Sandpiper, 7½″, p. 486

204 Purple Sandpiper, 9″, p. 488

205 Baird's Sandpiper, 7½″, p. 487

206 Pectoral Sandpiper, 9″, p. 488

207 Buff-breasted Sandpiper, 8″, p. 491

208 Curlew Sandpiper juv., 8″, p. 490

209 Stilt Sandpiper, 8½", p. 491

210 Spotted Sandpiper, 7½", p. 477

211 Solitary Sandpiper, 8½", p. 475

212 Sanderling, 8″, p. 483

213 Ruddy Turnstone, 8–10″, p. 482

214 Red Knot, 10½″, p. 483

215 Ruff winter plumage, 11″, p. 492

216 Ruddy Turnstone winter plumage, 8–10″, p. 482

217 Upland Sandpiper, 11–12½″, p. 478

218 Spotted Sandpiper winter plumage, 7½″, p. 477

219 Purple Sandpiper winter plumage, 9″, p. 488

220 Least Sandpiper winter plumage, 6″, p. 485

221 Red Knot winter plumage, 10½", p. 483

222 Semipalmated Sandpiper winter plumage, p. 484

223 Stilt Sandpiper winter plumage, 8½", p. 491

224 Sanderling winter plumage, 8″, p. 483

225 Willet winter plumage, 15″, p. 476

226 Dunlin winter plumage, 8½″, p. 489

227 Short-billed Dowitcher winter plumage, p. 493

228 Willet, 15″, p. 476

229 Dunlin, 8½″, p. 489

230 Whimbrel, 17″, p. 479

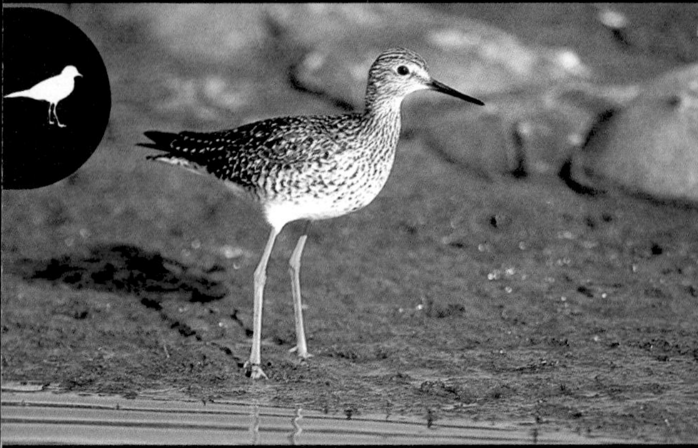

231 Lesser Yellowlegs, 10½″, p. 475

232 Short-billed Dowitcher, 12″, p. 493

233 Long-billed Curlew, 23″, p. 479

234 Greater Yellowlegs, 14″, p. 474

235 Long-billed Dowitcher, 12″, p. 494

236 Hudsonian Godwit, 15″, p. 480

237 Marbled Godwit, 18″, p. 481

238 Hudsonian Godwit winter plumage, 15″, p. 480

239 American Avocet, 16–20″, p. 472

240 American Avocet winter plumage, 16–20″, p. 472

241 Black-necked Stilt, 13–16″, p. 471

242 Common Snipe, 10½″, p. 495

243 Red-necked Phalarope winter plumage, 7″, p. 497

244 American Oystercatcher, 17–21″, p. 470

245 Red-necked Phalarope ♀ breeding plumage, p. 497

246 Wilson's Phalarope ♀ breeding plumage, p. 496

247 Red Phalarope ♀ breeding plumage, 8″, p. 498

248 Red Phalarope winter plumage, 8″, p. 498

249 Wilson's Phalarope winter plumage, 9″, p. 496

250 American Golden-Plover winter plumage, p. 465

251 American Golden-Plover, 9–11″, p. 465

252 Black-bellied Plover, 10–13″, p. 464

253 Black-bellied Plover winter plumage, p. 464

254 Wilson's Plover, 7–8″, p. 467

255 Piping Plover, 6–7″, p. 468

256 Snowy Plover, 5–7″, p. 466

257 Semipalmated Plover, 6–8″, p. 467

258 Killdeer, 9–11″, p. 469

## Chicken-like Marsh Birds

These are small to medium-sized marsh birds, most of which keep themselves well concealed in the reeds or marsh grasses. The bill may be long and slender, as in the Clapper Rail or Virginia Rail, or stubby and chicken-like, as in the Sora. The two gallinules, allied to the modestly plumaged rails that make up the rest of this group, are more often seen in the open and are more brightly colored.

259 Clapper Rail, 14–16″, p. 455

260 King Rail, 15–19″, p. 455

261 Sora, 8–10″, p. 457

262 Yellow Rail, 6–8″, p. 453

263 Virginia Rail, 9–11″, p. 456

264 Black Rail, 5–6″, p. 454

265 Purple Gallinule, 11–13″, p. 458

266 Common Moorhen, 13″, p. 459

267 Northern Jacana, 8–9″, p. 473

## Upland Ground Birds

This group contains the familiar game birds—grouse, quail, and pheasants—as well as certain other cryptically colored birds of woodlands, such as the nightjars. Many of these birds are difficult to detect against a background of dead leaves or grass until they flush unexpectedly into the air.

268 Plain Chachalaca, 18–21″, p. 442

269 Gray Partridge, 12–14″, p. 443

270 Ring-necked Pheasant, 30–36″, p. 444

271 Ring-necked Pheasant ♀, 30–36″, p. 444

272 Sharp-tailed Grouse, 15–20″, p. 450

273 Spruce Grouse, 15–17″, p. 444

274 Scaled Quail, 10–12″, p. 452

275 Ruffed Grouse, 16–19″, p. 447

276 Rock Ptarmigan winter plumage, 13–14″, p. 446

277 Rock Ptarmigan, 13–14″, p. 446

278 Willow Ptarmigan winter plumage, p. 445

279 Willow Ptarmigan, 15–17″, p. 445

280 Greater Prairie-Chicken displaying, p. 448

281 Lesser Prairie-Chicken displaying, 16″, p. 449

282 Lesser Prairie-Chicken, 16″, p. 449

283 Greater Prairie-Chicken, 16–18″, p. 448

284 Wild Turkey, 48″, p. 450

285 Wild Turkey ♀, 36″, p. 450

286 Northern Bobwhite, 8–11″, p. 451

287 Northern Bobwhite ♀, 8–11″, p. 451

288 American Woodcock, 11″, p. 495

289 Greater Roadrunner, 24″, p. 543

290 Pauraque, 12″, p. 558

291 Common Poor-will, 7–8½″, p. 559

292 Whip-poor-will, 10″, p. 560

293 Chuck-will's-widow, 12″, p. 559

294 Antillean Nighthawk, 9½″, p. 557

295 Common Nighthawk, 10″, p. 557

296 Lesser Nighthawk, 8–9″, p. 556

## Owls

This well-known group of birds scarcely needs a description. They are small to large birds with large round heads, loose, fluffy plumage, and disk-like faces. Many are nocturnal and are usually seen roosting quietly in trees during the day, but a few, such as the all-white Snowy Owl or the Short-eared Owl, often hunt by day and may be seen in open country.

297 Short-eared Owl, 16″, p. 553

298 Barred Owl, 20″, p. 551

299 Great Gray Owl, 24–33″, p. 552

300 Northern Hawk Owl, 15–17″, p. 549

301 Ferruginous Pygmy-Owl, 6½–7″, p. 549

302 Elf Owl, 5½″, p. 550

303 Northern Saw-whet Owl, 7″, p. 555

304 Burrowing Owl, 9″, p. 550

305 Great Horned Owl, 25″, p. 547

306 Long-eared Owl, 15″, p. 553

307 Boreal Owl, 9–12″, p. 554

308 Eastern Screech Owl red and gray phases, p. 546

309 Snowy Owl, 24″, p. 548

310 Barn Owl, 18″, p. 545

## Hawk-like Birds

The hawks and their allies range in size from the American Kestrel, scarcely larger than a Blue Jay, to the huge eagles and vultures. All have sharply hooked bills for tearing their prey, and many are often seen soaring high in the air. The wings may be rounded, as in the Red-tailed and Sharp-shinned hawks, or pointed, as in the falcons and some of the kites.

311 Turkey Vulture, 25–32″, p. 417

312 Black Vulture, 22–24″, p. 416

313 Osprey, 21–24″, p. 419

314 Crested Caracara, 20–22″, p. 436

315 Hook-billed Kite ♀, 15–17″, p. 419

316 Mississippi Kite, 12–14″, p. 423

317 American Swallow-tailed Kite, 22–24″, p. 420

318 Hook-billed Kite, 15–17″, p. 419

319 Snail Kite, 16–18″, p. 422

320 White-tailed Kite, 15–16″, p. 421

321 Bald Eagle, 30–31″, p. 423

322 Bald Eagle imm., 30–31″, p. 423

323 Golden Eagle, 30–41″, p. 435

324 Northern Goshawk, 20–26″, p. 427

325 Northern Harrier, 16–24″, p. 424

326 Northern Harrier ♀, 16–24″, p. 424

327 Broad-winged Hawk, 13–15″, p. 429

328 Ferruginous Hawk, 22½–25″, p. 434

329 Swainson's Hawk light phase, 18–22″, p. 431

330 Red-shouldered Hawk, 16–24″, p. 428

331 Red-tailed Hawk light phase, 18–25″, p. 433

332 Rough-legged Hawk, 19–24″, p. 434

333 Cooper's Hawk, 14–20″, p. 426

334 Sharp-shinned Hawk, 10–14″, p. 425

335 Short-tailed Hawk light phase, 13–14″, p. 430

336 Harris' Hawk, 18–30″, p. 428

337 American Kestrel ♀, 9–12″, p. 437

338 White-tailed Hawk, 21–23″, p. 432

339 Merlin, 10–14″, p. 438

340 American Kestrel, 9–12″, p. 437

341 Prairie Falcon, 17–20″, p. 439

342 Gyrfalcon, 22″, p. 441

343 Peregrine Falcon, 15–21″, p. 440

## Pigeon-like Birds

This group includes the familiar Rock Dove, or city pigeon, and its allies. These are small to medium-sized birds, small-headed, and clad in soft browns and grays. On the ground they walk with a characteristic mincing gait.

344 Inca Dove, 8″, p. 536

345 Mourning Dove, 12″, p. 535

346 Common Ground-Dove, 6½″, p. 537

347 White-tipped Dove, 12″, p. 537

348 Ringed Turtle-Dove, 12″, p. 534

349 White-winged Dove, 12″, p. 535

350 Rock Dove, 13½″, p. 532

351 White-crowned Pigeon, 13″, p. 533

352 Red-billed Pigeon, 14″, p. 533

## Swallow-like Birds

Included here are the swallows and martins and the similar but unrelated swifts. These are small birds that spend most of their time in the air, flying gracefully about in pursuit of their insect prey. They have pointed wings and often gather in large flocks.

353 Purple Martin, 7–8½", p. 596

354 Purple Martin ♀, 7–8½", p. 596

355 Violet-green Swallow, 5–5½″, p. 598

356 Tree Swallow, 5–6¼″, p. 597

357 Barn Swallow, 5¾–7¾″, p. 601

358 Northern Rough-winged Swallow, 5–5¾″, p. 598

359 Bank Swallow, 4¾–5½″, p. 599

360 Cliff Swallow, 5–6″, p. 600

361 Cave Swallow, 5½″, p. 601

362 Chimney Swift, 4¾–5½″, p. 561

## Tree-clinging Birds

The woodpeckers, nuthatches, and creepers are usually seen climbing about on the trunks of trees, in search of insects hidden in the bark. Most of the woodpeckers are clad in black and white, although a few, like the Northern Flicker, are mainly brown. The nuthatches are soft gray above and whitish or rusty below, and the creepers are brown and streaked.

363 Downy Woodpecker, 6″, p. 572

364 Yellow-bellied Sapsucker, 8½″, p. 571

365 Ladder-backed Woodpecker, 7″, p. 572

366 Red-headed Woodpecker, 10″, p. 569

367 Red-bellied Woodpecker, 10″, p. 570

368 Pileated Woodpecker, 17″, p. 576

369 Hairy Woodpecker, 9″, p. 573

370 Lewis' Woodpecker, 10½–11½″, p. 568

371 Northern "Yellow-shafted" Flicker, 12″, p. 576

372 Golden-fronted Woodpecker, 9½″, p. 569

373 Black-backed Woodpecker, 9″, p. 575

374 Three-toed Woodpecker, 8½″, p. 574

375 Black-backed Woodpecker ♀, 9″, p. 575

376 Three-toed Woodpecker ♀, 8½″, p. 574

377 Red-cockaded Woodpecker, 8″, p. 573

378 Downy Woodpecker ♀, 6″, p. 572

379 Red-breasted Nuthatch, 4½–4¾", p. 616

380 White-breasted Nuthatch, 5–6", p. 616

381 Brown-headed Nuthatch, 4–5″, p. 617

382 Brown Creeper, 5–5¾″, p. 618

## Perching Birds

This very large group includes nearly all of the songbirds, as well as cuckoos, kingfishers, and hummingbirds, which, while unrelated, resemble songbirds rather closely. They range in size from the three- or four-inch hummingbirds and kinglets to the large crows and ravens. They occur in a great variety of habitats and show an even greater variety of patterns and colors.

383 Black-headed Grosbeak, 7½″, p. 693

384 Rufous-sided Towhee, 7–8½″, p. 701

385 American Robin, 9–11″, p. 636

386 Northern "Baltimore" Oriole, 7–8½", p. 741

387 Orchard Oriole, 7", p. 738

388 Dark-eyed "Oregon" Junco, 5–6½", p. 722

389 Great Kiskadee, 10½″, p. 589

390 Dickcissel, 6″, p. 698

391 Lapland Longspur, 6–7″, p. 724

392 Chestnut-collared Longspur, 5½–6½″, p. 726

393 White-throated Sparrow, 6–7″, p. 719

394 White-crowned Sparrow, 6–7½″, p. 720

395 Harris' Sparrow, 7½″, p. 721

396 House Sparrow, 5–6½″, p. 752

397 Black-throated Sparrow, 5¼″, p. 709

398 Lark Sparrow, 5½–6½″, p. 709

399 House Sparrow ♀, 5–6½″, p. 752

400 Bachman's Sparrow, 6″, p. 702

401 Olive Sparrow, 5¾″, p. 699

402 Cassin's Sparrow, 5¼–5¾″, p. 703

403 Seaside Sparrow, 6″, p. 715

405 Vesper Sparrow, 5–6½″, p. 708

406 Clay-colored Sparrow, 5–5½″, p. 706

407 Field Sparrow, 5¼″, p. 707

408 Song Sparrow, 5–7″, p. 717

409 Lincoln's Sparrow, 5–6″, p. 718

410 Swamp Sparrow, 5″, p. 718

411 Savannah Sparrow, 4½–6″, p. 711

412 Savannah "Ipswich" Sparrow, 4½–6″, p. 711

413 Baird's Sparrow, 5–5½″, p. 712

414 Grasshopper Sparrow, 4½–5″, p. 712

415 Henslow's Sparrow, 5″, p. 713

416 Le Conte's Sparrow, 5″, p. 714

417 Sharp-tailed Sparrow, 5½", p. 714

418 Botteri's Sparrow, 5¼–6¼", p. 702

419 Fox Sparrow, 6–7½", p. 716

420 Chipping Sparrow, 5–5½″, p. 705

421 Eurasian Tree Sparrow, 6″, p. 753

422 American Tree Sparrow, 5½–6½″, p. 705

423 American Pipit, 6–7″, p. 642

424 Sprague's Pipit, 6¼–7″, p. 643

425 Bobolink ♀, 6–8″, p. 727

426 Smith's Longspur, 5¾–6½", p. 725

427 McCown's Longspur, 5¾–6", p. 723

428 Lapland Longspur winter plumage, 6–7", p. 724

429 Snow Bunting winter plumage, 6–7¼″, p. 726

430 Indigo Bunting ♀, 5½″, p. 696

431 Brewer's Blackbird ♀, 8–10″, p. 732

432 Red-winged Blackbird ♀, 7–9½″, p. 728

433 Rusty Blackbird ♀, 9″, p. 732

434 Yellow-headed Blackbird ♀, 8–11″, p. 731

435 Gray-cheeked Thrush, 6½–8″, p. 633

436 Swainson's Thrush, 6½–7¾″, p. 634

437 Hermit Thrush, 6½–7½″, p. 634

438 Wood Thrush, 8″, p. 635

439 Northern Waterthrush, 6″, p. 680

440 Louisiana Waterthrush, 6½″, p. 681

441 Brown Thrasher, 11½″, p. 640

442 Curve-billed Thrasher, 9½–11½″, p. 641

443 Long-billed Thrasher, 11″, p. 640

444 Sage Thrasher, 8½", p. 639

445 Veery, 6½–7¼", p. 632

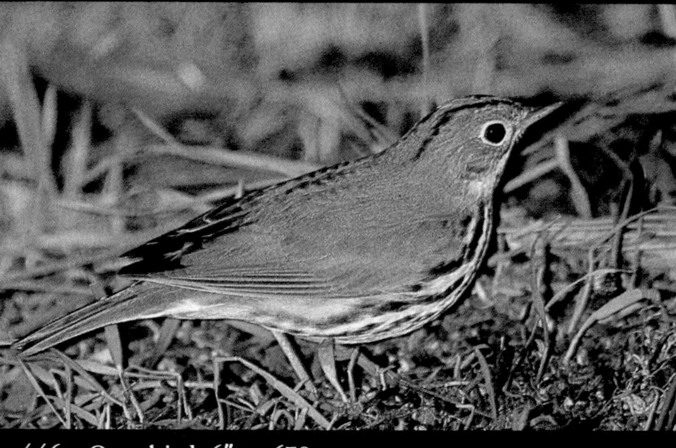

446 Ovenbird, 6", p. 679

447 Mangrove Cuckoo, 12″, p. 542

448 Yellow-billed Cuckoo, 10½–12½″, p. 541

449 Black-billed Cuckoo, 12″, p. 541

450 Bohemian Waxwing, 7½–8½″, p. 644

451 Cedar Waxwing, 6½–8″, p. 645

452 Horned Lark, 7–8″, p. 595

453 Pine Grosbeak ♀, 8–10″, p. 743

454 Evening Grosbeak ♀, 7½–8½″, p. 751

455 Rose-breasted Grosbeak ♀, 8″, p. 693

456 Blu Grosbeak ♀, 6–7½″, p. 694

457 B k-headed Grosbeak ♀, 7½″, p. 693

458 hern Wheatear, 5½–6″, p. 630

459 Yellow-rumped Warbler ♀, 5–6″, p. 667

460 Worm-eating Warbler, 5½″, p. 678

461 Swainson's Warbler, 5″, p. 678

462 House Finch ♀, 5–6″, p. 744

463 Purple Finch ♀, 5½–6½″, p. 744

464 Pine Siskin, 4½–5″, p. 748

465 Cactus Wren, 7–8¼″, p. 620

466 Rock Wren, 5–6½″, p. 621

467 Canyon Wren, 5½–6″, p. 622

468 Carolina Wren, 5½″, p. 622

469 Bewick's Wren, 5½″, p. 623

470 House Wren, 4½–5¼″, p. 624

471 Winter Wren, 4–4½″, p. 624

472 Sedge Wren, 4–4½″, p. 625

473 Marsh Wren, 4–5½″, p. 626

474 Rufous-sided Towhee ♀, 7–8½″, p. 701

475 Brown Jay, 14–18″, p. 605

476 Scissor-tailed Flycatcher 14″, p. 593

477 Brown-headed Cowbird ♀, 6–8″, p. 737

478 Brown-headed Cowbird, 6–8″, p. 737

479 Common Grackle juv., 12″, p. 735

480 Boat-tailed Grackle ♀, 12–13″, p. 734

481 Common Redpoll, 5–5½″, p. 747

482 Pine Grosbeak, 8–10″, p. 743

483 House Finch, 5–6″, p. 744

484 Purple Finch, 5½–6½″, p. 744

485 Northern Cardinal, 8–9″, p. 691

486 Red Crossbill, 5¼–6½″, p. 745

487 White-winged Crossbill, 6–6½″, p. 746

488 Summer Tanager, 7–8″, p. 688

489 Scarlet Tanager, 7½″, p. 689

490 Vermilion Flycatcher, 6″, p. 586

491 Hooded Oriole, 7–7¾″, p. 739

492 Altamira Oriole, 9″, p. 740

493 Northern "Bullock's" Oriole, 7–8½″, p. 741

494 Spot-breasted Oriole, 8″, p. 739

495 Western Tanager, 6–7½″, p. 690

496 Summer Tanager ♀, 7–8″, p. 688

497 Yellow-headed Blackbird, 8–11″, p. 731

498 Eastern Meadowlark, 9–11″, p. 729

499 Western Meadowlark, 8½–11″, p. 730

500 Tropical Parula, 4–5″, p. 662

501 Evening Grosbeak, 7½–8½″, p. 751

502 Audubon's Oriole, 9″, p. 741

503 American Goldfinch, 4½–5″, p. 750

504 Yellow Warbler, 4½–5″, p. 663

505 Blue-winged Warbler, 4½″, p. 658

506 Prothonotary Warbler, 5½″, p. 677

507 Wilson's Warbler, 4½–5″, p. 685

508 Bachman's Warbler, 4½″, p. 657

509 Hooded Warbler, 5½″, p. 684

510 Cape May Warbler, 5″, p. 665

511 Canada Warbler, 5″, p. 686

512 Prairie Warbler, 5″, p. 672

513 Magnolia Warbler, 5″, p. 665

514 Kentucky Warbler, 5½″, p. 681

515 Blackburnian Warbler, 5″, p. 669

516 Black-throated Green Warbler, 5″, p. 668

517 Yellow-rumped "Myrtle" Warbler, 5–6″, p. 667

518 Verdin, 4–4½″, p. 615

519 Golden-winged Warbler, 4½″, p. 659

520 Northern Parula ♀, 4½″, p. 662

521 Northern Parula, 4½″, p. 662

522 Nashville Warbler, 4–5″, p. 661

523 Chestnut-sided Warbler imm., 5″, p. 664

524 Connecticut Warbler, 5½″, p. 682

525 Tennessee Warbler, 5″, p. 659

526 Bay-breasted Warbler imm., 5½″, p. 673

527 Orange-crowned Warbler, 4½–5½″, p. 660

528 Mourning Warbler, 5½″, p. 683

529 Yellow-breasted Chat, 6½–7½″, p. 687

530 American Redstart ♀, 4½–5½″, p. 676

531 Chestnut-sided Warbler, 5″, p. 664

532 Bay-breasted Warbler, 5½″, p. 673

533 Yellow-throated Warbler, 5″, p. 670

534 Golden-cheeked Warbler, 4½–5″, p. 668

535 Palm Warbler, 5½″, p. 672

536 Kirtland's Warbler, 6″, p. 671

537 Pine Warbler, 5½″, p. 670

538 Blackpoll Warbler, 5½″, p. 674

539 Lesser Goldfinch, 3½–4″, p. 749

540 Couch's Kingbird, 8½″, p. 590

541 Western Kingbird, 8–9″, p. 591

542 Gray Kingbird, 9″, p. 592

543 Common Yellowthroat, 4½–6″, p. 684

544 Common Yellowthroat ♀, 4½–6″, p. 684

545 Northern "Baltimore" Oriole ♀, 7–8½″, p. 741

546 Orchard Oriole ♀, 7″, p. 738

547 Yellow-throated Vireo, 6″, p. 652

548 American Goldfinch ♀, 4½–5″, p. 750

549 Scarlet Tanager ♀, 7½″, p. 689

550 Western Tanager ♀, 6–7½″, p. 690

551 Yellow-bellied Flycatcher, 5½″, p. 580

552 Great Crested Flycatcher, 9″, p. 588

553 Acadian Flycatcher, 6″, p. 581

554 Olive-sided Flycatcher, 7½″, p. 578

555 Ash-throated Flycatcher, 8″, p. 587

556 Vermilion Flycatcher ♀, 6″, p. 586

557 Alder Flycatcher, 5–6″, p. 582

558 Willow Flycatcher, 6″, p. 583

559 Least Flycatcher, 5¼″, p. 584

560 Black Phoebe, 6–7″, p. 584

561 Eastern Phoebe, 7″, p. 585

562 Say's Phoebe, 7–8″, p. 586

563 Eastern Wood-Pewee imm., 6½", p. 580

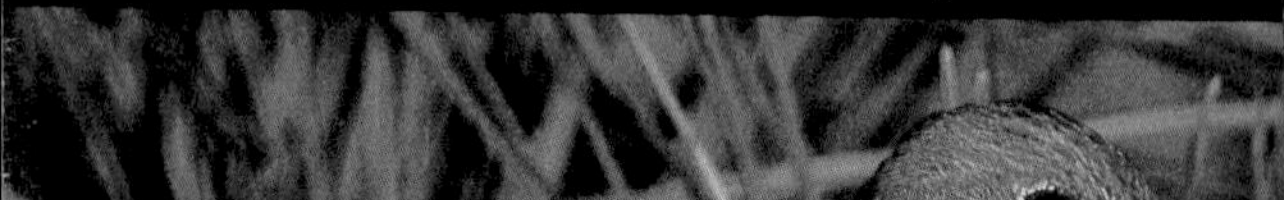

564 Western Wood-Pewee, 6½", p. 579

565 Northern Beardless-Tyrannulet, 4″, p. 578

566 Bell's Vireo, 4¾–5″, p. 650

567 Black-whiskered Vireo, 5½″, p. 656

568 Solitary Vireo, 5–6″, p. 651

569 Yellow-green Vireo, 6–7″, p. 655

570 Warbling Vireo, 5–6″, p. 653

571 Red-eyed Vireo, 5½–6½″, p. 654

572 Philadelphia Vireo, 6″, p. 654

573 White-eyed Vireo, 5″, p. 649

574 Cape May Warbler imm., 5″, p. 665

575 Rose-throated Becard, 6½″, p. 594

576 Golden-crowned Kinglet, 3½–4", p. 627

577 Ruby-crowned Kinglet, 3¾–4½", p. 628

578 Green-tailed Towhee, 6¼–7", p. 700

579 Buff-bellied Hummingbird, 4½″, p. 562

580 Ruby-throated Hummingbird ♀, 3½″, p. 563

581 Black-chinned Hummingbird, 3¼–3¾", p. 564

582 Ruby-throated Hummingbird, 3½", p. 563

583 Rufous Hummingbird, 3½–4", p. 564

584 Painted Bunting ♀, 5½", p. 697

585 Budgerigar, 7", p. 538

586 Green Jay, 12", p. 604

587 Monk Parakeet, 11″, p. 539

588 Rose-ringed Parakeet, 15–17″, p. 539

589 Canary-winged Parakeet, 9″, p. 540

590 Green Kingfisher, 8″, p. 567

591 Belted Kingfisher, 13″, p. 566

592 Blue Grosbeak, 6–7½″, p. 694

593 Lazuli Bunting, 5–5¼″, p. 695

594 Indigo Bunting, 5½″, p. 696

595 Blue-Gray Tanager, 7″, p. 690

596 Blue Jay, 12″, p. 603

597 Scrub Jay, 11–13″, p. 605

598 Eastern Bluebird, 7″, p. 631

599 Mountain Bluebird, 7″, p. 632

600 Black-throated Blue Warbler, 5″, p. 666

601 Cerulean Warbler, 4½″, p. 675

602 Painted Bunting, 5½″, p. 697

603 Varied Bunting, 4½– 5½″, p. 697

604 Eastern Kingbird, 8–9″, p. 591

605 Gray Jay, 10–13″, p. 602

606 European Starling juv., 7½–8½″, p. 648

607 Blue-gray Gnatcatcher, 4½–5″, p. 629

608 Pyrrhuloxia, 7½–8½″, p. 692

609 Northern Cardinal ♀, 8–9″, p. 691

610 Black-throated Blue Warbler ♀, 5″, p. 666

611 Northern Mockingbird, 9–11″, p. 638

612 Gray Catbird, 8–9¼″, p. 637

614 Northern Shrike, 9–10½″, p. 646

615 Loggerhead Shrike, 8–10″, p. 647

616 Tufted "Black-crested" Titmouse, 6″, p. 614

617 Tufted Titmouse, 6″, p. 614

618 Blackpoll Warbler, 5½″, p. 674

619 Black-and-White Warbler, 5″, p. 675

620 Snow Bunting, 6–7¼″, p. 726

621 Black-capped Chickadee, 4¾–5¾″, p. 611

622 Boreal Chickadee, 5–5½″, p. 613

623 Carolina Chickadee, 4–5″, p. 612

624 Rose-breasted Grosbeak, 8″, p. 693

625 Red-whiskered Bulbul, 8″, p. 619

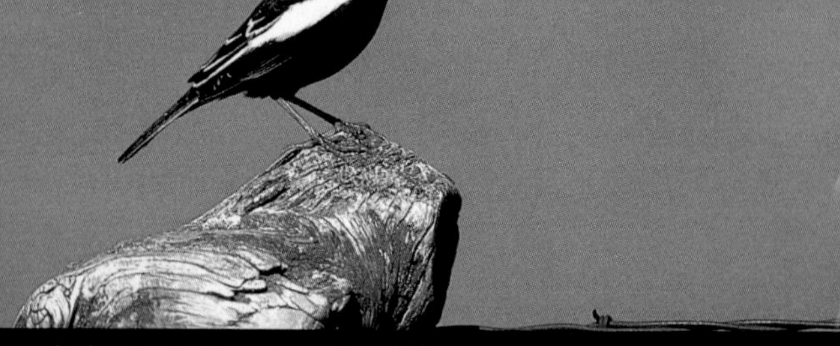

626 Lark Bunting, 6–7½″, p. 710

627 Black-billed Magpie, 17½–22″, p. 606

628 Bobolink, 6–8″, p. 727

629 American Redstart, 4½–5½″, p. 676

630 Boat-tailed Grackle, 16–17″, p. 734

631 Great-tailed Grackle, 16–17″, p. 733

632 Common Grackle, 12", p. 735

633 European Starling, 7½–8½", p. 648

634 Red-winged Blackbird, 7–9½″, p. 728

635 Rusty Blackbird, 9″, p. 732

636 Brewers Blackbird, 8–10″, p. 732

637 Bronzed Cowbird, 8½″, p. 736

638 Bronzed Cowbird ♀, 8½″, p. 736

639 Shiny Cowbird, 7–8″, p. 736

640 Groove-billed Ani, 12″, p. 544

641 Smooth-billed Ani, 14″, p. 543

642 Common Raven, 21–27″, p. 610

643 Chihuahuan Raven, 19–21″, p. 609

644 Mexican Crow, 15″, p. 608

645 American Crow, 17–21″, p. 607

646 Fish Crow, 17″, p. 609

# Part II
# Species Accounts

The number preceding each species description in the following pages corresponds to the number of the illustration in the color plates section. If the description has no number, there is no color plate.

## Family Gaviidae
Loons

5 species: Northern Hemisphere. All five species breed or have bred in North America. These birds are excellent swimmers and divers that prey mainly on fish. They have long bodies with webbed feet set far back and long pointed bills. When swimming they ride low in the water. On the wing loons hold both their heads and feet below the level of the body, which gives them a distinctive humpbacked flight silhouette. Loons nest on lakes and along rivers and spend the winter mostly in coastal waters.

---

189, 191 **Red-throated Loon**
*Gavia stellata*

Description: 24–27" (61–69 cm). A small loon seldom seen far from salt water. In breeding plumage, has *gray head and neck, rusty throat,* black back spotted with white. In winter, similar to Common Loon, but smaller, paler, with *bill thinner and seemingly upturned.*

Voice: Call, rarely sounded away from breeding grounds, is a series of high-pitched wails and shrieks.

Habitat: Coastal and tundra ponds during summer; large lakes, bays, estuaries, and ocean during migration and winter.

Nesting: 2 brownish-olive, usually spotted eggs in nest of aquatic vegetation, beside or in water.

Range: Breeds from Aleutian Islands, Alaska, and Canadian Arctic south to British Columbia, northern Manitoba, and Newfoundland. Winters south along Pacific Coast to southern California, and along Gulf Coast and both coasts of Florida. Also in northern Eurasia.

The attractive breeding plumage of this loon is seldom seen in temperate latitudes, because the birds molt just before they depart for their nesting grounds. Because their legs are located so far back, loons have difficulty walking on land and are rarely found far from water. They are extremely vulnerable to oil pollution; many have been killed along both coasts as a result of recent spills.

## 192 Pacific Loon
*Gavia pacifica*

Description: 24″ (61 cm). A *small* loon with a *slender straight bill.* In breeding plumage, head pale gray; neck and back black with white stripes; throat black with purple reflections. In winter plumage, blackish above, white below; sometimes shows suggestion of thin chin strap. Red-throated Loon in winter is paler, with less contrast between dark crown and hindneck and white throat, and a seemingly upturned bill; Common Loon is larger, with stouter bill.

Voice: A harsh *kok-kok-kok-kok;* wailing notes on breeding grounds.

Habitat: Breeds on lakes and ponds in tundra and northern forests; winters on coastal bays and inlets, and on the ocean.

Nesting: 2 spotted olive-brown eggs in a slight depression lined with aquatic vegetation (sometimes on bare ground) at edge of water.

Range: Breeds from Alaska east to Hudson Bay, and south to northern British Columbia, Manitoba, and Ontario. Winters chiefly along Pacific Coast; very rare along coast of northeastern United States.

Until recently, this bird was considered a form of the Arctic Loon (*Gavia arctica*) of Eurasia. It is the rarest and least known of the three loons found in the East. The Pacific Loon usually feeds closer to shore than other loons; its diet consists mainly of fish, but on the breeding grounds it also takes crustaceans.

188, 190 **Common Loon**
*Gavia immer*

Description: 28–36″ (71–91 cm). A large, heavy-bodied loon with a *thick, pointed, usually black or dark gray bill held horizontally.* In breeding plumage, head and neck black with white bands on neck; back black with white spots. In winter, crown, hindneck, and upperparts dark grayish; throat and underparts white.

Voice: Best-known call a loud, wailing laugh; also a mournful, yodeled *oo-AH-ho* with middle note higher, and a loud, ringing *kee-a-ree, kee-a-ree* with middle note lower. Often calls at night, and sometimes on migration.

Habitat: Nests on forested lakes and rivers; winters mainly on coastal bays and ocean.

Nesting: 2 olive-brown or greenish, lightly spotted eggs in a bulky mass of vegetation near water's edge, usually on an island.

Range: Breeds from Aleutian Islands and Alaska across northern Canada, and south to California, Montana, and Massachusetts. Winters along Great Lakes, Gulf Coast, and Atlantic and Pacific coasts. Also breeds in Greenland and Iceland.

The Common Loon is famous for its loud, wailing call, a characteristic sound of the North Woods. Diving deeply in pursuit of their prey, loons have been caught in nets as much as 200 feet (60 meters) below the water's surface. Their principal food is fish, but they also eat shellfish, frogs, and aquatic insects. In recent decades, acid rain has sterilized many lakes where these birds formerly bred, and their numbers are declining.

## FAMILY PODICIPEDIDAE
Grebes

21 species: Worldwide. Seven species breed in North America. Grebes are similar to loons, but smaller, and have lobed rather than webbed feet. Like loons, grebes dive expertly; they can also sink gradually out of sight, leaving only their bills and nostrils above the surface. They eat fish but also take crayfish and other small aquatic animals. Grebes often ingest large quantities of their own feathers to protect their stomach linings from fish bones. Grebes breed on lakes, ponds, and marshes, and build floating nests of aquatic vegetation. They winter mainly on the coasts.

### 193 Least Grebe
*Tachybaptus dominicus*

Description: 8–10″ (20–25 cm). Robin-sized. Similar to Pied-billed Grebe, but smaller, with a more slender bill. Brownish gray with orange-yellow eyes and small dark bill.

Voice: Loud *peek!* and other calls.

Habitat: Dense floating vegetation on quiet ponds and slow-moving streams.

Nesting: 3–6 bluish-white eggs that become stained with brown, in a floating nest of aquatic vegetation usually anchored to reeds or other emergent plants.

Range: Resident in southern Texas and West Indies to South America.

This is the smallest of North America's grebes and has the smallest range. It feeds mainly on insects but has also been known to feed on algae. Least Grebes seldom fly, and they rarely leave the immediate vicinity of their nesting places. When not nesting, they are often found in small flocks.

## 185, 195 Pied-billed Grebe
*Podilymbus podiceps*

Description: 12–15″ (30–38 cm). Pigeon-sized. A stocky, uniformly brownish water bird, with *stout whitish bill* that has black ring around it during breeding season.

Voice: A series of hollow, cuckoo-like notes, *cow-cow-cow-cow, cow, cow, cowp, cowp, cowp,* that slows down at the end; various clucking sounds.

Habitat: Marshes, ponds; salt water in winter if freshwater habitats freeze.

Nesting: 5–7 whitish eggs, stained brown, in a well-hidden, floating mass of dead marsh vegetation anchored to adjacent plants.

Range: Breeds from British Columbia east through southern Mackenzie to Nova Scotia, and southward. Winters in southern states or wherever water remains open.

This is the most common nesting grebe in the East. On ponds and marshes where it breeds, the Pied-billed Grebe advertises its presence by loud, barking calls. It eats small fish, crustaceans, and aquatic insects but is especially fond of crayfish, which it crushes easily with its stout bill. When alarmed, this bird often sinks slowly into the water, surfacing again out of sight among the reeds. But it can also dive with amazing speed, a habit that has earned it the local name "Hell-diver."

## 186, 199 Horned Grebe
*Podiceps auritus*

Description: 12–15″ (30–38 cm). Small, slender-necked, with short, sharply pointed bill. In breeding plumage, body dark, with rufous neck and flanks; head blackish, with *conspicuous buff ear tufts.* In winter, upperparts dark, chin and foreneck white. The most common saltwater grebe in the East.

Voice: Usually silent. On breeding grounds, a variety of croaks, shrieks, and chatters.

Habitat: Breeds on marshes and lakes; winters mainly on salt water, but also on the Great Lakes and other large inland bodies of water.

Nesting: 4–7 bluish-white eggs, stained buff, on nest of floating vegetation anchored to marsh plants.

Range: Breeds from Alaska and northern Canada south to Washington and Oregon, Dakotas, and northern Great Lakes. Winters in Aleutians and along coasts to southern California and Texas. Also in Eurasia.

Although the Horned Grebe breeds in freshwater marshes, each fall most of the population moves to the coast; it is therefore thought of as a saltwater bird. These grebes are only occasionally seen in flight; once on the wintering grounds they seldom fly, and they migrate almost entirely at night. Like other grebes, the young can swim and dive immediately after hatching but are often seen riding on the parents' backs.

---

184, 194 **Red-necked Grebe**
*Podiceps grisegena*

Description: 18–20″ (46–51 cm). A slender bird, the largest grebe in eastern North America. In breeding plumage, has rufous neck, black cap, *whitish cheeks,* and a *long, pointed, yellowish bill.* In winter, mainly gray, with paler cheeks and pale (not necessarily yellow) bill. In flight, distinguished from loons by smaller size and white wing patches.

Voice: Usually silent. On breeding grounds, a variety of squeaks, growls, and wailing calls.

Habitat: Marshy ponds and lakes in summer; large lakes, coastal bays, and estuaries during migration and winter.

Nesting: 4–5 bluish-white eggs, stained brown, on a floating mass of dead reeds and grass in reedy lakes. Rarely nests in colonies.

Range: Breeds from Alaska and northern Canada south to Oregon, Idaho, southern Minnesota, and Ontario; rarely east to southern Quebec. Winters along coasts south to California and Georgia, rarely to Florida. Also in Eurasia.

Highly aquatic, grebes can swim with only their head above water, concealing themselves in low pond vegetation. The young, striped in black and white, are often seen riding on the parents' backs. Like loons, grebes are expert divers, propelling themselves with their lobed toes as they pursue fish, crustaceans, and aquatic insects.

---

187, 198 **Eared Grebe**
*Podiceps nigricollis*

Description: 12–14″ (30–36 cm). A small, slender-necked, slender-billed grebe. In breeding plumage, head and back black with *golden ear tufts* and *black crest.* In winter, dark gray above, white below, neck dusky. In winter, similar to Horned Grebe, but chunkier, and *bill appears slightly upturned;* sides of face smudged with gray, with whitish patch behind ear.

Voice: On breeding grounds, frog-like cheeping notes.

Habitat: Marshy lakes and ponds; open bays and ocean in winter.

Nesting: 3–5 bluish-white eggs, stained brown, on a floating mass of vegetation in a marsh. Usually nests in dense colonies.

Range: Breeds from British Columbia, southern Manitoba, and Dakotas south to California and New Mexico. Winters on Pacific, Gulf, and Atlantic (rare) coasts, and occasionally on open water in interior Southwest and Texas. Also in Eurasia.

Although most Eared Grebes migrate southwestward in the fall to the Pacific, a very few turn up each year on the East Coast. Unlike the Horned Grebe, which supplements its diet with small fish, the Eared Grebe feeds almost exclusively on aquatic insects and small crustaceans. These birds are highly gregarious, not only nesting in large, dense, and noisy colonies but also assembling in large flocks in winter.

## 197 Western Grebe
*Aechmophorus occidentalis*

Description: 22–29″ (56–74 cm). A large slender grebe with a *long neck*. Blackish above with *black of cap extending below eyes;* white below and on front of neck. *Bill long, slender, and greenish yellow.* Long white wing stripe shows in flight. See Clark's Grebe.

Voice: A rolling *kr-r-rick, kr-r-rick!* sounded most often on breeding grounds, but sometimes heard in winter.

Habitat: Breeds on large lakes with tules or rushes; winters mainly on shallow coastal bays and estuaries.

Nesting: 3 or 4 bluish-white eggs, stained brown or buff, on a floating nest anchored to reeds. Nests in dense, noisy colonies.

Range: Breeds from British Columbia, Saskatchewan, and Minnesota south to southern California; sparsely in Arizona, New Mexico, and Colorado. Winters along Pacific Coast, on Gulf Coast, and on large river systems in West. Rare on East Coast.

The mating display of the Western Grebe is spectacular, with both members of a pair paddling vigorously and churning across the surface of the water in an upright posture. During migration Western Grebes fly in loose flocks but spread out to feed during the day. On their coastal wintering grounds these birds often fall victim to oil spills and to insecticides that accumulate in their food, build up in their bodies, and reduce their breeding success.

---

196 **Clark's Grebe**
*Aechmophorus clarkii*

Description: 22–29″ (56–74 cm). Very similar to Western Grebe, but black of cap does not reach eyes, so *face is largely white; bill bright yellow or orange-yellow.*

Voice: A loud *kr-r-rick,* not doubled as in Western Grebe; heard most often on breeding grounds.

Habitat: Breeds on large lakes with tules or rushes; winters mainly on shallow coastal bays and estuaries.

Nesting: 3 or 4 bluish-white eggs, stained brown or buff, on a floating nest anchored to reeds. Nests in dense, noisy colonies.

Range: Breeding range broadly overlaps that of Western Grebe, from British Columbia, Saskatchewan, and Minnesota south to southern California, and sparsely to Arizona, New Mexico, and Colorado. Winters along coast from southeastern Alaska to California, along Gulf Coast, and on large river systems in West.

First described in 1858, at the same time as the Western Grebe, Clark's Grebe was originally regarded as a distinct species and then as a color phase of the Western Grebe. These two birds are once again considered separate species because they nest side by side with very little interbreeding. In most respects the two are alike. Clark's Grebe is more common in the southern portions of the combined range of the two species, and relatively rare in the northern part.

## Family Procellariidae
Shearwaters and Petrels

80 species: Worldwide. Only three species breed in North America, but many winter here. Shearwaters and petrels are chiefly oceanic in the nonbreeding season, nesting in burrows on islands and along coasts, where they are mainly nocturnal. These birds have tubular nostrils, webbed feet, and long pointed wings that are held stiffly during prolonged effortless glides low over the waves. Most species feed on fish, squid, crustaceans, or plankton.

### 79 Northern Fulmar
*Fulmarus glacialis*

Description: 18″ (46 cm). A stocky, gull-like seabird seldom seen from shore. Most eastern birds are pale gray on back and wings, white elsewhere, but uniformly dark gray individuals occur, as do intermediates between pale and dark gray. *Bill yellow*. Easily distinguished from a gull by its flight: several fast wingbeats followed by a stiff-winged glide.

Voice: Chuckling and grunting notes when feeding; various guttural calls during breeding season.

Habitat: Rocky cliffs for nesting; open seas most of year.

Nesting: 1 white egg on a bare rock or in a shallow depression lined with plant material.

Range: Breeds on Arctic coasts and islands. Winters at sea south to southern California and North Carolina. Also in northern Eurasia.

The Northern Fulmar feeds on fish, squid, shrimp, and the refuse of the fishing industry. The expansion of commercial fishing in the 20th century caused a great increase in the population of this species, especially in the North Atlantic, but newly mechanized methods of processing fish at sea have reduced the amount of refuse thrown overboard, and the numbers of these birds have begun to decline.

**Black-capped Petrel**
*Pterodroma hasitata*

Description: 14–18″ (36–46 cm). A long-winged, long-tailed petrel, dark above with black cap; *white collar and rump* (lacking in Manx and Audubon's shearwaters); white underparts. Viewed from below, wings have *broad dark margins.*

Voice: Usually silent at sea.

Habitat: Open ocean, especially Gulf Stream waters.

Nesting: 1 white egg in a burrow or rocky crevice on an isolated mountain ridge.

Range: Breeds on larger islands in West Indies; visits Gulf Stream, regularly as far north as Carolinas.

The Black-capped Petrel is a little-known seabird that visits its Caribbean nesting colonies only at night. The total population is small, and a mere handful drift northward along the Gulf Stream in summer and fall, after the breeding season. There they feed chiefly on squid, which they snatch from the surface of the water.

75 **Cory's Shearwater**
*Calonectris diomedea*

Description: 20–22″ (51–56 cm). A large stocky shearwater, dull gray-brown above and whitish below; *bill pale* (*usually yellow,* sometimes marked with dusky color). Similar to Greater Shearwater, but dull gray crown of Cory's blends evenly with white sides of face, without abruptly contrasting "cap" seen in Greater Shearwater; Greater is darker above, with dusky belly and black bill.

Voice: Howling, gurgling calls heard only on breeding grounds.

Habitat: Open ocean.

Nesting: 1 white egg in a rock crevice or on open ground on an island, occasionally in a cave or burrow. Nests in colonies.

Range: Breeds in eastern Atlantic and Mediterranean; in late spring, summer, and fall, frequents East Coast of North America.

This is the only large shearwater found off the East Coast that breeds in the Northern Hemisphere. At sea off our coasts, these birds forage at night, feeding on squid and crustaceans; they also follow schools of mackerel and other large fish, catching smaller fish driven close to the surface. Unlike many shearwaters, they seldom follow ships in search of food.

## 78 Greater Shearwater
*Puffinus gravis*

Description: 18–20″ (46–51 cm). A large shearwater, more slender than Cory's, dull brown above with pale scaling; white below, with dusky belly; *cap dark, contrasting with white face;* may show white at base of tail; *bill black*. Cory's Shearwater is paler above and whiter below, lacks the contrast between crown and face, and has a pale bill.

Voice: Usually silent at sea, but birds resting on water have a low nasal, squealing call.

Habitat: Open ocean.

Nesting: 1 white egg in a burrow on a grassy slope. Nests in large dense colonies.

Range: Breeds on islands of Tristan de Cunha in South Atlantic. Spends northern summer, from May to early November, as a nonbreeding visitor to North Atlantic.

At the end of the breeding season in the Southern Hemisphere, Greater Shearwaters follow a "Great Circle" route around the Atlantic, appearing in North American waters as early as May, then moving on to the eastern Atlantic by late summer. Adept divers, they feed mainly on small fish and squid, which they pursue underwater with partially open wings and paddling feet.

## 77 Sooty Shearwater
*Puffinus griseus*

Description: 16–18″ (41–46 cm). A large shearwater, the only one in the Atlantic that appears *uniformly dark sooty brown above and below;* wing linings silvery white. This slender, narrow-winged seabird skims on stiff wings over the waves, alternately gliding and flapping.

Voice: Silent at sea; a variety of cooing and croaking notes heard on breeding grounds.

Habitat: Open ocean.

Nesting: 1 white egg in a burrow. Nests in colonies.

Range: Breeds on islands in cold southern oceans. Spends Northern Hemisphere summer in North Atlantic and North Pacific oceans.

This is one of the most abundant birds in the world. Millions of individuals of this species nest on islands off New Zealand. Most that appear off the American East Coast breed around Tierra del Fuego, off the southern tip of South America. After breeding, they begin a great circular migration around the Atlantic Ocean, arriving off the East Coast of North America in May, continuing on to Europe, then down the west coast of Africa, and returning to their nesting islands in November.

76 **Manx Shearwater**
*Puffinus puffinus*

Description: 12½–15″ (32–38 cm). A small shearwater, *uniform blackish above and white below.* Greater Shearwater is larger, with pale scaling on brown upperparts, a distinct blackish cap—darker than the back—and usually a distinct white patch at base of tail. Audubon's Shearwater very similar, but has longer tail and dark undertail coverts (white in Manx).

Voice: Cooing and clucking notes heard at night in breeding colonies.

Habitat: Open ocean.

Nesting: 1 white egg in a burrow or rock crevice on an island. Nests in colonies.

Range: Breeds mainly in eastern Atlantic, but also on islands off Newfoundland, and in Massachusetts (one record). An uncommon visitor off East Coast.

Unlike the large shearwaters of the western Atlantic, the Manx Shearwater seldom follows ships and is usually seen skimming past them at some distance. A few Manx Shearwaters are known to breed in North America, but because they visit their nesting islands only at night, they may be breeding more frequently and in more places on our shores than is presently known. These birds are great travelers whose movements are poorly understood; one bird banded in Britain was later recovered off Australia.

74 **Audubon's Shearwater**
*Puffinus lherminieri*

Description: 11–12″ (28–30 cm). A small shearwater, brownish-black above and white below except for *dark undertail coverts.* Half the size of Greater Shearwater. The rarer Manx Shearwater is blacker, has white undertail coverts, and less fluttery flight.

Voice: Twittering calls and mewing notes heard at night in breeding colonies.

Habitat: Open ocean.

Nesting: 1 white egg in a burrow or rock crevice on an island. Nests in colonies.

Range: Breeds on islands in tropical seas around the world. Wanders northward along Gulf Stream from Caribbean and Bermuda as far as Carolinas and, rarely, New England.

Very similar to the Manx Shearwater, this tropical species appears regularly on the Gulf Stream during the summer, sometimes in large numbers. There is no evidence that Audubon's Shearwaters undertake the great migrations of many other shearwaters. Like the similar Manx, it does not follow ships in search of food, and so is often difficult to observe at close range.

## FAMILY HYDROBATIDAE
Storm-Petrels

21 species. Worldwide in tropical and temperate oceans. Four species breed in North America. These small birds flutter over the surface of the water, where they feed on small crustaceans, fish, and plankton. Like the shearwaters, they have tubular nostrils on top of the bill. Most species are black, and some have white on the rump, but a few are gray. Because they are small and usually seen from the deck of a pitching boat, they can be difficult to identify; flight characteristics, rather than color and pattern, are often the best clues. Storm-petrels nest in burrows on offshore islands and isolated coasts, which they visit only at night.

## 80 Wilson's Storm-Petrel
*Oceanites oceanicus*

Description: 7″ (18 cm). A small seabird that darts and skims over the waves like a swallow. Black with *white rump; tail rounded or square-tipped.* Leach's Storm-Petrel is similar, but has notched tail and flies like a nighthawk.

Voice: A soft peeping, heard at close range when birds are feeding.

Habitat: Open ocean.

Nesting: 1 white egg placed in a crevice among rocks or in a burrow in soft earth.

Range: Breeds on islands in Antarctic and subantarctic seas; in nonbreeding season ranges northward over Atlantic, Pacific, and Indian oceans, in western Atlantic north to Labrador.

Perhaps the most abundant bird in the world, this species nests in countless millions on islands in the Southern Hemisphere and visits the Northern Hemisphere during our summer months. Wilson's Storm-Petrel often hovers at the surface of the water, its wings held over its back and its feet gently touching the water. Although normally a bird of the open ocean, it sometimes enters bays and estuaries, and often follows ships. This bird is named after American ornithologist Alexander Wilson (1766–1813).

---

## 81 Leach's Storm-Petrel
*Oceanodroma leucorhoa*

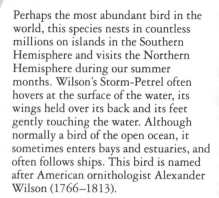

Description: 8–9″ (20–23 cm). Small, swallow-like seabird, all black with white rump. Differs from Wilson's Storm-Petrel in having longer, more pointed wings, and a *somewhat forked tail.* Flies like a nighthawk, with much bounding and veering. Unlike Wilson's, this species seldom follows boats.

Voice: A variety of trills, screams, and cooing notes.

Habitat: Open ocean; nests on spruce-covered islands and rocky coasts.

Nesting: 1 white egg in a shallow burrow in the ground or hidden under a log or board. Nests in colonies.

Range: Breeds on coasts and offshore islands from Labrador south to Maine and Massachusetts. Winters mainly in tropical seas. Also breeds in eastern Atlantic and on both sides of Pacific Ocean.

Even near their nesting islands, Leach's Storm-Petrels are seldom seen because they feed far out at sea and visit their burrows only at night. The presence of the birds is not difficult to detect, however; their burrows have an unmistakable musky odor, produced by an oily orange liquid that the birds emit when disturbed, and at night the air is filled with their eerie calls. These birds are vulnerable to many terrestrial predators, but their nocturnal habits save them from being taken by predatory gulls. Like other storm-petrels, they feed mainly on small shrimp and other planktonic animals, which they pluck deftly from the surface of the water.

---

**Family Phaethontidae**
Tropicbirds

3 species: Tropical and subtropical oceans of the world. These birds resemble huge terns with long tail streamers. They are locally numerous and easy to see near their nesting colonies on oceanic islands, but outside the breeding season they roam widely over the ocean and are usually solitary. They feed on squid and small fish.

## 85 White-tailed Tropicbird
*Phaethon lepturus*

Description: 32″ (81 cm). W. 3′1″ (94 cm). Adult is a *white,* pigeon-sized seabird with *very long central tail feathers,* bold black wing markings, and *yellow bill.* Young birds lack the long tail feathers and are white, with fine black barring above.

Voice: A piping *keck-keck-keck* and other tern-like calls, given in flight.

Habitat: Tropical oceans.

Nesting: 1 pinkish egg, speckled with brown, on bare soil or a rock or in a crevice among rocks on an island.

Range: Breeds on Bermuda and Bahamas, and on other islands in tropical Atlantic, Indian, and Pacific oceans. A rare visitor off coast of Florida and Carolinas.

In pursuit of fish and squid, tropicbirds engage in graceful dives from the air. They fly with rapid wingbeats and glide occasionally. Tropicbirds forage far from land, sometimes following ships. After the breeding season, many gather in the Sargasso Sea, in the middle of the Atlantic Ocean.

---

## Family Sulidae
Boobies and Gannets

9 species: Nearly worldwide on islands and coasts. Only one species breeds in North America. Boobies and gannets are large birds with long pointed bills, webbed feet, and pointed wings, adapted for plunge diving for fish from great heights into the ocean. They nest on steep sea cliffs and rocky islands, and sometimes in trees.

## 87 Masked Booby
**"Blue-faced Booby"**
*Sula dactylatra*

Description: 32″ (81 cm). A stocky white seabird with black tail, black tips and trailing edges to the wings, and stout pinkish or orange bill. In breeding season, birds have patch of bare, bluish skin at base of bill. Northern Gannet similar but larger, with only wing tips black.

Voice: Usually silent; a variety of hissing and quacking notes on breeding grounds.

Habitat: Tropical seas.

Nesting: 2 chalky, pale blue eggs in a shallow depression on the ground. Nests in colonies.

Range: Breeds in Bahamas and West Indies, and on other islands in tropical Atlantic, Indian, and Pacific oceans. A rare visitor to coasts of Florida, Louisiana, and Texas, and in Gulf Stream to Carolinas.

Like many birds that nest on remote oceanic islands, boobies have little fear of humans. Because of their tameness they were easily killed for food by early mariners, who gave them their name (from the Spanish *bobo,* "stupid") for this reason. Boobies obtain their prey in spectacular plunges from the air into the sea. Principal foods include flying fish and squid; boobies are seldom found in areas where these marine creatures are not plentiful.

## 88 Brown Booby
*Sula leucogaster*

Description: 30″ (76 cm). Adult has dark brown head, upperparts, and breast, with *sharply contrasting white belly* and white underwing coverts. Immature gray-brown, darker on head, wings, and tail.

Voice: Usually silent, but gives a variety of quacking, grunting, and screeching calls on breeding grounds.

Habitat: Tropical and subtropical seas; breeds on coastal islands.

Nesting: 1–3 pale blue or green eggs on bare ground in a slight mound of broken shells and scattered vegetation, usually at the edge of a cliff.

Range: Worldwide in tropical seas. In America, breeds on islands north to Gulf of Mexico and Caribbean Sea; wanders occasionally to coasts of Florida, Louisiana, and Texas; casually farther north in western Atlantic.

Of the boobies seen off the beaches of the Gulf of Mexico, this species is by far the most plentiful. Like the Northern Gannet, they dive for fish by plunging into the sea, but they also skim the surface to catch flying fish that leap clear of the surf. On land, these birds are dependent on a strong wind for takeoff from a tree or other elevated perch. On calm days they rest in vegetation or on the ground.

---

82, 86 **Northern Gannet**
*Morus bassanus*

Description: 35–40″ (89–102 cm). Adult white with *black wing tips;* head tinged with orange-buff. Long pointed tail and wings. Immature dark gray, variously speckled and patterned with white, depending on age. Alternately flaps and glides in flight; plunge dives when feeding. The gleaming white of the adult is visible at great distances.

Voice: Guttural croak or grunt, heard only on breeding islands.

Habitat: Open seas. Nests on northern rocky sea cliffs.

Nesting: 1 bluish-white egg that soon changes to brown, in a shallow nest of dried seaweed high on a precipitous cliff or along the top of a bluff. Nests in colonies, with nests close together.

Range: Breeds on a few isolated islands off Newfoundland, in Gulf of Saint Lawrence, and off Nova Scotia. Winters in coastal waters south to Florida and occasionally to Texas; also on northwest coast of Europe.

The only northern member of the booby family, the Northern Gannet is one of the most spectacular sea birds. During migrations gannets may be observed offshore, either gliding above the water or diving into the sea after fish, sometimes plunging headlong from heights as great as 50 feet (15 meters) or more. An intricate system of air sacs under the skin of the breast cushions the impact when a bird strikes the water. Gannets, like boobies, engage in an elaborate series of breeding displays. When one bird returns to a nest site, it is greeted by its mate. Both birds raise their heads and cross bills, which they clash together like swords, then bow to each other with wings and tails raised. This is followed by mutual preening of the head and neck. Usually the bird who has been relieved at the nest will pick up sticks or seaweed to present to its mate. Finally, the departing bird stands with head and neck extended straight up and wings raised over the back, then launches itself into the air.

---

## Family Pelecanidae
Pelicans

8 species: Nearly worldwide. Two species breed in North America. Pelicans are huge birds with webbed feet, very long bills, and enormous gular (throat) pouches. The American White Pelican inhabits inland waters and coastal lagoons, catching fish at the surface, while the Brown Pelican is exclusively coastal and plunge dives from the air to catch its prey. Flocks of

both species fly in long lines, alternately flapping and gliding, or occasionally soaring high in the sky.

## 182 American White Pelican

*Pelecanus erythrorhynchos*

Description: 55–70″ (1.4–1.8 m). W. 8′ (2.4 m). A *huge white bird* with a *long flat bill* and black wing tips. In breeding season, has short yellowish crest on back of head, and horny plate on upper mandible. Young birds are duskier than adults.

Voice: Usually silent; grunts or croaks on nesting grounds.

Habitat: Marshy lakes and coastal lagoons.

Nesting: 1–6 whitish eggs on a low mound of earth and debris on a marshy island. Nests in colonies.

Range: Breeds from British Columbia and Mackenzie south to northern California, Utah, and Manitoba, and along Texas Gulf Coast. Winters from central California, Gulf Coast, and Florida south to Panama.

A flock of migrating American White Pelicans is a majestic sight—a long line of ponderous birds, flapping and coasting. Each bird seems to take its cue from the one in front of it, beginning to flap and starting a glide when its predecessor does. These birds ride rising air currents to great heights, where they soar slowly and gracefully in circles. They often capture fish cooperatively, swimming in a long line, beating their wings, and driving the prey into shallow water, where they seize the fish in their large pouched bills. They take in both water and fish, and then hold their bills vertically to drain out the water before swallowing the food.

183 **Brown Pelican**
*Pelecanus occidentalis*

Description: 45–54" (1.1–1.4 m). W. 7′6" (2.3 m). A *very large,* stocky bird with a *dark brown body* and a *long flat bill.* Head whitish in adults, with dark brown on hindneck during breeding season. Young birds have dark brown heads and whitish bellies.

Voice: Usually silent, but utters low grunts on nesting grounds.

Habitat: Sandy coastal beaches and lagoons; waterfronts and pilings.

Nesting: 2 or 3 chalky white eggs in a nest of sticks, straw, or other debris, placed in a tree or low bush or on the ground on an island. Nests in colonies.

Range: Resident on Atlantic Coast from North Carolina south to Venezuela; on Pacific Coast from southern California to Chile. After nesting season, disperses northward as far as southern British Columbia.

The only nonwhite pelican in the world, this marine bird obtains its food by diving from the air, its wings half folded as it plunges into the surf. During one of these dives, the pouched bill takes in both fish and water; the bird drains out the water before throwing its head back and swallowing the fish. A few decades ago, pesticides accumulated in the birds' bodies and caused thinning of their eggshells. The Brown Pelican ceased to breed in many parts of its range. Today, with a reduction of pesticides, these familiar birds are reclaiming much of the territory they lost. They are once again a familiar sight in harbors and along sandy coastlines in the South.

## Family Phalacrocoracidae
Cormorants

38 species: Worldwide. Six species breed in North America. These are large birds, usually black, with long necks, long hooked bills, and webbed feet. The feet of these expert divers are located far back on the body to give them forward thrust under water; on land cormorants stand upright, often with their wings partially extended to dry. In the air, they fly in long lines or wedge-shaped formations.

### 96 Great Cormorant
*Phalacrocorax carbo*

Description: 35–40″ (89–102 cm). A large, thick-necked cormorant. Adult black with *white throat* and yellow chin pouch; in breeding plumage, has white flank patches. Immature is dull brown, with dusky neck and white on belly.

Voice: Deep guttural grunts.

Habitat: Sea cliffs, rocky coasts, and inshore waters.

Nesting: 3 or 4 chalky, pale blue-green eggs in a nest of sticks lined with seaweed, placed on isolated cliffs or rocky islands.

Range: Breeds from Newfoundland and Gulf of Saint Lawrence south to Nova Scotia, Bay of Fundy, and Maine. Winters south to New Jersey, rarely to Florida. Also in Old World.

The largest member of its family, the well-named Great Cormorant is widespread in the Old World but nests only along the eastern coast of Canada in the New World. In the Far East, birds of this species are trained to catch fish, wearing a neck ring to prevent them from swallowing what they catch; well-trained birds can be sent out without a ring. The Great Cormorant has increased in numbers in recent decades, and dozens may now be observed in winter on offshore rocks where a single bird would have been a real find just a few years ago.

98, 99 **Double-crested Cormorant**
*Phalacrocorax auritus*

Description: 30–35″ (76–89 cm). A solidly built black cormorant, with an *orange throat pouch* and long neck. Long hooked bill is tilted upward when bird swims. Adults have short tuft of feathers over each eye during breeding season. Young birds are browner, with tan or whitish color on neck and upper breast. In flight, neck shows a slight crook, not seen in larger Great Cormorant or smaller Neotropic.

Voice: Deep guttural grunts.

Habitat: Lakes, rivers, swamps, and coasts.

Nesting: 3–5 chalky, pale blue-green eggs in a well-made platform of sticks, or of seaweed on the coast, placed in a tree or on a cliff or rocky island. Nests in colonies.

Range: Breeds locally in interior from Alaska, Manitoba, and Newfoundland south to Mexico, and in Bahamas. Winters mainly on coasts, north to southern New England and Alaska.

The Double-crested is the most familiar cormorant in the East. Except in the Northeast during the winter, and along the Gulf Coast, it is the only cormorant likely to be seen. Occupying a wide variety of habitats, it nests and feeds as readily on inland waters as it does along the coast. Despite years of persecution by fishermen who viewed it as a competitor, the species is currently increasing in number and expanding its range. Like geese, cormorants migrate in large arcs or in wedge-shaped flocks, but are silent when flying. The word "cormorant" is derived, through French, from the Latin *corvus marinus,* or "sea crow."

## 95 Neotropic Cormorant
**"Olivaceous Cormorant"**
*Phalacrocorax brasilianus*

Description: 25″ (64 cm). A small, delicate-looking cormorant of southern lagoons and marshes. Black, glossed with olive, and with *orange throat pouch narrowly bordered with white.* Double-crested Cormorant is larger, lacks white border on throat pouch, has a shorter tail, and flies with crook in its neck.

Voice: Soft grunts.

Habitat: Brackish and fresh water.

Nesting: 2–6 chalky blue eggs, often stained with brown, in a shallow nest of sticks lined with grass and built in trees or bushes. Nests in small colonies.

Range: Resident along Gulf Coast of Louisiana and Texas to southern South America.

This is the smallest of the three cormorants inhabiting the East. Unlike the others, it often perches on telephone wires, where it can be seen spreading its wings to dry. When alarmed, it is more apt to escape by flying than by diving, as its larger relatives do. These birds sometimes engage in communal fishing, lining up across a stream and moving forward with flailing wings to drive fish into shallow water.

## Family Anhingidae
Anhingas or Darters

4 species: Tropical and subtropical regions of the world. One species breeds in North America. These large, web-footed birds have long slender necks and pointed spear-like bills with which they impale fish. They inhabit inland, freshwater lakes, streams, and marshes, and nest in trees and bushes.

94, 97 **Anhinga**
*Anhinga anhinga*

Description: 34–36″ (86–91 cm). A blackish bird of southern swamps, shaped like a cormorant but with a *very long, slender, S-shaped neck;* a *long, spear-like bill;* and a long, fan-shaped tail. Male's plumage has greenish iridescence; upper surface of wings silvery gray. Female has tawny-brown neck and breast, sharply set off from black belly.

Voice: Low grunts like those of cormorants.

Habitat: Freshwater ponds and swamps with thick vegetation, especially where there are large trees.

Nesting: 3–5 chalky blue eggs in a nest of sticks lined with fresh green leaves and built in trees. Often nests in colonies of Double-crested Cormorants.

Range: Breeds near Atlantic and Gulf coasts from North Carolina to Texas, in Florida, and in Mississippi Valley north to southern Missouri and Kentucky. Winters along Gulf Coast north to South Carolina. Also in tropical America.

Also known as the "Snakebird," the Anhinga often swims with its body submerged and only its head and long slender neck visible above the water. Its long, dagger-shaped, serrated bill is ideally suited for catching fish, which it stabs and then flips into the air and gulps down headfirst. Cormorants and Anhingas lack oil glands with which to preen and so must perch with their wings half open to dry them in the sun. Anhingas often soar in circles high overhead.

## Family Fregatidae
Frigatebirds

5 species: Tropical oceans of the world. In North America one species breeds in extreme southern Florida on the Marquesas Keys off Key West. These are large, extremely long-winged birds with long, deeply forked tails, hooked bills, and webbed feet. Males have inflatable throat pouches. Nesting chiefly on oceanic islands, they rob other seabirds, forcing them to disgorge the fish they have caught.

---

### 83, 84 Magnificent Frigatebird
*Fregata magnificens*

Description: 38–40″ (97–102 cm). W. 7′6″ (2.3 m). Black with very long, narrow, pointed wings, deeply forked tail, and long hooked bill. Male has brilliant red throat pouch in breeding season, which it inflates to huge size during courtship. Female has white breast. Young have white heads and underparts.

Voice: Usually silent at sea; harsh guttural calls during courtship.

Habitat: Open ocean and inshore waters; nests on mangrove islands.

Nesting: 1 white egg in a flimsy nest of sticks built in mangrove clumps.

Range: Breeds on a few mangrove islands in Florida Bay, and elsewhere in tropical Atlantic and Pacific oceans. In nonbreeding season, ranges to coasts of North Carolina, Texas, and California.

Frigatebirds, also called man-o'-war-birds, are among the most agile of birds on the wing. They have the largest wingspread in proportion to weight of any bird. In addition to stealing fish from other seabirds, their most famous method of obtaining food, they can soar for hours and often dip down to the surface to pick fish and other marine animals from the water, or skim past a breeding colony of boobies to snatch young birds from their nests. Frigatebirds never alight on the ground or water; their short legs and narrow wings make it difficult for them to take off except from a height, such as the limb of a tree or a rock.

## Family Ardeidae
Bitterns and Herons

64 species: Worldwide. Twelve species breed in North America. Some of these large to medium-sized, long-legged wading birds have long necks that they fold over their backs in flight. Bitterns and herons have long bills for catching prey, and their toes are unwebbed. Many species nest in colonies in trees and bushes. Some species have elaborate plumes during the breeding season.

### 25 American Bittern
*Botaurus lentiginosus*

Description: 23–34″ (58–86 cm). A secretive, medium-sized, streaked brown heron. *Outer wing appears blackish brown in flight,* contrasting with lighter brown of inner wing and body. At close range, adults show long black stripe down side of throat. Young night-herons are similar but stockier, with shorter necks and more rounded wings without dark tips; they lack the secretive habits of bitterns.

Voice: On breeding grounds, a loud pumping sound, *oong-KA-chunk!* repeated a few times and often audible for half a mile. Flight call a low *kok-kok-kok.*

Habitat: Freshwater and brackish marshes and marshy lakeshores; regular in salt marshes during migration and winter.

Nesting: 2–6 buff or olive-buff eggs on a

platform of reeds concealed in the marsh. Does not nest in colonies.

Range: Breeds from southeastern Alaska, Manitoba, and Newfoundland south to California, New Mexico, Arkansas, and Carolinas. Winters north to coastal British Columbia, Southwest, Illinois, and along Atlantic Coast to southern New England.

Known as the "Thunder-pumper" and "Stake-driver" because of its peculiar territorial call, the American Bittern is secretive and more likely to be heard than seen. When approached, it prefers to freeze and trust its concealing coloration rather than flush like other herons. When an observer is nearby, it will often stretch its neck up, point its bill skyward, and sway slowly from side to side, as if imitating waving reeds. If this doesn't fool the intruder, the bittern will fly off, uttering a low barking call.

## 26 Least Bittern
*Ixobrychus exilis*

Description: 11–14" (28–36 cm). A tiny, secretive heron with blackish back and *conspicuous buff wing patches* and underparts. Female and young are similar but duller, more buffy.

Voice: A soft *coo-coo-coo,* easily overlooked.

Habitat: Freshwater marshes where cattails and reeds predominate.

Nesting: 2–7 pale blue or green eggs on a flimsy platform of dead cattails or reeds, usually about a foot above the water.

Range: Breeds locally in Oregon, California, and Southwest, and from Manitoba and Texas east to Atlantic Coast. Winters from southern California, lower Colorado River, and Gulf Coast southward. Also in South America.

Although locally common in suitable habitat, this heron is very secretive. It is reluctant to fly, relying on its cryptic color pattern to escape detection. It often walks and climbs rapidly through reeds and cattails. The best way to see this bird is to wait at the edge of a cattail marsh, where eventually one may rise, fly over the cattails, and drop out of sight again. The very rare rufous form, once thought to be a separate species, is called "Cory's Least Bittern."

4, 19 **Great Blue Heron including "Great White Heron"**
*Ardea herodias*

Description: 39–52″ (99–132 cm). W. 5′10″ (1.8 m). A common, *large, mainly grayish* heron with pale or yellowish bill. Often mistaken for a Sandhill Crane, but flies with its neck folded, not extended like a crane's. In southern Florida an all-white form, "Great White Heron," differs from Great Egret in being larger, with greenish-yellow rather than black legs.

Voice: A harsh squawk.

Habitat: Lakes, ponds, rivers, and marshes.

Nesting: 3–7 pale greenish-blue eggs on a shallow platform of sticks lined with finer material, usually placed in a tree but sometimes on the ground or concealed in a reedbed. Nests in colonies.

Range: Breeds locally from coastal Alaska, south-central Canada, and Nova Scotia south to Mexico and West Indies. Winters as far north as southern Alaska, central United States, and southern New England. Also in Galápagos Islands.

This large heron is frequently found standing at the edge of a pond or marshy pool, watching for fish or frogs, which are its principal food. It also feeds on small mammals, reptiles, and occasionally birds. Most Great Blue Herons migrate south in the fall, but a few remain in the North during the winter; such lingering birds often fall victim to severe weather.

7, 8 **Great Egret**
*Casmerodius albus*

Description: 35–41″ (89–104 cm). W. 4′7″ (1.4 m). A large, all-white heron with a *yellow bill and black legs.* In breeding plumage, has long lacy plumes on back. In southern Florida, white form of Great Blue Heron, known as "Great White Heron," is similar but larger, with greenish-yellow legs. Much smaller Snowy Egret has black bill and black legs with yellow feet.

Voice: A guttural croak. Also loud squawks at nesting colonies.

Habitat: Freshwater and salt marshes, marshy ponds, and tidal flats.

Nesting: 3–5 pale blue-green eggs on a platform of sticks in a tree or bush. Nests in colonies, often with other species of herons.

Range: Breeds locally from Oregon south to western Mexico, from Minnesota to Mississippi Valley and Southeast, and along Atlantic Coast north to southern New England. Winters regularly north along Pacific Coast to Oregon, Southwest, Texas, and Gulf Coast states; on Atlantic Coast, north to New Jersey. Also in tropical America and warmer parts of Old World.

Formerly known as the "American Egret," "Common Egret," "Large Egret," "White Egret," "Great White Egret," and "Great White Heron," this bird's official name in North America is now Great Egret. One of the most magnificent of our herons, it has fortunately recovered from historic persecution by plume hunters. Like the Great Blue Heron, it usually feeds alone, stalking fish, frogs, snakes, and crayfish in shallow water. Each summer many individuals, especially young ones, wander far north of the breeding grounds.

**5, 6 Snowy Egret**
*Egretta thula*

Description: 20–27″ (51–69 cm). W. 3′2″ (97 cm). A small, delicate, white heron with a *slender black bill, black legs, and yellow feet.* In breeding season, has long lacy plumes on head, neck, and back. Immature similar, but lacks plumes and has yellow stripe up back of legs. Adult Cattle Egret has pale bill, legs, and feet; legs and feet dark in immatures. Much larger Great Egret has yellow bill, black legs and feet. Similar to immature of less common Little Blue Heron, but that species has stouter, gray-based, dark-tipped bill, has greenish-yellow legs and feet, and lacks yellow lores.

Voice: A harsh squawk.

Habitat: Marshes, ponds, swamps, and mudflats.

Nesting: 3–5 pale blue-green eggs on a platform of sticks placed in a bush or reedbed or on the ground. Nests in colonies, often with other species of herons.

Range: Breeds locally from Oregon and California east to New England, mainly along coasts but at scattered localities inland. Winters regularly north from California, Arizona, and Virginia south to West Indies and South America. Also resident in tropical America.

These delicate, agile birds often feed by sprinting rapidly through shallow water, chasing schools of minnows and shrimp. This habit makes them easy to identify without seeing their bills and feet. Often several Snowies will be found feeding together, and it is thought that their white color, visible at great distances, lets other birds know where the feeding is good; the sprinting behavior also attracts other birds that then join in the feast.

## 3, 17 Little Blue Heron
*Egretta caerulea*

Description: 25–30″ (64–76 cm). W. 3′5″ (1 m). Adult slate-blue with maroon neck. Immatures white, usually with dusky tips to primaries. Bill grayish with black tip; legs greenish. Young birds acquiring adult plumage have a piebald appearance. Snowy Egret somewhat smaller and all white, with black bill and legs, yellow lores and feet.

Voice: Usually silent but squawks when alarmed. Various croaks and screams at nesting colonies.

Habitat: Freshwater swamps and lagoons in the South; coastal thickets on islands in the North.

Nesting: 3–5 pale blue-green eggs in a nest of sticks in a small tree or bush. Nests in colonies.

Range: Breeds from southern California (rare), southern New Mexico, Texas, Oklahoma, Illinois, and southern New England south to Gulf Coast; more common along coasts. Winters along Gulf Coast, in Florida, and on Atlantic Coast north to New Jersey. Also in tropical America.

This is one of the most numerous herons in the South and may be observed in large mixed concentrations of herons and egrets. It eats more insects than the larger herons and is sometimes seen following a plow to pick up exposed insect larvae. Unlike the egrets, it has no fancy plumes and was thus spared by plume hunters.

## 18 Tricolored Heron
## "Louisiana Heron"
*Egretta tricolor*

Description: 25–30″ (64–76 cm). W. 3′2″ (97 cm). A *slender,* gray-blue heron with rufous neck and *white belly.*

Voice: Guttural croaks and squawks.
Habitat: Swamps, bayous, coastal ponds, salt marshes, mangrove islands, mudflats, and lagoons.
Nesting: 3 or 4 blue-green eggs in a nest of sticks placed in a tree or reedbed, or on the ground.
Range: Breeds in southeastern New Mexico and Texas, on Gulf Coast, and along Atlantic Coast, casually north to southern Maine. Winters from New Jersey south to northern South America and West Indies. Also resident in tropical America.

Formerly called the "Louisiana Heron," this is one of the most abundant herons in the Deep South. It is extremely slender and moves gracefully as it searches about for frogs or fish. Despite its relatively small size, it forages in deep water; often its legs are completely underwater, and the bird appears to be swimming.

9, 20 **Reddish Egret**
*Egretta rufescens*

Description: 30″ (76 cm). W. 3′10″ (1.2 m). A medium-sized heron, slate-gray with shaggy, pale rufous head and neck, *bluish legs,* and *pink bill with dark tip.* White phase has bluish legs and pink bill with dark tip. Adult Little Blue Heron darker, without shaggy neck, and with grayish (not pink) bill. Immature grayish with buff on head, neck, and wings; bill dark.
Voice: Squawks and croaks.
Habitat: Salt and brackish waters, breeding in shallow bays and lagoons; in mangroves (Florida); among cacti, willows, and other shrubs (Texas).
Nesting: 3 or 4 pale blue-green eggs in a nest of sticks placed in mangroves or low bushes, or on the ground.

Range: Locally resident in extreme southern Florida and along Gulf Coast of Texas and Louisiana. Also in Mexico and West Indies.

The Reddish Egret forages by rushing rapidly about in shallow salt water with its wings raised, chasing down fish, frogs, and crustaceans. It also brings its wings forward in front of its body, creating a "canopy" of shade from which it spots its prey more easily. Both color phases may be seen on the Gulf Coast, the dark one predominating in Florida waters, the white more numerous in Texas. During the nuptial display, this species erects the shaggy plumes on its head, neck, and back.

---

1, 2 **Cattle Egret**
*Bubulcus ibis*

Description: 20″ (51 cm). A small, stocky, white heron with buff on the crown, breast, and back during breeding season. Legs pale yellow or orange in adults, blackish in some immatures. Bill short and yellow or orange; dark in immatures.

Voice: Hoarse croaks.

Habitat: Forages mainly alongside livestock in open fields and pastures, but breeds near water with other herons.

Nesting: 3–5 pale blue eggs in a nest of sticks placed in a bush or tree, generally in a marsh. Usually nests in colonies with other herons.

Range: Breeds locally from California and most western states east to Great Lakes and Maine, and southward to Gulf Coast. Also in American tropics and Old World.

Originating in the Old World, the Cattle Egret crossed the Atlantic, probably flying from Africa to South America, where this species was first reported in the late 19th and early 20th centuries. The birds gradually spread northward through the West Indies and into Florida, then northward and westward. Originally adapted to feeding on insects stirred up by wild grazing animals, they now follow livestock.

28 **Green Heron**
**"Green-backed Heron"**
*Butorides virescens*

Description: 16–22" (41–56 cm). A *dark, crow-sized* heron. Crown black, *back and wings dark gray-green or gray-blue* (depending on lighting); *neck chestnut colored.* Bill dark; legs bright orange. Immature has streaks on neck, breast, and sides.

Voice: Call a sharp *kyowk!* or *skyow!*

Habitat: Breeds mainly in freshwater or brackish marshes with clumps of trees. Feeds along margin of any body of water.

Nesting: 3–6 pale green or pale blue eggs in a loose nest of sticks built in a tree or dense thicket.

Range: Breeds over a wide region from Canadian border to Gulf of Mexico, west to Great Plains, western Texas, and southwestern New Mexico; in West from Fraser River delta of British Columbia south to California and Arizona. Winters from coastal California south to southern Arizona and Texas, along Gulf Coast, and along Atlantic Coast north to South Carolina.

The most common heron in much of its range, the Green Heron requires only a pond or stream with thick bushes or trees nearby for nesting and soft muddy borders in which to search for its prey. It stretches its neck and bill forward as if taking aim, nervously flicking its short tail, and, after a few elaborately cautious steps, seizes the fish with a jab of its bill. A retiring bird, it is often first noticed when it flushes unexpectedly from the edge of the water and flies off uttering its sharp call.

13, 14 **Black-crowned Night-Heron**
*Nycticorax nycticorax*

Description: 23–28″ (58–71 cm). W. 3′8″ (1.1 m). A medium-sized, stocky, rather short-necked heron with *black crown,* gray wings, and *white underparts;* short black bill; pinkish or yellowish legs. In breeding season, has 2 or more long white plumes on back of head. Young birds are dull gray-brown lightly spotted with white. Young Yellow-crowned Night-Herons are grayer, with stouter bills and longer legs.

Voice: Loud barking *kwok!* or *quawk!* often heard at night or at dusk. Utters a variety of croaks, barks, and other harsh calls in nesting colonies.

Habitat: Marshes, swamps, and wooded streams.

Nesting: 3–5 pale blue-green eggs in a shallow saucer of sticks or reeds placed in a thicket or reedbed, occasionally in tall trees. Nests in colonies, sometimes with other species of herons.

Range: Breeds throughout United States (except Rocky Mountain region), from Washington, Saskatchewan, Minnesota, and New Brunswick to southern South America. Winters in southern half of United States. Also occurs in much of Old World.

As its name implies, this noisy bird is largely nocturnal, beginning to forage at dusk, when other herons are on their way to roosts. Night-herons are less likely to nest in mixed colonies than other herons; when they do, they often keep to themselves in a separate corner.

15, 16 **Yellow-crowned Night-Heron**
*Nyctanassa violacea*

Description: 22–27″ (56–69 cm). W 3′8″ (1.1 m). Medium-sized heron. Adult slate-gray with black head, *white cheeks, yellowish crown and plumes,* black bill, and yellow or orange legs. In flight, feet and part of legs extend beyond tail. Immature grayish brown, finely speckled with white above. Young Black-crowned Night-Herons similar but browner, with legs and feet that scarcely project beyond tail in flight.

Voice: A loud *quawk!* that is higher pitched than that of Black-crowned Night-Heron.

Habitat: Wooded swamps and coastal thickets.

Nesting: 3–5 blue-green eggs in a nest of sticks in a tree or occasionally on the ground. Nests singly or in small colonies, occasionally with other herons.

Range: Breeds from southern New England to Florida and west to Texas, mainly near coasts but in the interior north to Minnesota and along Mississippi River and its larger tributaries. Ranges more widely after nesting season. Winters along Gulf Coast and on Atlantic Coast north to South Carolina. Also in tropical America.

Like other herons with a southerly distribution, this species has increased and expanded its range northward in recent decades. Unlike the Black-crowned Night-Heron, the Yellow-crowned preys chiefly on crabs and crayfish, which it crushes with its short, powerful bill.

## Family Threskiornithidae
Ibises and Spoonbills

33 species: Chiefly tropical regions of the world. Four species breed in North America, including the colorful Roseate Spoonbill. The bills of ibises are long and curved downward; those of spoonbills are straight and spatulate. They are aquatic birds that feed on fish, frogs, insects, and other small animals in the water. They nest in colonies in trees and bushes, often with herons.

## 12, 24 White Ibis
*Eudocimus albus*

Description: 23–27″ (58–69 cm). W. 3′2″ (97 cm). Adult white with black wing tips (usually hidden at rest); bare face and down-curved bill are red; legs red in breeding season, otherwise slate-gray. Immatures brown above and white below, with brown bill and legs.

Voice: Grunts and growls.

Habitat: Marshes, mudflats, lagoons, and swampy forests.

Nesting: 3 or 4 greenish-white eggs with dark spots or blotches in a stick nest in trees over water. Nests in colonies.

Range: Coastal resident from North Carolina to Florida and Texas. Also in American tropics.

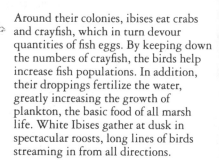

Around their colonies, ibises eat crabs and crayfish, which in turn devour quantities of fish eggs. By keeping down the numbers of crayfish, the birds help increase fish populations. In addition, their droppings fertilize the water, greatly increasing the growth of plankton, the basic food of all marsh life. White Ibises gather at dusk in spectacular roosts, long lines of birds streaming in from all directions.

## 22 Glossy Ibis
*Plegadis falcinellus*

Description: 22–25″ (56–64 cm). W. 3′1″ (94 cm). A large, all-dark marsh bird with a down-curved bill. Plumage rich chestnut in breeding season; wings glossy greenish; eyes brown. The bare face is outlined by a thin line of white. Breeding White-faced Ibis similar, but has broader band of white feathers around bare face, red eyes, and all-red legs. Outside the breeding season, both species have streaks on the head and neck, and brown eyes; they are then very difficult to distinguish.

Voice: Low grunts and higher-pitched bleats.

Habitat: Marshes, swamps, flooded fields, coastal bays, and estuaries.

Nesting: 3 or 4 pale blue-green eggs in a stick nest in a bush or tree, rarely on the ground. Nests in colonies, often along with herons.

Range: Breeds on or near the coast, chiefly from Maine to Florida and Texas. Resident and in winter along Gulf Coast and on Atlantic Coast south from Carolinas. Also in Old World.

The Glossy Ibis probably crossed the Atlantic from Africa to northern South America in the 19th century, dispersing northward into the United States by way of the Caribbean region. In recent years it has expanded its range considerably and is now a common breeder in areas where it was formerly rare or absent. Away from salt water it frequently eats crayfish, but along the coast it feeds mostly on fiddler crabs. It also eats insects and snakes, including the poisonous water moccasin.

---

## 23 White-faced Ibis
*Plegadis chihi*

Description: 22–25″ (56–64 cm). W. 3′1″ (94 cm). A large, chestnut-bronze marsh bird with a long, down-curved bill. Very similar to Glossy Ibis, but with band of white feathers around the bare face, red eyes, and all-red legs. The Glossy Ibis has a narrow band of white skin around the edge of the bare face, and brown eyes. In winter, the White-faced has streaks on the head and neck, and brown eyes; it is then virtually impossible to distinguish from the Glossy.

Voice: Low croaks and grunts.

Habitat: Salt marshes and brushy coastal islands in Louisiana and Texas, freshwater marshes in the West.

Nesting: 3 or 4 pale blue-green eggs in a shallow cup of reeds lined with grass placed in low bushes in a marsh.

Range: Breeds from Oregon sporadically east to Minnesota and south to southeast New Mexico and Texas, and east to coastal Louisiana. Winters in Southwest and along Gulf Coast.

This western bird enters our area only in western Louisiana and Texas, where the White-faced Ibis is common and the Glossy Ibis is rare; in these areas most dark ibises can be assumed to be White-faced. This bird probably represents an earlier invasion of the New World by the Glossy Ibis, which in isolation evolved into a separate species.

---

## 29 Roseate Spoonbill
*Ajaia ajaja*

Description: 30–32″ (76–81 cm). W. 4′5″ (1.3 m). Bill long and straight with *broad spatulate tip* from which the bird gets its name. Mainly white, with brilliant pink wings and flanks, and orange tail; shoulder rich crimson. Immature pale pink and white.

Voice: Low croaks and clucking sounds.

Habitat: Mangroves and saltwater lagoons.

Nesting: 2 or 3 dull-white eggs, with dark spots and blotches, in a bulky nest of sticks built in a low bush or tree. Nests in colonies.

Range: Resident locally on coasts of Texas, Louisiana (rare), and southern Florida. Also in American tropics.

These birds spend much time feeding in the shallow waters of Florida Bay and the Gulf of Mexico on shrimp, small fish, snails, and aquatic insects, which they detect by their sense of touch as they rhythmically sweep their "spoon-shaped" bills from side to side. Early in the century their numbers were severely depleted by plume hunters, but with protective laws they have increased once again.

## FAMILY CICONIIDAE
Storks

17 species: Chiefly tropical regions of the world. Only one species breeds in North America. Storks are large, long-legged, long-necked, and long-billed birds that live chiefly in open, marshy country. They nest either singly or in colonies in trees and bushes, often with herons and ibises. They feed on all sorts of animal matter, and a few species eat carrion.

### 10 Wood Stork
*Mycteria americana*

Description: 40–44″ (1.0–1.1 m). W. 5′6″ (1.7 m). White with black flight feathers and tail. Head and neck bare, dark gray. Bill long, stout, and slightly curved, black in adults and dull yellow in immatures. Unlike herons, storks fly with the neck extended.

Voice: Dull croak. Usually silent except around nest. Young make clattering noises with their bills.

Habitat: On or near the coast, breeding chiefly in cypress swamps; also in mangroves.

Nesting: 2 or 3 white eggs on a huge stick platform in a tree. Nests in colonies.

Range: More or less resident in Florida and Georgia, very rarely elsewhere along coast from South Carolina to Texas. Outside breeding season has wandered as far as California and Massachusetts (very rarely). Also breeds in tropical America.

Formerly called the "Wood Ibis," this is a true stork. Its naked gray head has earned it the local name "Flinthead." These birds perch motionless on a bare branch or slowly stalk through marshes in search of food. Expert at soaring, they are sometimes seen circling high in the air on rising air currents. They nest in enormous colonies numbering up to 10,000 pairs, but in recent years their numbers have declined drastically due to land development, lumbering, and draining of their feeding grounds.

## FAMILY PHOENICOPTERIDAE
Flamingos

6 species: Widely distributed in saline desert areas of the world. These slender, long-legged, long-necked birds feed on aquatic microorganisms, filtering them with a peculiarly modified bill. All species have some pink on their plumage.

### 30 Greater Flamingo "American Flamingo"
*Phoenicopterus ruber*

Description: 48″ (1.2 m). W. 4′7″ (1.4 m). Unmistakable. A tall, long-legged, long-necked *pink* bird with a short, *down-curved bill.* Wings have black tips and trailing edges.

Voice: Goose-like honking and cackling notes.

Habitat: Shallow coastal lagoons and mudflats.

Nesting: 1 white egg on a low mound of mud on a mudflat. Nests in dense colonies.

Range: Resident in Bahamas, West Indies, Yucatán, northern South America, and Galápagos Islands. A casual visitor to U.S. coast from Carolinas to Texas.

This species was formerly more numerous and probably bred at one time along the coast of Florida. Flamingos are extremely sensitive to disturbance and today nest only in a few very isolated localities. The birds use their curiously shaped bills to strain small animals from the mud. Flamingo-like birds, known today only as fossils, lived in western North America 50 million years ago.

## Family Anatidae

Swans, Geese, and Ducks

150 species: Worldwide. At least 40 species breed in North America. In swans and geese, the sexes are alike, but many species of ducks have marked sexual dimorphism, with the males the more brightly colored. All members of the family have webbed feet and most are aquatic, although the geese are primarily terrestrial. As might be expected from such a diverse family, food habits are extremely varied; some forms are vegetarians, others eat fish, snails, and insects. This successful family has been able to colonize very remote oceanic islands in all parts of the globe.

### 173 Fulvous Whistling-Duck

*Dendrocygna bicolor*

Description: 18–21″ (46–53 cm). A long-legged, long-necked, goose-like duck. Body mainly *tawny, with a white stripe on the side;* wings dark; rump and undertail coverts white.

Voice: A hoarse whistle, *ka-wheee.*

Habitat: Rice fields, freshwater marshes, wet meadows, and lagoons.

Nesting: 12–15 buff-white eggs in a shallow cup of grass or a well-woven basket of reeds in a marsh. Sometimes several females lay in the same nest.

Range: Resident in southern California, coastal Texas and Louisiana, and southern Florida. Also in American tropics and Old World.

Although Fulvous Whistling-Ducks in North America breed only in California, Texas, Louisiana, and Florida, they sometimes wander. Small flocks have turned up as far north as British Columbia and Nova Scotia. These long-legged ducks do most of their feeding on land, eating green grass, seeds, and acorns. This species was formerly known as the "Fulvous Tree Duck." The name "fulvous" refers to its tawny color.

## 172 Black-bellied Whistling-Duck
*Dendrocygna autumnalis*

Description: 20–22″ (51–56 cm). A tall, long-necked, long-legged duck. Body of adult mainly chestnut and black, bill red, legs pink; large white wing patch visible in flight. Immature similar, but much duller.

Voice: Mellow whistles.

Habitat: Wooded or tree-lined streams and ponds.

Nesting: 12–16 white eggs without a nest lining in a tree cavity or artificial nest box, occasionally on the ground among reeds.

Range: Breeds in southern Arizona and resident in southern Texas; introduced birds have bred in southern Florida. Also in American tropics.

These handsome, conspicuous birds often rest on large tree branches, stakes, or poles in the water or, less commonly, on the ground. Almost entirely herbivorous, they feed in shallow water on tubers and other aquatic vegetation, as well as in grain fields. Unlike many ducks, this species is largely nocturnal, migrating at night and resting and feeding during the day. They are easily domesticated and are quite tame even in the wild. This species was formerly known as the "Black-bellied Tree Duck."

181 **Tundra Swan**
**"Whistling Swan"**
*Cygnus columbianus*

Description: 48–55″ (1.2–1.4 m). The only native swan in the East. Large, all white; bill black, usually with small yellow spot in front of eye. Holds neck straight up, unlike Mute Swan, which bends its neck in a graceful curve.

Voice: Mellow, bugling call, *hoo-ho-hoo,* usually heard from a flock of migrating birds.

Habitat: Arctic tundra; winters on marshy lakes and bays.

Nesting: 4–6 creamy-white eggs on a large mound of grass and moss on an island or beside a marshy tundra lake.

Range: Breeds in Alaska and far northern Canada east to Baffin Island. Winters from southern Alaska south to Nevada, Utah, and Baja California and on mid-Atlantic Coast, rarely to Gulf Coast of Texas; also occasionally on Great Lakes.

Each fall large numbers of Tundra Swans bound for the Atlantic Coast pause briefly on the Great Lakes before moving to their winter headquarters from Delaware Bay to North Carolina. Often traveling in flocks of several hundred, they present a spectacular sight. Many stop on the Niagara River, where some are swept over the falls to their death. Because they breed in remote and little disturbed areas, they have so far escaped the fate of the closely related Trumpeter Swan (*Cygnus buccinator*) of the West, which was reduced to near extinction by hunting and habitat destruction.

180 **Mute Swan**
*Cygnus olor*

Description: 58–60″ (1.47–1.52 m). W. 7′11″ (2.4 m). Adults all white; *bill orange with black knob at base.* Young birds similar but dingy gray-brown, becoming whiter with age. The Mute Swan holds its neck in a graceful curve; native swans hold their necks straight up.

Voice: Usually silent, but utters hissing and barking notes. A loud trumpeting call is rarely heard; wings make loud whirring sound in flight.

Habitat: Ponds, rivers, coastal lagoons, and bays.

Nesting: 4–6 gray or blue-green eggs in a huge mound-like nest lined with feathers and down, conspicuously placed at the edge of a pond or marsh.

Range: Introduced from Europe into northeastern United States; resident and most common in southern New England, southeastern New York, New Jersey, and Maryland; also established locally in Michigan.

With its wings arched over its back and its neck in a graceful S-curve, the male is extremely handsome on the water. Breeding pairs are highly aggressive and will defend the nest and young against all comers, using their powerful wings and strong bills to drive away other waterfowl and even humans.

---

175 **Greater White-fronted Goose**
**"White-fronted Goose"**
*Anser albifrons*

Description: 27–30″ (69–76 cm). A dusky brown goose with conspicuous white belly and undertail coverts; *white patch on front of face;* underparts barred and flecked with black; bill usually pink; legs orange. Birds from Greenland have orange bills. Young birds lack white face and black bars on underparts.

Voice: A distinctive bark, *kla-ha!* or *kla-hah-luk!*

Habitat: Breeds on marshy tundra; winters on marshes and bays.

Nesting: 5 or 6 cream-colored eggs in a down-lined grassy depression on the tundra.

Range: Breeds in Alaska, far northern Canada, and Greenland. Winters from coastal British Columbia to California and along Gulf Coast in Texas and Louisiana, more rarely on East Coast and in interior. Also breeds in northern Eurasia.

This is the least common goose in the eastern states, occurring in numbers only along the Gulf Coast in Louisiana and Texas; its winter headquarters is California's Sacramento Valley. Along the eastern edge of the Great Plains the birds often migrate at night, when they can be identified by their distinctive call. Like other geese, they often leave the marshes to feed in nearby stubble fields; here they are frequently concealed from view until the observer is very close, when they explode noisily into the air. The "Tule Goose" of the West Coast is considered a large race of the White-fronted Goose, but its status is still uncertain and its nesting grounds are unknown.

177, 178 **Snow Goose including "Blue Goose"**
*Chen caerulescens*

Description: 25–31″ (64–79 cm). Smaller than the domestic goose. *Pure white with black wing tips; bill pink with black "lip"; legs pink.* Young birds have dark bills and are mottled with brownish gray above. A dark phase, once considered a separate species called the "Blue Goose," has bluish-gray upperparts, brownish underparts, and *white head and neck.* Blue-phase birds have increased in recent decades and can now be found along the East Coast among the thousands of white Snow Geese wintering there.

Voice: A high-pitched, barking *bow-wow!* or *howk-howk!*

Habitat: Breeds on the tundra. Winters in salt marshes and marshy coastal bays, less commonly in freshwater marshes and adjacent grain fields.

Nesting: 4–8 white eggs in a nest sparsely lined with down placed on the tundra. Nests in colonies.

Range: Breeds in arctic regions of North America and extreme eastern Siberia. In the West, winters from southern British Columbia and central California south to Baja California; also along mid-Atlantic Coast and Gulf Coast from Mississippi to Texas. In smaller numbers in the interior.

Snow Geese migrate long distances, sometimes flying so high that they can barely be seen. Even at this distance, however, they can often be identified by the shifting curved lines and arcs they form as they fly. Hunters call these birds "Wavies," but not because of the shape of their flocks; the word is derived from *wewe,* the Chippewa name for the species. The "Blue Goose," once confined to the central Arctic and wintering mainly along the Gulf Coast, has increased in recent decades and now turns up throughout the species' winter range.

## 176 Ross' Goose
*Chen rossii*

Description: 24″ (61 cm). A Mallard-sized edition of the Snow Goose. White wings, black wing tips, pink bill, and pink legs. Differs from the Snow Goose in its smaller size, *very stubby bill,* and rounder head. The rare blue phase looks like a miniature "Blue Goose."

Voice: Soft cackling and grunting notes.

Habitat: Arctic tundra in breeding season; salt or fresh marshes in winter.

Nesting: 4 or 5 creamy-white eggs in a down-lined grass nest placed on a small island in a lake or river. Nests in loose colonies.

Range: Breeds in northeastern Mackenzie and on Southampton Island in Hudson Bay. Winters mainly in California, but is now appearing in increasing numbers in lower Mississippi Valley and on East Coast.

This species is very similar to the white phase of the Snow Goose; when it appears in the East, it is usually in the company of the larger species. It occasionally hybridizes with the Snow Goose, and there is some evidence that many of the Ross' Geese that appear in the eastern states in winter are actually hybrids. The great majority of Ross' Geese spend the winter in the Far West.

---

## 174 Brant
**including "Black Brant"**
*Branta bernicla*

Description: 22–30″ (56–76 cm). Similar to the Canada Goose but smaller, shorter-necked, and lacking conspicuous white cheek patch. Dark brown above with black head and neck, and inconspicuous white mark on side of neck; whitish on belly and flanks.

Voice: A low guttural *ruk-ruk.*

Habitat: Tundra and coastal islands in the Arctic; salt marshes and estuaries in winter.

Nesting: 3–5 dull-white eggs in a large mass of moss and down placed on the tundra. Often nests in loose colonies.

Range: Breeds in coastal Alaska and Canadian Arctic. Winters along coasts south to California and Carolinas. Also in Eurasia.

In the 1930s a disease virtually wiped out eelgrass, until then the favorite food of the Brant, and numbers of this species declined sharply. The survivors switched to the seaweed called sea lettuce. Eelgrass is abundant again in coastal bays, and the numbers of Brant have risen; there are now more than 100,000 wintering on the East Coast, and more than 150,000 on the Pacific Coast. Migrating flocks can be identified at a great distance as they travel in erratic, constantly shifting bunches unlike the V-shaped flocks of Canada Geese or the long curved lines of Snow Geese. Birds from far western North America have black underparts and until recently were considered a separate species, the "Black Brant."

179 **Canada Goose**
*Branta canadensis*

Description: Small races 22–26″ (56–66 cm); large races 35–45″ (89–114 cm). Brownish body with *black head, long black neck, and conspicuous white cheek patch.* The smaller Brant has a shorter neck and lacks the white cheek patch.

Voice: Rich musical honking in larger races; high-pitched cackling in smaller races.

Habitat: Lakes, bays, rivers, and marshes. Often feeds in open grasslands and stubble fields.

Nesting: 4–8 whitish eggs in a large mass of grass and moss lined with down; usually on the ground near water or on a muskrat lodge, but sometimes in a tree, in an abandoned Osprey or Bald Eagle nest.

Range: Breeds from Alaska east to Baffin Island and south to California, Illinois, and Massachusetts. Winters south to northern Mexico and Gulf Coast. Widespread as a semidomesticated bird in city parks and on reservoirs.

When people speak of "wild geese," it is generally this familiar species they have in mind. Their V-shaped migrating flocks are a common sight in spring and fall. There is much geographical variation in size. Some birds, including the so-called "Cackling Goose," are scarcely larger than Mallards, while others are at least twice that size. The largest is the "Giant Canada Goose," which inhabits the northern Great Plains. Increasingly tolerant of humans, some Canadas even nest in city parks and suburbs. They are especially noticeable in late summer and early fall, when they form molting flocks on golf courses and large lawns; at such times, they have come to be regarded as pests.

116, 149 **Wood Duck**
*Aix sponsa*

Description: 17–20″ (43–51 cm). A beautiful, crested, multicolored duck. Male patterned in iridescent greens, purples, and blues, with a distinctive white chin patch and face stripes; bill mainly red; tail long. Female grayish with broad white eye ring.

Voice: Female, loud *wooo-eeek!;* male, softer *jeee?* or *ter-weeeee?*

Habitat: Wooded rivers and ponds; wooded swamps. Visits freshwater marshes in late summer and fall.

Nesting: 9–12 whitish or tan eggs in a nest made of down and placed in a natural tree cavity or artificial nest box, sometimes up to 50′ (15 m) off the ground.

Range: Breeds from British Columbia south to California, and from Montana east to Nova Scotia and south to Texas and Florida; absent from Rocky Mountains and Great Plains. Winters near Pacific Coast north to Washington, and to New Jersey in East, rarely farther north.

The Wood Duck's habit of nesting in cavities enables it to breed in areas lacking suitable ground cover. The young leave the nest soon after hatching, jumping from the nesting cavity to the ground or water. Once out of the nest, they travel through wooded ponds with their mother. Snapping turtles take a heavy toll of the young.

114, 160 **Green-winged Teal including "Common Teal"**
*Anas crecca*

Description: 12–16" (30–41 cm). A small *dark* duck. Male has chestnut head, green ear patch, flashing *green speculum,* pale gray sides, and pinkish breast with a vertical white stripe down the side. Female dark brown, without distinctive markings. "Common Teal," race in Old World, has horizontal white stripe above flanks, no vertical white stripe on side.

Voice: Clear, repeated whistle. Females quack.

Habitat: Marshes, ponds, and marshy lakes.

Nesting: 10–12 whitish or pale buff eggs in a down-lined cup in tall grass, often several hundred yards from water.

Range: Breeds in northern Alaska, Manitoba, and Quebec south to California, Colorado, Nebraska, and New York. Winters in southern states and along coasts. Also in Eurasia.

Until recently, the North American and Eurasian forms were considered distinct species. Each year a few males—and doubtless females—of the Eurasian form turn up in North America, giving rise to speculation that somewhere in North America a few of these so-called "Common Teal" may be breeding. Green-winged Teal are among the fastest-flying ducks and are therefore popular game birds. They wheel in compact flocks like shorebirds. A hardy species, they are among the last ducks to reach their winter habitat in fall and the first to depart in spring.

164 **American Black Duck**
*Anas rubripes*

Description: 19–22" (48–56 cm). Sooty brown with paler head and *conspicuous white wing linings* and violet speculum; olive or dull yellow bill. Sexes similar. Female

Mallard paler and sandier, with bill mottled with orange and black, and whitish tail feathers.

Voice: Typical duck quack.

Habitat: Marshes, lakes, streams, coastal mudflats, and estuaries.

Nesting: 9–12 greenish-buff eggs in a ground nest of feathers and down.

Range: Breeds in eastern and central North America, from Manitoba and Labrador to Texas and Florida. Winters from southern Minnesota and Nova Scotia south to southern Texas and central Florida.

Habitat destruction and widespread interbreeding between American Black Ducks and Mallards has resulted in recent years in a decrease of "pure" Blacks. Actually the bird is not black, but only appears so at a distance; it was formerly more aptly known as the "Dusky Duck." In areas of heavy shooting, these and other dabbling ducks ingest enough lead shot to cause extensive mortality from lead poisoning. If hunters used steel shot such damage would be much reduced.

161 **Mottled Duck**
*Anas fulvigula*

Description: 21″ (53 cm). Mottled dark brown and sandy. Similar to a female Mallard, but bill clear yellow or orange-yellow, throat plain tawny, and tail dark rather than whitish.

Voice: A loud quack, like that of a Mallard.

Habitat: Coastal marshes and lagoons.

Nesting: 9–13 pale greenish eggs in a down-lined nest of grass concealed in vegetation near a shore.

Range: Resident in southern Florida and along Gulf Coast of Louisiana and Texas.

This southern duck is a very close relative of the widespread Mallard.

Until recently, no other duck of the genus *Anas* nested in these coastal marshes, and so the distinctive male plumage, which among these birds enables females to identify mates of their own species, was gradually lost. After thousands of years of evolutionary change, the two sexes are colored alike.

---

119, 158 **Mallard**
*Anas platyrhynchos*

Description: 18–27" (46–69 cm). Male has a *green head, white neck ring,* chestnut breast, and grayish body. Speculum metallic purplish blue, bordered in front and back with white. Female mottled brown with *white tail* and purplish-blue speculum; bill mottled orange and black. See Mottled Duck.

Voice: Males utter soft, reedy notes; females, a loud quack.

Habitat: Ponds, lakes, and marshes. Semi-domesticated birds may be found on almost any body of water.

Nesting: 8–10 pale greenish-buff eggs in a shallow bowl of grass lined with down, hidden in marsh grass or on a brush pile near the shore.

Range: Breeds from Alaska east to Quebec, and south to southern California, Virginia, Texas, and northern Mexico. Winters throughout United States south to Central America and West Indies. Also in Eurasia.

The Mallard is undoubtedly the most abundant duck in the world. Nearly 10 million live in North America, and millions more are found in Eurasia. Since the Mallard is the ancestor of the common white domestic duck, still more can be added to the total. Mallards frequently interbreed with domestic stock, producing a bewildering variety of patterns and colors. They also hybridize with wild species such as the closely related American Black Duck and even occasionally with Northern Pintails. Strong fliers, Mallards sometimes reach remote oceanic islands where isolated populations have evolved into new species. Like the Mottled Duck, these isolated populations often differ from the Mallard mainly in that they lack the colorful plumage of the male.

112, 168 **Northern Pintail**
*Anas acuta*

Description: Males 25–29″ (64–74 cm); females 21–23″ (53–58 cm). Slim, graceful duck with a slender neck. Male has *brown head and white neck with white line extending onto side of head.* Central tail feathers long, black, and pointed. Female mottled brown, similar to female Mallard, but paler, grayer, and more slender, with brown speculum bordered with white at rear edge only; tail is more pointed than in female Mallard.

Voice: Distinctive two-toned whistle; females quack.

Habitat: Marshes, prairie ponds, and tundra; sometimes salt marshes in winter.

Nesting: 6–9 pale greenish-buff eggs in a shallow bowl of grass lined with down, often some distance from water.

Range: Breeds from Alaska east to Labrador and south to California, Nebraska, and Maine. Locally and occasionally elsewhere in East. Winters south to Central America and West Indies. Also in Eurasia.

The Northern Pintail, a widely distributed and common duck, is a strong flier and long-distance migrant like the Mallard. Seeds of aquatic plants are its main food, but in winter it also eats small aquatic animals; when freshwater habitats freeze over, the Pintail resorts to tidal flats, where it feeds on snails and small crabs. A popular game bird because of its tasty flesh and fast flight, it is one of our wariest ducks.

134, 162 **Blue-winged Teal**
*Anas discors*

Description: 14–16″ (36–41 cm). A small brown duck with *pale blue shoulder patches.* Male has gray head and *white crescent in front of eye.* Female mottled brown, similar to female Green-winged Teal, but grayer and larger-billed, with pale blue shoulder patches like the male.

Voice: Soft lisping or peeping note; female utters a soft quack.

Habitat: Marshes, shallow ponds, and lakes.

Nesting: 9–12 dull-white eggs in a down-lined hollow concealed in grass near water.

Range: Breeds from southeastern Alaska and western Canada to Canadian Maritimes, and south to northeastern California, New Mexico, and New York. Winters from southern California, southern Texas, and Carolinas southward through tropical America.

On low, marshy prairies in the central part of the continent, where this duck is most numerous, virtually every pond and pothole has a breeding pair. The male commonly "stands guard" on the pond while the female is incubating. Unlike other dabbling ducks that form pairs in the fall, this teal begins courting in the spring and often does not acquire the familiar breeding plumage until December or January. Like most ducks, it goes through an eclipse plumage and molts most of its feathers simultaneously, including the primaries, and so is flightless until new feathers grow in. In fall, this species migrates early, often passing through the United States in August and September; most Blue-wings winter south of the United States.

111, 163 **Cinnamon Teal**
*Anas cyanoptera*

Description: 14–17" (36–43 cm). Male bright rufous with pale blue shoulder patches. Female mottled sandy-brown and dusky, with pale blue shoulder patches; face plainer than female Blue-wing's, but the two are often not distinguishable in the field.
Voice: A soft quack; various chattering and clucking notes.
Habitat: Marshes, ponds, and streams bordered with reeds.
Nesting: 9–12 pale buff or whitish eggs in a down-lined nest of grass concealed in vegetation, usually near water.
Range: Breeds in western North America from southern British Columbia and eastern Montana south to Texas. Winters in southern part of breeding range south to tropical America. Rare in East, usually in flocks of Blue-winged Teals. Also in South America.

This western relative of the Blue-winged Teal often associates with that species in areas where both occur. Like the Blue-winged, these birds migrate south in late summer and early fall, a month or two ahead of other dabbling ducks. Records of the Cinnamon Teal from east of their normal range are based mainly on sightings of the adult male, because the female is almost indistinguishable from the female Blue-winged Teal.

118, 159 **Northern Shoveler**
*Anas clypeata*

Description: 17–20" (43–51 cm). *Large shovel-shaped bill.* Male has green head, white body, and *chestnut flanks.* Female mottled brown with pale blue shoulder patches; similar to female Blue-winged Teal, but bill much larger.
Voice: Low croak, cluck, or quack.

Habitat: Marshes and prairie potholes. Sometimes on salt or brackish marshes.

Nesting: 8–12 pale buff or greenish eggs in a down-lined cup of grass concealed in vegetation, often some distance from water.

Range: Breeds from Alaska east to northern Manitoba, and south to California and Great Lakes region. Winters from Oregon across southern half of United States to Gulf Coast and north to New Jersey.

Like the closely related Blue-winged Teal, the Northern Shoveler is among the first ducks to arrive in the fall and the last to leave in the spring. It feeds on minute aquatic animals by straining water through comb-like teeth along the edges of its long, expanded bill. It also eats seeds and aquatic plants. Because it often feeds in stagnant ponds, it is particularly susceptible to botulism, a fatal bacterial food poisoning.

---

156, 157 **Gadwall**
*Anas strepera*

Description: 18–21″ (46–53 cm). Male is a medium-sized grayish duck with a *white patch on hind edge of wing,* black rump, and sandy-brown head. Female mottled brown, with white patch on hind edge of wing.

Voice: Utters duck-like quack; also chatters and whistles.

Habitat: Freshwater marshes, ponds, and rivers; locally in salt marshes.

Nesting: 9–11 cream-white eggs in a down-lined nest of grass, usually hidden near water but sometimes in upland fields.

Range: Breeds from southern Alaska, British Columbia, and Minnesota south to California and western Texas; locally in East. Winters in much of central and southern United States. Also in Old World.

This species has the widest range of any duck, breeding almost throughout the North Temperate Zone. Known to hunters as the "Gray Duck," it is a popular game bird and is abundant in winter in southern marshes. It feeds mainly on seeds, leaves, and stems of aquatic plants.

---

108 **Eurasian Wigeon**
*Anas penelope*

Description: 18–20″ (46–51 cm). Male has *rusty head, buff crown,* pinkish-buff breast, and gray body. Female is mottled gray-brown or rust-brown. Both sexes have *large white shoulder patches* and dull blue bill. Female very similar to female American Wigeon, but often has reddish-brown head.

Voice: Piping two-noted whistle, seldom heard in America.

Habitat: Marshes, ponds, and lakes; tidal flats in nonbreeding season.

Nesting: 7 or 8 cream-white eggs in a down-lined nest of grass hidden in vegetation, often some distance from water.

Range: Breeds in Eurasia; an uncommon but regular visitor to North America, mainly along Atlantic and Pacific coasts.

An Old World relative of the American Wigeon, this bird in recent years has been turning up more frequently in North America, usually found in a flock with its American cousin. Known in Europe as one of the shyest of ducks, it is a popular game bird. Wigeons often feed at night; unlike most other ducks, they obtain a good deal of food by grazing.

**117, 165** **American Wigeon**
*Anas americana*

Description: 18–23″ (46–58 cm). Male is brownish with *white crown*, green ear patch, and bold *white shoulder patches* easily visible in flight. Female is mottled brown with grayish head and whitish shoulder patches. Bill pale blue in both sexes.

Voice: Distinctive whistled *whew-whee-whew;* also quacks.

Habitat: Marshes, ponds, and shallow lakes.

Nesting: 9–11 whitish or cream-colored eggs in a down-lined nest of grass, often several hundred yards from water.

Range: Breeds from Alaska, northern Manitoba, and southern Quebec south to Nevada, Dakotas, and Great Lakes region; rarely farther east. Winters mainly along Pacific, Atlantic, and Gulf coasts.

The American Wigeon, or "Baldpate," is a wary species, often seen on marshy ponds in the company of diving birds such as coots, Redheads, and Canvasbacks. Wigeons wait at the surface while the other birds dive, then snatch the food away when the birds reappear. They also visit grain fields and meadows to graze like geese on tender shoots. The birds found in winter along the Atlantic Coast seem to come mainly from the Far North, while birds that nest in the interior of the continent move south to the Gulf Coast.

---

**109, 167** **Canvasback**
*Aythya valisineria*

Description: 19–24″ (48–61 cm). Male has a *whitish body,* black chest, and reddish head with low forehead. *Long bill gives the head a distinctive sloping profile.* Female grayish, with sandy-brown head. At a distance, males can be distinguished from Redheads by their white bodies, the male Redhead's body being largely gray.

Voice: Males grunt or croak; females quack.
Habitat: Nests on marshes; winters on lakes, bays, and estuaries.
Nesting: 7–10 greenish eggs in a floating mass of reeds and grass anchored to stems of marsh plants.
Range: Breeds from Alaska south and east to Nebraska and Minnesota. Winters from British Columbia south to interior West, from Massachusetts south to Gulf Coast, and in Mississippi Valley.

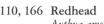

Although they breed mainly in the West, each fall large numbers of Canvasbacks migrate eastward to the Great Lakes and the Atlantic Coast. They are considered among the best-tasting ducks, and many thousands are shot annually. In recent years their numbers have declined drastically, chiefly because of the draining of the large marshes they require to breed. Where they are still relatively numerous, their long, V-shaped flocks are a striking sight as they move from one feeding ground to another.

---

**110, 166 Redhead**
*Aythya americana*

Description: 18–22″ (46–56 cm). Male *gray, with brick-red head and black breast.* Female duller and browner, with a light area around base of bill; larger and rounder-headed than female Ring-necked Duck. Both sexes have a pale gray wing stripe and a pale blue-gray bill. Similar Canvasback has a whiter body and sloping forehead and bill.

Voice: Like the meow of a cat; also quacks.
Habitat: Nests in marshes, but at other times is found on open lakes and bays; often on salt water in winter.
Nesting: 10–16 buff eggs in a woven cup of reeds lined with white down and attached to marsh vegetation.
Range: Breeds from Alaska and British Columbia east to Minnesota and south

to California and Colorado. Winters in southern half of United States, Mississippi Valley, and Great Lakes region.

Redheads do most of their feeding at night, spending the daylight hours resting on water. This species has suffered greatly from hunting and the destruction of its habitat; it has declined in numbers until it is now one of the least common North American ducks. In many areas the introduction of carp from Eurasia has caused the destruction of its aquatic food plants.

---

123, 150 **Ring-necked Duck**
*Aythya collaris*

Description: 14–18″ (36–46 cm). Male has black back and breast; angular, purple-glossed, black-appearing head; pale gray flanks; vertical white mark on side of breast. Female brownish, paler around base of bill, with narrow white eye ring. Bill pale gray with white ring. The high, angular shape of the head distinguishes this bird from the scaup.

Voice: Soft purring notes, but usually silent.
Habitat: Wooded lakes, ponds, and rivers; seldom on salt water except in southern states.
Nesting: 8–12 buff or olive eggs in a down-lined cup concealed in vegetation near the edge of a pond.
Range: Alaska east through Manitoba to Newfoundland, and south to California, Arizona, Great Lakes, and Maine. Winters from Washington south along Pacific Coast, east through Southwest and Gulf states, and north to New England.

This species might better be called the "Ring-billed Duck," for its chestnut neck ring is usually seen only at close range, while the white ring on the bill can be a prominent field mark. More partial to acid ponds and lakes in wooded regions than other diving ducks, it eats the seeds of aquatic plants as well as snails and insects.

122, 148 **Tufted Duck**
*Aythya fuligula*

Description: 17″ (43 cm). Male a stocky blackish duck with flashing *white flanks* and *wispy crest*. Female warm brown, paler on flanks, with small white patch at base of bill; little or no crest.

Voice: Various soft, growling notes; low whistles.

Habitat: Wooded lakes, streams, and marshes; in winter, often in estuaries and shallow coastal bays.

Nesting: 8–10 pale buff or greenish eggs in a down-lined bowl of grass concealed under a bush or tussock, usually near water.

Range: Breeds in northern Eurasia; very rare in North America, chiefly along coasts in Alaska, California, and northeastern states. Most often seen near urban areas.

This Old World bird is a counterpart of the Ring-necked Duck of North America. Indeed, on those rare occasions when a Tufted Duck turns up in our area, it may be seen with a small flock of Ring-necks. But the fact that many Tufted Ducks in the Northeast are seen in or near large cities suggests that they may be birds that have escaped from captivity, and not genuinely wild birds that have crossed the Atlantic on their own.

121, 140 **Greater Scaup**
*Aythya marila*

Description: 15–20″ (38–51 cm). Male has very light gray body; blackish chest; and *black-appearing, green-glossed head*. Female a uniform dark brown with white patch at base of bill. Both sexes have long whitish wing stripe. See Lesser Scaup.

Voice: Usually silent; discordant croaking calls on breeding grounds.

Habitat: Lakes, bays, and ponds; in winter, often on salt water.

Nesting: 8–12 olive-buff eggs in a down-lined cup of grass concealed in a clump of grass on land or in marsh vegetation well out from shore.

Range: Breeds in Alaska and northern Canada east to Hudson Bay and occasionally in Maritime Provinces. Winters mainly along Pacific, Gulf, and Atlantic coasts. Also in Eurasia.

The Greater Scaup is the more common of the two scaup in the northern United States, where it is usually seen in large rafts, often composed of thousands of birds, on large lakes or coastal bays. Although the two scaup can be difficult to tell apart, any very large flock of scaup on the northeast coast in winter may be assumed to be the Greater. Because it dives for mollusks and other animals and is not as much of a vegetarian as the Redhead or the Canvasback, the Greater Scaup is not considered as choice a game bird, although it is still shot in large numbers annually.

---

120, 141 **Lesser Scaup**
*Aythya affinis*

Description: 15–18″ (38–46 cm). Similar to Greater Scaup, but crown is higher and forehead steeper, giving head a more angular appearance. Male head glossed with purple, not green. Female dark brown, with small, white face patch, not easily distinguishable from female Greater Scaup. In flight, white wing stripe is shorter (extending about one-half of wing's length), whereas in Greater

Scaup stripe extends to three-fourths of wing's length.

Voice: Seldom heard; sharp whistles and guttural scolding notes.

Habitat: Ponds and marshes; during migration and winter, it occurs on lakes, rivers, and ponds, and in southern states on salt water.

Nesting: Usually 9–12 dark olive-buff eggs in a down-lined cup of grass hidden in vegetation, often some distance from the edge of the water.

Range: Breeds from interior Alaska and northern Canada south to Colorado and Iowa, occasionally farther east. Winters along the East and West coasts as well as inland south of Colorado and Great Lakes to Gulf of Mexico.

Confined to the New World, the Lesser Scaup is thought to be descended from an earlier invasion of North America by the ancestor of both modern species of scaup. Here it evolved into a distinct species, to be joined later by a second arrival, the Greater Scaup, found in both hemispheres. In the northern states, where the Greater Scaup is more common in winter, the Lesser is often found in small parties on fresh water, while in the South it is seen in large flocks on lakes and salt water.

---

137, 155 **Common Eider**
*Somateria mollissima*

Description: 23–27″ (58–69 cm). Our largest duck. Male has *black underparts, white back;* white head and breast; dark crown; greenish tinge on back of head. Female is mottled brown with barred flanks. Long sloping bill gives the bird a distinctive profile. Usually holds bill pointed slightly down toward surface of water. See King Eider.

Voice: During courtship the male gives a hollow moan and various cooing notes;

female quacks.

Habitat: Rocky coasts and coastal tundra.

Nesting: 4–7 olive or buff eggs in a substantial mass of grass thickly lined with down. Often several pairs form a loose colony.

Range: Breeds on Arctic coasts of Alaska and Canada south to Massachusetts. Winters along Alaska coast south to Washington and along Atlantic Coast south to Long Island, occasionally farther. Also northern Eurasia.

Eiders are best known for their down—very soft feathers plucked from the breast of the female. For hundreds of years eiderdown has been gathered from nests in northern Europe and used to line pillows, quilts, and parkas. Only eiders in the Arctic are strongly migratory; in the warmer parts of their range they may remain near the breeding grounds all year. Their principal foods are mussels and other shellfish; the birds gather in huge rafts where these are available. Since the persecution of eiders ended after the turn of the century, there has been a spectacular increase along the Maine coast, and they are once again nesting there in large numbers.

---

136, 154 **King Eider**
*Somateria spectabilis*

Description: 18–25″ (46–64 cm). A large duck. Similar to the Common Eider, but male has a *black back* and a conspicuous orange-yellow bill and "shield" on forehead. Female similar to female Common Eider, but bill is shorter, not extending as far back toward eye, and lacks the distinctive sloping profile; flanks marked with black crescents, not bars. Usually holds bill more horizontal to surface of water than Common Eider.

Voice: A guttural croaking.

Habitat: Rocky coasts and islands.

Nesting: 4–7 buff-olive eggs in a down-lined depression on rocky tundra, often some distance from the edge of the water.

Range: Breeds in freshwater ponds and lakes in Alaska and Arctic islands of Canada, south locally to Hudson Bay. Winters along coasts south to southern Alaska and from Labrador to New Jersey; rarely farther south and on Great Lakes. Also in Eurasia.

Although the world population of the King Eider is large, the birds are seldom seen in the United States; most winter farther north and favor deeper water than the Common Eider. They often dive far for food and have been caught in nets as much as 150 feet (50 meters) below the surface. Like the Common Eider, they take large numbers of mussels and other shellfish but vary their diet with small fish, squid, sand dollars, and sea urchins. Their breeding grounds are so remote that their down is not collected as extensively as that of the Common Eider.

135, 153 **Harlequin Duck**
*Histrionicus histrionicus*

Description: 14–20″ (36–51 cm). A small dark duck. Male blue-gray (appearing black at a distance), with chestnut flanks and distinctive white patches on head and body. Female dusky brown with two or three whitish patches on sides of face. In flight, this species lacks large white patches on wings.

Voice: A mouse-like squeak and various low whistles.

Habitat: Swift-moving streams in summer; rocky, wave-lashed coasts and jetties in winter.

Nesting: 6–8 pale buff or cream-colored eggs in a mass of down concealed in a crevice in rocks along a stream.

Range: Breeds from Alaska and Yukon south to Wyoming and Sierra Nevada of

California, and from southern Baffin Island south to Labrador and the Gaspé Peninsula. Winters along coasts south to central California and Long Island. Also in Eurasia.

In the Northeast these ducks are known locally as "Lords and Ladies." They spend most of their lives on salt water, visiting inland streams only during the breeding season. As soon as the female begins incubating, her mate returns to the ocean and undergoes the annual molt. The preferred habitat—rugged seacoast—offers food that few other species can exploit. The birds are adept at riding a wave up against the rocks and quickly tearing loose snails, limpets, and barnacles. They also feed on small shrimp, crabs, and small fish, which they catch by diving. In their stay on freshwater streams, they feed mainly on the larvae of aquatic insects.

---

138, 139, 152 **Oldsquaw**
*Clangula hyemalis*

Description: Males 19–22″ (48–56 cm); females 15–17″ (38–43 cm). Male boldly patterned in black and white (mainly white in winter, mainly black in summer), with very long, slender central tail feathers. Females are duller and lack the long tail feathers. In all plumages has *all-dark, unpatterned wings.*

Voice: Various clucking and growling notes; male's courtship call a musical *ow-owdle-ow, ow-owdle-ow,* frequently repeated.

Habitat: Breeds on tundra; winters on open bays and inshore waters.

Nesting: 5–11 yellowish or cream-colored eggs in a down-lined cup of grass concealed on tundra near water.

Range: Breeds in Alaska and Arctic Canada. Winters along coasts from Bering Sea south to Oregon, from Labrador south to Carolinas, along portions of Gulf

Coast, and on Great Lakes. Also in Eurasia.

While most diving ducks paddle with their webbed feet, the Oldsquaw uses its partially folded wings to propel itself underwater. It is one of the deepest-diving ducks; birds have been caught in nets as much as 200 feet (60 meters) below the surface. Its food consists mainly of mussels, crabs, shrimp, and other crustaceans. These birds are noisy in early spring, when males gather and utter their mellow, barking courtship calls; this pleasing sound is audible for a mile or two on a still spring morning.

125, 146 **Black Scoter**
**"Common Scoter"**
*Melanitta nigra*

Description: 17–21″ (43–53 cm). Male black; bill black with *large yellow knob at base.* Female duller, with pale cheeks and all-dark bill. Both sexes show silvery wing linings in flight.
Voice: In spring, a musical, whistled *cour-loo.*
Habitat: Breeds on ponds in boreal forests; winters on ocean and in large salt bays.
Nesting: 5–8 pale buff eggs in a down-lined cup of grass hidden in a rock crevice or clump of grass near the edge of water.
Range: Breeds in western Alaska and in Labrador and Newfoundland. Winters along coasts from Alaska south to California and from Newfoundland south to Carolinas, as well as on portions of Gulf Coast and on Great Lakes. Also in Eurasia.

Formerly called the "Common Scoter," this is actually the least common of the three scoters, being more abundant in the Old World than in North America. Like the other scoters, it preys on mussels and other mollusks, and also tears barnacles, chitons, and limpets

from submerged rocks and reefs. Newly hatched young remain on fresh water for several days, feeding on small freshwater mussels and the larvae of aquatic insects before moving to salt water.

126, 145 **Surf Scoter**
*Melanitta perspicillata*

Description: 17–21″ (43–53 cm). Male black with *white patches on crown and nape.* Multicolored bill swollen at base and bearing a large black spot. Female brownish-black, with two whitish patches on cheek. Both sexes lack white wing patch.

Voice: A low guttural croaking.

Habitat: Breeds on northern lakes; winters almost entirely on the ocean and in large coastal bays.

Nesting: 5–8 pinkish-buff eggs in a down-lined depression hidden under bushes or in marsh vegetation, not necessarily near water.

Range: Breeds in Alaska and across northern Canada to Labrador. Winters mainly along coasts, from Alaska south to California and from Newfoundland south to Florida, and rarely to Texas.

The so-called "Skunk-head" is the only one of the three scoters confined to the New World. These birds are similar in their habits to the other scoters but are more often seen diving for mollusks and crustaceans along the line of breaking surf. Because they consume little plant food, hunters do not consider their flesh good to eat. Yet many thousands are shot each year for sport, while others fall victim to oil pollution.

124, 147 **White-winged Scoter**
*Melanitta fusca*

Description: 19–24″ (48–61 cm). Male black with *bold white wing patches,* white crescents around eyes, and yellow bill with black knob at base. Females dull brown, with two whitish facial spots and white wing patches.

Voice: Soft whistles and guttural croaks.

Habitat: Breeds on large lakes; winters mainly on the ocean and on large coastal bays, but a few remain on lakes in the interior.

Nesting: 5–17 buff or pink eggs in a hollow lined with sticks and down, under a bush or in a crevice near water, often on an island in a lake.

Range: Breeds in Alaska and much of western and central Canada. Winters along coasts, from Alaska south to California and from Newfoundland south to Carolinas, rarely to Florida and Texas. Also in Eurasia.

During migration, long irregular lines consisting of thousands of White-winged Scoters move southward, just offshore and only a few feet above the waves. The most abundant and widespread of the three scoters—there are over a million in North America—this species feeds chiefly on mollusks, which it collects from mussel beds at depths of 15 to 40 feet (5 to 12 meters). These birds also feed on crabs, starfish, sea urchins, and some fish.

131, 143 **Common Goldeneye**
*Bucephala clangula*

Description: 16–20″ (41–51 cm). Male has white body, black back; black-appearing (actually glossy *greenish*) head, and *large, round, white spot in front of eye;* eye bright yellow. Female grayish, with warm-brown head, white neck ring, and *dark bill.* Both sexes have distinctive puffy head shape and large white wing patch, conspicuous in flight. See Barrow's Goldeneye.

Voice: Courtship call of male a high-pitched *jeee-ep!* Females utter a low quack.

Habitat: Breeds on wooded lakes and ponds; winters mainly on coastal bays and estuaries.

Nesting: 8–12 pale green eggs in a mass of down in a natural tree cavity, up to 60′ (18 m) above ground.

Range: Breeds in Alaska and across Canada to Newfoundland and Maritime Provinces, south to mountains of Montana and Great Lakes. Winters in much of United States, wherever water is open. Also in Eurasia.

During its courtship display in late winter, the male stretches his head forward along the water and then snaps it rapidly upward over his back, bill pointed skyward, while uttering a shrill, two-noted call. Then he swings his orange feet forward, sending up a small shower in front of him. The wings of this species produce a loud whistling sound in flight, easily identified even when the birds cannot be seen; hunters call this species the "Whistler." Wintering in small groups or large flocks, goldeneyes feed mainly on mollusks; in summer, their diet shifts to aquatic plants and insects.

---

130, 142 **Barrow's Goldeneye**
*Bucephala islandica*

Description: 16½–20″ (42–51 cm). Male has white body, black back, and black-appearing (actually glossed with *purple*) head. Similar to male Common Goldeneye, but has more black on sides, stubbier bill, and *crescent-shaped, rather than round, white spot in front of eye.* Female gray with brown head, white collar, and (usually) entirely *orange-yellow bill.* Both sexes differ from Common Goldeneye in having steeper forehead and smaller white wing patches.

Voice: Soft grunts and croaks during courtship; otherwise usually silent.

Habitat: Breeds on forested lakes and rivers; winters mainly on open bays and estuaries along coast.

Nesting: 5–15 pale green eggs on a bed of down in a hollow tree or, in treeless areas, in a crevice among rocks.

Range: Breeds from Alaska south in mountains to central California and Wyoming, and in northern Quebec and Labrador. Winters along Pacific Coast from Alaska south to California and in smaller numbers from Maritime Provinces south to Long Island. Also breeds in western Greenland and Iceland.

Barrow's Goldeneye favors alpine lakes, often breeding at elevations of 10,000 feet (3,000 meters) or more. Its patchy distribution suggests that it is an ancient species that was once more widespread and is now in decline. In the East, it is greatly outnumbered by the Common Goldeneye but may occur in flocks of hundreds in the Canadian Maritimes.

---

115, 144 **Bufflehead**
*Bucephala albeola*

Description: 13–15″ (33–38 cm). Small chubby duck, also known as the "Butterball." Male largely white, with black back, black head with greenish and purplish gloss, and *large white patch from behind eye to top and back of head.* Female all dark with single whitish patch on cheek. A fast flier with a rapid wingbeat.

Voice: Male has a squeaky whistle; female has a soft, hoarse quack.

Habitat: Breeds on wooded lakes and ponds; winters mainly on salt bays and estuaries.

Nesting: 6–12 pale buff or ivory eggs in a mass of down placed in a woodpecker hole up to 20′ (6 m) above ground.

Range: Breeds in Alaska and east to western Quebec, and south in mountains to Washington and Montana. Winters in southern United States, south to Mexico, Gulf Coast, and northern Florida.

A small relative of the two goldeneyes, the "Butterball" shares with them the habit of nesting in cavities in trees. In winter, it is one of the most familiar and easily identified ducks along the coast, where it travels in small parties, never forming large rafts like other diving ducks. Unlike its larger relatives, it makes no loud whistling sound in flight.

---

132, 170 **Hooded Merganser**
*Lophodytes cucullatus*

Description: 16–19″ (41–48 cm). A small duck with a slender pointed bill. Male has *white, fan-shaped, black-bordered crest;* blackish body with dull rusty flanks; and white breast with two black stripes down the side. Female is dull gray-brown with head and crest warmer brown. Both sexes show a white wing patch in flight.

Voice: Hoarse grunts and chatters.

Habitat: Breeds on wooded ponds, lakes, and rivers; winters in coastal marshes and inlets.

Nesting: 8–12 white eggs in a down-lined cup placed in a natural tree cavity or sometimes in a fallen hollow log.

Range: Breeds from southern Alaska south to Oregon and Montana, and from Manitoba and Nova Scotia south to Arkansas and northern Alabama. Winters near coasts from British Columbia south to California and from New England south to Florida and Texas.

The smallest of our mergansers, Hoodeds are most often seen along rivers and in estuaries during the fall and winter. They are usually found in pairs or in flocks of up to a dozen; when startled, they are among the fastest-flying of our ducks. They feed chiefly on small fish, which they pursue in long, rapid, underwater dives, but also take frogs and aquatic insects.

128, 171 **Common Merganser**
*Mergus merganser*

Description: 22–27″ (56–69 cm). Male has *flashing white sides, green head,* white breast, and long, thin red bill. Female has gray body and sides; reddish-brown, crested head sharply set off from white throat. Red-breasted Merganser is similar, but male has gray sides, white neck ring, and rust-colored breast; female has reddish-brown head that blends into gray of neck.

Voice: Low rasping croaks.

Habitat: Breeds on wooded rivers and ponds; winters mainly on lakes and rivers, occasionally on salt water.

Nesting: 9–12 pale buff or ivory eggs placed in a down-lined tree cavity, or sometimes on the ground or in an abandoned hawk's nest.

Range: Breeds across Canada from eastern Alaska, Manitoba, and Newfoundland south in mountains to California, northern New Mexico, Great Lakes, and northern New England. Winters south to northern Mexico and Georgia (rarely farther). Also in Eurasia.

Although preferring to feed on lakes, Common Mergansers are often driven to rivers by cold weather; there they are found in flocks of 10 to 20 birds, all facing upstream and diving in pursuit of fish. Pairs are formed in late winter, and until then one is likely to find flocks composed entirely of males or of females. Often called "Sawbills," mergansers have fine, tooth-like serrations along the sides of their bills that help in grasping slippery fish.

---

129, 169 **Red-breasted Merganser**
*Mergus serrator*

Description: 19–26″ (48–66 cm). Male has green head with wispy crest, *gray sides, white neck ring, and rusty breast.* Female grayish, with reddish-brown head shading gradually into gray of neck. Both sexes are crested and have red bills.

Voice: Usually silent; various croaking and grunting notes during courtship.

Habitat: Breeds on wooded lakes and tundra ponds; winters mainly on salt water.

Nesting: 8–10 olive-buff eggs in a down-lined depression concealed under a bush or in a brush pile.

Range: Breeds in Alaska and across northern Canada to Newfoundland and south to Great Lakes. Winters chiefly along coasts from Alaska south to California, from Maritime Provinces south to Florida, and along Gulf Coast. Also in Eurasia.

This is the merganser most likely to be found on salt water. Like the other two species, it lives mainly on fish, which it captures in swift underwater dives, aided by its long pointed bill lined with sharp, tooth-like projections.

---

133, 151 **Ruddy Duck**
*Oxyura jamaicensis*

Description: 14–16″ (36–41 cm). A small chunky duck with a long tail that is often held straight up. Male in breeding plumage has a chestnut body, black crown, and *white cheeks.* Female and winter male are dusky brown, with whitish cheeks of female crossed by a dark stripe. Male's bill is blue in breeding season, black at other times.

Voice: Usually silent. Courting male produces ticking and clapping sounds by pressing its bill against its breast.

Habitat: Breeds on freshwater marshes, marshy lakes, and ponds; winters on marshes and in shallow coastal bays.

Nesting: 6–20 white or cream-colored eggs in a floating nest of dry stems lined with down, concealed among reeds or bulrushes in a marsh.

Range: Breeds from British Columbia, Mackenzie, and Quebec south to California, southern New Mexico, and southern Texas, with occasional breeding farther east. Winters around the coastal perimeter of United States north to British Columbia and Massachusetts, and as far inland as Missouri.

This duck is one of the most aquatic members of the family and, like a grebe, can sink slowly out of sight. Although it can avoid danger by diving or by hiding in marsh vegetation, it is a strong flier and undertakes long migrations to and from its nesting places. Largely vegetarian, it favors pondweeds and the seeds of other aquatic plants, but also consumes large numbers of midge larvae during the breeding season.

113 **Masked Duck**
*Oxyura dominica*

Description: 12–14″ (30–36 cm). A small brown duck with a white speculum. Breeding male mainly reddish brown, with black face and crown, and pale blue bill. Female and winter male brown, marked with blackish bars or spots, blackish line through eye, and dark line across cheek.

Voice: Usually silent; low grunts and whistling calls.

Habitat: Freshwater marshes, rice fields, and weedy ponds and lake margins.

Nesting: 4–6 buff eggs on a large mass of marsh vegetation concealed near shore.

Range: Breeds irregularly on Gulf Coast in Texas; a few winter in southern Florida. Also in American tropics.

A tropical relative of the Ruddy Duck, the Masked Duck can be as secretive as a grebe, spending most of its time hidden in marsh vegetation, where it dives for food and paddles away quickly at the first sign of danger. It flies readily and swiftly, however, and can take flight directly from the surface of the water. It seems to be more willing to fly than the Ruddy, and is most active at dusk and at dawn.

## Family Cathartidae
American Vultures

7 species: Tropical and temperate America. Three species, including the nearly extinct California Condor, breed in North America. These scavengers feed on carrion and refuse. They possess weak feet and blunt claws instead of sharp talons like those of hawks. Vultures are large, mostly blackish birds with broad wings and bare heads; their naked heads prevent their feathers from becoming fouled while they feed on carrion. They nest in tree cavities or on the ground.

### 312 Black Vulture
*Coragyps atratus*

Description: 22–24″ (56–61 cm). W. 4′6″ (1.4 m). Black with white patch near each wing tip, conspicuous in flight; head bare, grayish; feet extend beyond the short tail. Flaps its shorter and rounder wings more often and more rapidly than the Turkey Vulture.

Voice: Hisses or grunts; seldom heard.

Habitat: Open country, but breeds in light woodlands and thickets.

Nesting: 2 white or gray-green eggs, blotched with brown, under a bush, in a hollow log, under large rocks, or in a cave.

Range: More or less resident from Texas and Arkansas north and east to New Jersey (rarely to Massachusetts and Maine) and south to Florida. Also in American tropics.

Black Vultures are scavengers that feed on carrion, but they also take weak, sick, or unprotected young birds and mammals. They are smaller but more aggressive than Turkey Vultures and will drive the latter from a carcass. Both species are often found perched in trees, on fence posts, and on the ground, or flying high overhead, especially on windy days, taking advantage of thermals or updrafts. Unlike Turkey Vultures, Black Vultures depend on their vision to find food.

## 311 Turkey Vulture
*Cathartes aura*

Description: 25–32″ (64–81 cm). W. 6′ (1.8 m). Eagle-sized, blackish bird usually seen soaring over the countryside. In flight, the long wings are held upward in a wide, shallow V; wings narrower than those of Black Vulture; flight feathers silvery below; it flaps its wings less frequently than the Black Vulture, and rolls and sways from side to side. Tail long; head small, bare, and reddish (gray in immature).

Voice: Usually silent; when feeding or at the nest, hisses or grunts.

Habitat: Mainly deciduous forests and woodlands; often seen over adjacent farmlands.

Nesting: 2 whitish eggs, heavily marked with dark brown, placed without nest or lining in a crevice in rocks, in a hollow tree, or in a fallen hollow log.

Range: Breeds from southern British Columbia, central Saskatchewan, Great Lakes, and New Hampshire southward. Winters in Southwest, and in East northward to southern New England.

The most common and widespread of the New World vultures, this species nests throughout all of the United States except northern New England. Soaring for hours over woodland and nearby open country, the Turkey Vulture searches for carcasses, locating them at least partly by means of its acute sense of smell. Turkey Vultures are valuable for their removal of garbage and disease-causing carrion. At night they often gather in large roosts.

## Family Accipitridae
Hawks and Eagles

240 species: Worldwide. Twenty-four species breed in North America. This varied group of birds ranges from the very large eagles to small hawks not much bigger than an American Robin. All are predators, with hooked bills and sharply pointed talons. Some, the buteos (eagles, the Red-tailed Hawk, and similar birds), have short broad tails and wide rounded wings adapted for soaring as they search for prey. Others, the accipiters, have short rounded wings and long narrow tails well suited for darting and twisting among dense branches in pursuit of prey. Some of the kites have narrow pointed wings and are expert gliders, while the Osprey, a fish eater, has long talons and sharp spines on the soles of its feet for grasping slippery prey.

313 **Osprey**
*Pandion haliaetus*

Description: 21–24″ (53–61 cm). W. 4′6″–6′ (1.4–1.8 m). A large, long-winged "fish hawk." Brown above and white below; head white with dark line through eye and on side of face. Wing shows distinctive bend at the "wrist." At a distance, can resemble a gull.

Voice: Loud, musical chirping.

Habitat: Lakes, rivers, and seacoasts.

Nesting: 2–4 white, pink, or buff eggs, blotched with brown, in a bulky mass of sticks and debris placed in a tree, on a telephone pole, on rocks, or on flat ground.

Range: Breeds from Alaska east to Newfoundland and south to Arizona and New Mexico; also along Gulf Coast and on Atlantic Coast south to Florida. Winters regularly north to Gulf Coast and California. Also in South America and Old World.

Ospreys search for fish by flying and hovering over the water, watching the surface below. When prey is sighted, an Osprey dives steeply, its talons outspread, and splashes into the water. It quickly resurfaces and, if it has made a catch, flies off, adjusting the fish in its claws so that the head is pointed forward. Ospreys declined drastically because of pesticides during the 1950s and 1960s, but since then they have made a comeback and are nesting again in areas from which they had disappeared.

315, 318 **Hook-billed Kite**
*Chondrohierax uncinatus*

Description: 15–17″ (38–43 cm). W. 33″ (84 cm). A small bird of prey with long hooked bill, short rounded wings, and tail boldly banded with black and white.

Male slate-gray above, barred below with gray. Female brown on back with rufous collar, and with rufous barring on underparts.

Voice: Musical whistles; harsh chattering during courtship or when disturbed.

Habitat: Mesquite woods along rivers and streams.

Nesting: 2 white eggs in a nest of twigs placed in a tree.

Range: Resident in extreme southern Texas. Also in American tropics.

A tropical species that enters the United States only along the Rio Grande, the Hooked-billed Kite feeds mainly on tree snails, which it deftly extracts from their shells with its long hooked bill. This bird often has a favorite feeding perch, marked by a pile of empty snail shells on the ground below. As it flies through the dense mesquites, this kite flaps its short wings several times and then glides unsteadily.

---

## 317 American Swallow-tailed Kite
*Elanoides forficatus*

Description: 22–24″ (56–61 cm). W. 4′2″ (1.3 m). A graceful bird of prey, with long pointed wings and deeply forked tail; head and underparts white; back, wings, and tail black.

Voice: A shrill *klee-klee-klee.*

Habitat: Swamps, marshes, river bottoms, and glades in open forests.

Nesting: 2–4 creamy-white eggs, boldly marked with brown, in a stick nest often lined with Spanish moss and usually in a tall tree.

Range: Breeds mainly on or near coasts from Texas east to Florida, and north to South Carolina; local farther inland in Gulf states. Winters in American tropics. Also breeds in tropics.

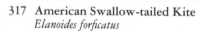

The Swallow-tailed Kite is the most aerial of our birds of prey. It catches much of its insect food on the wing, snatches lizards from the trunks of trees, eats what it has caught while flying, drinks by skimming the surface of ponds and marshes, and even gathers nesting material by breaking dead twigs from the tops of trees as it flies past. Formerly more abundant, this distinctive bird nested as far north as Minnesota and Illinois, but habitat destruction and indiscriminate shooting reduced it to its present range.

### 320 White-tailed Kite "Black-shouldered Kite"
*Elanus leucurus*

Description: 15–16″ (38–41 cm). W. 3′4″ (1 m). A delicate, graceful, gull-like bird of prey. *Largely white,* with gray back, black patch on shoulder and undersurface of the pointed wing, and *white tail.* The back and breast of young birds are streaked with warm brown. Often dangles its feet in flight.

Voice: A whistled *keep-keep-keep;* also a longer, plaintive *kreep.*

Habitat: Open country and farmlands with scattered trees or fencerows; mesquite grasslands.

Nesting: 4 or 5 white eggs, heavily spotted with brown, in a nest of sticks and twigs lined with grass and placed in a tall tree, usually near water.

Range: Resident in coastal and interior California, Arizona, and southern Texas. Also in American tropics.

The tame, elegant White-tailed Kite was formerly shot in large numbers by farmers who thought it threatened their chickens, although the birds feed almost entirely on insects and a few small rodents. The North American population was reduced to a pitiful remnant, and it was feared that the species might become extinct here. Recently, however, it has staged a surprising and unexplained comeback, and is again rather numerous in Texas and California. At the same time, a related species in southern Europe and Africa has also increased in number; the reason for these increases is unknown.

## 319 Snail Kite
**"Everglade Kite"**
*Rostrhamus sociabilis*

Description: 16–18″ (41–46 cm). W. 3′8″ (1.1 m). A crow-sized bird of prey with long, thin, strongly hooked bill; broad, rounded wings; and dark tail with white base. Male dark slate in color, with base of bill, face, and feet reddish. Female and immature have brown upperparts and heavily streaked breast; base of bill yellowish; feet dull orange or pinkish.

Voice: Low cackles and chatters when disturbed.

Habitat: Freshwater marshes and lakes.

Nesting: 2–5 white eggs, heavily spotted and blotched with brown, in a stick nest placed in low bushes or in marsh grasses.

Range: Resident mainly on Lake Okeechobee and in Everglades in southern Florida. Widespread in American tropics.

This round-winged kite feeds exclusively on apple snails of the genus *Pomacea,* found in shallow ponds and swampy places. The kite's slender, sharply hooked bill easily extracts the living animal from the unbroken shell. The Florida population has become seriously reduced due to draining of its habitat, but there is evidence that it is presently on the increase again.

316 **Mississippi Kite**
*Ictinia mississippiensis*

Description: 12–14″ (30–36 cm). W. 36″ (91 cm). A small bird of prey with narrow pointed wings. Adult gray, paler below and on head; tail and outer flight feathers in wings blackish, inner flight feathers whitish. Young bird streaked below, with banded tail.

Voice: Two or three high, clear whistles, but seldom heard.
Habitat: Open woodlands and thickets, usually near water.
Nesting: 2 or 3 white eggs in a stick nest placed in a tree.
Range: Breeds from Arizona and southern Great Plains east to Carolinas and south to Gulf Coast; rare in spring migration north to New England. Winters in tropics.

This graceful, buoyant kite is a marvelous flier and spends hours in the air. It is quite gregarious, often seen in flocks and even nesting in loose colonies. Although chiefly insectivorous, feeding largely on grasshoppers and dragonflies, it occasionally takes small snakes and frogs. Its range has expanded somewhat in recent years, and the species now occurs annually in spring north to southern New England.

321, 322 **Bald Eagle**
*Haliaeetus leucocephalus*

Description: 30–31″ (76–79 cm). W. 6′–7′6″ (1.8–2.3 m). A large blackish eagle with a *white head and tail* and a heavy yellow bill. Young birds lack the white head and tail, and resemble adult Golden Eagles, but are variably marked with white and have a black, more massive bill.
Voice: Squeaky cackling and thin squeals.
Habitat: Lakes, rivers, marshes, and seacoasts.

Nesting: 2 or 3 white eggs in a massive nest of sticks in a tall tree or, less frequently, on top of a cliff.

Range: Breeds from Alaska east to Newfoundland and south locally to California, Great Lakes, and Virginia; also in Arizona, along Gulf Coast, and in Florida. Formerly more widespread. Winters along coasts and large rivers in much of United States.

Following a dramatic decline caused by pesticides, our national bird is now making a slow but steady comeback, and once again nests in areas where it was wiped out during the 1960s. However, it is still not as numerous as it was in colonial times, when it was a familiar sight along almost every coastline. Bald Eagles are fish eaters, like Ospreys; when they pursue their prey they rarely enter the water as an Osprey does, but instead snatch the fish from the surface with their talons. Where Ospreys are common, the eagles obtain much of their food by stealing it from the smaller "fish hawk."

---

325, 326 **Northern Harrier**
**"Marsh Hawk"**
*Circus cyaneus*

Description: 16–24" (41–61 cm). W. 3′6" (1.1 m). A long-winged, long-tailed hawk with a *white rump,* usually seen gliding unsteadily over marshes with its wings held in a shallow V. Male has pale gray back, head, and breast. Female and young are brown above, streaked below, young birds with a rusty tone.

Voice: Usually silent. At the nest it utters a *kee-kee-kee-kee* or a sharp whistle.

Habitat: Marshes and open grasslands.

Nesting: 4 or 5 pale blue or white eggs, unmarked or with light brown spots, on a mound of dead reeds and grass in a marsh or shrubby meadow.

Range: Breeds from Alaska east to Canadian Maritimes and south to southern California, Arizona, Kansas, and Virginia. Winters from South America north to British Columbia, Great Lakes, and New Brunswick. Also in Eurasia.

This is the only North American member of a group of hawks known as harriers. All hunt by flying close to the ground and taking small animals by surprise. They seldom pursue their prey in the air or watch quietly from an exposed perch, as do other birds of prey. Harriers have keener hearing than other hawks; their disk-shaped faces, not unlike those of owls, enable them to amplify sound.

---

334 **Sharp-shinned Hawk**
*Accipiter striatus*

Description: 10–14″ (25–36 cm). W. 21″ (53 cm). A jay-sized, fast-flying hawk with a *long, narrow, square-tipped tail and short, rounded wings.* Adult slate-gray above, pale below, with fine rust-colored barring. Immature brown above with whitish spots, creamy-white below, with streaks on breast, barring on flanks. The bigger Cooper's Hawk has a proportionately larger head, more rounded tail tip, and slower wingbeat.

Voice: Sharp *kik-kik-kik-kik;* also a shrill squeal.

Habitat: Breeds in dense coniferous forests, less often in deciduous forests. In migration and winter, may be seen in almost any habitat.

Nesting: 4 or 5 whitish eggs, marked with brown, on a shallow, well-made platform of twigs concealed in a dense conifer.

Range: Breeds from Alaska through Mackenzie to Newfoundland, and south to California, New Mexico, northern Gulf states, and Carolinas. Winters across

United States north to British Columbia and Canadian Maritimes.

The smallest and most numerous of the accipiters, the Sharp-shinned Hawk feeds mainly on birds, which it catches in sudden and swift attacks. Its rounded wings and long narrow tail enable it to pursue birds through the woods, making sharp turns to avoid branches. In the East, this species seems to be undergoing a decrease in number, perhaps because some of its prey species are also declining. Nonetheless, it is still one of the most common species at hawk-migration lookouts both in the East and in the West.

---

## 333 Cooper's Hawk
*Accipiter cooperii*

Description: 14–20″ (36–51 cm). W. 28″ (71 cm). A crow-sized hawk, with long tail and short rounded wings. Adult slate-gray above, with dark cap, and finely rust-barred below. Immature brown above, whitish below with fine streaks. Tail tip rounded, not squared-off. See Sharp-shinned Hawk.

Voice: Loud *cack-cack-cack-cack.*

Habitat: Deciduous and, less often, coniferous forests, especially those interrupted by meadows and clearings.

Nesting: 4 or 5 dull-white eggs, spotted with brown, on a bulky platform of sticks and twigs, usually more than 20′ (6 m) above the ground.

Range: Breeds from British Columbia east to Manitoba and Canadian Maritimes, and south to Mexico, Gulf Coast, and northern Florida; absent or local throughout much of Great Plains. Winters from Central America north to British Columbia and southern New England.

Like its smaller look-alike the Sharp-shinned Hawk, Cooper's feeds mainly on birds, which it chases relentlessly through the woods. It also takes small mammals. During incubation and the early stages of brooding the young, the male bird does all the hunting, bringing food both to his mate and to the nestlings. Cooper's Hawks mature rapidly for birds their size; a full 25 percent of young birds breed the year after they are hatched, and the rest the year after that.

## 324 Northern Goshawk
*Accipiter gentilis*

Description: 20–26″ (51–66 cm). W. 3′6″ (1.1 m). A robust hawk with a long narrow tail, short rounded wings, and *bold white eyebrow.* Adults blue-gray above with a black crown and pale underparts finely barred with gray. Young bird similar in size and shape, but brown above, streaked below.

Voice: Loud *kak-kak-kak-kak-kak* when disturbed.

Habitat: Breeds in coniferous forests; winters in farmland, woodland edges, and open country.

Nesting: 3 or 4 white or pale bluish eggs in a large mass of sticks lined with fresh sprigs of evergreen and placed in a tree.

Range: Breeds from Alaska east through Mackenzie and northern Quebec to Newfoundland, and south to New Mexico, Great Lakes, and New England; also southward to northern Appalachians. Winters south to Virginia and Southwest.

This big raptor is mainly an uncommon winter visitor from the North; it is seldom present in large numbers, remaining mostly in the northern coniferous forests unless forced to move south by a periodic decline in populations of the grouse that are a staple of its diet. It is fearless in defense of its nest and will boldly attack anyone who ventures too close. It has recently begun extending its range to the south, and now breeds in small numbers in deciduous forests.

---

## 336 Harris' Hawk
*Parabuteo unicinctus*

Description: 18–30″ (46–76 cm). W. 3′7″ (1.1 m). Black with chestnut shoulders and thighs, white on rump and base of tail, and with white tail tip. Immatures similar but more streaked.

Voice: A low, harsh hissing sound.

Habitat: Semiarid regions in scrub with mesquite, cacti, and yucca.

Nesting: 2–4 dull-white eggs, faintly spotted with brown, in a stick nest lined with grass, usually placed low in scrubby brush, cacti, or small trees.

Range: Resident in southern Arizona, southeastern New Mexico, and southern Texas. Also in American tropics.

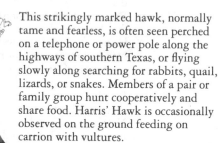

This strikingly marked hawk, normally tame and fearless, is often seen perched on a telephone or power pole along the highways of southern Texas, or flying slowly along searching for rabbits, quail, lizards, or snakes. Members of a pair or family group hunt cooperatively and share food. Harris' Hawk is occasionally observed on the ground feeding on carrion with vultures.

---

## 330 Red-shouldered Hawk
*Buteo lineatus*

Description: 16–24″ (41–61 cm). W. 3′4″ (1 m). A large, long-winged hawk with white barring on dark wings, *rusty shoulders,* pale underparts barred with rust, and a

*narrowly banded tail.* In flight, shows translucent area near tip of wing, visible from below. Young birds streaked below; best distinguished from young Red-tailed Hawks by their somewhat smaller size, narrower tail, and longer, narrower wings, and absence of white chest.

Voice: Shrill scream, *kee-yeeear,* with a downward inflection.

Habitat: Deciduous woodlands, especially where there is standing water.

Nesting: 2 or 3 white eggs, spotted with brown, in a large mass of leaves and twigs, placed 20 to 60′ (6 to 18 m) up in a forest tree.

Range: Breeds from Minnesota east to New Brunswick and south to Gulf Coast and Florida, and on Pacific Coast in California. Winters in breeding range north to southern New England.

The Red-shouldered Hawk prefers lowlands, especially swampy woods and bogs. There it hunts by watching quietly from a low perch, dropping down to capture snakes and frogs. It also eats insects and small mammals. Normally shy, these birds become tame if they are not persecuted. During courtship a pair can be quite noisy, wheeling in the sky above their nesting territory and uttering their distinctive whistled scream.

---

327 **Broad-winged Hawk**
*Buteo platypterus*

Description: 13–15″ (33–38 cm). W. 33″ (84 cm). A stocky, pigeon-sized hawk. Adult plain brown above, barred with rusty color below, with *broad black-and-white tail bands.* Immatures similar, but sparsely spotted or blotched below, and with tail bands less distinct.

Voice: Thin whistle, *pe-heeeeeeeee?*

Habitat: Breeds mainly in deciduous woodlands.

Nesting: 3 or 4 white eggs, with irregular brown spots, in a nest of sticks lined with green leaves placed in the crotch of a tree.

Range: Breeds from Alberta east to Manitoba and Nova Scotia, south to Gulf Coast and Florida. Winters from southern Florida southward into tropics.

The Broad-winged Hawk is an eastern species, best known for its spectacular migrations; often thousands of birds travel together, with single flocks numbering up to several hundred individuals. Great numbers migrate along the eastern ridges in mid-September; more than 19,000 were counted in one day as they passed over the lookout at Hawk Mountain, Pennsylvania. During breeding, this hawk is secretive or, rather, unobtrusive. It lives mainly in the woods, beneath the canopy or hidden among the foliage. Often one is made aware of it only through its call. Its food consists mainly of snakes, mice, frogs, and insects.

---

## 335 Short-tailed Hawk
*Buteo brachyurus*

Description: 13–14" (33–36 cm). W. 35" (89 cm). A stocky, pigeon-sized hawk with two color phases. The light phase is dark above and white below; the dark phase (more common in Florida) is black above and below except for the light bases of the primaries. Both phases have *banded, black-and-white tail,* yellow cere, and yellow legs and feet. Immatures are like adults, but with more numerous tail bands.

Voice: A high-pitched squeal, *kleeeea,* dropping in pitch at end; usually silent away from nest.

Habitat: Open woodlands of pine and oak, cypress swamps, and mangroves.

Nesting: 2 white eggs, sometimes spotted or blotched with brown, in a stick nest lined with leaves and sometimes decorated with Spanish moss, placed in a tree.

Range: Local resident in southern Florida. Also in tropical America.

This rare and wary hawk is easily identified in either color phase, as it is the only hawk in the area that is pure black or pure white below. It often perches low on poles or trees near swampy areas and darts out after birds, rodents, lizards, or insects. But it also hunts from high in the air, obtaining its prey in deep and swift dives.

---

## 329 Swainson's Hawk
*Buteo swainsoni*

Description: 18–22″ (46–56 cm). W. 4′1″ (1.2 m). A large hawk with longer, more pointed wings than the Red-tailed; soars with wings held in shallow V. Uniform brown above, white below with warm-brown breast; tail dark brown and indistinctly banded. Young bird similar to immature Red-tail, but tends to have darker markings on the breast, whereas young Red-tails are more heavily marked on flanks and belly. A less-common all-dark form also occurs.

Voice: Long, plaintive, whistled *kreee.*

Habitat: Open plains, grasslands, and prairies.

Nesting: 2–4 white eggs, unmarked or lightly spotted with brown or black, in a large nest of sticks often placed conspicuously in an isolated tree.

Range: Breeds locally in Alaska, Yukon, and Mackenzie, and across much of western United States south to northern Mexico and Texas. Winters chiefly in tropics, but small numbers winter in Florida.

Named after the English naturalist William Swainson (1789–1855), this species is highly gregarious, often migrating in great soaring flocks containing thousands of birds. Its migrations are longer than those of the other species; most individuals go all the way to Argentina to spend the winter, making a round trip of as much as 17,000 miles (27,000 kilometers). On its breeding grounds in the western plains, this hawk preys mainly on rodents and huge numbers of grasshoppers.

## 338 White-tailed Hawk
*Buteo albicaudatus*

Description: 21–23″ (53–58 cm). W. 4′ (1.2 m). A large stocky hawk. Adult gray above, white below, with narrow but conspicuous black band on its short white tail, and rufous shoulder patch. Immature birds dark with gray tail.

Voice: A musical *ke-ke-ke-ke-ke* or *cutta-cutta-cutta-cutta.*

Habitat: Coastal prairies, grasslands, and semiarid scrub.

Nesting: 2 dull-white or pale bluish eggs, unmarked or lightly spotted with brown, in a grass-lined nest of sticks in a low bush, cactus, or small tree.

Range: Resident in southern Texas. Also in American tropics.

This handsome and conspicuous hawk is a common sight in south Texas, where it is usually seen perched along highways on telephone poles, fence posts, or dead trees. It mainly preys on rabbits, but this bird is an opportunist, gathering in flocks with other hawks at brush fires to feed on rodents, rabbits, lizards, and insects driven out by the flames. Like related hawks, it rides the air currents on motionless wings, often soaring to great heights.

## 331 Red-tailed Hawk including "Harlan's Hawk"
*Buteo jamaicensis*

Description: 18–25″ (46–64 cm). W. 4′ (1.2 m). A large stocky hawk. Typical light-phase birds have whitish breast and *rust-colored tail.* Young birds are duller, more streaked, and lack rust-colored tail of adult; they are distinguished from Red-shouldered and Swainson's hawks by their white chest, stocky build, and broader, more rounded wings. This species is quite variable in color, especially in the West, where blackish individuals occur; these usually retain the rusty tail.

Voice: High-pitched descending scream with a hoarse quality, *keeeeer.*

Habitat: Deciduous forests and open country of various kinds, including tundra, plains, and farmlands.

Nesting: 2 or 3 white eggs, spotted with brown, in a bulky nest of sticks lined with shreds of bark and bits of fresh green vegetation, placed in a tall tree or on a rock ledge.

Range: Breeds throughout North America, from Alaska east to Nova Scotia and southward. Winters north to southern British Columbia and Maritime Provinces.

The Red-tail is the most common and widespread American member of the genus *Buteo,* which also includes the Red-shouldered, Swainson's, and Broad-winged hawks, among others. Like other hawks of this group, it soars over open country in search of its prey, but just as often perches in a tree at the edge of a meadow, watching for the slightest movement in the grass below. The Red-tail rarely takes poultry, feeding mainly on small rodents. Certain western birds with grayish or faintly streaked or mottled tails were formerly considered a separate species called "Harlan's Hawk."

328 **Ferruginous Hawk**
*Buteo regalis*

Description: 22½–25″ (57–64 cm). W. 4′8″ (1.4 m). A large hawk. Light-phase adult *rufous above, mainly whitish below,* with rufous "wrist" patch and leg feathers, and black primary tips. In rare dark phase, deep rufous above and below, with whitish tail. Legs and feet feathered down to talons. Immatures resemble light-phase adults, but with few or no rufous markings.

Voice: A loud descending *kree-e-ah.*

Habitat: Prairies, brushy open country, badlands.

Nesting: 3–5 white eggs, blotched or spotted with brown, in a nest of roots, sticks, sagebrush, cow dung, or even old cattle bones, placed in a tree or bush, or on a rocky hillside.

Range: Nests from Canadian prairie provinces south to eastern Oregon, Nevada, Arizona, New Mexico, and western Oklahoma. Rare east of Minnesota and central Texas. Winters in southern half of breeding range and southwestern states from central California to southwestern Texas into Mexico.

The clutch of three to five eggs is large for a *Buteo* hawk and may result from a fluctuating food supply. Ferruginous Hawks, which feed mainly on prairie dogs and ground squirrels, lay more eggs when prey abounds, fewer eggs in years when rodent populations decrease. They also eat grasshoppers, birds, and lizards.

332 **Rough-legged Hawk**
*Buteo lagopus*

Description: 19–24″ (48–61 cm). W. 4′4″ (1.3 m). A large, long-winged hawk that often hovers. Tail white at base with dark terminal band. Light-phase adult has sandy-brown head and neck, blackish belly, and dark "wrist" marks on underside of wing. All-dark forms can usually be identified by underwing and tail pattern.

Voice: Loud or soft whistles, often in a descending scale.

Habitat: Tundra; winters on open plains, agricultural areas, and marshes.

Nesting: 2–7 white eggs, speckled with brown and black, in a nest of moss and sticks placed on a cliff or rocky outcropping on the tundra.

Range: Breeds in Aleutians and northern Alaska east to Baffin Island, and south to northern Manitoba and Newfoundland. Winters across United States irregularly south to California, northern Texas, and Virginia. Also in Eurasia.

The number of eggs laid by the Rough-leg, like the Snowy Owl, depends on the food supply, with larger clutches occurring in years when lemmings are abundant. At a distance this hawk can be identified by its habit of hovering and by the way it perches: balancing precariously on the most slender twigs at the top of a tree.

## 323 Golden Eagle
*Aquila chrysaetos*

Description: 30–41″ (76–104 cm). W. 6′6″ (2 m). A large, all-dark eagle with a pale golden nape. Bill smaller and darker than that of Bald Eagle. Young birds have white at base of tail and black at tip, and white patches on undersides of wings.

Voice: A high-pitched *kee-kee-kee;* also a high scream or squeal, but usually silent.

Habitat: Mountain forests and open grasslands; some winter on salt marshes in the East; found in any habitat during migration.

Nesting: 1–4 whitish eggs, unmarked or lightly speckled with dark brown, in a large mass of sticks placed on a rocky ledge or in a tall tree.

Range: Breeds from Alaska east across northern

Canada south to Mexico, Canadian prairie provinces, and Labrador. Winters in southern part of breeding range and in much of United States, except Southeast. Also in Eurasia.

Although widespread in the Northern Hemisphere, the Golden Eagle has probably never been numerous in eastern North America; after long persecution, only a very few breeding pairs now survive. In recent years a few nests have been found, and some have produced young, but it is unlikely that the species will ever be more than a rarity in the eastern part of its range.

## Family Falconidae
Caracaras and Falcons

63 species: Worldwide. Seven species breed in North America. This family includes the true falcons (genus *Falco*) and also the caracaras, which are larger and often feed on carrion, as vultures do. True falcons have long pointed wings and long tails, and are among the fastest-flying birds in the world. They mainly inhabit open country, and many pursue birds on the wing. Unlike other birds of prey, true falcons do not build nests of their own but utilize other birds' nests or lay eggs in hollow trees, on cliffs, or on the ground. Caracaras build nests like other birds of prey.

### 314 Crested Caracara
*Caracara plancus*

Description: 20–22″ (51–56 cm). W. 4′ (1.2 m). A large, long-legged, hawk-like bird with rounded wings, often seen on the ground. Dark brown with black cap and bare red face; throat, neck, and base of tail white; tip of tail has black band. In flight, shows large white patches near wing tips.

Voice: High, harsh cackle.

Habitat: Prairies, savannas, and semiarid areas with open groves of palms, mesquite, and cacti.

Nesting: 2 or 3 white eggs, with heavy brown spots and blotches, in a nest of twigs, grasses, weeds, and briars lined with leaves and moss, placed in palmetto hammock or live oak, rarely on the ground.

Range: Resident in southern Arizona, southern Texas, southwestern Louisiana (rarely), and central and southern Florida. Also in American tropics.

This scavenger has probably the most varied diet of any bird of prey. It often accompanies and dominates vultures at fresh kills or carrion and also eats small animals. It is primarily a ground-inhabiting falcon of open prairies, with long legs that enable it to walk and run with ease. The Crested Caracara is the national bird of Mexico.

---

337, 340 **American Kestrel**
**"Sparrow Hawk"**
*Falco sparverius*

Description: 9–12″ (23–30 cm). W. 21″ (53 cm). A jay-sized falcon, often seen hovering. May be recognized in any plumage by its *rusty tail and back.* Adult male has slate-blue wings. Female has wings rusty like back, narrow bands on tail. Both sexes have 2 black stripes on face.

Voice: Shrill *killy-killy-killy.*

Habitat: Towns and cities, parks, farmlands, and open country.

Nesting: 4 or 5 white or pinkish eggs, blotched with brown, placed without nest or lining in a natural or man-made cavity.

Range: Breeds from Alaska and Northwest Territories east through Maritime Provinces, and south throughout

continent. Winters north to British Columbia, Great Lakes, and New England. Also in American tropics.

Unlike larger falcons, the "Sparrow Hawk" has adapted to humans and nests even in our largest cities, where it preys chiefly on House Sparrows. In the countryside it takes insects, small birds, and rodents, capturing its prey on the ground rather than in midair like other falcons. The female does most of the incubating and is fed by the male. As he nears the nest with food, he calls; the female flies to him, receives the food, and returns to the nest. After the eggs hatch, the male continues to bring most of the food. The young stay with the adults for a time after fledging, and it is not uncommon to see family parties in late summer.

---

339 **Merlin**
**"Pigeon Hawk"**
*Falco columbarius*

Description: 10–14″ (25–36 cm). W. 23″ (58 cm). A jay-sized falcon, stockier than the American Kestrel. Slate colored (males) or brownish (females) above; light and streaked below. Long tail boldly banded. Lacks facial stripes of most other falcons.
Voice: Usually silent. High, loud cackle; also *klee-klee-klee* like an American Kestrel.
Habitat: Coniferous forests; more widespread in winter.
Nesting: 5 or 6 buff eggs, stippled with purple and brown, placed in a tree cavity without a nest or lining, on a rocky ledge, or in an abandoned crow's nest.
Range: Breeds from Alaska east through Mackenzie to Newfoundland, and south to Wyoming, Montana, and northern New England (rarely). Winters from British Columbia south to New Mexico, central Texas, and Carolinas, casually

north to southern Canada. Also in Eurasia.

The "Pigeon Hawk" is best known as a migrant along our larger rivers and coastal marshes and dunes. It is most abundant during the migrations of smaller birds, on which it feeds. This little falcon is swift and aggressive, harassing larger hawks and gulls and attacking intruders at its nest. As with other falcons, the female begins incubating as soon as the first egg is laid, so that the young hatch at intervals; when food is scarce, the larger young are fed first, the smaller ones sometimes dying of starvation. This seemingly heartless procedure ensures that some young will be raised successfully even in hard times.

341 **Prairie Falcon**
*Falco mexicanus*

Description: 17–20″ (43–51 cm). W. 3′6″ (1.1 m). A large falcon, sandy brown above, whitish or pale buff below with fine spots and streaks, narrow brown "mustache" stripe, and *dark wing linings.*

Voice: A loud *kree-kree-kree,* most often heard near nest.

Habitat: Barren mountains, dry plains, and prairies.

Nesting: 4 or 5 white or pinkish eggs, blotched with brown, placed without a nest on a cliff ledge or in the abandoned nest of some other large bird.

Range: Breeds from British Columbia and Canadian prairie provinces south to Mexico and northern Texas. Winters in breeding range, and sparingly farther east.

The Prairie Falcon is usually found in places far from water, while the Peregrine is nearly always found near a river or lake. The Prairie Falcon's diet consists mainly of birds, which it pursues on the wing but usually captures on the ground. Its numbers are declining, due to rodent-poisoning programs and nest-robbing by falconers

## 343 Peregrine Falcon<br>"Duck Hawk"<br>*Falco peregrinus*

Description: 15–21″ (38–53 cm). W. 3′4″ (1 m). A large robust falcon with a black hood and wide black "mustaches." Adults slate-gray above and pale below, with fine black bars and spots. Young birds are brown or brownish slate above and heavily streaked below.

Voice: Rasping *kack-kack-kack-kack,* usually heard at nest; otherwise generally silent.

Habitat: Open country, especially along rivers; also near lakes and along coasts, and in cities. Migrates chiefly along coasts.

Nesting: 2–4 cream or buff eggs, spotted with reddish brown, placed in a scrape with little lining on a cliff or in an abandoned bird's nest.

Range: Breeds from Alaska and Canadian Arctic south locally through mountainous West, and sparingly in East; increasing. Winters near coasts north to British Columbia and Massachusetts. Also in southern South America and Old World.

Following an alarming decline during the 1950s and 1960s, the spectacular "Duck Hawk" is on the increase again, now that pesticides that caused thinning of eggshells have been banned. After an intensive program of rearing birds in captivity and releasing them in the wild (a process called "hacking"), this large falcon is reclaiming nesting grounds from which it disappeared a few decades ago. A favorite nesting site nowadays is a tall building or bridge in a city; these urban Peregrines subsist mainly on pigeons.

342 **Gyrfalcon**
*Falco rusticolus*

Description: 22″ (56 cm). W. 4′ (1.2 m). The largest of the true falcons. Three color phases occur: blackish, white, and gray-brown. All are more uniformly colored than the Peregrine Falcon, which has bold dark "mustaches" and hood, and a proportionately larger head.

Voice: A chattering scream, *kak-kak-kak-kak.*

Habitat: Arctic tundra and rocky cliffs, usually near water. Each winter, a few move south to coastal beaches and marshes.

Nesting: Usually 4 whitish or buff eggs, finely spotted with reddish brown, on a rock ledge or in the abandoned nest of a Rough-legged Hawk or Common Raven.

Range: Breeds on tundra of northern Alaska and northern Canada. Winters in breeding range, and also rarely but regularly south to northern tier of states, especially along coasts.

It is a memorable occasion when a Gyrfalcon is sighted on a coastal salt marsh or over open country inland. In the Far North, it feeds mainly on ptarmigan, but during the summer months it also takes shorebirds, eiders, and gulls, and makes frequent raids on the great colonies of murres and dovekies.

## Family Cracidae
Curassows, Guans, and Chachalacas

50 species: Tropical and subtropical regions of the Western Hemisphere. One species occurs as far north as the Rio Grande Valley in Texas. These large, long-legged, long-tailed, chicken-like birds spend much time in trees, where they run nimbly along the branches, searching for the buds and tender new leaves that are an important part of their diet.

268 **Plain Chachalaca**
*Ortalis vetula*

Description: 18–21″ (46–53 cm). W. 26″ (66 cm). Crow-sized. Olive-brown, with a long tail glossed with green and tipped with white. Slightly crested, with patches of bare, pinkish-red skin at sides of throat.
Voice: Loud, raucous *cha-cha-lac,* often in chorus at dawn and dusk. Call of male lower pitched than female's.
Habitat: Riverside woodlands and thickets.
Nesting: Usually 3 dull-white eggs in a stick nest lined with leaves and moss, usually on a low tree limb.
Range: Resident from extreme southern Texas to Nicaragua.

These noisy, gregarious birds are a feature of the Rio Grande delta and locally common in the Santa Ana National Wildlife Refuge, where they are fed by tourists and have become remarkably tame. Although primarily arboreal in habits, they often come to the ground to feed on leaves, buds, berries, nuts, insects, and human handouts. Where they are not protected, they are hunted as game.

---

**Family Phasianidae**
Partridges, Grouse, Turkeys, and Quail

189 species: Worldwide except Australian region. This large and varied family contains almost all the birds that resemble chickens. They have stocky bodies; thick, short legs; large toes that are adapted for walking and scratching; and short, blunt bills that are well suited for crushing seeds and feeding on a variety of insects and other small creatures. In North America these birds can be divided into four groups: the introduced pheasants and partridges; the

grouse, which have feathered legs and feet; the turkeys; and the native quail, of which the Northern Bobwhite is the most widespread.

## 269 Gray Partridge
*Perdix perdix*

Description: 12–14" (30–36 cm). A small, stocky, chicken-like bird, largely gray with a black U-shaped mark on underparts and *bright, rust-colored tail,* most easily seen when the bird flies.

Voice: Hoarse *kee-ah;* when flushed, a rapid cackle.

Habitat: Grainfields, agricultural grasslands.

Nesting: 10–20 olive, unmarked eggs in a shallow depression lined with grass and concealed in vegetation.

Range: Introduced and locally established in Nova Scotia, New Brunswick, northern New York, Ontario, Ohio, Indiana, southern Michigan, Iowa, Minnesota, and across northern part of western United States to British Columbia. Introduction in East has been generally unsuccessful. Native to Eurasia.

Also called the "Hungarian Partridge," this species is well adapted to areas of intensive agriculture, where no native game bird can exist. It forms coveys outside the breeding season, like the Northern Bobwhite, but does not defend a territory. In the spring the flocks break up into pairs. While the male takes no part in incubating the eggs, he does help care for the young, which leave the nest soon after hatching. The Gray Partridge's high reproductive rate enables it to withstand hunting, predators, and cold, snowy northern winters, all of which take a heavy toll.

270, 271 **Ring-necked Pheasant**
*Phasianus colchicus*

Description: 30–36″ (76–91 cm). Long pointed tail. Male has red eye patch, brilliant green head, and (usually) white neck ring; body patterned in soft brown and iridescent russet. Female is a mottled sandy brown, with shorter tail.

Voice: Loud, crowing *caw-cawk!* followed by a resonant beating of the wings. When alarmed, flies off with a loud cackle.

Habitat: Farmlands, pastures, and grassy woodland edges.

Nesting: 6–15 buff-olive eggs in a grass-lined depression concealed in dense grass or weeds.

Range: Introduced from British Columbia, Alberta, Minnesota, Ontario, and Maritime Provinces south to central California, Oklahoma, and Maryland. Native to Asia.

The North American birds of this species are descended from stock brought from several different parts of the Old World and thus are somewhat variable. They are very tolerant of humans, and can get by with a minimum of cover; they often nest on the outskirts of large cities. Although successful in most grassland habitats, this species has its North American headquarters in the central plains. After the breakup of winter flocks, males establish large territories and mate with several females. At first the chicks feed largely on insects but soon shift to the adult diet of berries, seeds, buds, and leaves.

273 **Spruce Grouse**
*Dendragapus canadensis*

Description: 15–17″ (38–43 cm). A dark, chicken-like bird with a fan-shaped tail. Male dusky gray-brown with red comb over eye, black throat and upper breast, white-spotted sides, and chestnut-tipped tail. Female browner, underparts barred with brown.

Voice: Males give a low *krrrrk, krrrk, krrk, krrk, krrk,* said to be lowest-pitched vocal sound of any North American bird. Females produce low clucking notes.

Habitat: Coniferous forests, especially those with a mixture of spruce and pine; edges of bogs.

Nesting: 8–11 buff eggs, plain or spotted with brown, in a hollow lined with grass and leaves, concealed on the ground under low branches of a young spruce.

Range: Resident from Alaska, northern Manitoba, Quebec, and Nova Scotia south to Washington, Wyoming, central Manitoba, Michigan, and northern New England.

This northern grouse is extraordinarily tame and can occasionally be approached and caught; hence its local name, "Fool Hen." It is generally a quiet bird, thinly distributed in its habitat and therefore difficult to find. Its principal foods are the needles and buds of evergreens, although insects are eaten in large quantities by young birds. Spruce Grouse are generally found singly or in small family groups, picking their way quietly over the forest floor or sitting in dense conifers.

278, 279 **Willow Ptarmigan**
*Lagopus lagopus*

Description: 15–17″ (38–43 cm). A small tundra grouse with a red comb over each eye. In winter, *entirely white except for black tail.* In summer, male is rusty red with white wings and belly; female is mottled and barred with brown but has white wings. Spring and fall molting plumages show a variety of checkered patterns. Summer male Rock Ptarmigan more grayish; winter Rock Ptarmigan has black stripe through eye.

Voice: In flight, courting males have a loud, staccato *go-back, go-back, go-back* and other guttural calls.

Habitat: Tundra; also thickets in valleys and foothills; muskeg.

Nesting: 7–10 yellowish eggs, blotched with brown, in a scrape lined with grass and feathers, often sheltered by vegetation, rocks, or logs.

Range: Breeds from Alaska east to Labrador, and south to central British Columbia, northern Ontario, and central Quebec. Winters south to forested regions of central Canada. Also in Eurasia.

The most widespread ptarmigan of the Far North, this species increases in number in some years but in others is very scarce. While the female incubates, the male guards the territory. When the chicks grow up, several families gather in large flocks and often migrate southward together when winter arrives. In summer, ptarmigans feed on green shoots, buds, flowers, and insects; in winter, they take mainly twigs and buds of willows and alders.

---

276, 277 **Rock Ptarmigan**
*Lagopus mutus*

Description: 13–14″ (33–36 cm). Smaller than Willow Ptarmigan. In winter, *entirely white except for black tail and black line through eye* in males and most females. In summer, male is flecked with dark gray-brown, and has white wings and belly. Female is paler, with gray, yellowish, and brown on most feathers. Bill smaller than in Willow Ptarmigan.

Voice: Courting male gives a snoring *kurr-kurr.* Female has clucking and purring notes.

Habitat: Upland tundra with thickets of willows and heaths.

Nesting: 6–9 buff eggs, spotted with dark brown, in a sheltered hollow lined with grass and moss.

Range: Breeds in Alaska and northern Canada. Winters south to tree line.

Pairs of Rock Ptarmigans remain together until midway through incubation, when the male deserts his mate. The female raises the chicks, which move about on the tundra in search of insects, buds, and berries. They become independent when about three months old. The white winter plumage of ptarmigans provides both good camouflage and protection against the cold, because white feathers have empty cells filled with air that help in insulation, whereas colored feathers contain pigment.

## 275 Ruffed Grouse
*Bonasa umbellus*

Description: 16–19″ (41–48 cm). A brown or gray-brown, slightly crested, chicken-like bird with *fan-shaped, black-banded tail,* barred flanks, and black ruffs on sides of neck.

Voice: Female gives soft, hen-like clucks. In spring, the displaying male sits on a log and beats the air with his wings, creating a drumming sound that increases rapidly in tempo.

Habitat: Deciduous and mixed forests, especially those with scattered clearings and dense undergrowth; overgrown pastures.

Nesting: 9–12 pinkish-buff eggs, plain or spotted with dull brown, in a shallow depression lined with leaves and concealed under a bush.

Range: Resident from tree line in Alaska and northern Canada south to California, Wyoming, Minnesota, Missouri, and Carolinas, and in Appalachians to Georgia.

Long one of the most highly esteemed game birds in North America, the Ruffed Grouse can withstand hunting pressure as long as suitable habitat exists. But in many areas forests are maturing, eliminating the undergrowth this species needs; where this is happening, reintroduced Wild Turkeys are increasing and the grouse are decreasing.

---

280, 283 **Greater Prairie-Chicken**
*Tympanuchus cupido*

Description: 16–18″ (41–46 cm). A chicken-like bird, heavily *barred* above and below with grayish brown. Has *short black tail.* Male has yellow-orange air sacs inflated during courtship display, and long black feathers on sides of neck, erected into "horns" during courtship; horns of female are shorter. See Lesser Prairie-Chicken.

Voice: Hollow "booming" call during display; also cackles and clucks.

Habitat: Undisturbed tall-grass prairie.

Nesting: 8–12 olive eggs, finely spotted and blotched with brown, in a well-concealed, grass-lined depression in the ground.

Range: Resident locally in Wisconsin, Illinois, and Michigan, and from Manitoba south through Great Plains to Oklahoma; also on coastal prairies of Texas.

Once found from the Atlantic Coast west to Wyoming, the Greater Prairie-Chicken has been exterminated from much of this vast range through the destruction of the undisturbed prairies on which it breeds. The East Coast subspecies, known as the "Heath Hen" (*Tympanuchus cupido cupido*), is extinct. The form inhabiting the prairies along the Texas Gulf Coast, "Attwater's Prairie-Chicken" (*Tympanuchus cupido attwateri*), may follow its eastern relative into extinction in a few years. Where they still survive, Greater Prairie-Chickens perform striking courtship dances on communal display grounds: the males strut about and stamp their feet, with "horns" erect and yellow-orange sacs of skin inflated on the sides of the neck, meanwhile uttering a deep cooing call that may carry a mile. They leap and whirl in the air, and threaten each other by short runs with tail raised, head down, and horns erect.

281, 282 **Lesser Prairie-Chicken**
*Tympanuchus pallidicinctus*

Description: 16″ (41 cm). Similar to Greater Prairie-Chicken, but smaller, paler, and more finely barred. In the male, air sacs on the neck are reddish, rather than yellow-orange.

Voice: Various cackling and clucking notes; male gives "booming" call during courtship.

Habitat: Dry grasslands with shrubs and short trees.

Nesting: 11–13 creamy or buff-colored eggs in a grass-lined depression, usually under a low bush or shrub.

Range: Resident in southern Colorado and Kansas, south locally in western Oklahoma, Texas, and eastern New Mexico.

As with the Greater Prairie-Chicken, males of this species gather and engage in communal courtship displays in which the birds dance about with the colorful air sacs on their necks inflated and uttering low cooing or "booming" notes. This species replaces the Greater Prairie-Chicken in higher, drier grasslands.

272 **Sharp-tailed Grouse**
*Tympanuchus phasianellus*

Description: 15–20″ (38–51 cm). Slightly smaller than a female pheasant, which it resembles. Mottled with buff, slightly paler below. Tail short and *pointed, with white outer tail feathers.* Tail of male longer than that of female. Male has purple neck patch and yellow comb over eye. Prairie-chickens are barred, not mottled, and show no white in tail.

Voice: During courtship, a low single or double cooing note.

Habitat: Grasslands, scrub forest, and arid sagebrush.

Nesting: 10–13 buff-brown eggs in a grass-lined depression in tall grass or brush.

Range: Resident from Alaska east to Hudson Bay, and south to Utah, northeastern New Mexico, and Michigan.

The habitat requirements of this grouse are not as specialized as those of the prairie-chickens, and so this species has a wider range and has managed to survive in much larger numbers. The cutting of large areas of northern coniferous forest, which has created vast tracts of brushland, has helped the Sharp-tail. Like their relatives the prairie-chickens and the Sage Grouse (*Centrocercus urophasianus*), these birds gather each spring on communal display grounds, the males bobbing and strutting with inflated sacs of purplish skin on the sides of the neck.

284, 285 **Wild Turkey**
*Meleagris gallopavo*

Description: Male 48″ (122 cm); female 36″ (91 cm). Unmistakable. Dusky brown with iridescent bronze sheen and barred with black; head and neck naked, with bluish and reddish wattles; tail fan-shaped, with chestnut or buff tail tips. Male has spurs and long "beard" on breast. Female smaller, lacks spurs, and usually lacks "beard." Domestic turkeys are similar, but usually tamer and stockier.

Voice: Gobbling calls similar to those of domestic turkey.

Habitat: Oak woodlands, pine-oak forests.

Nesting: 8–15 buffy eggs, spotted with brown, in a shallow depression lined with grass and leaves.

Range: Resident in much of southern United States, from Arizona east, as far north as New England. Introduced to many western states, including California.

By the end of the 19th century, the Wild Turkey had been hunted almost to extinction in much of its original range. Now, with protection, restocking programs, and the return of the mature forests favored by turkeys, this species is making a marked comeback. It is now common in areas where it was totally absent a few decades ago.

---

286, 287 **Northern Bobwhite**
*Colinus virginianus*

Description: 8–11″ (20–28 cm). A small, chunky, brown bird; underparts pale and streaked; *face patterned in black and white in males, and in buff and white in females.* Usually seen in groups called coveys.

Voice: Clear whistled *bob-WHITE* or *poor-bob-WHITE.*

Habitat: Brushy pastures, grassy roadsides, farmlands, and open woodlands.

Nesting: 10–15 white eggs in a grass-lined hollow concealed in weeds or grass.

Range: Permanent resident from Kansas, Iowa, Pennsylvania, and Cape Cod southward. Fluctuating populations farther north and west. Introduced locally elsewhere.

One of our most popular game birds, the Northern Bobwhite is more numerous now than it was when unbroken forest covered most of the eastern United States; but in recent years the species has declined somewhat due to the cutting of roadside brush, the trimming of farmland borders, and the gradual replacement of former pastures with dense stands of young trees. Outside the breeding season, Northern Bobwhites gather in coveys of roughly two dozen birds, vigorously defending their territory from other coveys.

274 **Scaled Quail**
*Callipepla squamata*

Description: 10–12″ (25–30 cm). A small stocky quail, gray-brown above, with *buff-white crest.* Bluish-gray feathers on breast and mantle have black, semicircular edges, creating *scaled effect;* belly also has brown "scales." Sexes alike.
Voice: The call is a low, nasal *pe-cos.* Also harsh clucking calls.
Habitat: Dry grasslands and brushy deserts.
Nesting: 12–14 pale buff eggs, evenly spotted with reddish brown, in a grass-lined hollow.
Range: Resident in Arizona, Colorado, western Kansas, and western Oklahoma south to central Mexico.

These modestly plumaged quail, often called "Cotton Tops" by hunters, are characteristic birds of the drier desert areas of the Southwest. Their numbers fluctuate markedly from year to year, because the birds are sensitive to drought and heavy rains. They spend most of the year in small flocks, which break up into pairs at the beginning of the breeding season.

## Family Rallidae
Rails, Gallinules, and Coots

130 species: Worldwide. Nine species breed in North America. Rails are mainly marsh-dwelling birds, with short, rounded wings, large feet, long toes, and bodies that are laterally compressed to enable them to slip between reeds and cattails. This family also contains the moorhens, gallinules, and coots, the last having lobed feet adapted for swimming in open water. Gallinules are brightly colored, but most other rails are cryptically colored in grays, browns, and buffs, blending in with the reeds. Their nests are well hidden among the dense rushes and other aquatic growth of the marsh.

262 **Yellow Rail**
*Coturnicops noveboracensis*

Description: 6–8″ (15–20 cm). A sparrow-sized rail. *Brownish buff,* with a short yellow bill and yellow feet. Shows a *white wing patch* in flight.

Voice: A series of clicks in groups of two or three, sounding like pebbles being tapped together; usually heard at night.

Habitat: Grassy marshes and wet meadows.

Nesting: 7–10 buff eggs, with a ring of dark spots around larger end, in a firm cup of grass well concealed in a grassy marsh.

Range: Breeds from northern Alberta east to Quebec and New Brunswick, and south to North Dakota, northern Michigan, and Maine. Winters from Carolinas south to Florida, and along Gulf Coast; rarely in southern California.

All rails are secretive, but none more so than this tiny bird. It is also rare, and many veteran bird-watchers have never seen one. It can conceal itself in very short grass and can seldom be induced to fly. The best way to see one is to follow a mowing machine in a damp meadow in the Deep South during September or October. When the uncut grass is reduced to a small patch, one or more birds may flush into view, fly weakly away, and disappear into the nearest patch of tall grass.

264 **Black Rail**
*Laterallus jamaicensis*

Description: 5–6″ (13–15 cm). A sparrow-sized rail. *Black,* with rusty nape and white flecks on the back, black bill, and greenish legs and feet. Can be confused with the downy black young of larger rails.

Voice: A piping *ki-ki-doo,* the last note lower in pitch.

Habitat: Coastal salt marshes; more rarely, inland freshwater marshes.

Nesting: 6–8 pale buff eggs, lightly spotted with brown, in a loose cup of grass, usually concealed under a mat of dead marsh vegetation.

Range: Breeds along Pacific and Atlantic coasts from California and Long Island southward, and locally in Midwestern interior and along lower Colorado River. Winters north to Gulf Coast and Florida and in its breeding range in West.

This tiny rail may be relatively common in some areas but is so secretive that many consider it rare. The birds spend much of their time creeping about under mats of dead marsh grass. The best way to detect them is to enter a salt marsh after dark during the breeding season and listen for the male's high-pitched, piping call notes, which carry as far as a mile on a still night. These birds respond to an imitation of their call and may sometimes be lured within range of a flashlight.

259 **Clapper Rail**
*Rallus longirostris*

Description: 14–16″ (36–41 cm). A long-billed rail of salt marshes. All birds have black-and-white barred flanks. Eastern populations are *grayish brown* without rusty underparts of similar King Rail. Birds on Gulf Coast and in Far West are rustier and more like the King Rail, but do not show rust on shoulders or sides of face. King Rail prefers freshwater marshes.

Voice: Harsh, clattering *kek-kek-kek-kek-kek.*

Habitat: Salt marshes and some freshwater marshes.

Nesting: 9–12 buff eggs, spotted or blotched with brown, in a shallow saucer or deep bowl of dead marsh grasses, often domed.

Range: Breeds along coasts from central California and Massachusetts southward. Also on inland California's Salton Sea and lower Colorado River. Winters north to central California and New Jersey, rarely farther north.

The rattling call of the Clapper Rail is one of the most familiar sounds in the salt marshes in summer. Generally secretive, the birds are sometimes forced into view by high tides, when they may be seen along roads in the marsh or standing on floating boards. Otherwise they are most often glimpsed as they dart across tidal creeks between sheltering grasses. This species may be confused with the rustier King Rail when the latter enters the salt meadows for the winter.

260 **King Rail**
*Rallus elegans*

Description: 15–19″ (38–48 cm). Similar to the Clapper Rail of salt marshes but *head, neck, shoulders, and underparts rusty.*

Flanks barred with black and white. Virginia Rail is smaller, with gray patch on face.

Voice: A harsh, clattering *kek-kek-kek-kek-kek,* almost identical to that of Clapper Rail.

Habitat: Freshwater marshes and roadside ditches; wanders to salt marshes in fall and winter.

Nesting: 8–11 buff eggs, spotted with brown, in a deep bowl of grass, often with surrounding marsh grass pulled down and woven into a dome.

Range: Breeds from North Dakota east to Massachusetts, and south to Florida and Texas. Winters regularly along Gulf Coast, in Mississippi Valley, and rarely northward to southern New England.

This large eastern rail is common in the larger freshwater marshes of the interior. Although difficult to see, it has a loud call that often reveals its presence. It occasionally hybridizes with the similar Clapper Rail where freshwater and salt marshes occur together. They may eventually be found to be two forms of a single species.

## 263 Virginia Rail
*Rallus limicola*

Description: 9–11″ (23–28 cm). A small rail with a long *reddish bill,* rusty underparts, and *gray cheeks.* Much larger King Rail has dark bill and buff or rusty cheeks. Late-summer young birds are similar to adults, but have blackish breasts and dark bills.

Voice: A far-carrying *ticket, ticket, ticket, ticket;* various grunting notes.

Habitat: Freshwater and brackish marshes; may visit salt marshes in winter.

Nesting: 5–12 pale buff eggs, spotted with brown, in a shallow and loosely constructed saucer often woven into surrounding marsh vegetation.

Range: Breeds from British Columbia east to Maritime Provinces, and south to southern California, Oklahoma, and Virginia. Winters regularly on coasts north to Washington, Virginia, and occasionally farther north.

This common but elusive marsh bird is most often detected by its call. It seldom flies, preferring to escape intruders by running through protective marsh vegetation. When the Virginia Rail does take wing, it often flies only a few yards before dropping back out of sight into the marsh. Despite its apparently weak flight, this bird migrates long distances each year; it has been recorded as far out of its normal range as Bermuda and Greenland.

---

261 Sora
*Porzana carolina*

Description: 8–10″ (20–25 cm). A quail-sized rail with a *short yellow bill. Gray breasted with a black face.* Upperparts mottled brown; lower abdomen banded with black and white. Young birds in fall lack black face and have buff breast.

Voice: Most familiar call a musical series of piping notes rapidly descending the scale; also a repeated *ker-wee,* with rising inflection. Near the nest, birds utter an explosive *keek!*

Habitat: Freshwater marshes and marshy ponds; rice fields and salt marshes in winter.

Nesting: 6–15 pale yellow-buff eggs, spotted with brown, in a cup of cattails and dead leaves, usually placed in a clump of reeds in an open part of the marsh.

Range: Breeds from British Columbia east through Mackenzie to Maritime Provinces, and south to Pennsylvania, Oklahoma, Arizona, and central California. Winters mainly along coasts north to California and Virginia.

These birds are especially numerous in fall and winter in southern marshes and rice fields, where they are primarily seed eaters. Although shot in large numbers every year, their high reproductive rate enables them to maintain a stable population. The greatest threat to the Sora is the destruction of the freshwater marshes where they breed: they have consequently become scarce in heavily populated areas.

---

## 265 Purple Gallinule
*Porphyrula martinica*

Description: 11–13″ (28–33 cm). A strikingly colored, chicken-sized marsh bird. Purplish blue with green upperparts, white undertail coverts, yellowish-green legs, red-and-yellow bill, and light blue frontal shield. Immature buffy-brown, with greenish wings and dark bill.

Voice: Squawking and cackling; also guttural grunts.

Habitat: Freshwater marshes with lily pads, pickerelweed, and other aquatic vegetation.

Nesting: 6–10 pinkish-buff eggs with fine dark spots in a nest of dead stems and leaves of water plants, placed on a floating tussock or in a clump of sawgrass or thicket over water.

Range: Breeds from southern Texas, Arkansas, and Carolinas south to Florida and Gulf Coast. Winters along Gulf Coast in Texas, Louisiana, and Florida.

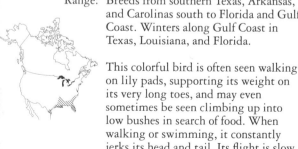

This colorful bird is often seen walking on lily pads, supporting its weight on its very long toes, and may even sometimes be seen climbing up into low bushes in search of food. When walking or swimming, it constantly jerks its head and tail. Its flight is slow and weak, but this has not prevented individual birds from traveling far out of their normal range. They have turned up in California, southern Canada, Bermuda, and even South Africa.

## 266 Common Moorhen
**"Common Gallinule"**
*Gallinula chloropus*

Description: 13″ (33 cm). A duck-like swimming bird that constantly bobs its head while moving. Adult slate-gray, with a conspicuous *red frontal shield and red bill with yellow tip.* White stripe on side, and white undertail coverts. Young birds are similar but duller, without colorful bill.

Voice: Squawking and croaking notes similar to those of coots.

Habitat: Freshwater marshes and ponds with cattails and other aquatic vegetation.

Nesting: 7–14 cinnamon or buff eggs, lightly spotted with brown, on a shallow platform of dead cattails, rushes, and other marsh plants, usually a few inches above water level.

Range: Breeds in California, Nevada, Arizona, and New Mexico, and from Minnesota east to New Brunswick, and south to Gulf Coast and Florida. Winters in California, Arizona, and along Atlantic and Gulf coasts from Virginia to Texas. Also in American tropics and in Old World.

Like coots, Common Moorhens are rails that often swim in open water, bobbing their heads as they cross a pond or pool. Their long toes enable them to walk through marsh vegetation, where they feed on seeds, other plant material, snails, and insects. Males build several nests on the pair's territory; once the young have hatched and left their original nests to wander through the marsh, they use these extra nests as places to spend the night.

## 127 American Coot
*Fulica americana*

Description: 15″ (38 cm). A gray, duck-like bird with a *white bill and frontal shield,* white undertail coverts, and lobed toes. The frontal shield has a red swelling at its upper edge, visible at close range. Immatures similar but paler, with duller bill. The Caribbean Coot (*Fulica caribbaea*), a rare winter visitor to southern Florida, has a more bulbous white frontal shield, without the red swelling.

Voice: A variety of clucks, cackles, grunts, and other harsh notes.

Habitat: Open ponds and marshes; in winter, also on coastal bays and inlets.

Nesting: 8–10 pinkish eggs, spotted with brown, on a shallow platform of dead leaves and stems, usually on the water but anchored to a clump of reeds.

Range: Breeds from western Canada and New York locally southward. Winters north to British Columbia, Kansas, Illinois, and Massachusetts. Also in American tropics.

Coots are the most aquatic members of their family, moving on open water like ducks and often feeding with them. They are excellent swimmers and divers, and they eat various aquatic plants. They also come out on land to feed on seeds, grass, and waste grain. They often become tame when fed scraps and bits of bread. These are heavy birds that must patter over the water before becoming airborne.

---

## Family Aramidae
Limpkins

1 species: Restricted to tropical America, and breeding as far north as southern Georgia. This is a swamp-loving, secretive, rail-like bird. It feeds

exclusively on aquatic snails, which it extracts without breaking the shell. It lays up to eight eggs in a nest in reeds.

## 21 Limpkin
*Aramus guarauna*

Description: 25–28″ (64–71 cm). A long-legged, long-necked, goose-sized marsh bird. Grayish brown with white spots and streaks; long, slender, down-curved bill. In flight, wings have rapid upstroke and slower downstroke.

Voice: A loud, wailing *krrr-eeeow.*

Habitat: Wooded swamps and marshes.

Nesting: 5–8 buff eggs, with dark brown spots and blotches, in a shallow nest of marsh vegetation just above the water; more rarely in a stick nest in low trees or bushes.

Range: Resident locally in southern Georgia and Florida. Also in American tropics.

Related to cranes and rails, the Limpkin is active mainly at night. For food, it depends chiefly on apple snails (*Pomacea*) but also takes frogs, tadpoles, and aquatic insects. Its loud, strident, eerie call, familiar at night in the Florida marshes, sounds like a human in distress, so the Limpkin is known locally as the "Crying Bird."

## Family Gruidae
Cranes

15 species: Fairly widespread, but absent in South America. Two species breed in North America. One, the nearly extinct Whooping Crane, is strictly protected; the other, the Sandhill Crane, is more numerous and has a fairly wide range. Cranes superficially resemble herons but are not related to them. Unlike herons, cranes fly with the neck outstretched

and with the upstroke faster than the downstroke. They are among the tallest birds in the world and inhabit open country, where they nest on the ground and lay only two eggs. Their colors run to black, white, and gray; most of them have a bare patch on the head.

27 **Sandhill Crane**
*Grus canadensis*

Description: 34–48″ (86–122 cm). W. 6′8″ (2 m). Very tall, with long neck and long legs. Largely gray, with red forehead. Immature browner, no red on head. Plumage often appears rusty because of iron stains from the water of tundra ponds.

Voice: A loud, rattling *kar-r-r-r-o-o-o.*

Habitat: Large freshwater marshes, prairie ponds, and marshy tundra; also on prairies and grainfields during migration and in winter.

Nesting: 2 buff eggs, spotted with brown, in a large mound of grass and aquatic plants in an undisturbed marsh.

Range: Breeds from Siberia and Alaska east across Arctic Canada to Hudson Bay, and south to western Ontario, with isolated populations in Rocky Mountains, northern prairies, and Great Lakes region, and in Mississippi, Georgia, and Florida. Winters in California's Central Valley, and across southern states from Arizona to Florida. Also in Cuba.

The mating dance of the Sandhill Crane is spectacular. Facing each other, members of a pair leap into the air with wings extended and feet thrown forward. Then they bow to each other and repeat the performance, uttering loud croaking calls. Courting birds also run about with their wings outstretched and toss tufts of grass in the air.

## 11 Whooping Crane
*Grus americana*

Description: 45–50″ (1.1–1.3 m). W. 7′6″ (2.3 m). A very large crane, *pure white with black wing tips,* and with red on forehead and cheeks. Young birds are similar, but strongly tinged with brown.

Voice: A trumpet-like call that can be heard for several miles.

Habitat: Breeds in northern freshwater bogs; winters on coastal prairies.

Nesting: 2 buff eggs, blotched with brown, on a mound of marsh vegetation.

Range: Breeds in Wood Buffalo National Park on Alberta-Mackenzie border. Winters on Gulf Coast of Texas at Aransas National Wildlife Refuge. A second flock, recently introduced but not yet fully established, breeds at Grays Lake National Wildlife Refuge in Idaho and winters at Bosque del Apache National Wildlife Refuge in New Mexico.

One of our most spectacular birds, the Whooping Crane was reduced by hunting and habitat destruction to about 15 birds in 1937. Strictly protected and monitored since then, the population wintering at Aransas has grown to about 130 birds. In recent decades, an attempt has been made to augment this number by placing eggs of this species in the nests of Sandhill Cranes at Grays Lake National Wildlife Refuge in Idaho. This effort has not yet been declared a complete success, but, including captives, there are now more than 170 Whooping Cranes in existence.

---

## Family Charadriidae
Plovers

60 species: Worldwide. Nine species breed in North America. Plovers are small to medium-sized shorebirds with

short bills slightly swollen at the tip. These birds run along the sand or mud for a way, suddenly stop and probe for food in the soft ooze, and snatch worms snails, small crustaceans, and insects from the ground. Most of the species have characteristic black or brown breast bands on a white background.

## 252, 253 Black-bellied Plover
*Pluvialis squatarola*

Description: 10–13″ (25–33 cm). A quail-sized plover. Breeding adults are gray, with flecks of light and dark above, black on face and breast, and white on belly. Winter adults are similar, but have face and breast white like the belly. Young birds have upperparts flecked with yellow, and breast and belly finely streaked. All plumages have bold white wing stripe, *white rump,* and *black patch under wing.* See American Golden-Plover.

Voice: A clear, whistled *pee-a-wee.*

Habitat: Breeds on tundra; winters on beaches, mudflats, and coastal marshes, less commonly on inland marshes, lakeshores, and plowed fields.

Nesting: 3 or 4 buff eggs, spotted with brown, in a shallow depression lined with moss, lichens, and grass.

Range: Breeds in northwestern Alaska and Arctic Canada. Winters mainly along coasts from British Columbia and Massachusetts southward. Also in Eurasia.

Unlike the related American Golden-Plover, this species usually travels alone or in small groups. Our largest plover, it stands out among its usual companions, the smaller plovers, turnstones, and sandpipers. When disturbed, it commonly flies out over water, circles, and lands again behind the observer. It is one of the familiar winter shorebirds along the Atlantic Coast, and a few—mostly fledged the previous summer—spend the summer south of the breeding range. Its principal foods are small crabs and sandworms.

## 250, 251 American Golden-Plover "Lesser Golden-Plover"

*Pluvialis dominica*

Description: 9–11″ (23–28 cm). A quail-sized plover. In breeding plumage, dull golden-brown above, with black throat, breast, flanks, belly, and undertail coverts; bold white stripe runs from forehead, over eye, and down side of neck and breast. In winter, has bold whitish eyebrow, grayish-white underparts. Lacks white wing stripe, white rump, and black patch under the wing of larger and paler Black-bellied Plover.

Voice: A mellow *quee-lee-la.*

Habitat: Breeds on tundra; during migration, coastal beaches and mudflats, and inland on prairies and plowed fields.

Nesting: 3 or 4 buff eggs, spotted with brown, in a shallow depression lined with reindeer moss, usually on a ridge or other elevated spot in the tundra.

Range: Breeds from Alaska east to Baffin Island. On migration, most birds travel south from Canadian Maritimes over Atlantic Ocean to South America, and return northward in spring over Great Plains.

The American Golden-Plover annually performs one of the longest migrations of any American bird. In late summer, birds from the eastern Arctic gather in eastern Canada, where they fatten on insects and crowberries and other small fruits before beginning their nonstop flight over the ocean to the northern coast of South America, a journey of some 2,500 miles (4,000 kilometers). Smaller numbers move southward in the fall across the Great Plains. Relatively few of these birds are found along the East Coast of the United States. Once in South America, they make another long flight across the vast Amazon Basin, finally arriving at their principal wintering grounds on the pampas of central Argentina, and in Patagonia and Tierra del Fuego. In former times they gathered there in enormous numbers, but heavy shooting in both North and South America took a serious toll, from which the species has not fully recovered. In the spring, the birds return to the Arctic, but at that time they move north by way of the Great Plains.

256 **Snowy Plover**
*Charadrius alexandrinus*

Description: 5–7″ (13–18 cm). A small whitish plover with pale brown upperparts, black legs, *slender black bill,* and small black mark on each side of breast. The similar Piping Plover has stubbier yellow bill and yellow legs.
Voice: A plaintive *chu-we* or *o-wee-ah.*
Habitat: Flat sandy beaches, salt flats, and sandy areas with little vegetation.
Nesting: 2 or 3 buff eggs, spotted with black, in a sandy depression lined with a few shell fragments or bits of grass.
Range: Resident along Pacific Coast from British Columbia to Mexico, and along Gulf Coast from Texas to Florida Panhandle. Also breeds locally in interior from California and Nevada east to Oklahoma and Texas. Also in Old World.

The Snowy Plover's patchy distribution, not only in North America but elsewhere in the world, is due to its specialized habitat requirements. Keeping to large, flat expanses of sand, it avoids competition for food in a habitat in which few other birds can exist. Here these plovers, with their pale coloration, are difficult to see even when they run nimbly over the hard, pavement-like ground.

254 **Wilson's Plover**
*Charadrius wilsonia*

Description: 7–8″ (18–20 cm). Male brown above and white below with a broad black eye patch and breast band, and *heavy black bill.* Female similar, but breast band is brown.
Voice: A clear, whistled *queet* or *quit-keet,* but usually silent.
Habitat: Sandy beaches and mudflats.
Nesting: 3 or 4 buff eggs with small, blackish spots and blotches, placed in a slight depression on open, level sand or occasionally in dunes. Sometimes nests in loose colonies.
Range: Breeds on Atlantic and Gulf coasts from southern New Jersey (rare) and Maryland to Florida and Texas. Winters chiefly along Gulf Coast and in Florida.

The long stout bill that makes this bird easy to distinguish from other plovers also enables it to partake of a more varied diet than its relatives. In addition to the usual fare of crustaceans, worms, and small mollusks, it also takes hard-shelled crabs, including fiddler crabs. Wilson's Plover feeds both day and night, males feeding during the day because they incubate the eggs at night while the female is foraging.

257 **Semipalmated Plover**
*Charadrius semipalmatus*

Description: 6–8″ (15–20 cm). A brown-backed plover with white underparts and *single black breast band.* Bill stubby, yellow-orange, with dark tip. Immature has all-black bill and brownish breast band. Piping Plover similar, but much paler above. Larger Killdeer has 2 black breast bands.

Voice: A plaintive, two-noted whistle, *tu-wee.* Also a soft, rather musical rattle.

Habitat: Breeds on sandy or mossy tundra; during migration, on beaches, mudflats, shallow pools in salt marshes, and lakeshores.

Nesting: 4 buff eggs, spotted with dark brown and black, placed in a shallow depression sparsely lined with shell fragments, pebbles, and bits of vegetation on the tundra.

Range: Breeds from Alaska east to Newfoundland and Nova Scotia. Winters regularly from California and Carolinas south and along Gulf Coast; rarely farther north.

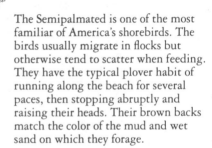

The Semipalmated is one of the most familiar of America's shorebirds. The birds usually migrate in flocks but otherwise tend to scatter when feeding. They have the typical plover habit of running along the beach for several paces, then stopping abruptly and raising their heads. Their brown backs match the color of the mud and wet sand on which they forage.

---

## 255 Piping Plover
*Charadrius melodus*

Description: 6–7″ (15–18 cm). A pale plover with sandy upperparts, narrow, incomplete black breast band, stubby bill with an orange base, and yellowish legs. Young birds are similar, with black bill and broken gray breast band. Snowy Plover has thin black bill and black legs. Semipalmated Plover has much darker upperparts.

Voice: A clear, whistled *peep-lo.*

Habitat: Bare, dry, sandy areas, both inland and on the coast.

Nesting: 4 buff-white eggs, evenly marked with small dark spots, in a depression in the sand lined with pebbles and bits of shells.

Range: Breeds along Atlantic Coast from Quebec and Newfoundland south to North Carolina, and locally from Alberta east to Minnesota and Great Lakes. Winters on Atlantic and Gulf coasts, north regularly to Carolinas.

The color of dry sand, the Piping Plover is difficult to see on the beach. The eggs and downy chicks also blend with the sand. With the rapid expansion of summer resorts along the Atlantic Coast, many of the former nesting sites have been destroyed. This species arrives much earlier in spring and departs for the South much earlier in fall than does the Semipalmated Plover.

---

## 258 Killdeer

*Charadrius vociferus*

Description: 9–11″ (23–28 cm). Our largest "ringed" plover. Brown above and white below, with *2 black bands across breast,* long legs, and a relatively long tail. In flight, shows rusty uppertail coverts and rump.

Voice: A shrill *kill-deee, kill-deee* or *killdeer, killdeer.* Also *dee-dee-dee.*

Habitat: Open country generally: plowed fields, golf courses, and short-grass prairies.

Nesting: 4 pale buff eggs, spotted with blackish brown, in a shallow depression lined with grass on bare ground.

Range: Breeds from Alaska east to Newfoundland and southward. Winters regularly north to British Columbia, Utah, the Ohio Valley, and Massachusetts. Also in South America.

This noisy plover is probably our best-known shorebird. Few golf courses or extensive vacant lots are without their breeding pair of Killdeers. When a nest is approached, the adult feigns injury, hobbling along with wings dragging as if badly wounded. This behavior usually succeeds in luring a predator away from the eggs or young; the bird then "recovers" and flies off, calling loudly.

## Family Haematopodidae
Oystercatchers

7 species: Widespread in warm regions. Two species breed in North America. Oystercatchers are large and boldly patterned in black or in black and white, with reddish bills and legs. They inhabit seacoasts and, less often, inland rivers, where they feed on shellfish, crustaceans, and sandworms. They are conspicuous birds whether feeding on mud banks or nesting on the sand, where they lay from two to five eggs.

### 244 American Oystercatcher
*Haematopus palliatus*

Description: 17–21″ (43–53 cm). A large stocky shorebird, boldly patterned in blackish brown and white. Bill long and red; legs and feet pink. Shows bold white wing patch in flight.

Voice: A piercing *kleep!* and a plover-like *cle-ar.*

Habitat: Sandy and pebbly beaches, mudflats, borders of salt marshes.

Nesting: 2–4 buff eggs, sparsely marked with brown, in a shallow depression lined with shell fragments.

Range: Breeds along coasts from Baja California and Massachusetts southward. Winters from North Carolina southward.

Oystercatchers are large, conspicuous birds that were hunted to near-extinction along the Atlantic Coast. Given total protection, they have once again become numerous and now nest in numbers as far north as Massachusetts, where just a few years ago they were very rare. Oystercatchers insert their long blade-like bills into mussels and other bivalves, severing the powerful adductor muscles before the shells can close. They also feed on barnacles and snails. Although they do not breed in colonies, these birds gather in large flocks during migration and in winter.

## Family Recurvirostridae
Stilts and Avocets

7 species: Fairly widespread in warmer regions. Two species breed in North America. Avocets and stilts are flashy shorebirds with vivid patterns of black, white, tan, and pink. Both are long-legged and long-necked; the long bills are upturned in avocets, straight in stilts. Avocets have partially webbed feet, presumably as an aid in swimming in deeper water than most waders attempt.

### 241 Black-necked Stilt
*Himantopus mexicanus*

Description: 13–16″ (33–41 cm). A slender, long-legged shorebird. Black above, white below; head patterned in black and white; neck long; bill long and thin; legs very long, red, and slender.

Voice: A sharp *kip-kip-kip-kip.*

Habitat: Salt marshes, shallow coastal bays in the East; also freshwater marshes in the West.

Nesting: 3 or 4 buff eggs, spotted with brown, in a shallow depression lined with grass or shell fragments in a marsh. Nests in loose colonies.

Range: Breeds along coasts from Oregon and Delaware southward, and locally in western interior states east to Idaho, Kansas, and Texas. Winters along Pacific Coast north to central California; also in Florida and Gulf Coast states.

Noisy and conspicuous, Black-necked Stilts declined due to hunting. In the nesting season they are particularly aggressive and will often fly low over an approaching human, uttering a loud alarm call, with their long red legs trailing behind them.

239, 240 **American Avocet**
*Recurvirostra americana*

Description: 16–20″ (41–51 cm). A large, long-legged shorebird with a *slender upturned bill.* Upperparts and wings patterned in black and white; underparts white. Head and neck rust-colored in summer, white in winter.

Voice: A loud repeated *wheep.*

Habitat: Freshwater marshes and shallow marshy lakes; breeds locally in salt or brackish marshes. Many move to coasts in winter.

Nesting: 4 olive-buff eggs, spotted with brown and black, in a shallow depression sparsely lined with grass, on a beach or mudflat. Often nests in loose colonies.

Range: Breeds from interior Washington, Saskatchewan, and Minnesota south to California and Texas. Winters north to California, Gulf Coast, and Florida. Rare but regular visitor on Atlantic Coast in fall.

During their southward migration every fall, a few American Avocets stray eastward to the Atlantic Coast, where they may be seen singly or in small flocks on shallow lagoons and coastal ponds. In the 19th century, there was a small breeding population in southern New Jersey, but they were hunted to near-extinction. Avocets feed much like spoonbills, sweeping their bills from side to side along the surface of the water to pick up crustaceans, aquatic insects, and floating seeds. Recently given complete protection, they seem to be gaining in number and before long may be reported breeding on the Atlantic Coast once again.

## Family Jacanidae
Jacanas

8 species: Worldwide in the tropics. One species is an occasional breeder in North America. Jacanas have very long toes and claws, and are adapted for walking on lily pads and other floating marsh vegetation. They are aggressive birds, several species being armed with spurs with which they defend their territories. In their exposed habitat, they have no need for cryptic coloration; most species are boldly patterned, and several have brilliantly colored frontal shields.

---

### 267 Northern Jacana
*Jacana spinosa*

Description: 8–9″ (20–23 cm). A dark, robin-sized marsh bird with very long toes. Head and neck black, body and folded wings dark rufous. *Large, pale-green wing patches visible in flight; bright yellow frontal shield.*

Voice: Various high-pitched squeaking and bickering notes.

Habitat: Marshes and ponds with heavy growth of lily pads and other floating plants.

Nesting: 4 pale buff eggs, heavily scrawled with black, in a loose cup of leaves and stems placed in the open on floating vegetation.

Range: Rare wanderer and occasional breeder in southern Texas; also in American tropics.

With their strikingly long toes, Northern Jacanas are adept at balancing on floating plants and are therefore able to exploit a habitat available to few other birds. They are quarrelsome and often engage in combat with one another, using sharp spurs on the bend of the wing. Females are somewhat larger than males and defend a large territory in which several males build nests and care for the eggs and young.

**Family Scolopacidae**
Sandpipers, Phalaropes, and Allies

90 species: Worldwide. Thirty-six species breed in North America. The members of this family that frequent our waters range in size from the large Long-billed Curlew to one of the smallest, the Least Sandpiper. They are wading birds that are found on seacoasts and on inland lakes and rivers, and most of them nest on the Arctic tundra. Many perform tremendous migrations to the Southern Hemisphere in autumn and back north again in spring. This family includes curlews, godwits, snipes, woodcocks, turnstones, phalaropes, dowitchers, yellowlegs, and the "peeps"—the smallest sandpipers of the genus *Calidris.*

---

234 **Greater Yellowlegs**
*Tringa melanoleuca*

Description: 14″ (36 cm). A slender, gray-streaked wader with conspicuous white rump and long *yellow legs.* Lesser Yellowlegs is similar, but smaller, with a shorter, straighter, and more slender bill and a different call.

Voice: A series of musical, whistled notes, *whew-whew-whew.*

Habitat: Breeds on tundra and marshy ground; pools, lakeshores, and tidal mudflats during migration.

Nesting: 4 tawny eggs, heavily marked with brown, in a slight depression on the ground in a damp open spot.

Range: Breeds from south-central Alaska across central Canada to Maritime Provinces and Newfoundland. Winters mainly along coasts from Washington and Virginia southward, and along Gulf Coast.

The larger of the two yellowlegs is a noisy and conspicuous bird. It is also more wary than its smaller relative and flushes at a greater distance. It often runs about wildly in shallow water or wades up to its belly and occasionally even swims. With its long legs, it easily obtains food in pools.

231 **Lesser Yellowlegs**
*Tringa flavipes*

Description: 10½″ (27 cm). A smaller, more slender edition of the Greater Yellowlegs, with a proportionately shorter, straighter, more slender bill. Looks longer-legged than Greater Yellowlegs.

Voice: A flat *tu-tu,* less musical than call of Greater Yellowlegs.

Habitat: Breeds in northern bogs; on marshy ponds, lake and river shores, and mudflats during migration.

Nesting: 4 buff eggs, blotched with brown, in a slight depression on the open ground near water.

Range: Breeds from Alaska to Hudson Bay. Winters along coasts from southern California and Virginia southward, and along Gulf Coast.

This species usually occurs in larger flocks and is a tamer bird than the Greater Yellowlegs, allowing an observer a much closer approach before flying off a short distance. Both species of yellowlegs bob their heads up and down when watching an intruder.

211 **Solitary Sandpiper**
*Tringa solitaria*

Description: 8½″ (22 cm). A small dark sandpiper with dark olive legs, speckled upperparts, white tail barred with black, and *prominent eye ring.* Flight is swallow-like. No white wing stripe, as seen in Spotted Sandpiper.

Voice: A high-pitched *peet-weet* or *peet-weet-*

*weet;* more shrill than call of Spotted Sandpiper.

Habitat: Ponds, bogs, wet swampy places, and woodland streams.

Nesting: 4 pale green or buff eggs, thickly spotted with gray and brown, in deserted tree nests of thrushes, jays, or blackbirds.

Range: Breeds in Alaska and across Canada to Labrador, south to northeastern Minnesota. Winters in American tropics.

As its name suggests, this bird is most often seen by itself—a single migrant foraging along the margin of a wooded pond or stream. It is wary and, when approached, will spring quickly into the air, uttering its ringing call note, and dart away. In the spring, most Solitary Sandpipers seem to migrate north through Central America, and there an observer may be surprised to see flocks of several dozen feeding in flooded fields.

---

225, 228 **Willet**
*Catoptrophorus semipalmatus*

Description: 15″ (38 cm). A large shorebird, gray-brown with a long straight bill. Best identified in flight by its flashy *black-and-white wing pattern.* Gray legs and thicker bill distinguish it from the Greater Yellowlegs.

Voice: A loud, ringing *pill-will-willet* and a quieter *kuk-kuk-kuk-kuk-kuk.*

Habitat: Coastal beaches, freshwater and salt marshes, lakeshores, and wet prairies.

Nesting: 4 olive-buff eggs, spotted with brown, in a nest lined with weeds or bits of shell placed in a depression on open ground or in a grass clump.

Range: Breeds from central Canada to northeastern California and Nevada; also along Atlantic and Gulf coasts south from Nova Scotia. Winters along coasts from Oregon and Carolinas southward.

Willets look quite nondescript on the ground and superficially resemble yellowlegs, but once in flight or even with wings spread out, they are distinguished by their striking black-and-white color pattern. They frequently forage with godwits on migration.

210, 218 **Spotted Sandpiper**
*Actitis macularia*

Description: 7½″ (19 cm). A medium-sized shorebird that bobs its tail almost constantly. Breeding adults brown above, white below with bold black spots on breast and belly. Fall birds lack black spots below, have brownish smudge at side of breast.

Voice: A clear *peet-weet;* also a soft trill.
Habitat: Ponds, streams, and other waterways, both inland and along the shore.
Nesting: 4 buff eggs, spotted with brown, in a nest lined with grass or moss in a slight depression on the ground.
Range: Breeds from northern Alaska east throughout Canada, and south throughout United States. Winters along Pacific Coast south from British Columbia and across southern states south to South America.

This is one of the best known of American shorebirds. Its habit of endlessly bobbing the rear part of its body up and down has earned it the vernacular name "Teeter-tail." When flushed from the margin of a pond or stream, it is easily identified by its distinctive flight—short bursts of rapidly vibrating wingbeats alternating with brief glides. Most of our shorebirds breed in the Far North; this is one of the few that nests in the United States.

## 217 Upland Sandpiper
*Bartramia longicauda*

Description: 11–12½″ (28–32 cm). A sandpiper of open meadows with *long yellowish legs,* slender neck and small head, and short bill. Upperparts brown and scaly, underparts streaked and barred. Ends of wings are dark in flight; tail long and wedge-shaped. Often holds wings upward briefly on alighting, exposing black-and-white barring on underwing.

Voice: Alarm call a mellow *quip-ip-ip-ip;* on breeding grounds and at night during migration, a long mournful, rolling whistle.

Habitat: Breeds in open grasslands, prairies, and hayfields; open country generally during migration.

Nesting: 4 pinkish-buff eggs, with brown spots, in a grass-lined nest in a hollow on the ground.

Range: Breeds from Alaska east to New Brunswick and south to northeastern Oregon, Oklahoma, and Virginia. Winters in southern South America.

Formerly abundant, this attractive bird of open grasslands was shot in such large numbers for food and sport that it became very scarce. Now given complete protection, it has increased once again; its principal danger is now habitat destruction. The Upland Sandpiper often flies with wings held stiffly in a downward curve, like a Spotted Sandpiper, especially on its nesting grounds. When alighting, the "Grass Plover," as it was known to hunters, holds its wings over its back before folding them down in a resting position. In old books this bird is called the "Upland Plover."

230 **Whimbrel**
*Numenius phaeopus*

Description: 17″ (43 cm). A large shorebird with a *down-curved bill.* Uniform brown or gray-brown above, with bold head stripes and long legs. Eskimo Curlew (*Numenius borealis*), now near extinction, is much smaller and buffier, with very slender, down-curved bill, cinnamon wing linings, and no bold head pattern.

Voice: A series of 5 to 7 loud, clear, whistled notes: *pip-pip-pip-pip-pip.*

Habitat: Breeds on Arctic tundra, especially near coasts; coastal salt meadows, mudflats, and grassy shoreline slopes during migration.

Nesting: 4 olive eggs, heavily marked with brown, in a depression in moss or in a sedge clump on the ground.

Range: Breeds in Arctic Alaska and Canada. Winters in southern California, along Gulf Coast, and along Atlantic Coast north to Virginia. Also in Eurasia.

The Whimbrel is found along both coasts, as well as in the interior of the continent. It is still numerous because of its wary behavior and the remoteness of its nesting grounds on the Arctic tundra. Like many other tundra breeders, Whimbrels in the East fly offshore over the Atlantic during their autumn migration to South America, returning in spring mainly along an interior route.

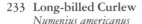

233 **Long-billed Curlew**
*Numenius americanus*

Description: 23″ (58 cm). A large curlew, warm brown and buff below, with cinnamon wing linings, no head pattern, and a *very long, sickle-shaped bill.*

Voice: A clear *curleee;* a sharp *whit-whit, whit, whit, whit, whit.*

Habitat: Breeds on plains and prairies; during

migration, on lake and river shores, mudflats, salt marshes, and sandy beaches.

Nesting: 4 olive-buff eggs, spotted with brown, in a grass-lined nest in a hollow on the ground.

Range: Breeds from southern Canada to northern California, Utah, northern New Mexico, and Texas. Winters from California, Texas, Louisiana, South Carolina, and Florida southward.

Our largest shorebird, the "Sicklebill" was once a plentiful game bird of the Great Plains and the formerly extensive prairies to the east. It is now so scarce that it is protected by law. Its prolonged, musical whistles carry far, signaling the birds' arrival in spring. While they incubate, their warm colors blend with the brown grass, making them difficult to detect. On grasslands, they consume grasshoppers, crickets, and beetles; on shores and beaches during migration, they feast on small crustaceans and mollusks or on berries and seeds.

---

236, 238 **Hudsonian Godwit**
*Limosa haemastica*

Description: 15″ (38 cm). A large slender shorebird with a long, slightly upturned bill. Breeding adult has *barred, chestnut underparts,* mottled brown upperparts. Fall birds grayish above, whitish below. All plumages have *black-and-white tail,* broad white wing stripe, and *black wing linings.*

Voice: Similar to call of Marbled Godwit, but higher pitched; usually silent.

Habitat: Breeds on tundra; mainly mudflats during migration.

Nesting: 4 olive-buff eggs, spotted with brown and black, in a shallow, grass-lined hollow on the ground.

Range: Breeds in Alaska, Mackenzie,

northwestern British Columbia, and around Hudson Bay. Winters in southern parts of South America.

Never common, the Hudsonian Godwit was for many years hunted for food and became scarce. Now completely protected, it has increased in number considerably. This large shorebird can be seen in flocks of up to several dozen or more during fall passage on the coastal mudflats of the northeastern states.

---

237 **Marbled Godwit**
*Limosa fedoa*

Description: 18″ (46 cm). A crow-sized shorebird, dark and mottled above, cinnamon-buff below, with cinnamon wing linings, and *long, pinkish, upturned bill.*

Voice: A loud *kerreck* or *god-wit,* usually heard on breeding grounds.

Habitat: Breeds on grassy plains; during migration, on salt marshes, tidal creeks, mudflats, and sea beaches.

Nesting: 4 olive-buff eggs, blotched with brown, in a slight depression lined with grass on the ground.

Range: Breeds on central plains from Saskatchewan to Minnesota. Winters from California and Virginia southward, and along Gulf Coast.

One of our largest shorebirds, the Marbled Godwit breeds on the vast grassy plains of the West but in smaller numbers than in former times. Like the Long-billed Curlew, it is a rich buff color, blending perfectly with the brown grass of the plains.

213, 216 **Ruddy Turnstone**
*Arenaria interpres*

Description: 8–10″ (20–25 cm). A stocky shorebird with orange legs. Upperparts mainly rusty red in summer, brown in winter; underparts white. Face and breast have conspicuous black markings, duller but still visible in winter. Bold pattern of black and white visible in flight.

Voice: A metallic but musical *netticut* or *kek-kek.*

Habitat: Breeds on coastal tundra; winters on rocky, pebbly, and sandy coasts and beaches.

Nesting: 4 buff-olive eggs, spotted with brown, in a hollow sparsely lined with grass and dead leaves and concealed under a low bush.

Range: Breeds in northwestern Alaska and islands of Canadian Arctic. Winters along coasts from Oregon and Connecticut southward, and along Gulf Coast. Also in Eurasia.

Turnstones are named for their method of feeding, in which they walk along the beach, deftly overturning small stones and pebbles and seizing the animals hiding underneath. They also dig holes in the sand, often larger than themselves, in pursuit of burrowing crustaceans. Although Ruddy Turnstones are usually encountered in small groups, they are very abundant; during the winter they scatter over a huge area, regularly occurring as far south as Australia, New Zealand, southern Africa, and South America, as well as on remote islands in the South Pacific, where they sometimes prey on nesting terns' eggs.

214, 221 **Red Knot**
*Calidris canutus*

Description: 10½″ (27 cm). A robin-sized shorebird. Breeding adults have *pinkish-rufous face and underparts,* dark brown upperparts with pale feather edgings. Fall birds gray above, whitish below. Rump dark; wing stripe faint; bill straight and slightly tapered; legs greenish.
Voice: A soft *quer-wer;* also a soft *knut.*
Habitat: Breeds on tundra; during migration, on tidal flats, rocky shores, and beaches.
Nesting: 4 olive-buff eggs, spotted with brown, in a slight depression lined with lichens, often among rocks.
Range: Breeds on islands in High Arctic of Canada. Winters along coasts from California and Massachusetts southward to southern South America. Also in Eurasia.

In breeding plumage, with their rich rufous underparts set off by marbled gray backs, Red Knots are among the handsomest of shorebirds. Those that winter in southern South America may make a round trip of nearly 20,000 miles (32,000 kilometers) each year.

212, 224 **Sanderling**
*Calidris alba*

Description: 8″ (20 cm). A starling-sized shorebird with a *conspicuous white wing stripe.* Summer adults have rufous head and breast, and white belly. In winter, rufous areas are replaced by pale gray and look almost white. *Bill and legs black.*
Voice: A sharp *kip;* conversational chatter while feeding.
Habitat: Breeds on tundra; winters on ocean beaches, sandbars, mudflats, and shores of lakes and rivers.
Nesting: 4 olive eggs, spotted with brown, in a hollow on the ground lined with grasses and lichens.

Range: Breeds on islands of high Arctic in Canada. Winters along coasts from British Columbia and Massachusetts southward to southern South America. Also in Eurasia.

Practically every day of the year, these birds may be found on any ocean beach. As a wave comes roaring in, the birds run up on the beach just ahead of the breaker, then sprint after the retreating water to feed on the tiny crustaceans and mollusks left exposed.

200, 222 **Semipalmated Sandpiper**
*Calidris pusilla*

Description: 5½–6¾″ (14–17 cm). Slightly larger than a Least Sandpiper. In all plumages, grayer above with less-streaked breast than other "peeps" (small sandpipers). *Feet black. Bill black and short,* drooping slightly at tip, noticeably stouter than bill of Least Sandpiper.

Voice: A sharp *cheh* or *churk,* not as drawn out as the notes of the Least and Western sandpipers.

Habitat: Breeds on tundra; winters on and migrates along coastal beaches, lake and river shores, flats, and pools in salt marshes.

Nesting: 4 buff eggs, marked with brown, in a depression on the ground.

Range: Breeds in northern Alaska and Canada south to Hudson Bay. Migrates commonly through eastern and central states, rarely but regularly in West. Winters in South America.

These small sandpipers are perhaps the most numerous shorebirds in North America, sometimes occurring by the thousands during migration. Often they are found on flats feeding together with their close relative, the Least and Western sandpipers. The word "Semipalmated," referring to the birds'

toes, means "half-webbed." Actually the toes are only slightly lobed at their bases, but they do help the birds to walk on mud without sinking.

202 **Western Sandpiper**
*Calidris mauri*

Description: 6½″ (17 cm). Similar to Semipalmated Sandpiper and not always easy to distinguish, but *bill tends to be longer, with more evident droop at tip.* In summer, *crown and upper back rusty;* in winter, crown and upper back dull gray.

Voice: A soft *cheep* or *kreep,* higher and thinner than that of Semipalmated Sandpiper.

Habitat: Shores, mudflats, grassy pools, and wet meadows.

Nesting: 4 creamy eggs, with red-brown spots, in a grass-lined depression on either wet or dry tundra.

Range: Breeds in northern and western Alaska. Winters mainly along coasts from California and Virginia southward to South America.

This species often associates with the slightly smaller Semipalmated Sandpipers. Western Sandpipers usually feed in deeper water than the other "peeps" (small sandpipers) and sometimes immerse their bills completely. In all other respects, these sandpipers are much alike in their behavior and are difficult to distinguish in the field.

201, 220 **Least Sandpiper**
*Calidris minutilla*

Description: 6″ (15 cm). The smallest of American shorebirds. Brownish above with *yellowish or greenish legs,* short thin bill, and streaked breast. Grayer in winter plumage. Bill shorter, thinner, and more pointed than in Semipalmated or Western sandpipers.

Voice: A clear *treep;* when feeding, a soft chuckle.

Habitat: Grassy pools, bogs, and marshes with open areas; also flooded fields and mudflats.

Nesting: 4 pinkish-buff eggs, spotted with brown, in a nest lined with moss and grass, and placed on a dry hummock in a depression on boggy tundra.

Range: Breeds from Alaska east across northern Canada to Newfoundland and Nova Scotia. Winters along coasts from Oregon and North Carolina southward; also in Southwest and Southeast.

These are probably the tamest of shorebirds; at times they fly off only when almost underfoot. With their yellowish legs, they look like miniature Pectoral Sandpipers; like Pectorals, they prefer grassy areas to the more open flats frequented by most shorebirds. The name *minutilla* is Latin for "tiny."

---

## 203 White-rumped Sandpiper
*Calidris fuscicollis*

Description: 7½" (19 cm). A slender "peep" (small sandpiper) with a short straight bill and a *white rump.* About the same size as Baird's Sandpiper; larger than Least, Semipalmated, and Western sandpipers. Wing tips extend beyond end of tail, giving bird a "pointed" look behind. Breeding adults have tinge of rusty color on crown and ear coverts, dark brown streaks or spots on flanks. Fall adults have gray upperparts and gray wash on breast, and a narrow, pale eyebrow. Young birds brighter, with feathers of upperparts edged with rufous.

Voice: A very high-pitched *tzeet;* also a swallow-like twitter.

Habitat: Breeds on tundra; flats, grassy pools, wet meadows, and shores during migration.

Nesting: 4 olive eggs, spotted with brown, in a grass-lined nest in a slight depression on the ground.

Range: Breeds in northern Alaska and Canadian Arctic. Migrates mainly though eastern and central United States. Winters in South America.

A long-distance flier, the White-rumped Sandpiper performs annual migrations between the Arctic and the subantarctic region. On its wintering grounds in Argentina, this is the most common of the smaller sandpipers. With its conspicuous white rump, this species is the easiest to identify of the "peeps."

## 205 Baird's Sandpiper
*Calidris bairdii*

Description: 7½″ (19 cm). A slender "peep" (small sandpiper) with a short straight bill. About the same size as White-rumped Sandpiper; larger than Least, Semipalmated, and Western sandpipers. Wing tips extend beyond end of tail, giving bird a "pointed" look behind. Breeding adults have buff tinge on face, splotchy pattern on upperparts. Juveniles have buff face and breast, bold white scaling on upperparts.

Voice: A soft *krrrrt;* also a loud trill similar to that of other "peeps."

Habitat: Breeds on tundra; grassy pools, wet meadows, and lake and river shores during migration.

Nesting: 4 tawny eggs, spotted with brown, in a dry depression on the ground, often among rocks.

Range: Breeds in northern Alaska and Canadian Arctic. Migrates mainly through Great Plains and along Pacific Coast in fall, through Great Plains in spring. Regular in small numbers on East Coast in fall. Winters in South America.

In the East, Baird's Sandpiper is the least common of the "peeps" and is often overlooked because of its similarity to the others. It was named in honor of Spencer Fullerton Baird (1823–1887), for many years Secretary of the Smithsonian Institution.

---

206 **Pectoral Sandpiper**
*Calidris melanotos*

Description: 9″ (23 cm). A chunky, somewhat short-legged wader, with *heavily streaked breast sharply delimited from unmarked white belly.* Legs yellow. In flight, the wings are dark and have no prominent stripe.
Voice: A dull *krrrrp.*
Habitat: Breeds on tundra; during migration, on moist grassy places, grass-lined pools, golf courses and airports after heavy rains, and salt creeks and meadows.
Nesting: 4 buff-white eggs, marked with brown, in a slight depression in boggy tundra.
Range: Breeds on Arctic Coast from Alaska east to Hudson Bay. Migrates along both coasts and through interior. Winters in southern South America.

In the days when shorebirds were shot as game, hunters called this species the "Grass Snipe," referring to its liking for grassy meadows, or "Krieker," because of its grating snipe-like flight call. They are as numerous in the interior as on the coasts and are another of the many shorebirds that make the long migration from the Arctic to the Southern Hemisphere and back again.

---

204, 219 **Purple Sandpiper**
*Calidris maritima*

Description: 9″ (23 cm). A stocky sandpiper of wave-lashed rocks. Breeding birds finely streaked with brown and black on head and neck, heavily spotted on breast. Winter adults mainly *dark slate,* with whitish spot in front of eye, and yellow legs. Bill dull orange with black tip.

Voice: A single or double *twit* or *twit-twit.*

Habitat: Breeds on tundra; rocky coasts and promontories in winter.

Nesting: 4 buff eggs, spotted with brown, in a depression lined with grass and leaves on the ground.

Range: Breeds on islands in High Arctic of Canada. Winters along East Coast from Newfoundland to Virginia. Also in Eurasia.

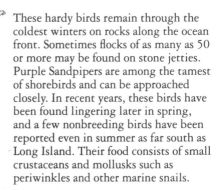

These hardy birds remain through the coldest winters on rocks along the ocean front. Sometimes flocks of as many as 50 or more may be found on stone jetties. Purple Sandpipers are among the tamest of shorebirds and can be approached closely. In recent years, these birds have been found lingering later in spring, and a few nonbreeding birds have been reported even in summer as far south as Long Island. Their food consists of small crustaceans and mollusks such as periwinkles and other marine snails.

---

226, 229 **Dunlin**
*Calidris alpina*

Description: 8½″ (22 cm). A starling-sized shorebird. Bill fairly long with *distinct droop at tip.* Breeding adults have reddish back, whitish underparts with *black patch* in center of belly. Winter birds are dull gray, paler below.

Voice: A soft *cheerp* or *chit-lit.*

Habitat: Nests on tundra; winters on beaches, mudflats, sand flats, and inland lake and river shores.

Nesting: 4 olive eggs, blotched with brown, in a grass clump on a dry hummock on the open tundra.

Range: Breeds from western and northern Alaska east to Hudson Bay. Winters

along coasts from southern Alaska and Massachusetts southward. Also in Eurasia.

These handsome birds, formerly known as "Red-backed Sandpipers," are very tame and thus easy to approach and study. They are among the hardiest of shorebirds; thousands sometimes spend the winter months on sandbars or inlets along the coast as far north as southern New England, where they feed on mollusks, crustaceans, and marine worms.

## 208 Curlew Sandpiper
*Calidris ferruginea*

Description: 8″ (20 cm). Similar in size and shape to Dunlin, but entire bill noticeably curved. Summer adults rich cinnamon or chestnut. Winter birds gray above and white below. Immatures have buff breast, upperparts marked with buff scaling. *White rump* visible in flight.
Voice: A soft dry *chirrip.*
Habitat: Breeds on tundra; chiefly coastal mudflats during migration.
Nesting: 4 yellow-buff eggs, with dark brown spots, in a depression on the ground in tundra.
Range: Breeds in Eurasia and very rarely in northern Alaska. Rare but regular migrant to East Coast, less common on West Coast. Winters mainly in Old World.

Except for a small area on the Arctic Coast of Alaska, this Old World species breeds solely in northern Siberia. During spring migration, the adults are in their bright chestnut breeding plumage and, with their curved bills and white rumps, are easily distinguished in the field from their usual associates, the Red Knots and Dunlins. However, they are most likely to be seen in the fall, wearing their dull winter plumage; they are then much more difficult to spot among the hordes of other shorebirds.

209, 223 **Stilt Sandpiper**
*Calidris himantopus*

Description: 8½″ (22 cm). A starling-sized sandpiper with long greenish legs and long bill, slightly down-curved at tip. Wings lack stripe. Breeding adult has chestnut head stripes and barring below. Nonbreeding birds have much paler plumage, and a white line over the eye.

Voice: Simple *tu-tu,* similar to call of Lesser Yellowlegs.

Habitat: Grassy pools and shores of ponds and lakes.

Nesting: 4 pale buff eggs, marked with brown, on open ground in a clump of grass near water.

Range: Breeds in northern Alaska and northern Canada east to Hudson Bay. Winters in small numbers in southern California's Salton Sea, along Gulf Coast, and in Florida.

Often associated with dowitchers and yellowlegs, Stilt Sandpipers resemble both species and appear to be intermediate between the two. Yellowlegs move about continually in nervous, jerky motions, and dowitchers feed slowly, probing deep into the mud; Stilt Sandpipers move like yellowlegs but cover more ground, while feeding deliberately like dowitchers.

207 **Buff-breasted Sandpiper**
*Tryngites subruficollis*

Description: 8″ (20 cm). A starling-sized sandpiper with a small head. *Underparts and face buff, legs dull orange-yellow.* Bill short and straight.

Voice: A low *tik-tik-tik.*

Habitat: Breeds on dry tundra; during migration on short-grass prairie, fields, and meadows.

Nesting: 4 pale buff, brown-blotched eggs in a grass-lined nest on the Arctic tundra.

Range: Breeds in northernmost Alaska and Canada. Migrates mainly through Great Plains, but small numbers appear on East Coast and smaller numbers on West Coast. Winters in South America.

This species looks like a small buff edition of the Upland Sandpiper, at times its grassland associate. It is very tame and when approached merely trots through the short grass instead of flying off. Like the American Golden-Plover, it undertakes an amazing migration in both spring and fall. After the nesting season in the far Northwest, it migrates southward on a broad front, eventually ending up on the Argentine pampas, where it spends the winter. On the return passage in spring, its movements are much more confined, carrying it chiefly up the Mississippi Valley and to the West, but ultimately back to the Arctic shores of Alaska and Canada.

---

## 215 Ruff
*Philomachus pugnax*

Description: 11″ (28 cm). A stocky shorebird with a short tapered bill. Breeding males have extraordinarily variable plumage, showing ear tufts, ruffs, and gorgets in any combination of black, white, chestnut, gray, buff, etc. Females (called "Reeves") and winter males are much duller—gray or brown above with pale spot at base of bill, white below; leg color varies from yellow to green, brown, and red. In flight, two oval white patches are visible at sides of rump. In all seasons, male noticeably larger than female.

Voice: Usually silent, but occasionally a soft *tu-whit* when flushed.
Habitat: Short grassy meadows and marshy ponds.
Nesting: 4 gray, green, or buff eggs, heavily marked with deep brown blotches, in a grass-lined depression in a meadow or marsh.
Range: Breeds in northern Eurasia. A rare migrant along Pacific and Atlantic coasts and on Great Lakes.

The Ruff is one of the most remarkable of all shorebirds. It is one of the few waders in which the two sexes are dramatically different in color, pattern, and size during the breeding season. The males gather in communal leks, or displaying grounds, and engage in courting. After mating, the females build their nests away from the courtship area.

227, 232 **Short-billed Dowitcher**
*Limnodromus griseus*

Description: 12″ (30 cm). A snipe-like, *long-billed* shorebird with *white lower back and rump,* black-and-white checkered tail, dark bill, green legs. Summer adults have reddish underparts (belly often whitish) with variable spotting on breast and sides, barred flanks, and reddish edges on feathers of upperparts. Winter birds are gray overall, with pale eyebrow and white lower back and rump. See Long-billed Dowitcher.
Voice: A soft *tu-tu-tu,* quite unlike call of Long-billed Dowitcher.
Habitat: Breeds on moist tundra or beside forest pools; during migration and winter, on mudflats, creeks, salt marshes, and tidal estuaries.
Nesting: 4 greenish eggs spotted with brown, in a nest lined with grass and moss in a depression on the ground.
Range: Breeds in southern Alaska, central

interior Canada, and northern Quebec. Winters along coasts from California and Virginia southward.

Dowitchers often occur in large flocks—sometimes in the thousands—on coastal flats during migrations, remaining well bunched whether in flight or feeding on a mudflat. They probe deeply with their long bills, with rapid up-and-down movements like sewing machines, seeking marine worms, snails, tiny crustaceans, and aquatic larvae.

## 235 Long-billed Dowitcher
*Limnodromus scolopaceus*

Description: 12″ (30 cm). Similar to Short-billed Dowitcher, but breast and sides barred rather than spotted, belly more reddish. Best distinguished by call.

Voice: A high, sharp *keek,* quite unlike call of Short-billed Dowitcher.

Habitat: Breeds in muskeg; during migration and winter, on mudflats, marshy pools, and margins of freshwater ponds.

Nesting: 4 olive eggs, spotted with brown, in a grass and moss-lined nest on the ground.

Range: Breeds in western Alaska and extreme northwestern Mackenzie. Winters mainly along coasts from Washington and Virginia southward.

Dowitchers are most often seen during migration. This species favors freshwater habitats, while the Short-billed Dowitcher is more partial to salt water. The main fall migration of Long-bills takes place in September and October, when most of the Short-bills have already departed.

242 **Common Snipe**
*Gallinago gallinago*

Description: 10½" (27 cm). A long-billed, brownish shorebird with striped head and back, white belly, and rust in tail. Usually seen when flushed from edge of a marsh or a pond. Flight fast and erratic.

Voice: A sharp, rasping *scaip!* when flushed.

Habitat: Freshwater marshes, ponds, flooded meadows, and fields; more rarely in salt marshes.

Nesting: 4 pale olive-brown eggs, spotted with black, concealed in a grass-lined depression in a grass tussock in a marsh.

Range: Breeds from northern Alaska and Canada south to California, southwestern states, and New Jersey. Winters across much of United States north to British Columbia and Virginia. Also in Old World.

Although the Common Snipe generally migrates in flocks at night, during the day the birds scatter and usually feed alone. They seek food early in the morning and in late afternoon, and seem to be more active on cloudy days. In addition to the alarm note described above, these birds have a variety of calls heard only on the breeding ground, and they perform a spectacular aerial territorial display in which the feathers of the tail produce an eerie whistling sound.

288 **American Woodcock**
*Scolopax minor*

Description: 11" (28 cm). A chunky, quail-sized bird with a very long bill and rounded wings. Rufous below, "dead leaf" pattern above, with transverse black bands on head. Eyes large, bulging, and located close to back of head.

Voice: A loud, buzzy *bzeep!* similar to the call of a nighthawk and often repeated on the ground about every two seconds during courtship.

Habitat: Moist woodlands and thickets near open fields.

Nesting: 4 buff eggs, spotted with brown, in a hollow among dead leaves or under a bush.

Range: Breeds from southern Manitoba and Newfoundland south to Texas, Gulf Coast states, and central Florida. Winters in southeastern states.

The American Woodcock is seldom seen, for its protective coloring renders it virtually invisible against a background of dried leaves. When flushed from underfoot, it zigzags off through the brush with a whistling of wings. Those fortunate enough to live near their breeding grounds may see woodcocks perform their courtship flight in early spring each year. In these spectacular aerial displays, the male spirals up to a considerable height, circles, then plummets down to earth, twittering as he descends. Woodcocks subsist chiefly on earthworms, which they extract with their long bills; the tip of the upper mandible is flexible so that they can grasp a worm while probing in mud without opening the bill. Insect larvae and occasionally vegetable matter are also eaten.

---

246, 249 **Wilson's Phalarope**
*Phalaropus tricolor*

Description: 9″ (23 cm). A strikingly patterned shorebird with needle-like bill, pearl-gray head and back, white underparts, *black stripe through eye and down neck,* and *chestnut markings on breast and back.* In fall plumage, pale gray above, white below; in this plumage, pale color, more terrestrial habits, and slender bill distinguish it from other phalaropes. Females more boldly patterned than males.

Voice: A soft *quoit-quoit-quoit.*

Habitat: Prairie pools and marshes, lake and river shores, marshy pools along the coast.

Nesting: 4 pale buff eggs, spotted with brown, in a grass-lined nest placed in a slight depression on the ground near water.

Range: Breeds from southern Yukon and Minnesota south to California and Kansas; also in Great Lakes region and Massachusetts (rare). Winters mainly in American tropics, but a few birds winter in California and Texas.

Wilson's is larger than the Red and Red-necked phalaropes and has a much longer, thinner bill. Unlike the others, this species does not have fully lobed toes and so rarely swims, spending no time at sea. When it does feed in water, however, it spins in circles more rapidly than the other two. It is limited to the Western Hemisphere and breeds much farther south than the other phalaropes.

243, 245 **Red-necked Phalarope**
**"Northern Phalarope"**
*Phalaropus lobatus*

Description: 7″ (18 cm). A sparrow-sized, swimming shorebird with a conspicuous wing stripe. Breeding adults have dark head and back, white chin and belly separated by *chestnut upper breast and sides of neck.* Females more boldly patterned than males. In winter, darker above, with dark crown (typically) and dark line through eye, and entirely white below. Bill thin.

Voice: A sharp *twit* or *whit.*

Habitat: Breeds on tundra pools; open ocean, beaches, flats, lake and river shores during migration.

Nesting: 4 olive eggs, spotted with brown, in a slight hollow on the ground in marshy tundra.

Range: Breeds in Alaska and across northern Canada. Migrates along both coasts, more rarely in interior, and winters mainly at sea in Southern Hemisphere. Also in Old World.

Among phalaropes, the female is brighter than the male, and the male incubates the eggs and cares for the young. This species has fully lobed toes and swims buoyantly. In effect an oceangoing sandpiper, it spends nearly all of its nonbreeding life at sea, although on occasion it wades in pools and feeds on mudflats with many other shorebirds. Phalaropes often feed by spinning around in the water; the motion of their feet stirs up tiny organisms, which they pluck from the surface with rapid jabs of the bill.

---

247, 248 **Red Phalarope**
*Phalaropus fulicaria*

Description: 8″ (20 cm). A starling-sized, swimming shorebird with conspicuous wing stripe and short *yellow bill with black tip.* Breeding adults *rich chestnut,* with dark crown, white face. Females more boldly patterned than males. In winter, gray above and white below, with pale crown, dark line through eye, and dark bill.
Voice: Sharp metallic *kreeep.*
Habitat: Breeds on tundra; open ocean, bays, inlets, lakes, shores, and coasts during migration.
Nesting: 4 olive eggs, speckled with brown, placed in a grass-lined depression on an elevated spot in low marshy tundra.
Range: Breeds in Alaska and northern Canada. Migrates off both coasts, very rarely in interior. Winters mainly at sea in Southern Hemisphere; irregular along Pacific Coast. Also in Old World.

Hundreds of these shorebirds may be seen from fishing boats far at sea;

bobbing like corks, they look like miniature gulls riding the waves. While they are at sea the greater part of their diet is made up of tiny marine animals known as plankton. On land, they forage around tundra pools for the aquatic larvae of mosquitoes, midges, and beetles. After egg laying, the male takes over the duties of incubating the eggs and rearing the young.

## Family Laridae
Jaegers, Gulls, Terns, and Skimmers

129 species: Worldwide. Thirty-four species breed in North America. Jaegers and many gulls occur in colder latitudes, while most of the terns and the Black Skimmer are found in warmer climates. All species have webbed feet. The predatory jaegers have strongly hooked bills and elongated central tail feathers; gulls are mainly clad in gray or black and white, and have bills that are less hooked; terns have straight and pointed bills used chiefly for catching fish, and often have black caps; and the Black Skimmer is a black-and-white bird with an overshot lower mandible that it uses to skim fish from the surface of the water. These birds are primarily colonial nesters, breeding on sea islands and coastal beaches and on inland marshes, lakes, and rivers. Sizes range from the large Great Black-backed Gull to the diminutive Least Tern.

### 93 Pomarine Jaeger
*Stercorarius pomarinus*

Description: 22″ (56 cm). Larger and stockier than the Parasitic Jaeger, with a more extensive white flash on outer wing and with central tail feathers twisted and blunt or spoon-shaped, not pointed;

breast band often darker and wider; bill heavier; wings broader at base. Flight more direct. Dark-phase and light-phase individuals occur.

Voice: Harsh, chattering calls; a harsh *which-yeu*

Habitat: Breeds on swampy tundra; migrates and winters over ocean.

Nesting: 2 olive-brown eggs, with darker brown spots, in a grass-lined depression on the ground.

Range: Breeds above Arctic Circle in Alaska and across northern Canada. Winters at sea as far north as California and North Carolina. Very rare during migration on Great Lakes. Also in Eurasia.

The largest of our jaegers, the Pomarine preys on birds up to the size of terns and small gulls, as well as on lemmings, carrion, and the eggs and young of colonial seabirds. Like the Parasitic Jaeger, at sea it also pursues gulls and terns, forcing them to disgorge their food, which it snatches up in midair. Although it can be seen from land at times, it is much more often seen far offshore.

---

92 **Parasitic Jaeger**
*Stercorarius parasiticus*

Description: 21″ (53 cm). A fast-flying, gull-like seabird. Typical adults are brown above, white or light dusky colored below, with an incomplete, gray-brown band across the breast; dark, almost black, crown; and short (up to 4″) pointed central tail feathers. Dark-phase birds are uniform dusky brown with a darker cap; intermediates between the two color phases occur. Often seen harrying gulls and terns.

Voice: Usually silent; a variety of mewing and wailing notes on breeding grounds.

Habitat: Breeds on grassy tundra and stony ground near inland lakes; at other times on the ocean.

Nesting: 2 olive-brown eggs, with darker brown spots, in a grass-lined depression on the ground or among rocks.

Range: Breeds in Alaska and northern Canada. Winters in warm waters in Southern Hemisphere. Also in northern Eurasia.

This is the most familiar of our jaegers since it comes more readily into bays and estuaries and often feeds closer to shore. Like the other jaegers, it usually obtains food by pursuing gulls and terns and forcing them to drop food.

## 91 Long-tailed Jaeger
*Stercorarius longicaudus*

Description: 21″ (53 cm). Adult similar to light-phase Parasitic Jaeger, but smaller, more graceful, and with *very long central tail feathers* (up to 6″). Upperparts paler than in other jaegers, and blackish cap smaller and more sharply defined; flight more buoyant.

Voice: A harsh *kreeah;* other yelping and rattling notes on breeding grounds.

Habitat: Breeds on tundra and stony hillsides; at other times ranges over open ocean.

Nesting: 2 olive-brown eggs, with brown spots, in a grass-lined nest placed either on bare ground or among rocks.

Range: Breeds in Alaska and Canada north of Arctic Circle. Winters far offshore in both Atlantic and Pacific oceans.

Smallest of the three jaegers, the Long-tailed is the rarest in eastern North America, presumably because it migrates chiefly in mid-ocean. Although occasionally, like other jaegers, it harries terns and gulls, it feeds mainly by catching its own fish, taking flying insects in the air, and sometimes preying on small birds. On the breeding grounds, lemmings are its staple food.

## 89 Great Skua
*Catharacta skua*

Description: 23″ (58 cm). A large, dark, heavy-bodied, gull-like bird, mottled gray-brown with conspicuous white patches on the outer wing. Tail short and blunt. Immatures of larger gulls lack prominent white wing patches.

Voice: A harsh *hah-hah-hah-hah;* various quacking and croaking notes.

Habitat: Breeds on open bare ground near the sea; at other times, ranges over the ocean.

Nesting: 2 olive-brown eggs, with dark brown spots, in a grass-lined nest on the ground. Often nests in loose colonies.

Range: Nests in Iceland and on islands north of Britain. Winters off Atlantic Coast south to Maryland.

Great Skuas occur off the shores of the Northern Hemisphere most often in winter, where they are common on the fishing banks off Newfoundland. They feed on a variety of shrimp, fish, and rodents, and on the eggs and young of colonial seabirds. They are vigorous in the defense of their nests, diving boldly at human intruders.

## 90 South Polar Skua
*Catharacta maccormicki*

Description: 21″ (53 cm). Similar to Great Skua, but typically more uniform gray, not mottled.

Voice: Usually silent in American waters.

Habitat: Open ocean.

Nesting: 1 or 2 olive-brown eggs, with dark brown spots, in a depression on the ground. Often nests in colonies.

Range: Breeds in Southern Hemisphere; rare summer visitor off Pacific and Atlantic coasts.

Until recently, all the skuas of the world were thought to be a single species, but now some experts believe there may be as many as five species. On some southern islands, two forms nest side by side without interbreeding, proving that they are different species.

31, 52 **Laughing Gull**
*Larus atricilla*

Description: 15–17″ (38–43 cm). A slender, medium-sized gull with a *black hood* in breeding plumage. In summer, the adult's back and wings are dark gray; trailing edge of wing is white, and *wing tip is black, without white spots.* In winter, lacks a hood. Young bird is dark brown with *contrasting rump and broad black tail band.* See Franklin's Gull.

Voice: Loud, high-pitched *ha-ha-ha-ha-haah-haah-haah-haah-haah.*

Habitat: Salt marshes, bays, and estuaries. Very rare inland.

Nesting: 3 olive-brown eggs, with dark blotches, in a ground nest lined with grass and weed stems placed on sand or in a salt marsh. Nests in colonies.

Range: Breeds from Nova Scotia to Caribbean. Winters regularly north to Virginia, in smaller numbers farther north.

A common summer gull along the Atlantic and Gulf coasts, this species has declined in numbers in recent years due to the destruction of coastal marshes and the increase in Herring Gulls, which prey on its eggs and young. Very agile on the wing, Laughing Gulls easily catch bits of food tossed into the air. In winter, they forage on beaches and in harbors.

32 **Franklin's Gull**
*Larus pipixcan*

Description: 13–15″ (33–38 cm). Similar to Laughing Gull of seacoasts, but smaller, paler, with *black wing tip separated from gray by a white band.* Black hood in breeding plumage. Winter adults and young birds have dark half-hood.

Voice: A strident *ha-ha-ha-ha-ha-ha,* similar to Laughing Gull's but higher in pitch.

Habitat: Prairie marshes and sloughs. Often feeds in plowed fields.

Nesting: 3 buff-brown eggs, spotted with brown, on a loose platform in a marsh. Nests in large noisy colonies.

Range: Breeds on prairie marshes from southern Canada to South Dakota and Iowa; also in scattered marshes in West. Migrates to Gulf Coast and winters on Pacific coast of South America.

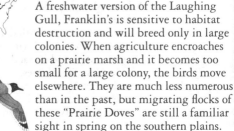

A freshwater version of the Laughing Gull, Franklin's is sensitive to habitat destruction and will breed only in large colonies. When agriculture encroaches on a prairie marsh and it becomes too small for a large colony, the birds move elsewhere. They are much less numerous than in the past, but migrating flocks of these "Prairie Doves" are still a familiar sight in spring on the southern plains.

---

45, 46 **Little Gull**
*Larus minutus*

Description: 11″ (28 cm). The *smallest* gull. Summer adult has pale gray back and wings, white underparts, *black hood,* and *blackish underwings.* Winter plumage similar, but head white with partial gray cap and dark spot behind eye. Dark red bill and legs. Immature has narrow black tail tip, diagonal dark bar on forewing, and dark primaries.

Voice: A soft *kek-kek-kek-kek.*

Habitat: Inland marshes, meadows, lakes, and

rivers; also coastal bays, flats, harbors, and estuaries.

Nesting: 3 olive-brown eggs, with dark spots, in a nest lined with grass and leaves, placed among marsh vegetation.

Range: Central Europe east to southern Siberia. In recent years, breeds locally in Ontario and Wisconsin; winters regularly in small numbers in eastern North America, especially along coast from New Brunswick to New Jersey and on Great Lakes.

This tiny gull was known for decades as a rare winter visitor to the Northeast before it was found nesting in Ontario. Its flight is rather buoyant and tern-like, and it often plucks food from the surface while on the wing or dives from the air after minnows and aquatic insects. Often consorts with Bonaparte's Gulls.

---

## 33 Common Black-headed Gull
*Larus ridibundus*

Description: 15″ (38 cm). A small gull with gray back and inner wings and *flashing white primaries.* In breeding plumage, has dark brown hood; in winter, head becomes white. Red bill and legs. Immature is darker above, but shows some white in primaries, and has narrow black tip to tail. *In all plumages, undersurface of primaries is blackish.* Bonaparte's Gull is smaller, has black bill, and lacks dark undersurface of primaries.

Voice: A harsh *kwup;* various squealing notes.

Habitat: Bays and estuaries.

Nesting: 3 buff-brown eggs, with black blotches, in a nest lined with grass, sticks, and seaweed, and placed in trees or bushes, on rocks, or on the ground. Nesting colonies located on sand dunes, beaches, marshes, and open fields.

Range: Breeds in northern portions of Europe, including Iceland, and Asia south to their southern parts. Winters from the southern portions of the breeding range south to Africa and southern Asia. Uncommon but regular winter visitor to eastern North America; also rarely on Great Lakes.

Like that of the Bonaparte's Gull, with which it is almost always found in America, the flight of the Common Black-headed Gull is light and buoyant. In the air it resembles a tern more than a gull. Although this Old World gull is uncommon in North America, it may be seen regularly in small numbers in northeastern coastal waters. In Europe it is one of the most familiar gulls.

34, 53 **Bonaparte's Gull**
*Larus philadelphia*

Description: 12–14″ (30–36 cm). A small delicate gull, silvery gray above with conspicuous white, wedge-shaped patches on the leading edge of the outer wing. Black on head of breeding adults, but not in winter. Bill black. Young birds have dark markings on the upper surface of the wing and a black tail band. The Common Black-headed Gull is similar, but is larger, and has a red bill and dark wing linings.

Voice: Rasping *tea-ar;* a soft, nasal snarling note.

Habitat: Forested lakes and rivers; winters along the coast, in estuaries, and at mouths of large rivers.

Nesting: 2–4 olive or buff spotted eggs in a well-made cup of grass, moss, and twigs, placed in a spruce or fir tree near a lake or river.

Range: Breeds in Alaska and interior northwestern Canada east to James Bay. Winters along both coasts, on Atlantic from southern New England southward, on Pacific from Washington to Mexico.

Because they breed in the Far North, these beautiful gulls are most often

seen on lakes and rivers during migration or along the coast in winter. They keep to themselves, seldom joining the larger gulls at dumps. They feed in tidal inlets and at sewage outlets, picking scraps of food from the water. During spring migration, they may often be seen flying northward along large rivers such as the Hudson and the Mississippi. The gull is named after a nephew of Napoleon, Charles Lucien Bonaparte, who was a leading 19th-century ornithologist in America and Europe.

41, 48 **Ring-billed Gull**
*Larus delawarensis*

Description: 18–20″ (46–51 cm). Adult silvery gray on back, white on head, tail, and underparts. Similar to Herring Gull but smaller, with *greenish-yellow legs and feet* and with narrow black ring around bill. Young birds are mottled brown, paler than young Herring Gulls, and have narrow blackish tail band and flesh-colored legs. Acquires adult plumage in three years.

Voice: Loud, raucous mewing cry, like that of Herring Gull but higher in pitch.

Habitat: Lakes and rivers; many move to salt water in winter.

Nesting: 2–4 spotted buff or olive eggs in a hollow in the ground, sometimes lined with grass or debris. In the North, they sometimes nest in low trees. Nests in colonies, often with other gulls or terns, usually on islands in lakes.

Range: Breeds in Northwest (locally south to California), northern Great Plains, and southern prairie provinces of Canada; also in Great Lakes region, Canadian Maritimes, and northern New England. Winters from southern New England south to Cuba, from Great Lakes to Gulf Coast, and from British Columbia to southern Mexico.

In most of the northern part of the United States the Ring-billed Gull is a winter visitor and less common than the Herring Gull. However, in some inland areas and in the Deep South it is the more numerous of the two species. It often nests in very large colonies; as many as 85,000 pairs nest on a single island in Lake Ontario. By contrast, colonies of Herring Gulls seldom number more than a few score pairs.

42, 51 **Herring Gull**
*Larus argentatus*

Description: 23–26" (58–66 cm). Adult white with light gray back and wings; black wing tip has white spots. Bill yellow with red spot on lower mandible. *Feet pink or flesh-colored.* First-year birds brownish. Acquires adult plumage in four years.

Voice: Loud rollicking call, *kuk-kuk-kuk, yucca-yucca-yucca,* and other raucous cries.

Habitat: Lakes, rivers, estuaries, and beaches; common in all aquatic habitats.

Nesting: 2–4 heavily spotted olive-brown eggs in a mass of seaweed or dead grass on the ground or a cliff; most often on islands. Nests in colonies.

Range: Breeds from Alaska east across northern Canada to Maritime Provinces, south to British Columbia, north-central Canada, and Great Lakes, and along Atlantic Coast to North Carolina. Winters in all but northernmost breeding areas and in Southeast and West from southern Alaska south to Baja, California. Also in Eurasia.

This is a common "seagull" inland and along the coast. Since the 1960s it has become abundant, probably due to the amount of food available at garbage dumps, and has extended its range southward along the Atlantic Coast, often to the detriment of colonial birds such as terns and Laughing Gulls.

Although a scavenger, it also eats large numbers of aquatic and marine animals, and feeds on berries. It often drops clams and other shellfish on exposed rocks or parking lots in order to break the shells and get at the soft interior.

37 **Thayer's Gull**
*Larus thayeri*

Description: 24″ (61 cm). In all plumages, very similar to Herring Gull, gray above, white below, but *eye of adult dark* instead of yellow. Adults have less white on underside of wing tips than do Herring Gulls.
Voice: Mewing and squealing notes.
Habitat: Arctic coasts and islands, usually on rocky cliffs.
Nesting: 3 bluish or greenish eggs, spotted with brown, in a nest lined with grass, moss, or lichens placed on a high rocky cliff.
Range: Breeds in arctic north-central Canada. Winters chiefly on Pacific Coast south to Baja California. Very rare winter visitor to Maritime Canada and northeastern United States.

This bird has variously been considered a species of its own, a subspecies of the Herring Gull, a subspecies of the Iceland Gull, or even a hybrid of the two. At the moment, it is treated as a species. Distinguishing young Thayer's Gulls from young Herrings is difficult.

40, 47 **Iceland Gull**
*Larus glaucoides*

Description: 23″ (58 cm). A smaller version of the Glaucous Gull, with relatively smaller bill and rounded head. Adults are pearl-gray above, white on head and below, Canadian breeders usually with darker gray markings at wing tips; feet are pinkish. Immatures are creamy buff; bill dark in first winter.

Voice: Like Herring Gull, a variety of croaks, squeaks, and screams.

Habitat: Lake and river shores, ocean beaches, sewer outlets, and refuse dumps.

Nesting: 2 or 3 light brown eggs, with darker blotches, in a nest lined with grass, moss, and seaweed placed either on a cliff or a sandy shore.

Range: Breeds on eastern Baffin Island and coastal Greenland. Winters in eastern North America south to New Jersey and Great Lakes. Also in Eurasia.

The habits of the two "white-winged" gulls are similar, but the smaller Iceland Gull is more buoyant and graceful on the wing. It is also more of a scavenger and much less predatory. In addition to garbage dumps and sewage outlets, this species frequents places where fish are being cleaned. Both this species and the Glaucous Gull, being relatively scarce, are eagerly sought by birders.

38 **Lesser Black-backed Gull**
*Larus fuscus*

Description: 23″ (58 cm). Slightly smaller than the Herring Gull. Adult has *yellow legs;* dark slate-gray back and wings. Immatures of this species and Herring Gull are very similar and hard to distinguish.

Voice: A strident *kyow,* deeper than that of Herring Gull.

Habitat: Nearly all types of open country—coasts, islands, fields, lakes, airports, refuse dumps, etc.

Nesting: 3 pale blue-green eggs, spotted with brown, in a nest sparsely lined with grass or laden with debris, placed on open ground or on rocky islets. Usually nests in colonies.

Range: Breeds in northern Europe. An uncommon but increasingly regular visitor to eastern North America; rarer inland and in West.

Although this Old World species is rare on the American side of the Atlantic, it can be found in and around larger cities, not only along the coast but also in the Great Lakes region. During the colder months it may be found at garbage dumps, sewer outlets, and reservoirs.

39, 50 **Glaucous Gull**
*Larus hyperboreus*

Description: 28″ (71 cm). A large gull. Adults pearl-gray above, *with no black on wing tips;* white on head and underparts. Bill yellowish; feet pinkish. Immatures creamy buff; bill pinkish with dark tip.
Voice: Hoarse croaks and screams.
Habitat: Shores of lakes and rivers, and the seacoast; also refuse dumps and sewage outflows.
Nesting: 3 light brown eggs, with dark chocolate blotches, placed in a cliff nest lined with moss and grass.
Range: Breeds in Alaska and northern Canada. Winters south to Oregon, Great Lakes, and Virginia; rare elsewhere in United States. Also in Eurasia.

The Glaucous Gull is ordinarily uncommon south of Canada; it is usually found with flocks of the abundant Herring Gull when it visits the United States. This is one of the most predatory of gulls; it captures and eats auks, plovers, small ducks, ptarmigans, and songbirds as well as lemmings and fish. It is also a scavenger, feeding on garbage, dead animal matter, and even bird droppings.

36, 49 **Great Black-backed Gull**
*Larus marinus*

Description: 30″ (76 cm). A very large gull. Adult has black back and wings, with rest of plumage white. Bill yellow and legs pinkish. Immature mottled with brown, paler on head and breast, with black tail tip and a dark bill.

Voice: Similar to that of Herring Gull, but deeper and more guttural, a deep *keeow.*

Habitat: Coastal beaches, estuaries, and lagoons; also at refuse dumps. Less commonly on inland lakes and rivers.

Nesting: 3 olive eggs, with dark brown blotches, placed in a ground nest lined with grass

Range: Breeds from Labrador south to Carolinas, rarely farther; also on Great Lakes. Winters south to Florida. Also in Eurasia.

Our largest gull, this coastal species accompanies the ever-present Herring Gull at all times of the year, even during the summer, when they nest together in mixed colonies. However, the Black-backed always asserts dominance over its smaller relative. It preys on almost anything smaller than itself, including Dovekies, small ducks, petrels, fish, and shellfish, as well as the eggs and young of other gulls. Although found close to human habitations, it is a shyer bird than the Herring Gull.

---

54, 55 **Black-legged Kittiwake**
*Rissa tridactyla*

Description: 16–18″ (41–46 cm). A small, seagoing gull. Adult white with pale gray back and wings; *sharply defined black wing tip,* as if dipped in black ink; black feet; yellow bill; slightly forked tail. Winter adult has dusky gray patch on nape. Young bird has dusky band on nape, dark diagonal wing band, and black-tipped tail.

Voice: Variety of loud, harsh notes. Very noisy on breeding grounds. With a little imagination, its common call can be said to resemble its name, *kittiwake.*

Habitat: Cliffs and seacoasts in the Arctic; winters at sea.

Nesting: 2 pinkish-buff spotted eggs in a well-made cup of mosses and seaweed at the top of a cliff or on a ledge. Nests in colonies.

Range: Breeds in North Pacific, Arctic Ocean, and Atlantic south to Gulf of Saint Lawrence. Winters from edge of sea ice southward, rarely to Gulf of Mexico. Also in Eurasia.

This abundant gull is not commonly seen from shore, for it generally spends the entire winter on the open ocean, where it feeds on small fish and plankton. Most young gulls flee from the nest if disturbed, but the young of this cliff-nesting species stay put no matter how close a human observer gets; to leave a nest on a high, narrow ledge could result in a fatal plunge to the rocks below. This is the only gull that occasionally dives and swims underwater to capture food.

---

43 **Ross' Gull**
*Rhodostethia rosea*

Description: 12–14" (30–36 cm). A very rare visitor from the Arctic. Breeding adults have narrow black collar, pale gray back and wings (including underwings), pinkish tinge on underparts, and *wedge-shaped tail.* Winter adults lack collar and pinkish tinge. Flight is graceful and tern-like.

Voice: Usually silent in winter; a harsh *miaw.*

Habitat: Breeds on swampy tundra; winters near pack ice. Rarely visits river mouths and coastal beaches.

Nesting: 2 or 3 deep olive eggs, spotted with brown, in a grass-lined depression.

Range: Breeds mainly in Old World Arctic, but a few nest in Canada. Appears as migrant off northern Alaska. Winters very rarely south to British Columbia and mid-Atlantic Coast. Also in Eurasia.

This beautiful Siberian gull winters mainly above the Arctic Circle, only rarely visiting areas where it can be seen by most birders. The appearance of a Ross' Gull in settled areas attracts hundreds of observers and often makes headlines in newspapers.

---

35 **Sabine's Gull**
*Xema sabini*

Description: 13–14″ (33–36 cm). A small, *fork-tailed* gull with black primaries and *triangular white patch on rear edge of wing.* Hood dark in breeding plumage. Bill black with yellow tip. Immature lacks dark hood but can be identified by forked tail and striking wing pattern.

Voice: High-pitched grating or squeaking notes.

Habitat: Tundra ponds in summer; open ocean on migration and in winter.

Nesting: 3 or 4 olive-brown eggs, spotted with darker brown, placed in a grass-lined depression on the ground. Nests in small colonies.

Range: Coastal tundra around shores of Arctic Ocean, farther inland in Alaska. Migrates mainly at sea. Winter range not fully known; some birds winter off Pacific coast of northern South America.

This delicate gull is seldom seen outside of the breeding season as it is almost exclusively oceanic. On the tundra coastline, it gracefully plucks small crustaceans and insects from the surface of the water like a tern. It also takes eggs from nesting colonies of Arctic Terns.

## 44 Ivory Gull
*Pagophila eburnea*

Description: 17″ (43 cm). A rather small, *short-legged* gull; adults are pure white with yellowish bill and legs; immatures (more often seen in southern latitudes) similar, but with *black bars and spots* in varying quantities.
Voice: A harsh *eeeer.*
Habitat: Breeds on rocky cliffs or stony ground; winters at edge of pack ice in Arctic seas.
Nesting: 2 buff-olive eggs, marked with dark blotches, in a nest lined with moss, lichens, and seaweed, placed on bare ground among rocks or on gravel-covered polar ice.
Range: Known to breed in New World only on Somerset and Ellesmere islands in Canadian Arctic; more common in Eurasia. Winters in Arctic Ocean, appearing rarely farther south.

The Ivory Gull shares the realm of the Inuit and the polar bear. Indeed, it follows these hunters in quest of food, for it is largely a scavenger, feeding on the remains of their kills—mainly seals. It also eats wolf and fox dung, whale blubber, lemmings, crustaceans, and insects.

---

## 58 Gull-billed Tern
*Sterna nilotica*

Description: 13–15″ (33–38 cm). A pigeon-sized tern. Very pale with almost white back and wings, black cap, and *stout black bill;* tail not as deeply forked as in other terns. Winter birds lack black cap.
Voice: Rasping *katy-did,* similar to sound made by that insect.
Habitat: Coastal marshes and sandy beaches.
Nesting: 2 or 3 spotted buff eggs in a shell-lined shallow depression (occasionally a well-made cup of dead marsh grasses) on a

sandy island in a salt marsh. Nests in colonies, and often breeds with other species of terns.

Range: Breeds from Long Island south to Gulf of Mexico and West Indies. Winters north to Gulf Coast. Also in Eurasia, Africa, and Australia.

In addition to the usual tern diet of fish and crustaceans, this bird catches insects in flight, and pursues them on the ground in plowed fields or croplands. Although not numerous, it is widespread, breeding in scattered colonies. In America, it was one of the species hardest hit by the millinery trade and has never recovered its former numbers, although recently it has slowly extended its range to the north.

---

63 **Caspian Tern**
*Sterna caspia*

Description: 19–23″ (48–58 cm). The largest tern. Largely white, with black cap, slight crest, and pale gray back and wings; heavy *bright red bill* and *dusky underwing.* The similar Royal Tern has an orange-red bill, more obvious crest, and paler underwing, and is almost never seen away from the coast.

Voice: Low, harsh *kraa.* Also a shorter *kow.*

Habitat: Sandy or pebbly shores of lakes and large rivers, and along seacoasts.

Nesting: 2 or 3 spotted buff eggs in a shallow depression or a well-made cup of dead grass, most often on a sandy or rocky island. Nests alone or in small colonies.

Range: Breeds locally from Mackenzie, Great Lakes, and Newfoundland south to Gulf Coast and Baja California. Winters north to California and North Carolina. Also breeds in Eurasia, Africa, and Australia.

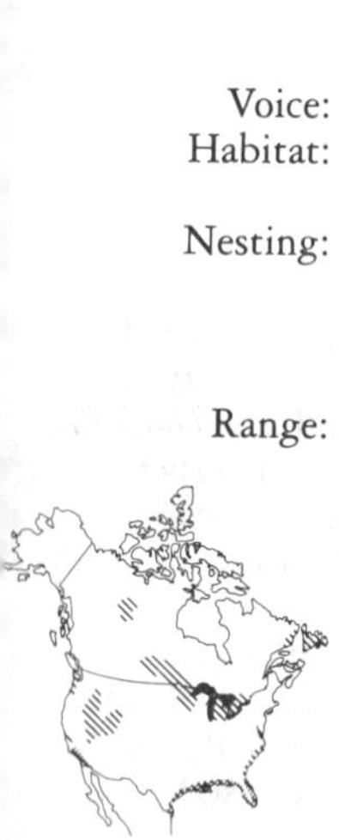

Much less gregarious than other terns, Caspians usually feed singly. Pairs breed by themselves or in small colonies, or may attach themselves to colonies of other birds such as the Ring-billed Gull. Caspians are more predatory than most other terns, readily taking small birds or the eggs and young of other terns.

62 **Royal Tern**
*Sterna maxima*

Description: 18–21″ (46–53 cm). Crow-sized. A large tern with a long, heavy, *yellow-orange to orange-red bill.* Black cap, wispy crest, pale gray back and wings, white forehead. Tail moderately forked. Similar Caspian Tern has blood-red bill, darker forehead and underwing, and shorter tail.

Voice: Harsh *kee-rare,* like Caspian Tern but higher pitched.

Habitat: Sandy beaches.

Nesting: Usually 1 buff, spotted egg in a sand scrape on an island or a sheltered peninsula.

Range: Breeds along coast from Maryland to Texas, wandering regularly farther north in summer. Winters from North Carolina, Gulf Coast, and southern California southward. Also in West Africa.

The Royal Tern breeds in large, dense colonies. Nests are sometimes washed away by storm tides, but the birds usually make a second attempt, often at a new location. This bird has fewer young than other terns but maintains its numbers wherever it has protection from disturbance. It feeds almost entirely on small fish, rather than the crustaceans and insects taken by most other terns.

72, 73 **Sandwich Tern**
*Sterna sandvicensis*

Description: 16″ (41 cm). A slender tern, white with gray mantle, black cap, short crest, and *long, black, yellow-tipped bill.*
Voice: Loud harsh *curr-it.*
Habitat: Coastal beaches and islands.
Nesting: 2 greenish, black-marked eggs on bare sand; usually nests with Royal Terns.
Range: Breeds locally on Atlantic and Gulf coasts from Virginia to Florida and Texas. Winters in tropics. Also in Eurasia.

The Sandwich Tern is one of three crested terns occurring along our coasts. It breeds much farther north in Europe than it does in America because of the warming influence of the Gulf Stream. Sandwich Terns feed offshore, diving for fish, shrimp, and squid; inshore they have been reported to eat marine worms as well.

60 **Roseate Tern**
*Sterna dougallii*

Description: 14–17″ (36–43 cm). White with a black cap and *very pale gray back and wings.* Similar to Common, Arctic, and Forster's terns, but bill usually solid black, upper parts paler, tail longer and more deeply forked.
Voice: Loud, harsh *zaap,* likened to sound of tearing cloth. Also a softer *chew-wick.*
Habitat: Coastal beaches, islands, and inshore waters.
Nesting: 2 or 3 spotted buff or olive eggs in a hollow in the ground, sometimes lined with dead grass; may be located in the open but more often concealed in vegetation or among rocks. Nests in colonies, often with other species of terns.
Range: Breeds along Atlantic Coast from Nova Scotia to Long Island. Winters in

tropics. Also in Eurasia, East Africa, and southwest Pacific.

The Roseate Tern is much less numerous than other terns of similar size, and its patchy distribution around the world suggests that it is an old species, perhaps more abundant and widespread ages ago. It probably suffers from competition for nesting sites with the Common Tern, at least in American waters; like that species, it is sensitive to disturbance by humans. For these reasons, our breeding population is small and dwindling, and the location of known colonies is often kept secret by those eager to protect the birds. It frequently nests in colonies of Common Terns, occupying less favorable, marginal sites.

56, 61 **Common Tern**
*Sterna hirundo*

Description: 13–16″ (33–41 cm). White with black cap and pale gray back and wings. Bill red with black tip; tail deeply forked. Similar to Forster's Tern, but lacks frosty wing tip. Also similar to Arctic and Roseate terns.

Voice: *Kip-kip-kip.* Also *tee-aar.*

Habitat: Lakes, ponds, rivers, coastal beaches, and islands.

Nesting: 2 or 3 spotted olive-buff eggs in a depression in sand or in a shallow cup of dead grass, located on sandy or pebbly beaches or in open rocky places, most often on islands or isolated peninsulas. Nests in colonies.

Range: Breeds from Labrador south along Atlantic Coast to Caribbean (locally) and inland locally west to Wisconsin and Alberta and Montana. Winters from Florida to southern South America. Also in Eurasia.

A grasp of the field marks of other terns is best gained by comparison with this most common of the "sea swallows." It is a familiar sight on almost all large bodies of water where protected nesting sites exist. Common Terns are seen flying gracefully over the water, searching for small fish and shrimp, which they capture by plunge diving from the air. Sensitive to disturbance during the breeding season, whole colonies often fail to breed successfully because of disruption by humans; as a result, their numbers are slowly declining. They will attack human intruders in the nesting colonies, often striking them on the head with their bills.

---

64 **Arctic Tern**
*Sterna paradisaea*

Description: 14–17″ (36–43 cm). Deeply forked tail. Similar to Common Tern, but *underparts grayer, bill blood-red,* legs shorter, tail longer.
Voice: Harsh *tee-ar* or *kip-kip-kip-tee-ar,* higher pitched than that of Common Tern.
Habitat: Coastal islands and beaches; also on tundra in summer.
Nesting: 2 spotted olive-buff eggs in a shallow depression in the ground, sometimes lined with grass or shells, usually on islands or protected sand spits. Nests in colonies.
Range: Breeds from Aleutians, northern Alaska, northern Canada east to Ellesmere Island and Newfoundland, and south to British Columbia, northern Manitoba and Quebec, and Massachusetts. Winters at sea in Southern Hemisphere. Also breeds in northern Eurasia.

Seldom seen in the East south of its breeding grounds, these terns annually perform spectacular migrations, every fall heading eastward across the Atlantic and down the west coasts of Europe and

Africa to winter in the Antarctic Ocean. In spring they return north, following the East Coast of South and North America, a round-trip that can total 22,000 miles (35,000 kilometers). They see more daylight than any other living creature since they are in both the Arctic and Antarctic during the periods of longest days. During the northern winter, this species is more truly oceanic than its close relatives, feeding chiefly on small seagoing shrimp and other planktonic animals. Like most other terns, it vigorously defends its nest, often making painful attacks on the heads of human intruders.

---

57, 59 **Forster's Tern**
*Sterna forsteri*

Description: 14–15" (36–38 cm). White with pale gray back and wings, black cap, and deeply forked tail. Bill orange with black tip. Similar to Common Tern, but *wing tips frosty white, bill more orange.* Lacks black cap in winter, but has distinctive black mark behind eye.

Voice: Harsh nasal *beep.*

Habitat: Salt marshes in the East; freshwater marshes in the West.

Nesting: 3 or 4 buff, spotted eggs on a large platform of dead grass lined with finer grasses, usually placed on masses of dead marsh vegetation. Nests in colonies.

Range: Breeds along Atlantic Coast from Massachusetts to Texas and in interior from Alberta and California east to Great Lakes. Winters along coasts from California and Virginia southward.

One of the few exclusively North American terns, Forster's is so similar to the Common Tern that it was not recognized as a distinct species until 1831. Its preference for marshes enables it to avoid competition with the

Common Tern, which favors sandy or pebbly beaches and rocky islands. It was named after Johann Reinhold Forster (1729–1798), a German pastor-naturalist who accompanied Captain Cook around the world in 1772.

71 **Least Tern**
*Sterna antillarum*

Description: 8–10″ (20–25 cm). A *very small* tern with black-tipped *yellow bill* and fast shallow wingbeat. White with black cap, pale gray back and wings, and forked tail; *forehead white.*

Voice: Sharp *killick* or *kip-kip-kip-kiddeek.*

Habitat: Sandy and pebbly beaches along the coast; sandbars in large rivers. Often on landfills.

Nesting: 2 or 3 buff, lightly spotted eggs in an unlined scrape on a sand spit or gravel beach. Nests in colonies.

Range: Breeds along California coast, rivers in Mississippi Valley, and coasts from Maine south to Florida. Winters on Pacific coasts of Mexico and South America.

Because of the Least Tern's habit of nesting on low sandbars, whole colonies are sometimes destroyed by very high tides. It is also vulnerable to human disturbance when bathers and beach strollers enter its nesting colonies. Most often seen hovering over the water, it peers downward in search of small minnows and other marine or freshwater organisms.

67 **Bridled Tern**
*Sterna anaethetus*

Description: 14–15″ (36–38 cm). A stocky oceanic tern, dark gray above, white below, with black cap; white forehead and eyebrow;

and conspicuous white collar, or "bridle," on hindneck. Sooty Tern similar, but lacks collar and is blacker on upperparts.

Voice: Usually silent; various high-pitched barking notes on breeding grounds.

Habitat: Open ocean; breeds on rocky or sandy islands.

Nesting: 1 white egg, spotted with brown, placed in a shallow depression among rocks on an island. Nests in colonies.

Range: Breeds in tropical Atlantic, Indian, and Pacific oceans; in nonbreeding season, ranges to offshore Gulf Stream waters from Carolinas to Florida.

This bird was long thought to be a casual visitor to the North American coast, but as more birders travel out to the Gulf Stream, it has become evident that the species is fairly common 20 or 30 miles (30 to 50 kilometers) offshore.

## 69 Sooty Tern
*Sterna fuscata*

Description: 16″ (41 cm). *Adult black above with white forehead; white below.* Deeply forked tail; thin black bill. Immature birds are dark brown, finely spotted with white on back and wings.

Voice: Harsh squeaky notes and croaks.

Habitat: Coastal and oceanic islands during breeding season; open ocean at other times.

Nesting: 1 white egg, with reddish-brown blotches, in a hollow in the sand; occasionally on rocks or ledges. Almost always nests in large colonies.

Range: Tropical seas; in North America breeds only on Dry Tortugas, Florida.

Sooty Terns are notorious wanderers; when not nesting they range far and wide over the seas. Perhaps this is why they are so often blown inland, sometimes many hundreds of miles, by hurricanes and tropical storms. These birds have a remarkable homing ability. When individuals marked with a dye were taken from their breeding grounds on the Dry Tortugas and released along the coasts of North Carolina and Texas, all returned to their breeding grounds within one to seven days. Sooty Terns feed largely at dusk and at night. Unlike most other terns, they do not dive but pluck small fish and squid from the surface of the water. They spend most of their time in the air, almost never perching or alighting on the water.

## 68 Black Tern
*Chlidonias niger*

Description: 9–10″ (23–25 cm). A medium-sized tern with *solid black head and underparts;* gray wing and moderately forked gray tail. In fall and winter, the head and underparts are white, with dusky smudging around eyes and back of neck.

Voice: Sharp *kick;* when disturbed, a shrill *kreek.*

Habitat: Freshwater marshes and marshy lakes in summer; sandy coasts during migration and winter.

Nesting: 2 spotted olive-buff eggs laid in a hollow on a mass of floating marsh vegetation or in a well-made cup of dead grass. Nests in colonies.

Range: Breeds from British Columbia east to New Brunswick and south to central California and New York. Winters south of U.S. border, rarely in California. Also in Eurasia.

This tern usually nests in small groups and in shallow water. The nests are sometimes conspicuous; perhaps this is why the young often leave the nest at the first sign of an intruder, swimming quietly away to hide in the surrounding marsh vegetation. It is not unusual to visit an active colony and find all the nests empty. Unlike other terns, these birds frequently fly over land areas as they hawk for insects. They also eat small fish and crustaceans, which they pick from the surface of the water.

## 65 Brown Noddy
*Anous stolidus*

Description: 15″ (38 cm). Dark sooty brown with pale grayish-white crown; wedge-shaped tail; slender black bill.
Voice: Low *cah,* similar to call of a young crow.
Habitat: Coastal and oceanic islands during breeding season; open ocean at other times.
Nesting: 1 buff egg, spotted with lilac and brown, in a stick nest lined with seaweed and often bits of shell and coral, placed on rocks, in trees or bushes, or on exposed coral reefs.
Range: Breeds on Dry Tortugas, Florida. Found nearly throughout warmer ocean regions of world.

These dark brown terns with light caps commonly associate with Sooty Terns, at least at breeding colonies. Unlike them, however, the Noddy does not wander northward after the nesting season; as a result, few are reported in our area north of southern Florida. They catch their food—primarily small fish—by pouncing on them at the water's surface rather than diving as most terns do. These oceangoing terns are fond of perching on floating pieces of driftwood, and they occasionally alight on the water and float.

## 66 Black Noddy
*Anous minutus*

Description: 12″ (30 cm). Smaller and darker than Brown Noddy, with a more extensive pure white cap. Rest of plumage dark brownish black, feet brownish black; bill long, thin, straight, and black; tail wedge-shaped.

Voice: A sharp *kit, kit.*

Habitat: Small oceanic and coastal islands in breeding season; otherwise wanders at sea.

Nesting: 1 whitish egg, spotted with brown, in a stick nest lined with grass or seaweed, placed in a tree or bush.

Range: Tropical portions of Atlantic, Pacific, and Indian oceans. In North America found only in Dry Tortugas, Florida (rare).

This pantropical tern is of extremely local occurrence in North America, but each year since 1960 birds have been found among nesting Brown Noddies in the Dry Tortugas. Although seen there regularly, the Black Noddy has not yet been known to nest there.

## 70 Black Skimmer
*Rynchops niger*

Description: 18″ (46 cm). Black above, white below, with red legs. *Bill red with black tip,* laterally compressed, blade-like. Unique among birds in having *lower mandible much longer (about one-third) than the upper.* Immature mottled above, with shorter bill.

Voice: Short barking notes.

Habitat: Breeds chiefly on sandbars and beaches; feeds in shallow bays, inlets, and estuaries.

Nesting: 3 or 4 brown-blotched buff eggs on bare sand, usually among shell fragments and scattered grass clumps.

Range: Breeds along Atlantic and Gulf coasts from Massachusetts and Long Island to Florida and Texas. Winters north to southern California and Virginia. Also in American tropics.

This extraordinary bird, especially when in flight, can hardly fail to impress even the most casual observer. Usually only one or two are seen as they skim the surface for fish, with the tip of the lower mandible cutting through the water. They also wade in shallow water, jabbing at the fish scattering before them. Compact flocks may be seen flying in unison, wheeling in one direction and then another—showing first the jet black of the wings, then the gleaming white of the underparts. They are especially attracted to the sand fill of newly dredged areas; such places sometimes contain colonies of up to 200 pairs. These sites are usually temporary, abandoned as soon as too much grass appears.

---

## Family Alcidae
Auks, Murres, and Puffins

22 species: Seacoasts of the Northern Hemisphere. Twenty species breed in North America. The alcids are chunky, penguin-like seabirds, chiefly dark above and white below, with short wings and large webbed feet located far back on the body. They live along rocky coasts, where they breed mainly on precipitous cliffs and lay their pointed eggs on bare ledges, in crevices, or in burrows. They spend the winter at sea, where they dive for their food, primarily small fish and squid, which they pursue by using their wings for propulsion.

---

103 **Dovekie**
*Alle alle*

Description: 8″ (20 cm). A starling-sized alcid. Chunky; black above and white below, with a very short bill. Breeding adults have a black head; winter birds have black crown and white cheeks.

Voice: Squeaking notes.

Habitat: Breeds on rocky cliffs; winters chiefly at sea.

Nesting: 1 bluish-white egg in a rock crevice. High Arctic south to Greenland.

Range: Breeds in eastern Arctic Canada. Winters south to New Jersey. Also in northern Europe.

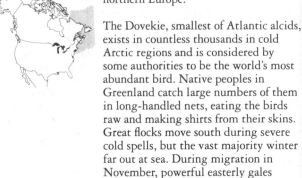

The Dovekie, smallest of Atlantic alcids, exists in countless thousands in cold Arctic regions and is considered by some authorities to be the world's most abundant bird. Native peoples in Greenland catch large numbers of them in long-handled nets, eating the birds raw and making shirts from their skins. Great flocks move south during severe cold spells, but the vast majority winter far out at sea. During migration in November, powerful easterly gales occasionally blow them great distances inland, where they usually succumb to the elements or die of starvation. Dovekies eat phytoplankton, krill, small fish, and crustaceans.

---

100, 106 **Common Murre**
*Uria aalge*

Description: 17″ (43 cm). Crow-sized. Blackish-brown above and on head, white below, with a long pointed bill. Winter birds have extensive white on the face, with a dark line behind the eye. See Thick-billed Murre.

Voice: Purring or murmuring, hence the name "murre." Also a guttural croak and higher-pitched bleat.

Habitat: Rocky coasts.

Nesting: 1 blue-green egg, with black marks, on a bare rock ledge.

Range: Breeds along Arctic and subarctic coasts south to central California and Gulf of Saint Lawrence. Winters south to southern California and Massachusetts. Also in Eurasia.

The murres, like all alcids, use their wings for swimming and diving, and seem to fly through the water. This species is more abundant on the Pacific Coast of the United States than on the Atlantic, where it is outnumbered by the Thick-billed Murre. In the Arctic, however, it nests in huge colonies, with incubating birds standing side by side on long narrow ledges.

101, 107 **Thick-billed Murre**
*Uria lomvia*

Description: 18″ (46 cm). Similar to Common Murre, but blacker above, with shorter, thicker bill. In winter, the face is mainly black, with white only on cheeks and throat.
Voice: Similar to Common Murre.
Habitat: Rocky coasts.
Nesting: 1 large bluish-green egg, scrawled with brown, on a narrow ledge. Nests in dense colonies.
Range: Breeds on Arctic and subarctic coasts south to southern Alaska and Gulf of Saint Lawrence. Winters south to southern Alaska and New Jersey. Also in Eurasia.

Unlike the other alcids, which are exclusively oceanic, this species occurs very rarely on the Great Lakes and other large inland bodies of water. Murre eggs are a rich source of food for native peoples, while the birds themselves are among the chief prey of Gyrfalcons and Peregrines. In turn, murres feed on fish, squid, and various crustaceans.

102 **Razorbill**
*Alca torda*

Description: 17″ (43 cm). A crow-sized diving bird. Black above and on head; white below; very deep, laterally compressed bill has white bands in adults. Winter birds have white on throat and cheek, and behind eye. Immatures have smaller, unmarked bills.

Voice: Low croaks and growls.

Habitat: Coastal waters.

Nesting: 1 brown-spotted, bluish egg on or under rocks.

Range: Breeds from Arctic south to Maine. Winters south to New Jersey, rarely to Carolinas. Also in Europe.

These birds often can be recognized at a distance on the water by their large heads, stout bills, and upward-pointed tails. As with many alcids, Razorbills migrate southward after severe cold spells and visit our shores in the midst of winter. They are hardy birds, spending most of their time at sea and approaching land only after strong easterly gales. During the breeding season, they prefer rocky coasts, where they lay their eggs and raise their young. Razorbills feed mostly on fish, shrimp, and squid. They are very adept at diving and have been caught in gill nets as deep as 60 feet (18 meters).

## 105 Black Guillemot
*Cepphus grylle*

Description: 13″ (33 cm). Pigeon-sized. In summer, *all black with large white wing patch; bright red feet;* pointed bill. In winter, the black is largely replaced by white. Murres are larger.

Voice: Shrill mouse-like squeaks.

Habitat: Rocky coasts, even in winter.

Nesting: 2 whitish eggs, with dark brown blotches, under rocks either on a bare surface or on loose pebbles.

Range: Breeds from Arctic Alaska and Canada south along Atlantic Coast to Maine. Winters south to Bering Sea and Long Island (rarely). Also in northern Europe, Scandinavia, and Alaska.

In summer plumage, these jet-black seabirds with large white wing patches and bright red feet are conspicuous, especially when in flight. A characteristic field mark is their habit of dipping their bills into the water. Guillemots are hardy birds, rarely migrating even in subzero weather. Their diet consists primarily of small fish, crustaceans, mollusks, and marine worms.

## 104 Atlantic Puffin
*Fratercula arctica*

Description: 12″ (30 cm). A short stocky bird. Black above and white below, with white face and red legs; its remarkable *triangular bill is brilliant red and yellow.* In fall, horny outer covering of bill is shed, leaving it smaller and duller.

Voice: Deep throaty purrs and croaks.

Habitat: Chiefly rocky coasts.

Nesting: 1 white egg in a burrow in soft soil or a rock crevice; nest cavity is lined with grass. Nests in colonies.

Range: Breeds from Canadian Maritimes south to Maine. Winters offshore near nesting colonies, rarely south to Long Island. Also in northern Europe.

This clown of the sea is a comical-looking bird with a dumpy figure, red-rimmed, gleaming yellow eyes, a gaudy bill, and a habit of waddling around, jumping from rock to rock. It nests in much smaller colonies than do most other alcids. Puffins hunt their food—small fish, shellfish, and shrimp—in rocky coastal waters and also at sea. They are excellent swimmers and divers. The birds breeding in Maine have only recently been established there as a result of a captive breeding program in which nestlings from Newfoundland were hand-reared on islands, with the hope that they would return to the area as adults.

## Family Columbidae
Pigeons and Doves

310 species: Worldwide. Only 11 species, three of them introduced but well established, breed in North America. Members of this family are stocky, short-legged birds with short necks and small heads; some have long tails. They walk with a mincing gait and, unlike most birds, can drink without raising their heads after each sip. There is no firm distinction between pigeons and doves, although species called pigeons tend to be larger. North American species are clad in soft browns and grays.

---

### 350 Rock Dove
*Columba livia*

Description: 13½" (34 cm). The common pigeon of towns and cities. Chunky, with short rounded tail. Typically bluish gray with 2 narrow black wing bands and a broad black terminal tail band; *white rump.* There are many color variants, ranging from all white through rusty to all black.

Voice: Soft guttural cooing.

Habitat: City parks, suburban gardens, and farmlands.

Nesting: 2 white eggs in a crude nest lined with sticks and debris, placed on a window ledge, building, bridge, or cliff.

Range: Native to Old World. Introduced and established in most of North America from central Canada southward.

Everyone knows the Rock Dove, or domestic pigeon, as a bird that, in the city, subsists on handouts or, in the country, nests in pigeon cotes on farms. Few have seen it nesting in its ancestral home—cliff ledges or high among rocks. Over the centuries, many strains and color varieties have been developed in captivity through selective breeding. Since pigeons have been accused of carrying human diseases, there have been several attempts to eradicate them from our cities, but they are so prolific that little progress has been made toward this end.

---

**351 White-crowned Pigeon**
*Columba leucocephala*

Description: 13″ (33 cm). *Dark gray,* with conspicuous *white crown.* Darker Rock Doves have shorter tails and white rather than blackish wing linings.
Voice: An owl-like *coo-coo-co-wooo.*
Habitat: Mangrove swamps and tropical hardwood hammocks.
Nesting: 1 or 2 white eggs in a grass-lined stick nest placed in a tree or bush; often nests in colonies.
Range: Breeds in Florida Keys and West Indies. Most winter farther south.

In the United States, the White-crowned Pigeon breeds only in the mangrove swamps of the Florida Keys and, to a lesser extent, among the gumbo-limbo and mahogany trees of the adjacent mainland. In former years, great numbers were shot for food, and they became very wary. After protective laws were passed in 1913, Rock Doves increased in number and nowadays are fairly tame. They eat mainly fruit, but also insects and seeds.

---

**352 Red-billed Pigeon**
*Columba flavirostris*

Description: 14″ (36 cm). A large pigeon, deep maroon and gray, without distinctive markings; bill red with pale tip.
Voice: Loud, high-pitched, clear *coo,* followed by a 3-syllable *coo* repeated 3 times.

**Habitat:** Thick forests and woodland borders, often near water.

**Nesting:** 1 white egg in a nest of sticks, lined with grass or fibers and placed in a bush or tree.

**Range:** Breeds in lower Rio Grande Valley of Texas to Costa Rica. Most winter farther south.

This tropical pigeon is found in the densely wooded bottomlands near the U.S.–Mexico border and occasionally in more open country around clearings in the forest, or in groves of large trees along rivers. It feeds in the crowns of tall trees on wild figs, other fruits, various nuts, and seeds. Like many other pigeons, it makes a series of cooing calls and a loud clapping noise with its wings as it rises in flight.

---

## 348 Ringed Turtle-Dove
*Streptopelia risoria*

**Description:** 12″ (30 cm). A slender, pale sandy dove; narrow black collar on hindneck; rounded, not pointed, tail. Mourning Dove similar but darker, with pointed tail, no collar.

**Voice:** Soft mellow *kooo-krooo,* rising and then falling in pitch.

**Habitat:** City parks and suburban areas, usually where trees are present.

**Nesting:** 2 white eggs in a flimsy saucer of twigs and grass, on a window ledge or in a dovecote.

**Range:** Introduced and established in southern California, Arizona, Alabama, and southern Florida. May be encountered elsewhere.

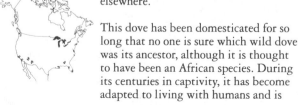

This dove has been domesticated for so long that no one is sure which wild dove was its ancestor, although it is thought to have been an African species. During its centuries in captivity, it has become adapted to living with humans and is unsuccessful in rural areas. Its pleasing call makes it a favorite cage bird; individuals frequently escape into the wild.

349 **White-winged Dove**
*Zenaida asiatica*

Description: 12″ (30 cm). A brownish-gray dove with blackish wings that have a *broad diagonal white bar;* rounded tail has *whitish corners,* noticeable in flight.
Voice: Drawn-out *hooo-hooo-ho-hooo* or *who-cooks-for-you.*
Habitat: Open country with dense thickets of shrubs and low trees; also in suburban and agricultural areas.
Nesting: 2 cream-buff eggs on a frail platform of loose twigs in low bushes.
Range: Breeds in southwestern United States and southern Texas. Winters south of United States; small numbers on Gulf Coast east to Florida. Also in American tropics.

In some areas, these doves nest in huge colonies covering many acres. When the birds rise, flashing their conspicuous white wing patches, they are a handsome sight.

345 **Mourning Dove**
*Zenaida macroura*

Description: 12″ (30 cm). A soft, sandy buff color, with long pointed tail bordered with white. Black spots on wings.
Voice: Low, mournful (hence its name) *coo-ah, coo, coo, coo.*
Habitat: Open fields, parks, and lawns with many trees and shrubs.
Nesting: 2 white eggs in a loosely made nest of sticks and twigs, placed in low bushes and tall trees, more rarely on the ground.

Range: Breeds from southeastern Alaska east to New Brunswick, and southward to Mexico and Panama. Winters north to northern United States.

This abundant bird has increased with the human practice of cutting the forest. The Mourning Dove is common in rural areas in all parts of the United States, as well as in city parks and, during winter, suburban feeders. In some states it is hunted as a game bird, while in others it is protected as a "songbird." Its species name, *macroura,* is Greek for "long-tailed." The young are fed regurgitated, partially digested food known as pigeon milk.

---

344 **Inca Dove**
*Columbina inca*

Description: 8″ (20 cm). A tiny, *long-tailed* dove with *scaly gray body* and contrasting *rufous in wings.*
Voice: A soft *coo-coo* or *no-hope,* often repeated.
Habitat: Semiarid country with mesquite thickets or cactus; also parks, yards, and ranches.
Nesting: 2 white eggs in a frail nest, usually of small twigs, placed low in a tree or bush.
Range: Resident in southeastern California, Arizona, New Mexico, and southern parts of Texas. Also in tropics.

This tiny bird is much like a Common Ground-Dove except for its long pointed tail. Perhaps because both of these species are too small to be considered game, they show little fear of humans. The Inca Dove is so tame it nests in city parks and gardens.

346 **Common Ground-Dove**
*Columbina passerina*

Description: 6½″ (17 cm). A sparrow-sized, short-tailed brown dove with *much rufous in wings.* Tail dark with white corners.
Voice: Soft cooing notes, *coo-oo, coo-oo, coo-oo,* each with rising inflection.
Habitat: Open areas such as fields, gardens, farmlands, and roadsides.
Nesting: 2 white eggs on or close to the ground. The nest is often hidden in a tuft of grass or among weeds.
Range: Resident in southern parts of California, Arizona, and Texas, and east to southern North Carolina.

This bird, as its name implies, spends much of its time on the ground and is most commonly seen when flushed from a roadside or path in a brushy pasture. A rather retiring bird, it is somewhat locally distributed.

347 **White-tipped Dove**
**"White-fronted Dove"**
*Leptotila verreauxi*

Description: 12″ (30 cm). Brown with whitish forehead, belly, and tail tips; chestnut wing linings.
Voice: Deep, drawn-out, descending *coo,* lower pitched than most of our pigeons and doves.
Habitat: Dense, moist woodlands and thickets.
Nesting: 2 white eggs in a stick nest lined with plant fibers and placed in a dense bush, vine, or tree.
Range: Resident in southernmost Texas. Also in American tropics.

Uncommon and local along the U.S.–Mexico border, the White-tipped Dove is primarily a forest species with a wide vertical range, feeding mostly on the ground but also flying to the tops of tall trees. When flushed, the bird makes a whistling sound with its sickle-shaped outermost primaries. It feeds on various seeds and nuts, and occasionally on small fruits such as wild figs, palm fruit, and various berries.

---

## Family Psittacidae
Parrots

358 species: Widespread in tropical regions. Only the now-extinct Carolina Parakeet (*Conuropsis carolinensis*) originally nested within the United States, but a few others have been introduced and are well established. Many additional species can be found in the United States; these are mainly birds that have escaped from captivity. Members of this well-known family are characterized by their strong hooked beaks and usually green plumage. Many have pointed tails.

---

### 585 Budgerigar
### "Parakeet"
*Melopsittacus undulatus*

Description: 7″ (18 cm). Typical adult barred above with black and yellow; rump and underparts green (occasionally blue). Tail long, pointed, and green.

Voice: A chattering warble, interspersed with screeching notes.

Habitat: Suburbs, parks, and gardens.

Nesting: 4–7 white eggs laid in a natural cavity or birdhouse.

Range: Introduced from Australia and established in west-central Florida and elsewhere in the state.

This familiar cage bird, which occurs in a variety of colors besides those of the wild type described above, escapes so frequently that birds may be seen almost anywhere in the United States, and not just in the area where it now nests successfully on its own.

588 **Rose-ringed Parakeet**
*Psittacula krameri*

Description: 15–17″ (38–43 cm). A slender green parakeet with long pointed tail, red bill. Male has *narrow red-and-black necklace.*
Voice: A loud screeching *eee-ak, eee-ak.*
Habitat: Suburban areas, parks, and gardens.
Nesting: 2–6 white eggs in a natural cavity, usually with no lining, or on a layer of sawdust or wood fragments.
Range: Native to Africa and Asia. Introduced in southern California and southern Florida.

A graceful and attractive bird, the Rose-ringed Parakeet has adapted well to life in warmer, settled parts of North America. It visits bird feeders and can even be seen scavenging in garbage cans.

587 **Monk Parakeet**
*Myiopsitta monachus*

Description: 11″ (28 cm). Bright green above and pale gray below, with scalloping on throat; dark blue primaries; long and pointed tail.
Voice: Loud, harsh, screeching *eeeh-eeeh.*
Habitat: City parks, suburban yards, and semi-open country.
Nesting: 5 or 6 white eggs in a huge, bulky stick nest, placed in a tree or on top of a power pole, or attached to a building wall. Nest is domed and has entrances to egg chambers on sides and bottom.
Range: Introduced from southern South America, and now established in northeastern United States and Florida.

This noisy but attractive parrot was first reported in the wild in the late 1960s, presumably having escaped from a shipment at New York's Kennedy Airport. Since that time, it has spread to surrounding regions. Its huge stick nests, used both for breeding and roosting, are conspicuous and may contain from one to as many as six pairs of birds.

589 **Canary-winged Parakeet**
*Brotogeris versicolurus*

Description: 9″ (23 cm). A small, stocky green parakeet with pointed tail and *flash of yellow and white in wing.*
Voice: A rapid series of shrill metallic notes.
Habitat: Suburban areas, parks, and gardens.
Nesting: 5 white eggs placed in a natural cavity or in a dense cluster of dead palm fronds.
Range: Native to tropical America. Introduced and established in southern California and southern Florida.

This boldly marked parakeet frequently escapes domestic confinement and can be seen occasionally in the heart of large cities like New York and San Francisco. It nests successfully in the wild only in California and Florida.

## Family Cuculidae
Cuckoos, Roadrunners, and Anis

143 species: Nearly worldwide. Six species breed in North America. Although some Old World species of this family are parasitic in their nesting habits, American cuckoos lay eggs in their own nests. Besides the familiar but secretive cuckoos, this mostly tropical family includes the comical, ground-inhabiting Greater Roadrunner of the Southwest and two all-black anis.

449 **Black-billed Cuckoo**
*Coccyzus erythopthalmus*

Description: 12″ (30 cm). Very similar to Yellow-billed Cuckoo, brown above, white below, but *bill entirely black,* wings brown, much less white at tips of tail feathers. Narrow red eye ring.

Voice: A series of soft mellow *cu-cu-cu-cu* notes in groups of 2 to 5, all on the same pitch.

Habitat: Moist thickets in low overgrown pastures and orchards; also in thicker undergrowth and sparse woodlands.

Nesting: 2–4 blue-green eggs in a flimsy shallow nest of twigs, lined with grass and plant down, and placed within a few feet of the ground in a dense thicket.

Range: Breeds from Alberta and Montana east to Maritime Provinces, and south to Texas, Arkansas, and South Carolina. Winters in South America.

Both widespread cuckoos—the Black-billed and the Yellow-billed—are adept at hiding and skulking in dense vegetation, and are more often heard than seen. Their distinctive notes, repeated over and over, are reminiscent of those of grebes and doves, but are deeper in tone and more repetitive. When tracked down, the birds slip away to another location and repeat the call. Cuckoos are beneficial to farmers and horticulturists, as they consume enormous quantities of destructive hairy caterpillars, especially gypsy moth and tent caterpillars. They are most numerous in years of heavy tent caterpillar infestations.

448 **Yellow-billed Cuckoo**
*Coccyzus americanus*

Description: 10½–12½″ (27–32 cm). Jay-sized. A slender, long-tailed bird, brown above and white below, with *large white spots on underside of tail and a flash of rufous in wings.* Bill slightly curved, with yellow lower mandible. Black-billed Cuckoo similar, but has very little rufous in wings and smaller white spots on tail.

Voice: A rapid, harsh, rattling *ka-ka-ka-ka-ka-ka-kow-kow-kowp, kowp, kowp, kowp,* slowing down at the end.

Habitat: Moist thickets, willows, overgrown pastures, and orchards.

Nesting: 2–4 pale blue-green eggs in a flimsy saucer of twigs placed in a bush or small sapling.

Range: Breeds from central California, Minnesota, and southern New Brunswick southward. Winters in South America.

This bird's tendency to utter its distinctive call at the approach of a storm has earned it the name "Rain Crow." Both the Yellow-billed and Black-billed cuckoos are fond of hairy caterpillars; during outbreaks of tent caterpillars, they are valuable in helping to keep these creatures in check. Usually shy and elusive, these birds are easy to overlook.

447 **Mangrove Cuckoo**
*Coccyzus minor*

Description: 12″ (30 cm). Brown above, *rich buff or tawny below,* with black facial mask; curved bill. Tail long and graduated, with black-and-white spots at tip.

Voice: Low guttural *gaw-gaw-gaw-gaw-gaw,* almost like a soft bark or the scolding of a squirrel.

Habitat: Mangrove swamps.

Nesting: 2 or 3 pale greenish-blue eggs in a stick nest in a low shrub.

Range: Breeds in southern Florida. A few remain during winter, but most leave for tropics.

In North America, this species is found only in the Florida Keys and on the

adjacent Gulf Coast of Florida as far north as Tampa Bay. It is difficult to observe, remaining hidden in dense thickets much of the time. Strictly insectivorous, it feeds on hairy caterpillars, grasshoppers, moths, larvae, and spiders.

## 289 Greater Roadrunner
*Geococcyx californianus*

Description: 24″ (61 cm). Bigger than a crow. A long-legged, *long-tailed,* streaked, gray-brown ground bird with a *bushy crest.* Bright yellow eyes.

Voice: Clucks, crows, dove-like coos, dog-like whines, and hoarse guttural notes.

Habitat: Open arid country with scattered thickets.

Nesting: 3–5 ivory-colored eggs in a flat stick nest lined with grass, usually not far above ground in thick shrub or cactus.

Range: Resident from northern California east to Arkansas and Louisiana, and southward into Mexico.

The comical-looking Roadrunner—or "Chaparral Cock," as it is called by cowboys—would rather run than fly. Twisting and turning in and out of cactus thickets, it can easily outdistance a human. The bird jerks its tail from side to side or up and down; it also elevates its bushy crest when excited. It eats a variety of animal foods, including small snakes, lizards, mice, scorpions, and insects.

## 641 Smooth-billed Ani
*Crotophaga ani*

Description: 14″ (36 cm). Pigeon-sized. Black, with a very long tail half the length of the bird. Bill huge, with arched ridge and no grooves.

Voice: Slurred double note with a rising inflection that has a whining, metallic quality; quite different from that of the Groove-billed Ani.

Habitat: Open agricultural country, often near cattle or other livestock; also found in scrub and thickets.

Nesting: 3–5 blue-green (often stained) eggs in a bulky stick nest in dense vegetation.

Range: Resident in southern Florida. Also in American tropics.

These birds have some peculiar traits. Usually several females lay eggs in a single nest, deposited in layers separated more or less by leaves or grass. Up to 30 eggs have been found in one nest. Those at the bottom do not hatch. The females share incubation, often two or more brooding simultaneously. Anis prefer cultivated country and rangelands, where they often alight on the backs of cattle to remove ticks.

## 640 Groove-billed Ani
*Crotophaga sulcirostris*

Description: 12″ (30 cm). Jay-sized. Black, with a very long tail half the length of the bird. Bill huge, with arched ridge and narrow grooves. Smooth-billed Ani lacks grooves on bill and does not occur in Texas.

Voice: Soft, liquid, gurgling notes and, if alarmed, rather loud harsh calls. Also a rollicking *wee-cup*.

Habitat: Arid agricultural land, especially where there are cattle.

Nesting: 3 or 4 pale blue eggs in a huge stick nest, often situated in thorny scrub.

Range: Resident in lower Rio Grande Valley. Also in American tropics.

In flight, both anis flap their wings loosely, alternating with short glides. The long tail, which appears as if on a hinge, swings up and down and from

side to side like a pendulum, and looks as though it might drop off. Both anis feed largely on a mixed diet of insects, seeds, and fruits. In the United States, the ranges of the two do not overlap.

FAMILY TYTONIDAE
Barn Owls

17 species: Worldwide. Only one species, the Barn Owl, occurs in North America. These long-legged, densely plumaged owls have conspicuous heart-shaped facial disks and dark eyes. They are found mostly in forests, but several species in the Old World tropics are adapted to open grasslands.

310 **Barn Owl**
*Tyto alba*

Description: 18″ (46 cm). W. 3′8″ (1.1 m). Crow-sized. Buff-brown above and white below, with *heart-shaped face* and numerous fine dark dots on white underparts; *dark eyes;* long legs.
Voice: Hissing notes, screams, guttural grunts, and bill snappings. Young give rapid grackle-like clicks.
Habitat: Open country, forest edges and clearings, cultivated areas, and cities.
Nesting: 5–10 white eggs on bare wood or stone in buildings, hollow trees, or caves, or even in burrows.
Range: Resident from southern British Columbia east through Dakotas and Michigan to southern New England, and southward. Also in South America and Old World.

This nocturnal ghost of a bird frequents such places as belfries, deserted buildings, and hollow trees. It hunts its food—almost entirely rodents—in garbage dumps, neglected cemeteries, run-down farms, and empty lots in large cities. Contrary to popular belief, owls see well by day, but their large eyes do give them especially good night vision. Experiments have shown, however, that Barn Owls depend on keen hearing to locate their prey. These owls appear to practice birth control: When food is scarce they lay fewer eggs or may not breed at all.

---

## Family Strigidae
True Owls

161 species: Worldwide. Eighteen species breed in North America. Members of this well-known family range from the huge Great Horned and Great Gray owls to the diminutive Elf Owl of the arid Southwest. Nearly all of the species are nocturnal, but some, such as the beautiful Snowy Owl of the Arctic, also hunt in the daytime. Owls do not build their own nests but use abandoned nests of other birds, such as stick nests in trees. They also nest in hollow trees and, more rarely, on cliffs or on the ground. All species lay white eggs. During the cold months, many of these birds roost in dense evergreens. Although, like hawks, they have sharp talons and hooked beaks for killing their prey, they are not related to hawks.

---

### 308 Eastern Screech-Owl
*Otus asio*

Description: 10″ (25 cm). A *small,* mottled owl with prominent *ear tufts;* yellow eyes. Both rufous and gray color phases occur, as well as brownish intermediates.

Voice: A tremulous, descending wail; soft purrs and trills.

Habitat: Open deciduous woods, woodlots, suburban areas, lakeshores, old orchards.

Nesting: 3–8 white eggs placed without a nest lining in a cavity in a tree or in a nest box.

Range: Resident from Canada's southern prairie provinces east to southern Maine, and south to Gulf of Mexico and Florida.

These common owls are fearless in defense of their nests and will often strike unsuspecting humans on the head as they pass nearby at night. When discovered during the day, they often freeze in an upright position, depending on their cryptic coloration to escape detection. The two color phases, which vary in their relative numbers according to geography, are not based on age, sex, or season.

---

305 **Great Horned Owl**
*Bubo virginianus*

Description: 25″ (64 cm). W. 4′7″ (1.4 m). A large owl, varying in color from nearly white (in Arctic) to dark brown and gray; mottled and streaked below, setting off the *white throat.* Prominent, *widely spaced ear tufts;* yellow eyes.

Voice: Series of low, sonorous, far-carrying hoots, *hoo, hoo-hoo, hoo, hoo,* with second and third notes shorter than the others.

Habitat: Forests, deserts, open country, swamps, and even city parks.

Nesting: 2 or 3 white eggs on the bare surface of a cliff or cave, or on the ground. In the East, it most often appropriates the unused stick nest of a heron, hawk, or crow.

Range: Resident from Alaska and northern Canada eastward and southward throughout the Americas.

The largest of American "eared" owls, the Great Horned is exceeded in size only by the rare Great Gray Owl. The Great Horned Owl preys on a wide variety of creatures, including grouse and rabbits as well as beetles, lizards, and frogs. It is one of the first birds to nest, laying its eggs as early as late January, even when there is still snow on the ground.

---

## 309 Snowy Owl
*Nyctea scandiaca*

Description: 24″ (61 cm). W. 4′7″ (1.4 m). A big, round-headed owl, ranging in color from nearly *pure white* to white with dark spotting or barring. Female larger and more heavily marked than male.

Voice: Usually silent; on breeding grounds, hoarse croak and shrill whistle.

Habitat: Open country: tundra, dunes, marshes, fields, plains, and airports in winter.

Nesting: 5–8 white eggs on a lining of feathers, mosses, and lichens placed on open tundra.

Range: Breeds in Alaska and northernmost Canada. Winters across continent south to northern United States, irregularly farther south. Also in Eurasia.

This great white owl is a beautiful sight as it perches upright on a fence post or flies over a marsh. Strictly a bird of open country, it is practically never seen in a tree; it sits on the ground, a rooftop, or other exposed resting place. In the Far North where it breeds, it depends largely on lemmings for food. The size of the lemming population periodically changes (due to population explosions and subsequent epidemics), and when lemming numbers decrease the owls must migrate southward to avoid starvation. In southern latitudes, the owls prey on rabbits, waterfowl, and other game, or on dead fish on ocean beaches. They prey on Norway rats in large refuse dumps.

300 **Northern Hawk Owl**
*Surnia ulula*

Description: 15–17″ (38–43 cm). W. 2′9″ (84 cm). Smaller than a crow. A *long-tailed, day-flying owl* that behaves more like a hawk. Barred breast; facial disks have bold black borders.

Voice: Whistling *ki-ki-ki-ki-ki-ki,* like the call of a kestrel.

Habitat: Clearings in boreal coniferous forests and muskeg.

Nesting: 3–7 white eggs in a tree cavity or an abandoned bird's nest, or (rarely) on a cliff.

Range: Resident from Alaska east to Labrador, and south to British Columbia, Newfoundland, and Gaspé Peninsula. May wander farther south in winter. Also in Eurasia.

The Northern Hawk Owl is a fast-flying, diurnal bird. It may often be seen on an exposed perch at the edge of a field or clearing, on the lookout for rodents and small birds. Because it does not depend on any one source of food, it is seldom subject to forced population shifts like other northern predators.

301 **Ferruginous Pygmy-Owl**
**"Ferruginous Owl"**
*Glaucidium brasilianum*

Description: 6½–7″ (17–18 cm). A sparrow-sized, rusty owl. Small round head and *long, finely barred tail,* often cocked at an angle. Especially characteristic are *rusty, faintly cross-barred tail* and streaked flanks. Crown streaked with white; underside streaked with red-brown. White-bordered black eye patch on each side of nape.

Voice: Monotonous, repeated, harsh *poip,* and other whistles.

Habitat: Mesquite or other streamside growth.

Nesting: 3 or 4 white eggs in a tree cavity.

Range: Resident in southern Arizona and New Mexico, and along lower Rio Grande Valley of Texas. Also in American tropics.

The male Ferruginous calls incessantly in spring, at a rate of 90 to 150 times a minute. (One is reported to have called for three solid hours.) This tiny tropical owl is rare and local in the United States, and the small population around Tucson, Arizona, is a great attraction to bird-watchers.

## 302 Elf Owl
*Micrathene whitneyi*

Description: 5½″ (14 cm). A tiny owl with short tail, no ear tufts, yellow eyes; buff with indistinct dark streaks.
Voice: Rapid series of high-pitched notes, higher in the middle.
Habitat: Deserts, dry open woodlands, and streamside thickets with trees.
Nesting: 3 white eggs in deserted woodpecker holes in cacti, oaks, pines, and other trees.
Range: Breeds in southeastern California, southern Arizona, southwestern New Mexico, and Rio Grande Valley of Texas. Winters in Mexico.

When captured, this tiny owl feigns death until sure that all danger has passed. It feeds almost exclusively on insects, catching them in the air or on the ground, but also eats mice and lizards.

## 304 Burrowing Owl
*Speotyto cunicularia*

Description: 9″ (23 cm). A robin-sized, terrestrial owl, short-tailed and long-legged; yellow eyes; no ear tufts. *Face framed in white with blackish collar.*

Voice: Liquid cackling; also a mellow *coo-coooo,* repeated twice.
Habitat: Plains, deserts, fields, and airports.
Nesting: 5–7 white eggs in a long underground burrow lined with grasses, roots, and dung.
Range: Breeds from Canada's southern prairie provinces south to southern California and Texas. Winters in southwestern states. Resident in central and southern Florida. Also in tropical America.

This comical little bird is one of the most diurnal of all owls. It often perches near its hole; when approached too closely, it will bob up and down and finally dive into its burrow rather than take flight. The burrows have usually been abandoned by prairie dogs or pocket gophers, but the owls are quite capable of digging their own.

298 **Barred Owl**
*Strix varia*

Description: 20″ (51 cm). W. 3′8″ (1.1 m). A large, stocky, dark-eyed owl, gray-brown with cross-barring on neck and breast, and streaks on belly; *no ear tufts* and brown eyes.
Voice: A loud barking *hoo, hoo, hoo-hoo; hoo, hoo; hoo, hooo-aw!* and a variety of other barking calls and screams.
Habitat: Low, wet woods and swampy forests.
Nesting: 2–4 white eggs, in an unlined cavity in a hollow tree or, rarely, an abandoned building; sometimes in an old crow's nest.
Range: Resident from British Columbia east to Nova Scotia, and south to northern California, and to Texas and Florida.

This owl is most often seen by those who seek it out in its dark retreat, usually a thick grove of trees in a lowland forest. There it rests quietly during the day, coming out at night to feed on rodents, birds, frogs, and crayfish. If disturbed, it will fly easily from one grove of trees to another. Barred Owls regularly call in the daytime.

---

## 299 Great Gray Owl
*Strix nebulosa*

Description: 24–33″ (61–84 cm). W. 5′ (1.5 m). A huge, dusky gray, earless owl of the North Woods, with yellow eyes, large facial disks, and distinctive black chin spot bordered by white patches resembling a bow tie. Barred Owl is smaller, stockier, and browner, with dark eyes.

Voice: Very deep, booming *whoo,* repeated 10 times or more and gradually descending the scale.

Habitat: Coniferous forests and muskeg.

Nesting: 2–5 white eggs in a bulky nest of sticks in a dense conifer.

Range: Resident in Alaska and across interior Canada south to northern California, northern Wyoming, Minnesota, and Quebec. In winter, wanders rarely southward into northern New England and Great Lakes region. Also in Eurasia.

Like other owls of the Far North, this species hunts during the day, often watching for prey from a low perch. Because it spends much of its time in dense conifers, it is often overlooked. One of the most elusive of owls, the Great Gray was discovered in America by Europeans before they realized that the species also occurs in Europe.

306 **Long-eared Owl**
*Asio otus*

Description: 15″ (38 cm). W. 3′3″ (1 m). A nearly crow-sized owl with *long ear tufts set close together;* heavily mottled brown, with *chestnut facial disks.*

Voice: Soft low hoots, also whistles, whines, shrieks, and cat-like meows. Seldom heard except during breeding time.

Habitat: Deciduous and coniferous forests.

Nesting: 4 or 5 white eggs in a deserted crow, hawk, or squirrel nest.

Range: Breeds from central British Columbia east across southern Mackenzie to Quebec, and south to California, Arkansas, and Virginia. Winters in southern part of breeding range and in southern tier of states. Also in Eurasia.

Although these woodland owls are gregarious in winter, they are so quiet during the day that up to a dozen may inhabit a dense evergreen grove without being detected. They have a tendency to roost near the trunk of a tree, and since they elongate themselves by compressing their feathers, they resemble part of the trunk itself. Only by peering intently upward can one detect the round face and telltale long ear tufts. A good way to locate an owl roost is to search in pine woods for groups of pellets on the ground. These regurgitated bundles of undigested fur and bones provide an excellent indication of the birds' food habits.

297 **Short-eared Owl**
*Asio flammeus*

Description: 16″ (41 cm). A crow-sized, long-winged owl of open country. Tawny-brown with rather heavy streaks below; blackish patch around each eye. Very short ear tufts rarely visible.

Voice: Usually silent; on nesting ground, gives a variety of barks, hisses, and squeals.
Habitat: Freshwater and salt marshes; open grasslands, prairies, dunes; open country generally during migration.
Nesting: 5–7 white eggs in a grass-lined depression on the ground, often concealed in weeds or beneath a bush.
Range: Breeds from Alaska across Canada, and south locally to California, Kansas, and New Jersey. Winters in southern part of breeding range and south throughout United States to Central America. Also in South America and most of Old World.

This owl is most commonly seen late in the afternoon as it begins to move about in preparation for a night of hunting. It can often be identified at a great distance by its habit of hovering; its flight is erratic and bounding. Occasionally several birds may be seen at once, an indication that small rodents are especially numerous below.

307 **Boreal Owl**
*Aegolius funereus*

Description: 9–12″ (23–30 cm). W. 24″ (61 cm). A rare robin-sized owl without ear tufts. Brown with white spots above, rust-streaked below. Similar to Northern Saw-whet Owl but larger, with dark borders on facial disks, *more spotting on upperparts, spotted (not streaked) forehead,* and *yellow (not dark) bill.*
Voice: Rapid series of whistled notes.
Habitat: Boreal coniferous forests and muskeg.
Nesting: 4–6 white eggs placed in a woodpecker hole or other tree cavity or in the abandoned nest of another bird.
Range: Breeds from Alaska and Yukon east across Canada to Labrador and Newfoundland, and south to northern British Columbia, Colorado (in Rocky Mountains), southern Manitoba, Ontario, and New Brunswick. In winter

wanders rarely south to northern tier of states. Also in Eurasia.

This small, secretive owl is considered one of the rarest winter visitors from the North. Its retiring habits cause it to be overlooked, and it is easily confused with its more common relative the Northern Saw-whet Owl. It is entirely nocturnal, spending the day concealed in dense spruce or in a hollow tree. It preys mainly on rodents.

## 303 Northern Saw-whet Owl
*Aegolius acadicus*

Description: 7″ (18 cm). A very small, earless, yellow-eyed owl; brown above, with white streaks on forehead, dark bill, and short tail. Juveniles are chocolate-brown above, buff below, with white triangle on forehead. See Boreal Owl.

Voice: Usually silent; in late winter and spring, utters a monotonous series of tooting whistles.

Habitat: Coniferous woodlands; in winter, also in evergreen thickets in parks, gardens, and estates; also isolated pines.

Nesting: 5 or 6 white eggs placed without a nest lining in a deserted woodpecker hole or natural cavity.

Range: Breeds from southeastern Alaska east across central Canada to Nova Scotia, and south to southern California, Arizona, Illinois, North Carolina (in mountains), and Connecticut. Winters in breeding range and south to Arkansas and North Carolina.

Northern Saw-whet Owls are almost entirely nocturnal, spending the day roosting quietly in dense foliage. At such times, they are extraordinarily tame and may be approached closely or even handled. At night this tiny owl becomes a rapacious hunter, preying on mice and other small rodents.

## Family Caprimulgidae
Nightjars

83 species: Worldwide. Eight species breed in North America. These mottled, cryptically colored birds spend most of their time resting on the ground, but they feed on flying insects at dusk or at night. They have long wings and short bills, with wide mouth openings for catching insects. Some American species, such as the Whip-poor-will, have loud rhythmic calls, but others have nasal or buzzy notes.

### 296 Lesser Nighthawk
*Chordeiles acutipennis*

**Description:** 8–9″ (20–23 cm). Similar to Common Nighthawk but smaller, with white wing patch (buff in female) nearer tip of wing, visible in flight. Both sexes have buff cast to underparts. Male's throat white; female's buff. Whereas Common Nighthawk hunts and calls from high up, Lesser Nighthawk flies low and utters no loud aerial calls.

**Voice:** A soft, sustained, tremolo whirring; very difficult to locate.

**Habitat:** Dry, open scrublands; desert valleys; prairies and pastures.

**Nesting:** 2 light gray, spotted eggs on open ground.

**Range:** Breeds from central California, Arizona, and parts of Nevada, Utah, New Mexico, and Texas southward. Winters in tropics.

The Lesser is more nocturnal than the Common Nighthawk and hunts its insect prey by flying low above the canopy of trees or the brush and grass of open plains. During courtship flight display, the male pursues the female close to the ground, flashing his white throat as he calls.

295 **Common Nighthawk**
*Chordeiles minor*

Description: 10″ (25 cm). W. 23″ 58 cm). Jay-sized; usually seen in flight. Dark with long pointed wings and *white patch on outer wing;* square-tipped or slightly notched tail. Flight high and fluttery. Perches motionless and lengthwise on branches. Male has white throat patch and white subterminal tail bar. Female has buffy throat patch and no tail bar.

Voice: Loud, nasal, buzzy *peent* or *pee-yah*, heard primarily at dusk.
Habitat: Open country generally; also cities and towns.
Nesting: 2 creamy or olive-gray, finely and densely speckled eggs, laid on soil, rocks, logs, or rooftop gravel.
Range: Breeds from southern Yukon east to northern Ontario and Nova Scotia, and south through most of United States. Winters in tropics.

This bird's name is somewhat inappropriate, since it is not strictly nocturnal, often flying in sunlight, and it is not a hawk, although it does hawk, catching flying insects on the wing. On its breeding grounds, the male does a power dive and then, as it swerves upward, makes a booming sound with its wings. Its capacity to consume insects is prodigious. Analysis of stomach contents has shown that in a single day one bird captured more than 500 mosquitoes and another ate 2,175 flying ants.

294 **Antillean Nighthawk**
*Chordeiles gundlachii*

Description: 9½″ (24 cm). Similar to Common Nighthawk, but slightly smaller and paler. Best distinguished by voice.
Voice: A dry *killy-ka-dick,* often repeated.
Habitat: Open country.

Nesting: 2 whitish to olive eggs, with dark blotches, laid on bare ground.

Range: Breeds in Florida Keys, wandering to southern peninsular Florida in summer. Probably winters in South America. Also in West Indies.

Once considered a form of the Common Nighthawk, this West Indian species barely reaches our area in the Florida Keys, where it has increased in recent decades because of the clearing of forests.

---

**290 Pauraque**
**"Common Pauraque"**
*Nyctidromus albicollis*

Description: 12″ (30 cm). Larger than the Whip-poor-will. Mottled brown. Brown body; wings and tail show white bands in flight, especially conspicuous in male. Identified mainly by voice.

Voice: A burry *pur-wheeer,* slurred downward and uttered at night.

Habitat: Semi-open scrub country with thickets, and light woodland clearings.

Nesting: 2 pinkish-buff, brown-blotched eggs on bare ground near a bush or a tree.

Range: Resident in extreme southern Texas. Also in American tropics.

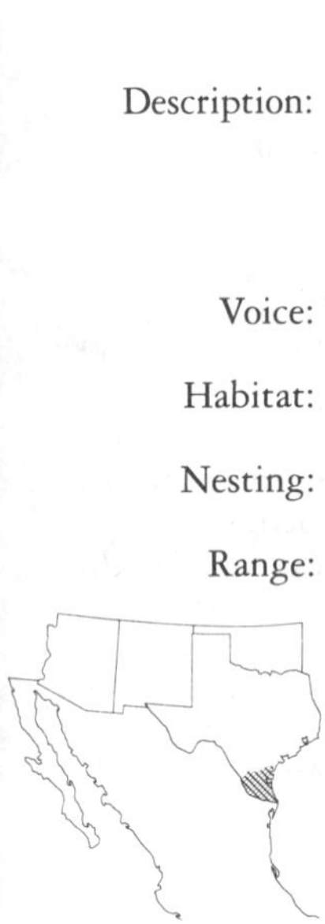

Pauraques are virtually impossible to see on the ground in daylight because they match dead leaves and twigs almost perfectly. But when one is flushed from the side of the road by car headlights, the white wing patch, like that of a nighthawk, may be seen distinctly, and the eyes shine a brilliant red. Like other nightjars, Pauraques have an enormously wide gape that enables them to catch large moths, beetles, crickets, and fireflies on the wing at night.

291 **Common Poorwill**
*Phalaenoptilus nuttallii*

Description: 7–8½″ (18–22 cm). Our smallest nightjar. Mottled gray-brown with *no white mark on wings;* whitish collar separates black throat from mottled underparts. Dark outer tail feathers are tipped with white, more conspicuously in male; *tail is rounded.*
Voice: A mellow *poor-will.*
Habitat: Deserts, chaparral, sagebrush, and other arid uplands.
Nesting: 2 pinkish-white eggs on bare ground.
Range: Breeds from southeastern British Columbia, Alberta, and Montana south throughout western United States, and east to central Kansas. Winters in southwestern states and Mexico.

Practically unique among birds, the Common Poorwill has been discovered hibernating in the desert in California, surviving long cold spells in a torpid condition, without food and with its body temperature lowered almost to that of its surroundings. These nightjars are seen most often sitting on roads at night.

293 **Chuck-will's-widow**
*Caprimulgus carolinensis*

Description: 12″ (30 cm). Pigeon-sized. Larger than the Whip-poor-will. Buff-brown body, *brown chin.*
Voice: A mellow *chuck-will's-widow,* repeated over and over, the *chuck* deep and low, the rest of the call whistled.
Habitat: Open woodlands and clearings near agricultural country.
Nesting: 2 creamy-white eggs, with purple and brown markings, on bare ground or dead leaves.
Range: Breeds from Kansas, Indiana, and Long Island south to Gulf Coast states. Winters chiefly in tropics, but a few winter in Florida and along Gulf Coast.

The "Chuck" is nocturnal and rarely seen during the day. When flushed, it flies off a short distance, then drops to the ground again. These birds hunt close to the ground, catching flying insects such as moths, beetles, and winged ants and termites. They have occasionally been reported to prey on warblers and sparrows.

---

## 292 Whip-poor-will
*Caprimulgus vociferus*

Description: 10″ (25 cm). Robin-sized. A leaf-brown, strictly nocturnal bird with *black throat.* Male has *broad white tips on outer tail feathers;* visible in flight. Female has all-brown tail. Chuck-will's-widow is larger and buffier.

Voice: A loud, rhythmic *whip-poor-will,* repeated over and over at night.

Habitat: Dry open woodlands near fields.

Nesting: 2 white eggs, scrawled with gray and brown, placed on ground among dead leaves.

Range: Breeds from Saskatchewan east to Maritime Provinces and south to Kansas, northern Louisiana, and northern Georgia, and in Arizona, New Mexico, and western Texas. Winters from Florida and Gulf Coast southward.

The Whip-poor-will is rarely seen because it sleeps by day on the forest floor, its coloration matching the dead leaves. At night, its eyes reflect ruby red in car headlights. It feeds exclusively on moths and other night insects caught on the wing.

## Family Apodidae
Swifts

99 species: Worldwide. Four species breed in North America, only one in the East. Members of this well-known family are aerial feeders, catching insects on the wing. They have long wings, short tails, and wide mouth openings. Swifts never perch but cling to vertical surfaces such as the walls of caves, buildings, and trees. These birds get their name from the fact that they are among the speediest of all birds. The sexes are alike, and colors run from drab grays and browns to black and white. The eggs are pure white, and clutches run from three to six eggs.

---

### 362 Chimney Swift
*Chaetura pelagica*

Description: 4¾–5½″ (12–14 cm). Sparrow-sized. Stubby, brownish-gray body (appearing black in flight) with very short tail; long, narrow, curved wings.
Voice: Loud chattering twitters.
Habitat: Breeds and roosts in chimneys; feeds entirely on the wing over forests, open country, and towns.
Nesting: 4 or 5 white eggs in a nest made of twigs cemented together with saliva and fastened to the inner wall of a chimney or, rarely, in a cave or hollow tree.
Range: Breeds from southeastern Saskatchewan east to southern Quebec and Nova Scotia, and south to Gulf states. Winters in tropics.

Members of this family are among the fastest fliers in the bird world. Swifts spend all of their daylight hours on the wing and come to rest only at evening. They feed exclusively on flying insects. They drink water and bathe by dipping into the water of a pond or river as they fly over it. Since they never perch, they

gather twigs in flight, snapping them off with their bills as they pass. Sometimes a twig fails to break and the bird is tossed backward, only to return again. These swifts gather in communal roosts in air shafts or large chimneys, often whirling in a huge circle as they funnel down for the night.

## FAMILY TROCHILIDAE
Hummingbirds

320 species: This strictly American family is most numerous in South America, especially in the Andes. Only 14 species breed regularly in North America, of which only the Ruby-throated is widespread in the East. Among the most colorful of birds, hummingbirds have glittering, iridescent plumage. They are the only birds known to fly backward, and like the related swifts, they do not perch while feeding. They hover in front of a flower and sip nectar, and pick off insects while on the wing. They lay two white eggs in a soft, very compact nest made of down.

### 579 Buff-bellied Hummingbird
*Amazilia yucatanensis*

Description: 4½″ (11 cm). Green above with glittering green throat, brown tail, and *tawny or rich buff belly. Bill long and thin, bright orange-red with black tip.*
Voice: Shrill squeaks.
Habitat: Woodland borders and thickets.
Nesting: 2 white eggs in woven nest of plant fibers decorated with lichens, saddled to the limb of a tree or shrub.
Range: Breeds in Lower Rio Grande Valley of Texas. Rare in winter there and elsewhere along Gulf Coast.

This mainly Mexican species may be found among dense tangled thickets and vines in light, open woodlands. It also feeds on flowers in gardens. Unlike most other hummers north of Mexico, the sexes are alike in color. It usually leaves the Rio Grande area in winter and retires southward into adjacent Mexico until the following spring.

580, 582 **Ruby-throated Hummingbird**
*Archilochus colubris*

Description: 3½″ (9 cm). Tiny. Needle-like bill. Metallic green above, white below; male has *brilliant, iridescent red throat.* Immature male lacks red throat. Female green above, with white throat and breast, buff sides, and white-tipped outer tail feathers.

Voice: Mouse-like, twittering squeaks.

Habitat: Suburban gardens, parks, and woodlands.

Nesting: 2 white eggs in a woven nest of plant down held together with spider silk and covered with lichens. Nest is saddled to the branch of a tree, usually in a forest clearing.

Range: The only hummingbird that breeds east of Mississippi River. Breeds from southern Canada to Gulf Coast. Winters mainly in tropics, rarely on Gulf Coast.

These diminutive birds are particularly attracted to tubular red flowers such as salvia and trumpet creeper, as well as bee balm, petunia, jewelweed, and thistle. Hummers are also attracted to artificial feeders—red glass tubes filled with sweet liquid. With their remarkable powers of flight, they are the only birds that can fly backward as well as hover in one spot like insects. They are constantly in motion, perching on twigs or wires only briefly to rest and to survey their surroundings, or when they are at the nest. During courtship, the female sits quietly on a perch while the male displays in a pendulum dance, swinging in a wide arc and buzzing loudly with each dip.

581 **Black-chinned Hummingbird**
*Archilochus alexandri*

Description: 3¼–3¾" (8–10 cm). Male green above with iridescent black chin, underlined by *violet-purple throat band.* Females and young birds not distinguishable in field from Ruby-throated Hummingbird.
Voice: A low *tup.*
Habitat: Woodlands, canyons with thickets, and orchards.
Nesting: 2 white eggs in a nest of fluffy plant wool and lichens woven together with spiderweb, placed in a shrub or low tree.
Range: Breeds from British Columbia south throughout West to Mexico and central Texas. Winters in Mexico.

The male Black-chinned, like all hummingbirds, maintains a mating and feeding territory in spring. He courts his female with a dazzling aerial display involving a pendulum-like flight pattern. When mating interest wanes, the male often takes up residence elsewhere, near a good food supply. Later, when the blooming season and insect swarming subside, the birds move south.

583 **Rufous Hummingbird**
*Selasphorus rufus*

Description: 3½–4" (9–10 cm). Male has *bright rufous upperparts* and flanks, and iridescent orange-red throat. Female green above, with rufous tinge on rump and flanks, and with much rufous in tail. Female Ruby-throated and Black-chinned similar, but lack rufous on rump and flanks.

Voice: An abrupt, high-pitched *zeee;* various thin squealing notes.

Habitat: Mountain meadows, forest edges; during migration and in winter, frequents gardens with hummingbird feeding stations.

Nesting: 2 white eggs in a lichen-covered cup of plant down and spiderweb attached to a horizontal branch.

Range: Breeds from southeastern Alaska, British Columbia, southwestern Alberta, and western Montana south to Washington, Oregon, Idaho, and northern California. Winters mainly in Mexico. Occurs in small numbers along Gulf Coast during migration and in winter.

This species is known in eastern North America mainly as a scarce migrant and winter visitor to Louisiana and Florida. While in that area it feeds chiefly on the flowers of hibiscus and salvia, which often bloom all winter long. A few birds generally spend the winter but may disappear abruptly when the first severe cold spell occurs; it is not known whether these birds succumb to the cold or quickly move farther south.

---

## Family Alcedinidae
Kingfishers

94 species: Chiefly tropical regions in the Old World. Three species breed in North America. Most kingfishers have large, powerful bills, and many are brilliantly colored, but North American species are relatively plain, although conspicuously crested. These birds dig tunnels into earthen banks where they lay their white eggs. As their name suggests, they feed on fish, but many tropical species also catch insects and lizards on land.

## Ringed Kingfisher
*Ceryle torquata*

Description: 13″ (33 cm). Pigeon-sized. Similar to Belted Kingfisher but larger, and with more chestnut on belly. Bushy crest and large, dagger-shaped bill. Blue-gray above, *chestnut below with white collar.* Female similar, but has gray band across upper breast.

Voice: Harsh rattle, louder than that of Belted Kingfisher. Also a loud *kleck.*

Habitat: Tree-lined rivers, streams, and lakes.

Nesting: 5–7 white eggs in a burrow in a sandbank.

Range: Resident from extreme southern Texas to southern South America.

The Ringed Kingfisher is the largest of the three species of kingfishers in the United States, where it is found only on the lower Rio Grande in Texas. Its habits are like those of the Belted Kingfisher.

## 591 Belted Kingfisher
*Ceryle alcyon*

Description: 13″ (33 cm). Pigeon-sized. *Bushy crest; dagger-like bill;* blue-gray above, white below. Male has blue-gray breast band; female similar, but also has *chestnut belly band.*

Voice: Loud, penetrating rattle, given on the wing and when perched.

Habitat: Rivers, lakes, and saltwater estuaries.

Nesting: 5–8 white eggs in an unlined chamber at the end of a tunnel up to 8′ (2.5 m) long, dug in a sand or gravel bank.

Range: Breeds from Alaska eastward across southern Canada and south throughout most of United States. Winters on Pacific Coast north to southeastern Alaska, and from Southwest north to Great Lakes and along Atlantic Coast to New England.

Kingfishers often hover like terns over water where a fish is visible, then dive vertically for the prey. In addition, they may eat crabs, crayfish, salamanders, lizards, mice, and insects. Kingfishers often patrol a regular beat along a stream or lakeshore, stopping at favorite exposed perches along the way.

590 **Green Kingfisher**
*Chloroceryle americana*

Description: 8″ (20 cm). Starling-sized. Dark glossy green above, white below; *male has broad rufous breast band, female has green breast band.* Both sexes have white collar.
Voice: An insect-like buzz. Also low clicking notes.
Habitat: Woodland streams and pools.
Nesting: 4–6 white eggs in a cavity at the end of a burrow dug in a sandy bank.
Range: Resident from extreme southern Texas south into tropics.

Smallest of the three species found in the United States, these birds may be observed in southern Texas near forest-fringed pools and streams of clear water, where they sit for long periods on a limb overhanging water until they spot a minnow or other small fish. They then plunge into the water after their prey. At other times, when at a considerable distance from water, they feed on small lizards or grasshoppers.

## Family Picidae
Woodpeckers

215 species: Widespread but absent from Australia, New Guinea, and Madagascar. Twenty-two species breed in North America, and one, the Ivory-billed Woodpecker (*Campephilus principalis*), recently became extinct.

Woodpeckers have sharp, chisel-like bills, which they use for drilling and digging into trees. They cling to the bark of trees with their strong claws, using their stiff tails as props. Most nest in holes in trees. The flight of most woodpeckers is undulating.

## 370 Lewis' Woodpecker
*Melanerpes lewis*

Description: 10½–11½″ (27–29 cm). Smaller than a flicker. Metallic *greenish black above; gray collar and breast; pinkish-red belly;* dark red face framed with greenish black. Sexes alike. Flight is crow-like, not undulating

Voice: Usually silent, but occasionally gives a low churring note.

Habitat: Open pine-oak woodlands, oak or cottonwood groves in grasslands, ponderosa pine country.

Nesting: 6–8 white eggs in a cavity in a dead stump or tree limb, often at a considerable height. Nests in loose colonies.

Range: Breeds from southern British Columbia and Alberta south to central California, northern Arizona, and northern New Mexico. Winters from southern British Columbia and Oregon to Colorado and south to northern Mexico; wanders east to Great Plains.

Unlike most woodpeckers, Lewis' does not peck at wood for food and is seen more often on top of a fence post than clinging to it vertically. As with the Acorn Woodpecker (*Melanerpes formicivorus*), its main method of getting food is catching flying insects; both species also store acorns and other nuts for winter, and sometimes damage fruit orchards. Lewis' is the common woodpecker of mountain ranchlands, and some ranchers call it the "Crow Woodpecker" because of its dark color, large size, and slow flight.

366 **Red-headed Woodpecker**
*Melanerpes erythrocephalus*

Description: 10″ (25 cm). *Whole head red,* wings and tail bluish black, with *large white patch on each wing;* white underparts; white rump, conspicuous in flight. Immature resembles adult, but has brown head, 2 dark bars on white wing patch.

Voice: A loud *churr-churr* and *yarrow-yarrow-yarrow.*

Habitat: Open country, farms, rural roads, open park-like woodlands, and golf courses.

Nesting: 5 white eggs placed without nest lining in a cavity in a tree, telephone pole, or fence post.

Range: Breeds from Saskatchewan, Manitoba, and Quebec south to Florida and Gulf Coast. Scarce in northeastern states. Winters in southern part of breeding range.

These woodpeckers are fond of open agricultural country with groves of dead and dying trees, particularly orchards. They often fly-catch, swooping low across a highway or along the shoulder of a road after flying insects. They store nuts and acorns, hiding them in holes and crevices. Red-headed Woodpeckers frequently are driven off by aggressive European Starlings, which occupy their nest holes, and by the removal of dead trees.

372 **Golden-fronted Woodpecker**
*Melanerpes aurifrons*

Description: 9½″ (24 cm). Barred with black and white above and buff below, like Red-bellied Woodpecker, but male has red restricted to cap; nape orange; forecrown yellow; female lacks red but has orange nape.

Voice: Loud *churrrr.* Call a burry *chuck-chuck-chuck.*

Habitat: Open woods in dry country and river bottoms with trees.

Nesting: 4 or 5 white eggs in holes in mesquite trees, poles, and posts.

Range: Resident in southwestern Oklahoma and central Texas.

This familiar woodpecker is common in the parks and shade trees of Texas towns and cities. A southwestern species, it is a close relative of and resembles the Red-bellied Woodpecker found mainly in the Southeast. The species name *aurifrons* is Latin for "gold-fronted."

## 367 Red-bellied Woodpecker

*Melanerpes carolinus*

Description: 10″ (25 cm). *Barred black and white* above; pale buff below and on face; sexes similar except that male has red crown and nape, female red nape only. Reddish patch on lower abdomen is seldom visible in the field.

Voice: *Chuck-chuck-chuck,* descending in pitch. Also a loud, often repeated *churrrr.*

Habitat: Open and swampy woodlands; comes into parks during migration and to feeders in winter.

Nesting: 4 or 5 white eggs in a tree cavity, often at edge of woodlands.

Range: Breeds from South Dakota, Great Lakes, and southern New England south to Gulf Coast and Florida. Northernmost birds sometimes migrate south for winter.

A common woodpecker over much of the South, the Red-bellied is scarcer farther north but has expanded its breeding range northward in recent decades. Like most woodpeckers, it is beneficial, consuming large numbers of wood-boring beetles as well as grasshoppers, ants, and other insect pests. It also feeds on acorns, beechnuts, and wild fruits. It is one of the woodpeckers that habitually stores food

## 364 Yellow-bellied Sapsucker
*Sphyrapicus varius*

Description: 8½″ (22 cm). A furtive woodpecker mottled with off-white and black; male has *red crown and throat;* female has only red crown. Both sexes dull yellowish below. Immatures dull brown. In all plumages, distinctive mark is *conspicuous white wing stripe,* visible both at rest and in flight.

Voice: Mewing and whining notes.

Habitat: Young, open deciduous or mixed forests with clearings; during migration, parks, yards, and gardens.

Nesting: 5 or 6 white eggs in a tree cavity excavated by the birds.

Range: Breeds from central Canada to Newfoundland, and south to British Columbia, North Dakota, Missouri, and central New England, and in mountains to North Carolina. Winters from Missouri east to New Jersey, and south to Florida and Texas; also in tropical America.

This species, at least on migration, is the quietest of the woodpeckers; aside from a few squeaks and whines, it is mainly silent. It is also the least conspicuous, hitching around to the opposite side of the tree trunk when approached. Sapsuckers get their name from their habit of boring holes into the cambium layer or inner bark, letting the sap exude and run down the trunk. The birds wipe up or suck the oozing sap with their brush-like tongues. They return again and again to the same tree and also consume the insects attracted to the sap. Unfortunately, sapsucker holes damage trees and sometimes provide points of entry for fungus and other tree diseases.

365 **Ladder-backed Woodpecker**
*Picoides scalaris*

Description: 7″ (18 cm). Barred black-and-white back, strong *black-and-white facial pattern forming a triangle;* male has red cap, female has black cap.
Voice: A sharp *pik,* similar to that of Downy Woodpecker; also a descending whinny.
Habitat: Arid areas with thickets and trees.
Nesting: 4 or 5 white eggs in holes of trees, cacti, poles, and posts.
Range: Resident of southwestern United States from California, Nevada, Utah, Colorado, Oklahoma, and Texas south into tropics.

Within most of its range, the Ladder-back is the only small woodpecker so marked. The most numerous of its family in Texas, it replaces the Downy in more arid areas. Familiar and trusting, it frequents ranches, village yards, and parks.

363, 378 **Downy Woodpecker**
*Picoides pubescens*

Description: 6″ (15 cm). A sparrow-sized woodpecker. Black and white, with small red patch on nape in males. Similar to Hairy Woodpecker, but smaller and with short stubby bill.
Voice: A quiet *pik*; also a descending rattle.
Habitat: Woodlands, parks, and gardens.
Nesting: 4 or 5 white eggs in a hole in a tree.
Range: Resident from Alaska across Canada, and south throughout United States except Southwest.

This is the smallest, tamest, and most abundant of our eastern woodpeckers. It comes readily to suet feeders in suburban yards and is a familiar sight in city parks and in roadside shade trees and shrubbery. It is often seen in the mixed flocks of chickadees, nuthatches, creepers, and kinglets that gather in the woods during migration and winter.

## 369 Hairy Woodpecker
*Picoides villosus*

Description: 9″ (23 cm). A robin-sized woodpecker. Black and white with *unspotted white back and long bill;* male has red head patch. Like most woodpeckers, has undulating flight. See Downy Woodpecker.
Voice: A sharp, distinctive *peek,* louder than that of Downy Woodpecker; also a loud rattle on one pitch.
Habitat: Deciduous forest; more widespread in winter and during migration.
Nesting: 4 white eggs in a hole in a tree.
Range: Resident from Alaska and across Canada south throughout United States to Gulf of Mexico. Some northern birds migrate south for winter.

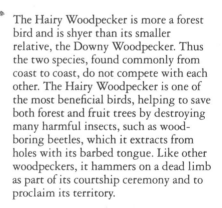

The Hairy Woodpecker is more a forest bird and is shyer than its smaller relative, the Downy Woodpecker. Thus the two species, found commonly from coast to coast, do not compete with each other. The Hairy Woodpecker is one of the most beneficial birds, helping to save both forest and fruit trees by destroying many harmful insects, such as wood-boring beetles, which it extracts from holes with its barbed tongue. Like other woodpeckers, it hammers on a dead limb as part of its courtship ceremony and to proclaim its territory.

## 377 Red-cockaded Woodpecker
*Picoides borealis*

Description: 8″ (20 cm). Cap and nape black; *large white cheek patch;* back barred black and white; white below with black spots on sides and flanks. Male has small, hard-to-see red spot behind eye.

Voice: A nuthatch-like *yank-yank.* Also a rattling scold note.
Habitat: Pine forests, especially yellow and longleaf pines.
Nesting: 4 white eggs in a tree cavity, usually in a live tree with decayed heartwood.
Range: Resident from southeastern Oklahoma and Maryland to Gulf Coast and central Florida.

The endangered Red-cockaded Woodpecker is one of the least known of the family. Although widespread in the Southeast, it is local and restricted to mature pine woods that contain trees whose heartwood has been softened by fungus, where the bird digs its nest cavity. Much less noisy and conspicuous than other woodpeckers and therefore seldom noticed, it travels in family groups of four to six. This woodpecker also has the peculiar trait of digging holes in trees adjacent to its nest, allowing pine gum or resin to ooze from the holes. Such signs of pitch may be evidence of its presence.

374, 376 **Three-toed Woodpecker**
**"Northern Three-toed Woodpecker"**
*Picoides tridactylus*

Description: 8½" (22 cm). A starling-sized woodpecker. Similar to Black-backed but smaller, with shorter bill, and *back barred black and white.* Sexes differ as in that species.
Voice: A soft *pik,* similar to call of Downy Woodpecker.
Habitat: Coniferous forests in boreal zone, especially where burned over, logged, or swampy.
Nesting: 4 white eggs in a tree hole. The nest holes of both three-toed woodpeckers are beveled on the lower side of the entrance to form a sort of doorstep for the birds.
Range: Resident of Alaska and Canada to

extreme northern United States, and in West to mountains of Arizona and New Mexico.

In the southern and eastern portions of its range, the Three-toed Woodpecker is less numerous than the Black-backed, but its range extends farther south in the Rockies. It is also more sedentary, rarely moving far from its home range.

373, 375 **Black-backed Woodpecker**
**"Black-backed Three-toed Woodpecker"**
*Picoides arcticus*

Description: 9″ (23 cm). A robin-sized woodpecker. *Solid black back,* barred flanks, white below. Male has *yellow crown;* female has solid *black crown.* See Three-toed Woodpecker.

Voice: A sharp fast *kyik,* and a scolding rattle.

Habitat: Coniferous forests in the boreal zone, especially where burned over, logged, or swampy.

Nesting: 4 white eggs in a cavity excavated in a tree, often rather close to the ground.

Range: Resident of Alaska and Canada to northernmost United States and to mountains of California, Wyoming, and South Dakota in West.

This and the Three-toed Woodpecker are the most northerly of the family. Both are rather tame. The Black-backed, found only in North America, is the more southerly. It is also somewhat more numerous, although neither of these birds is common anywhere. They visit dead and dying trees, scaling off bits of loose bark with vigorous sideways movements of the bill to get at the borers and beetle larvae underneath.

## 371 Northern Flicker including "Yellow-shafted Flicker" and "Red-shafted Flicker"

*Colaptes auratus*

Description: 12″ (30 cm). A large brownish woodpecker. *Brown back* with dark bars and spots, *whitish or buff below with black spots, black crescent* on breast, and *white rump* in flight. Eastern birds ("Yellow-shafted Flicker") have *red patch on nape and yellow wing linings; male has black "mustache."* Western birds ("Red-shafted Flicker") lack nape patch and have *salmon-pink wing linings;* males have red "mustache." These forms hybridize in mid-continent, where numerous intermediates can be found.

Voice: A loud, repeated *flicker* or *wicka-wicka-wicka*; also a loud *kleeer.*

Habitat: Open country with trees; parks and large gardens.

Nesting: 6–8 white eggs in a tree cavity, power pole, or birdhouse.

Range: Resident across continent from Alaska to Newfoundland, and south to southern Florida and Gulf Coast; also in Mexico. Northernmost birds are migratory.

Flickers are the only brown-backed woodpeckers in the East, and the only woodpeckers in North America that commonly feed on the ground, searching for ants and beetle larvae on lawns or even sidewalks. During courtship and to proclaim their territory, flickers hammer on dead limbs or tin roofs. On the Great Plains, the "Yellow-shafted" and "Red-shafted" forms meet and interbreed; they were formerly considered two species.

## 368 Pileated Woodpecker

*Dryocopus pileatus*

Description: 17″ (43 cm). A crow-sized woodpecker. Black with white neck stripes, conspicuous white wing linings, and prominent *red crest.* "Mustache" is red in male, black in female.

Voice: A loud, flicker-like *cuk-cuk-cuk-cuk-cuk,* rising and then falling in pitch and volume.

Habitat: Mature forests and borders.

Nesting: 4 white eggs in a tree cavity.

Range: Resident from British Columbia east across southern Canada to Nova Scotia, south to northern California, southern Idaho, eastern North Dakota, central Texas, and Florida.

Despite its size, this elegant woodpecker is often shy and hard to observe. Obtaining a close view of one usually requires careful stalking. Although primarily a forest bird, the "Logcock" has recently become adapted to civilization and has become relatively numerous even on the outskirts of large cities, where its presence is most easily detected by its loud, ringing call and by its large, characteristically rectangular excavations in trees.

---

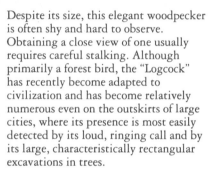

## Family Tyrannidae
Tyrant Flycatchers

416 species: An exclusively New World family, with by far the greatest number of its species in South America. In North America no fewer than 35 species breed. With few exceptions, the sexes are alike. These large-headed birds characteristically sit on wires and exposed branches waiting for flying insect prey. The flycatchers then dart out, grab the insect, and usually return to the very same spot before eating the insect. Other species glean foliage as warblers or vireos do; still others, such as the Rose-throated Becard, are fruit eaters. Species in the genera *Myiarchus* and *Empidonax* look much alike and are best identified by voice.

565 **Northern Beardless-Tyrannulet**
**"Beardless Flycatcher"**
*Camptostoma imberbe*

Description: 4″ (10 cm). A nondescript, dull-colored bird with a tiny bill. Olive-gray above with pale buff wing bars; whitish below with dusky throat and breast.

Voice: A thin *tee-tee-tee-tee-tee,* loudest in the middle. Also 3 long notes followed by a trill.

Habitat: Low thorn scrub, especially mesquite thickets and woodland borders.

Nesting: 2 or 3 white eggs, speckled with brown, in a globular nest of plant fibers; nest has a side entrance.

Range: Breeds in southeastern Arizona and southernmost Texas. Many birds migrate into Mexico for the winter. Also in tropics.

This tiny bird, the smallest flycatcher in the United States, lacks the stout bristles at the base of the bill that are present in most members of its family; hence its name. Instead of fly-catching on the wing, it looks and acts like a kinglet or small vireo, hopping among twigs and branches in search of insects.

---

554 **Olive-sided Flycatcher**
*Contopus borealis*

Description: 7½″ (19 cm). Large billed and heavy headed; deep olive-drab with dark sides of breast and flanks separated by *white down the center of breast;* white feather tufts protrude from lower back at base of tail; tail broad and prominently notched.

Voice: Song a distinctive and emphatic *quick-three-beers.* Call a loud *pip-pip-pip.*

Habitat: Boreal spruce and fir forests, usually near openings, burns, ponds, and bogs.

Nesting: 3 brown-spotted buff eggs in a twig nest lined with lichens, mosses, and grasses, placed near the end of a branch among the foliage well up in an evergreen tree.

Range: Breeds in northern portions of Alaska east across Canada to northern New England, and south to mountains of California, Arizona, and New Mexico, and to northern New York and New England. Winters in tropics.

This flycatcher almost always perches at or very near the tops of the tallest trees, in an exposed position on dead branches. Analysis of stomach contents shows that everything it feeds on is winged; it eats no caterpillars, spiders, or other larvae.

## 564 Western Wood-Pewee
*Contopus sordidulus*

Description: 6½″ (17 cm). A sparrow-sized flycatcher, dull olive-gray above, slightly paler below, with 2 whitish wing bars. Eastern Wood-Pewee extremely similar, but generally less dark below; two species best distinguished by voice. *Empidonax* flycatchers are smaller and usually have noticeable eye ring.

Voice: A harsh, nasal *pee-eeer,* very different from the sweet *peee-ah weee* of Eastern Wood-Pewee.

Habitat: Open woodlands and woodland edges; orchards.

Nesting: 3 or 4 white eggs, spotted with brown, in a shallow saucer of grass fastened to a horizontal branch.

Range: Breeds from eastern Alaska, Mackenzie, and Manitoba south through western United States. Winters in tropics.

This species is generally found in more open, park-like woodlands than the Eastern Wood-Pewee and is thus more readily observed. In a few areas along the western edge of the Great Plains, the two pewees occur together without interbreeding—conclusive evidence that, despite their great similarity, they are distinct species.

563 **Eastern Wood-Pewee**
*Contopus virens*

Description: 6½″ (17 cm). Almost identical to Western Wood-Pewee, and best distinguished by voice. *Empidonax* flycatchers are smaller and usually have noticeable eye ring.

Voice: A plaintive *pee-ah-weee* or *pee-weee,* falling in pitch on last note.

Habitat: Forests, open woodlands, orchards, and shade trees in parks and along roadsides.

Nesting: 3 or 4 creamy-white, brown-dotted eggs in finely woven, cup-shaped nest made of vegetable fiber and covered with lichens, saddled to a horizontal limb and blending in with the branch.

Range: Breeds from south-central and southeastern Canada to Gulf Coast and central Florida. Winters in tropics.

Eastern Wood-Pewees are more often heard than seen because of their dull coloration and because they frequent the dense upper canopy of the forest.

---

551 **Yellow-bellied Flycatcher**
*Empidonax flaviventris*

Description: 5½″ (14 cm). A very small flycatcher, olive-green above, yellowish below, including throat, with 2 white wing bars and yellowish eye ring. Other flycatchers of genus *Empidonax* (Acadian, Alder, Willow, and Least) have more whitish throats, underparts, and eye rings.

Voice: On breeding grounds, a flat *chilk* or *killic;* also a rising 2-note whistle, *per-wee?*

Habitat: Bogs and moist thickets in northern coniferous forests; on migration, in second-growth woodlands.

Nesting: 3 or 4 whitish eggs, with brown spots, in a nest of moss and rootlets on the ground.

Range: Breeds from central Canada and

Newfoundland south to Great Lakes region, northern New York, northern New England, and Maritime Provinces. Winters from Mexico to Panama.

This retiring little flycatcher spends most of its time on migration in dense thickets and so is easily overlooked. With its yellowish throat, underparts, and eye ring, it is the easiest of the eastern *Empidonax* flycatchers to identify.

---

553 **Acadian Flycatcher**
*Empidonax virescens*

Description: 6″ (15 cm). Olive green above, whitish or sometimes yellow below (especially on flanks and belly), with distinct white eye ring. Identified chiefly by voice and habitat.

Voice: An emphatic 2-note *flee-see* or *peet-seet!* with the second syllable accented and higher pitched, uttered on the breeding grounds and occasionally on migration.

Habitat: Beech and maple or hemlock forests, usually under the canopy but also in clearings; often in wooded ravines.

Nesting: 3 or 4 brown-spotted buff eggs in a woven nest of plant fibers in a bush or tree, sometimes over a stream.

Range: Breeds from southern Minnesota east through southern New England, south to Gulf Coast and central Florida. Winters in tropics.

The Acadian Flycatcher and its relatives in the genus *Empidonax* are difficult to distinguish, but in much of the South the Acadian is the only breeding species; between June and August, any *Empidonax* seen in the lowlands south of New Jersey and Missouri can safely be called an Acadian.

557 **Alder Flycatcher**
**"Traill's Flycatcher"**
*Empidonax alnorum*

Description: 5–6" (13–15 cm). The size of a House Sparrow. Dull gray-green above, whitish below, with 2 dull-white wing bars and narrow white eye ring (often not noticeable). Indistinguishable in appearance from Willow Flycatcher, and best identified by voice, breeding habitat, and nest.

Voice: A burry *fee-bee-o,* rather different from the wheezy *fitz-bew* of Willow Flycatcher.

Habitat: Alder swamps, streamside and lakeside thickets, and second-growth forests.

Nesting: 3 or 4 white eggs, finely speckled with brown, in a loose cup of grass with little or no plant down, placed in a low bush or sapling.

Range: Breeds from Alaska east through Manitoba to Newfoundland, and south to British Columbia, Great Lakes region, and southern New England. Winters in tropics.

This species has a more northerly distribution than its close relative the Willow Flycatcher. Although the habitats of the species differ, in a few places where their ranges meet the two can be heard singing in the same general area. It was in such an area in upstate New York that the small but constant differences between these birds were first noticed; research in the 1950s and 1960s showed that they are two distinct species. Previously the Willow and Alder flycatchers had been assumed to be one species, called "Traill's Flycatcher."

## 558 Willow Flycatcher "Traill's Flycatcher"
*Empidonax traillii*

Description: 6″ (15 cm). Distinguishable from Alder Flycatcher only by voice, breeding habitat, and nest. Other eastern *Empidonax* flycatchers have more conspicuous eye ring.

Voice: A wheezy *fitz-bew* or *pit-speer.* The song of the Alder Flycatcher is a burry *fee-bee-o,* descending more abruptly in pitch.

Habitat: Swampy thickets, upland pastures, and old abandoned orchards. Alder Flycatchers occur along wooded lakeshores and streams.

Nesting: 3 or 4 creamy-white eggs, with fine brown speckling, in a neat, compact cup of plant down and fibers placed in a low bush or sapling.

Range: Breeds from southern British Columbia east to Maine, and south to central California, Nevada, Southwest, Arkansas, and Virginia. Winters in tropics.

The species of the genus *Empidonax* are so similar in appearance that only an expert can tell them apart by sight alone. During the breeding season, each species lives in its characteristic habitat; but during their journey north migrants of different species may rest in a habitat where they are not usually found. Thus the only sure way to identify the breeding male is by the voice, which is different in each species. In seasons when the male does not sing, all that can readily be told is that a bird is an *Empidonax* flycatcher. Previously the Willow and Alder flycatchers had been assumed to be one species, called "Traill's Flycatcher."

559 **Least Flycatcher**
*Empidonax minimus*

Description: 5¼" (13 cm). Dull olive-gray above, whitish below, with 2 whitish wing bars and conspicuous white eye ring. Distinguished by voice and breeding habitat.

Voice: Dry, insect-like *che-bec,* snapped out and accented on the second syllable, and uttered incessantly through the hottest days of summer.

Habitat: Widely distributed in open country, nesting in shade trees and orchards, in villages and city parks, and along rural roadsides and woodland borders.

Nesting: 4 creamy-white eggs in a finely woven, cup-shaped nest made of vegetable fibers and lined with grass and feathers, firmly wedged in the fork or crotch of a tree.

Range: Breeds from southern Yukon east to central Quebec and Maritime Provinces, and south to Wyoming, Indiana, and New Jersey, and south in mountains to North Carolina. Winters in tropics.

Perhaps the most familiar member of the difficult-to-identify *Empidonax* group, the Least Flycatcher is a characteristic bird of large shade trees; its presence is most easily detected by its call. An incubating bird is surprisingly tame and will often allow itself to be touched or even lifted off the nest.

560 **Black Phoebe**
*Sayornis nigricans*

Description: 6–7" (15–18 cm). *Slate-black except for white belly, undertail coverts, and outer tail feathers.* Its *tail-wagging,* erect posture, and insectivorous feeding habits are helpful in field identification.

Voice: Song is a thin, buzzy *pi-tsee,* usually repeated. Call is a sharp, down-slurred *chip.*

Habitat: Shady areas near water, streams, and

pond and lake banks; in winter, city parks, open chaparral.

Nesting: 3–6 white eggs, with a few faint speckles, in a mud, moss, and grass nest lined with soft material, often feathers or cow hair, built under a bridge, on a sheltered ledge, in a crevice in an old building, or among hanging roots near the top of an embankment close to water.

Range: Resident from northern California south and east to southern Texas. Also in tropics.

Black Phoebes are territorial and solitary nesters, often remaining year-round in an established territory. The wanderers found in atypical winter habitats (chaparral or grassland) are thought to be first-year, nonbreeding birds.

---

561 **Eastern Phoebe**
*Sayornis phoebe*

Description: 7″ (18 cm). Dull olive green without an eye ring or wing bars. *Wags its tail.*

Voice: Clear *phoe-be,* repeated many times; the second syllable is alternately higher or lower than the first. Call note a distinctive, short *chip.*

Habitat: Open woodlands near streams; cliffs, bridges, and buildings with ledges.

Nesting: 4 or 5 white eggs in a mud-and-grass nest lined with moss and hair and attached to a ledge of a building, bridge, cliff, or quarry, or among roots of a fallen tree.

Range: Breeds in Canada and United States east of Rockies, south to northern edge of Gulf states. Winters from Virginia, Gulf Coast, and Florida southward.

The Eastern Phoebe arrives early in spring and departs late in fall, sometimes even staying through the winter in the northern states. In the absence of insects, its winter food is berries. Extraordinarily tame at the nest, the Eastern Phoebe was probably the first bird ever banded:

Audubon marked one with a silver wire on the leg in 1840 and recorded its return the following year.

562 **Say's Phoebe**
*Sayornis saya*

Description: 7–8″ (18–20 cm). Dusky head, breast, and back with darker wings and *black tail. Light rust-colored belly and undertail coverts.*

Voice: A mellow, whistled *pee-ur* with a plaintive quality.

Habitat: Plains, sparsely vegetated countryside, dry sunny locations, often near ranch houses, barns, and other buildings.

Nesting: 4 or 5 white eggs in a nest of grass and wool in a sheltered, elevated, dry site on a ledge, rock wall, or building.

Range: Breeds from central Alaska, Yukon, and northern Mackenzie south through western mountains to Mexico; not present west of the Cascades and Sierra Nevada except locally in south-central California and western Oregon. Winters in California and Southwest southward.

Although primarily insect eaters (as are all flycatchers), Say's Phoebes will eat other foods, such as berries, during long spells of cold inclement weather when insects are unavailable.

490, 556 **Vermilion Flycatcher**
*Pyrocephalus rubinus*

Description: 6″ (15 cm). Male has *brilliant scarlet crown and underparts,* with dark brown back, wings, and tail; female similar to male above, but *white below with dark streaks.* Belly of females and immatures varies from pink through yellow to white.

Voice: Call is *peet-peet* or *peet-a-weet.* Also has soft, tinkling flight song.

Habitat: Trees and shrubs along rivers and roadsides.

Nesting: 3 creamy-white eggs, with dark brown spots, in a well-made nest of fibers, feathers, and spiderweb lined with bits of lichen and placed on a horizontal branch.

Range: Breeds from southeastern California east to western Texas, and south into tropics. Winters in southern part of breeding range, but wanders as far east as Gulf Coast.

This species is unusual among flycatchers in that the sexes are differently colored. In southern Texas, it is conspicuous and tame, often nesting near houses and farmyards. The bright colors of the male have earned it the Mexican name *brasita de fuego,* "little coal of fire."

---

## 555 Ash-throated Flycatcher
*Myiarchus cinerascens*

Description: 8″ (20 cm). Dull olive above, yellowish below; like Great Crested and Brown-crested flycatchers, but smaller and less colorful; back browner, throat and breast grayish white.

Voice: *Purreeeer,* similar to call of Brown-crested Flycatcher but softer. Also a soft *ka-brick.*

Habitat: Deserts with cactus and mesquite thickets; also dry woods.

Nesting: 4 or 5 creamy-white, brown-spotted eggs in a nest lined with vegetable fibers in a tree or cactus hole.

Range: Breeds from Washington and Wyoming south to southwestern United States and east to Texas. Rare in East in fall. Winters in southern California and Arizona southward.

The Ash-throated Flycatcher lives in the hottest, driest parts of the West but is also found in dry, shady, open woodlands farther north. All flycatchers in the genus *Myiarchus* are similar in appearance. They may be identified according to their habitats and, where habitats overlap, by their voice.

552 **Great Crested Flycatcher**
*Myiarchus crinitus*

Description: 9″ (23 cm). Slightly crested. Brown above, with gray throat, yellow belly, *rufous wings and tail,* and *pale brown at base of lower mandible.*

Voice: A loud, whistled, slightly buzzy *wheep,* sometimes repeated. Also a raucous *whit-whit-whit-whit.*

Habitat: Open forests, orchards, and large trees in farm country.

Nesting: 5 or 6 creamy-white, brown-spotted eggs in tree cavities or bird boxes. The bulky nest is lined with all sorts of trash—cellophane, snakeskins, string, rags.

Range: Breeds from south-central and southeastern Canada to Gulf Coast. Winters in southern Florida; also in tropics.

This species is to woodlands what the Eastern Kingbird is to open country. It is noisy, aggressive, and even more colorful. Living mostly under the forest canopy, however, it is much more often heard than seen, and is much less in evidence than its black-and-white relative. A mystifying habit is its frequent use of shed snakeskins in its nest lining. Whether this is intended to frighten off predators or merely decorate the nest is not known. The Great Crested is the only eastern flycatcher that nests in holes.

**Brown-crested Flycatcher**
**"Wied's Crested Flycatcher"**
*Myiarchus tyrannulus*

Description: 9½″ (24 cm). A large flycatcher, olive above and yellow below, with cinnamon in wings and tail, and *black bill.* The Great Crested Flycatcher has brighter underparts and brown, not blackish, lower mandible; best distinguished by voice.

Voice: A burry *purreeeer,* or a sharp *wit!* or *way-burg,* very different from Great Crested Flycatcher's loud *wheep!*

Habitat: Arid lands in areas with cacti or large trees.

Nesting: 3–5 creamy-white, brown-spotted eggs in a nest lined with feathers, fibers, and hairs, placed in a tree cavity, in cacti, or on fence posts.

Range: Breeds from southern California, southern Nevada, central Arizona, and southern Texas southward. Winters mainly south of U.S. border, but a few winter in southern Florida.

This species replaces the Great Crested Flycatcher in arid country. Its old name, "Wied's Crested Flycatcher," was in honor of Prince Maximilian of Wied, a German naturalist and traveler in early-19th-century America.

---

389 **Great Kiskadee**
**"Kiskadee Flycatcher"**
*Pitangus sulphuratus*

Description: 10½″ (27 cm). A stocky, robin-sized flycatcher. Broad black bill; *black-and-white striped head;* olive-brown back; bright yellow underparts; rufous wings. Tail conspicuous in flight.

Voice: Loud, piercing *kis-ka-dee;* also an incessant, shrill chattering.

Habitat: Rivers, streams, and lakes bordered with dense vegetation; also in more open country and in parks in most of its range.

Nesting: 4 creamy-white, brown-spotted eggs in a bulky, domed stick nest with the entrance at the side, often in a thorn tree or bush.

Range: Resident from extreme southern Texas (lower Rio Grande Valley) southward.

This large and striking bird, named for its call, is common throughout Latin America. In addition to insects, it eats small fruits and even fish, diving straight into the water like a kingfisher, although not as deeply.

---

## 540 Couch's Kingbird
*Tyrannus couchii*

Description: 8½″ (22 cm). Bright yellow underparts, olive back, and dark patch through eye. *Slightly forked brown tail without white.* Tropical Kingbird (*Tyrannus melancholicus*), very rare in southern Texas, is identical in appearance but has distinctive twittering calls.

Voice: A series of *queer* notes, followed by *puit-puwit-puwit-pawitcheew.* Call a short *kip.*

Habitat: Borders of woodlands and brushy streamside thickets.

Nesting: 3 or 4 pinkish, brown-spotted eggs in a stick nest lined with grass and moss in a tree.

Range: Resident in extreme southern Texas (lower Rio Grande Valley).

Until recently, Couch's Kingbird was considered a form of the Tropical Kingbird, but the voices of the two differ consistently. Within the last few years, the Tropical Kingbird (see above) has become a rare visitor to the Rio Grande Valley, posing a challenge to local birders.

541 **Western Kingbird**
*Tyrannus verticalis*

Description: 8–9″ (20–23 cm). *Olive-brown above, yellow below;* gray head, lighter grayish throat and upper breast. Dusky wings and *blackish tail with white margins.* Red crown feathers not normally visible.
Voice: A loud, sharp *kit.* Various chattering notes.
Habitat: Open country; ranches, roadsides, streams, and ponds with trees.
Nesting: 4 creamy-white eggs in a stick nest lined with plant fibers and placed in a tree or bush.
Range: Breeds throughout West, from southern Canada south to Mexico, east to Great Plains; casual along Atlantic Coast in fall. Winters in tropics; also a few in southern Florida.

Like the Horned Lark, the Western Kingbird has benefited from the cutting of forests; the species has moved eastward in recent decades. In the Southwest, especially in arid regions, there are two other kingbirds, Cassin's (*Tyrannus vociferans*) and Tropical (*Tyrannus melancholicus*), that look like the Western; however, the Western is distinguished by white feathers on the sides of the black tail.

604 **Eastern Kingbird**
*Tyrannus tyrannus*

Description: 8–9″ (20–23 cm). Blackish head, blue-black mantle and wings, black tail *with white terminal band;* white below. Red feathers in middle of crown usually concealed. Long crown feathers and upright posture give this flycatcher a distinctive silhouette.
Voice: A sharp *dzee* or *dzeet.* Also a series of harsh, rapid *kit* and *kitter* calls.
Habitat: Savannas, rangelands, forest edges,

riverside groves, city parks, and roadsides.

Nesting: 3–5 white, spotted eggs in a large bulky nest consisting of heaps of twigs, straw, and twine lined with hair and rootlets. Nests are built on the horizontal limbs of trees, often near water.

Range: Breeds from British Columbia across Canada to Maritime Provinces, and south to northern California, central Texas, Gulf Coast, and Florida. Winters in tropics.

These noisy, conspicuous birds are named for their aggressive behavior, often driving away birds much larger than themselves, such as crows and hawks, especially near their nests. In late summer and early fall they often flock, and large numbers pursue flying insects; they also feed on wild berries, which they deftly pluck while on the wing.

## 542 Gray Kingbird

*Tyrannus dominicensis*

Description: 9″ (23 cm). A stocky, large-headed, pale gray flycatcher of coastal habitats. Underparts whitish; dusky blackish patch through eye; bill heavy; tail notched, without white.

Voice: A shrill, buzzy *pe-cheer-y.*

Habitat: Coastal, in mangrove thickets, on telephone wires, and in small groves of palms and oaks.

Nesting: 3 pinkish eggs, blotched with brown, in a grass-lined stick nest placed in a mangrove thicket, usually over or near salt water.

Range: Breeds in coastal regions of South Carolina, Georgia, Florida, and northern Gulf Coast. Winters in tropics.

Like other kingbirds, this species is fearless, even chasing hawks and crows. Noisy and belligerent, it frequently emits harsh notes as it sits on telephone wires or exposed branches, ready to dart after flying insects.

476 **Scissor-tailed Flycatcher**
*Tyrannus forficatus*

Description: 14″ (36 cm), of which more than half is a very *long and deeply forked black-and-white tail;* adult has *bright salmon-pink sides and belly;* head, upper back, and breast pale grayish white. Young birds similar, but have shorter tail and lack bright pink on sides and belly.

Voice: A harsh *kee-kee-kee-kee.* Also chattering notes like those of Eastern Kingbird.

Habitat: Open country along roadsides and on ranches with scattered trees and bushes; also fence wires and posts.

Nesting: 5 creamy, brown-spotted eggs in a bulky stick nest lined with soft fibrous material and placed in an isolated tree.

Range: Breeds from eastern Colorado and Nebraska south to Texas and western Louisiana. Winters south of the border; also a few in southern Florida.

These conspicuous flycatchers attract the attention of the most casual passerby. They are especially numerous in southern Texas, and one may see many in a day's drive by watching fence posts and wires along the road. Scissor-tails are as noisy and aggressive as kingbirds and will chase birds much larger than themselves. In spring, they put on a wonderful aerial courtship display. With their long scissor-like tail, they can maneuver and "sky-dance" gracefully. Nearly all of their food is captured on the wing; included in their diet are many insects harmful to agriculture.

575 **Rose-throated Becard**
*Pachyramphus aglaiae*

Description: 6½″ (17 cm). Sparrow-sized. Male gray above, with black cap and pale rose throat; whitish below. Female brown, paler below, and with dusky grayish cap.
Voice: A high-pitched whistle, *seeeeooo;* various chattering notes.
Habitat: Thick woodlands along streams; wooded canyons.
Nesting: 4 or 5 white eggs, spotted with brown, in a chamber in a globular nest of grass and plant fibers, suspended from the tip of a drooping branch.
Range: Breeds from southeastern Arizona and Rio Grande Valley of Texas southward. Winters from northern Mexico southward.

This quiet, unobtrusive bird spends most of its time foraging in tall trees and is therefore difficult to find. It is adept at catching flying insects like a flycatcher and also feeds on berries. The northern limit of its range is just within our borders, and it is common nowhere in our area.

## Family Alaudidae
Larks

91 species: This almost exclusively Old World family is represented in America by one native species, the Horned Lark, and by the Eurasian Skylark (*Alauda arvensis*), introduced in British Columbia. Larks are birds of open country, nesting on the ground. The Horned Lark is an exceedingly early breeder, laying its eggs in late winter, even with patches of snow on the ground. These birds feed on seeds and small insects.

452 **Horned Lark**
*Eremophila alpestris*

Description: 7–8″ (18–20 cm). Larger than a sparrow. Brown, with *black stripe below eye and white or yellowish stripe above, black crescent on breast, and black "horns"* (not always seen). Walks rather than hops. In flight, tail is black with white edges. Similar-looking pipits have brown tails and lack the face pattern.

Voice: A soft *ti-ti.* Song delivered in flight is high-pitched series of tinkling notes.

Habitat: Plains, fields, airports, and beaches.

Nesting: 3–5 brown-spotted gray eggs in a hollow in the ground lined with fine grass.

Range: Breeds in Alaska and Canadian Arctic south in coastal Canada and throughout all of United States except Southeast. Winters from southern Canada southward. Also Old World.

The only true lark native to the New World, this is one of our earliest nesting birds. Even in the northern states, nests may be found in February, when the first set of eggs is often destroyed by severe snowstorms. As many as three broods are raised each year. The species favors the most barren habitats; as soon as thick grass begins to grow in an area, the birds abandon it. In the fall, they roam over the open countryside in large flocks, often in company with pipits, longspurs, and Snow Buntings.

---

FAMILY HIRUNDINIDAE
Swallows and Martins

89 species: Worldwide. Eight species breed in North America. Swallows have long pointed wings and are expert flyers. Like swifts, they are aerial feeders. Their bills and legs are very short. They commonly perch on wires. Many species use man-made structures, such as

buildings, bridges, and culverts, as sites for their nests. In autumn, large flocks of swallows may be seen on their southward journey.

353, 354 **Purple Martin**
*Progne subis*

Description: 7–8½" (18–22 cm). Our largest swallow. Adult male dark steel-blue. Female and immature male duller above, pale gray below. Overhead, similar in shape to European Starling, but flight more buoyant and gliding.

Voice: Liquid, gurgling warble. Also a penetrating *tee-tee-tee.*

Habitat: Open woodlands, residential areas, and agricultural land.

Nesting: 4 or 5 white eggs in a mass of grass and other plant material placed in a natural cavity—sometimes a hole in a tree but more often in a martin house with many separate compartments, where the birds nest in a colony.

Range: Breeds from British Columbia, central interior Canada, and Nova Scotia southward, but absent from interior western mountains and Great Basin. Winters in tropics.

The custom of erecting a martin house to attract these beneficial birds was practiced by the early settlers and, before them, by the southern Indian tribes, who hung clusters of hollow gourds in trees near their gardens. In other areas, the species nested in tall dead trees riddled with woodpecker holes, but these original colonies never reached the size—as many as 200 pairs—of colonies found in large martin houses today.

356 **Tree Swallow**
*Tachycineta bicolor*

Description: 5–6¼" (13–16 cm). Sparrow-sized. The only swallow in the East with metallic blue or blue-green upperparts and clear white underparts. Young birds are dull brown above, but distinguished from Bank and Northern Rough-winged swallows by their clearer white underparts.

Voice: Cheerful series of liquid twitters.

Habitat: Lakeshores, flooded meadows, marshes, and streams.

Nesting: 4–6 white eggs in a feather-lined cup of grass placed in a hole in a tree or in a nest box.

Range: Breeds from Alaska across northern Manitoba to Newfoundland, and south to California, Colorado, Nebraska, and Maryland. Winters north to southern California, Gulf Coast, and Carolinas, occasionally farther.

This bird's habit of feeding on bayberries enables it to winter farther north than other swallows. Although most on the East Coast winter north to the Carolinas, a few occasionally are found on Long Island or Cape Cod. It is the first of our swallows to reappear in the spring. It sometimes breeds in unusual situations. Several pairs once nested on a ferry boat that shuttled across the Saint Lawrence River, foraging on both the American and Canadian sides. Tree Swallows often enjoy playing with a feather, which they drop and then retrieve as it floats in the air. They gather in enormous flocks along the coast in fall, where they circle in big eddies like leaves caught in a whirlwind.

355 **Violet-green Swallow**
*Tachycineta thalassina*

Description: 5–5½″ (13–14 cm). Dark, metallic, *bronze-green* upperparts; iridescent violet rump and tail, the latter slightly forked; *white underparts. White cheek* extending above eye and white on sides of rump distinguish it from Tree Swallow.
Voice: A high *dee-chip* given in flight. Also a series of varying *tweet* notes.
Habitat: Breeds in forests, wooded foothills, mountains, suburban areas.
Nesting: 4 or 5 white eggs in a grass-and-feather nest in a woodpecker hole, a natural cavity, under the eaves of a building, or in a nest box.
Range: Breeds from Alaska east to South Dakota, south to southern California and Texas. Winters mainly south of U.S.–Mexico border, but a few winter in southern California.

Like many other swallows, the Violet-green lives in colonies, basically because of its feeding needs. Where one finds food there is usually enough for all, and when feeding communally these birds can more readily detect and defend themselves from hawks.

358 **Northern Rough-winged Swallow**
*Stelgidopteryx serripennis*

Description: 5–5¾″ (13–15 cm). Pale brown above, white below with *dingy brown throat.* Bank Swallow similar but smaller, with white throat and brown breast band.
Voice: A low, unmusical *br-r-ret,* more drawn out than the call of Bank Swallow, and often doubled.
Habitat: Riverbanks. Prefers drier sites than Bank Swallow.
Nesting: 4–8 white eggs in a burrow or cavity. Not highly colonial; often nests singly. Will utilize ready-made cavities in bridges, culverts, or other streamside masonry.

Range: Breeds from southeastern Alaska and southern Canada southward throughout United States. Winters north to southern California, Gulf Coast, and southern Florida.

The name "Rough-winged" comes from tiny hooks on the outer primary, which give the feather a rough feel. The function of these hooks, found also in a group of unrelated African swallows, is unknown. Unlike the Bank Swallow, Rough-wings do not usually dig their own nesting burrows but use ready-made nesting sites along streams. Thus they do not nest in large colonies like the Bank Swallow, although occasionally a few pairs may be found close together.

## 359 Bank Swallow
*Riparia riparia*

Description: 4¾–5½" (12–14 cm). Sparrow-sized—our smallest swallow. Brown above, dull white below; *breast crossed by a distinct brown band;* tail notched. Northern Rough-winged Swallow is warmer brown, and has dusky throat and breast without distinct brown band.

Voice: Sharp, unmusical *pret* or *trit-trit.*

Habitat: Banks of rivers, creeks, and lakes; seashores.

Nesting: 4–6 white eggs in a grass-and-feather nest in a chamber at end of a deep tunnel that it digs near top of a steep bank. Since it breeds in large colonies, nesting banks may sometimes appear riddled with holes.

Range: Breeds across continent from Alaska and northern Canada south to California, Texas, and Virginia. Winters in tropics. Also in Old World.

Bank Swallows originally nested only in steep, sandy riverbanks, but, like other swallows, they have adapted to humans and now nest in the sides of man-made excavations. They breed in colonies of from two or three pairs to a few thousand. Most lay their eggs at the same time and thus later forage for their young at the same time. Such parents have an advantage: Swarms of flying insects are unevenly distributed and are more quickly located when many birds are searching together. The scientific name *riparia* is from the Latin word for "riverbank."

## 360 Cliff Swallow
*Hirundo pyrrhonota*

Description: 5–6″ (13–15 cm). Sparrow-sized. A stocky, square-tailed swallow with *pale buff rump.* Upperparts dull steel-blue, underparts buff-white; throat dark chestnut, forehead white. Cave Swallow of Texas and Southwest similar but smaller, with darker rump and pale buff throat.

Voice: Constant squeaky chattering and twittering.

Habitat: Open country near buildings or cliffs; lakeshores and marshes during migration.

Nesting: 4–6 white eggs in a gourd-shaped structure of mud lined with feathers and placed on a sheltered cliff face or under eaves. Nests in colonies.

Range: Breeds from Alaska east to Nova Scotia and southward through most of United States except Southeast. Winters in tropics.

As its name implies, this swallow originally nested on cliffs. The introduction of House Sparrows was a disaster for these birds, since the sparrows usurp their nests and often cause the swallows to abandon a colony. Long, cold, rainy spells while the young are in the nest also cause widespread mortality since the adults are unable to obtain enough insects.

361 **Cave Swallow**
*Hirundo fulva*

Description: 5½" (14 cm). A stocky swallow with square tail, steel-blue upperparts, *buff throat and rump,* and chestnut forehead. The more widespread Cliff Swallow similar, but has chestnut throat and white forehead.

Voice: A series of squeaks, twitters, and warbles.

Habitat: Chiefly open country near caves and cliffs.

Nesting: 4 brown-spotted, pinkish eggs in a mud nest lined with grass, roots, and feathers, attached to cliff walls and caves, and occasionally to bridges and old buildings.

Range: Breeds in southern Texas, southeastern New Mexico, and, rarely, in southern Arizona. Winters in tropics.

This bird is extremely local north of the U.S.–Mexico border, and relatively few nest within the United States. Most nests are in inaccessible places, plastered to walls far inside remote caves and crevices. Like all swallows, it catches its insect prey on the wing.

357 **Barn Swallow**
*Hirundo rustica*

Description: 5¾–7¾" (15–20 cm). Sparrow-sized. Our most familiar swallow, and the only one with a *deeply forked tail.* Upperparts dark steel-blue; underparts buff; throat and forehead rusty.

Voice: Constant liquid twittering and chattering.

Habitat: Agricultural land, suburban areas, marshes, lakeshores.

Nesting: 4–6 brown-spotted, white eggs in a solid cup of mud reinforced with grass, lined with feathers and soft plant material, and placed on a rafter in a building or on a sheltered ledge.

Range: Breeds from Alaska east across Canada to Newfoundland and south through all of United States except southern Texas, Gulf Coast, and peninsular Florida. Winters in tropics. Also in Eurasia.

The great majority of these birds now nest on or in buildings, but originally they used rocky ledges over streams and perhaps attached their nests to tree trunks in the shelter of branches (as do related species in Africa). Barn Swallows perform long migrations; some that breed in North America winter as far south as Argentina. Like other swallows, they migrate by day, often feeding as they travel. They are swift and graceful fliers; it is estimated that they cover as many as 600 miles (1,000 kilometers) a day in quest of food for their young.

## Family Corvidae
Jays, Magpies, and Crows

117 species: Worldwide. Sixteen species breed in North America, and an additional species is a regular visitor from Mexico. Birds in this family are among the largest of the perching birds. The crows and ravens are black, but the jays and magpies are a colorful group. The sexes are either alike or very similar. Their voices are mostly harsh and raucous, and can scarcely be called songs. These birds are omnivorous in their feeding habits and eat meat, fruit, insects, and various vegetable substances.

605 **Gray Jay**
*Perisoreus canadensis*

Description: 10–13″ (25–33 cm). Gray above, whitish below. Forehead and throat white; nape and stripe through eye dull black. Immatures sooty-gray.

Voice: *Whee-ah, chuck-chuck;* also scolds, screams, and whistles.
Habitat: Coniferous forests.
Nesting: 3–5 gray-green eggs spotted with dark olive-brown in a solid bowl of twigs and bark strips lined with feathers and fur, and placed near the trunk of a dense conifer.
Range: Resident from Alaska east across Canada to Labrador, and south to northern California, New Mexico, northern New York, and northern New England.

This bird is well known to anyone who has spent time in the North Woods. Like certain other birds of that region, it is very tame and habitually enters camps to take food; hence one of its many names, "Camp Robber." Gray Jays will eat almost anything, but in winter they are partial to conifer seeds. They glue together masses of seeds and buds with their thick saliva and store them for use when food is scarce. Because of their confiding nature and general coloration, they have often been likened to giant chickadees.

596 **Blue Jay**
*Cyanocitta cristata*

Description: 12″ (30 cm). *Bright blue* above with much white and black in the wings and tail; dingy white below; black facial markings; *prominent crest.*
Voice: A raucous *jay-jay,* harsh cries, and a rich variety of other calls. One is almost identical to the scream of the Red-shouldered Hawk. Also a musical *queedle-queedle.*
Habitat: Chiefly oak forest, but now also city parks and suburban yards, especially where oak trees predominate.
Nesting: 4–6 brown-spotted greenish eggs in a coarsely built nest of sticks, lined with grass and well concealed in a crotch or forked branch of a tree, often a conifer.

Range: Breeds east of Rockies, from southern Canada to Gulf of Mexico. In winter, often withdraws from northern parts of breeding range.

Although sometimes disliked because they chase smaller birds away from feeders, Blue Jays are among the handsomest of birds. They often bury seeds and acorns, and since many are never retrieved they are, in effect, tree planters. They regularly mob predators, and their raucous screaming makes it easy to locate a hawk or a roosting owl. Although seen throughout the year, they are migratory and travel in large loose flocks in both spring and fall. In the East, birds from farther north replace the local population in winter.

---

586 **Green Jay**
*Cyanocorax yncas*

Description: 12″ (30 cm). Strikingly colored, with *bright green body and green tail* with yellow on the sides; *brilliant blue crown and cheeks;* rest of head, throat, and breast black.
Voice: Variety of rattling calls. Also *shink, shink, shink.*
Habitat: Dry thickets and open forest with thick undergrowth; sometimes in more open country around ranch houses.
Nesting: 4 brown-spotted, grayish eggs in a loosely made stick nest of thorns, lined with rootlets or grass and placed in a bush or small tree.
Range: Resident in southernmost Texas (Rio Grande Valley) southward. Also in tropics.

In winter months and when not nesting, these inhabitants of dense thickets visit more open country, even near ranches and smaller towns. Like most jays, they are omnivorous, eating fruits, seeds, insects, and even corn. At times they visit feeders for meat scraps.

475 **Brown Jay**
*Cyanocorax morio*

Description: 14–18″ (36–46 cm). Large and long-tailed. Dusky brown above with darker brown head, paler on breast and whitish on belly and flanks. Bill thick, black in adults and yellow in immatures.
Voice: A shrill *pow!* or *kreeow!*
Habitat: Dense streamside woodlands and thickets.
Nesting: 3–5 blue-gray eggs marked with brown, in a cup of twigs, usually on a branch far out from trunk.
Range: Rare resident in extreme southern Texas. Also in tropics.

The largest North American jay, this species has only recently colonized the lower Rio Grande Valley, where it travels in noisy flocks. The birds have deep, slow wingbeats and pump their long tails as they fly.

597 **Scrub Jay**
*Aphelocoma coerulescens*

Description: 11–13″ (28–33 cm). Blue Jay–sized. Wings and tail dull blue, back gray, with dusky mask, and white throat set off by necklace of dull blue marks on breast. No crest.
Voice: Similar to Blue Jay's—loud, harsh, and rasping; also has a sweet song of trills and low warbles.
Habitat: Scrub oak, woodlands, and chaparral; also suburban gardens. Does not breed in low scrub because it needs watch posts.
Nesting: 3–6 buff or dull green eggs, spotted with dark brown, in a bulky nest of twigs concealed in a dense bush or low tree.

Range: Resident from Washington, Wyoming, and Colorado south to Texas, with an isolated population in central Florida; also in Mexico.

The isolated population in Florida is puzzling. Presumably a belt of scrub once extended from the western states across the South and into Florida. Today these birds are separated from their western relatives by more than 1,000 miles (1,600 kilometers). Scrub Jays feed on insects, seeds, and nuts, obtained chiefly on the ground. Rather shy for jays, they are often difficult to find even where they are common, except when perching on telephone wires. They soon become tame, however, and learn to come to feeders. Like others of their family, they often eat the eggs and young of other birds. They also share a tendency to carry off and hide brightly colored objects.

---

627 **Black-billed Magpie**
*Pica pica*

Description: 17½–22″ (44–56 cm). Large *black and white bird* with *long tail and dark bill.* Bill, head, breast, and underparts black, with green iridescence on wings and tail. White belly, shoulders, and primaries that are conspicuous as white wing patches in flight.

Voice: A rapid, nasal *mag? mag? mag?* or *yak-yak-yak.*

Habitat: Open woodlands, savannas, brush-covered country, streamside growth.

Nesting: 6–9 greenish, blotched eggs in a neat cup nest within a large, bulky, domed structure of strong, often thorny twigs. Nest has a double entrance, and is placed in a tree or bush.

Range: Resident from Alaska and western Canada south to east-central California, and east to Great Plains. Also in Eurasia.

Magpies are frequently shot because they steal grain, but since the most important items in their diet seem to be insects and small rodents, they are more beneficial than destructive to agriculture. In captivity a magpie may be trained to imitate the human voice. These birds frequently associate with cattle and sheep, perching on their backs and picking off ticks and maggots. In the process, they sometimes open sores on the animals that eventually prove fatal.

---

645 **American Crow**
**"Common Crow"**
*Corvus brachyrhynchos*

Description: 17–21″ (43–53 cm). A stocky black bird with stout bill and fan-shaped tail. Fish Crow smaller, slimmer, and glossier; larger ravens have wedge-shaped tails.

Voice: Familiar *caw-caw* or *caa-caa.*

Habitat: Woodlands, farmlands, and suburban areas.

Nesting: 4–6 dull green eggs, spotted with dark brown, in a large mass of twigs and sticks lined with feathers, grass, and rootlets, and placed in a tree.

Range: Breeds from British Columbia east to Newfoundland and south to southern California, Gulf Coast, and Florida. Winters north to southern Canada.

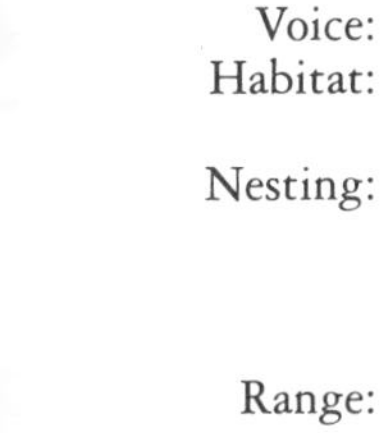

Every continent except South America has at least one familiar roadside crow, and this is the species in North America. It is almost impossible to go into the countryside without seeing these birds along highways or flying overhead. Intelligent, wary, virtually omnivorous, and with a high reproductive capacity, the American Crow is undoubtedly much more numerous than it was before the arrival of settlers. Crows may gather in roosts of over half a million birds and are so abundant that even an ardent defender of birds might not deny that they are destructive to crops and should be controlled, although they consume enormous amounts of grasshoppers, cutworms, and other harmful insects. Crows make interesting pets if obtained while quite young; some learn to mimic the human voice. They often carry off and hide bright objects.

644 **Mexican Crow**
*Corvus imparatus*

Description: 15″ (38 cm). A small glossy crow, all black, including bill and feet. Chihuahuan Raven larger, with wedge-shaped tail; American Crow slightly larger and best distinguished by voice.

Voice: A soft croaking *gar-lic,* very different from familiar *caw, caw* of American Crow.

Habitat: Arid open country, but with thickets and brush such as mesquite; also ranches and farms, as well as along woodland streams.

Nesting: 4 or 5 greenish eggs, blotched with brown, in a stick nest lined with leaves, grasses, or reeds, and set in a low bush or tree.

Range: A regular visitor to extreme southern Texas from Mexico.

This relatively little-known species occurs, like most crows, in flocks and feeds on a great variety of items, including seeds, grains, fruits, meat, carrion, and insects. Unknown north of the U.S.–Mexico border before the 1960s, it has in recent years become a regular visitor to the Brownsville region.

## 646 Fish Crow
*Corvus ossifragus*

Description: 17″ (43 cm). All black, somewhat smaller than American Crow, but size is deceptive in the field. Best told by voice.

Voice: Two calls, both distinct from the American Crow's familiar *caw*—a nasal *kwok* and a nasal, two-noted *ah-ah.* In breeding season, young American Crows have a similar *kwok* call.

Habitat: Low coastal country, near tidewater and pine barrens in North; in South, also lakes, rivers, and swamps far inland.

Nesting: 4 or 5 greenish eggs, with brown blotches, in a stick nest lined with pine needles, grass, hair, or bark flakes and placed in an evergreen or deciduous tree.

Range: Resident on Atlantic Coast from Massachusetts and extreme southern New England south to Florida, and along Gulf Coast west to Texas; also inland along larger rivers north to Illinois. Some northern birds migrate south in winter.

Many coastal heronries have attendant Fish Crows, ever ready to plunder the heron nests for eggs. Omnivorous feeders, like all crows, they also consume corn, insects, lizards, wild and cultivated fruits, and often carrion and dead fish—hence the name.

## 643 Chihuahuan Raven
## "White-necked Raven"
*Corvus cryptoleucus*

Description: 19–21″ (48–53 cm). Similar to Common Raven but somewhat smaller. White bases to feathers of neck seldom seen. Best told by voice.

Voice: Harsh *kraak,* higher pitched than Common Raven's.

Habitat: Arid grasslands and mesquite; plains and deserts.

Nesting: 5–7 dull green eggs, spotted and

streaked with brown and purple. Nest a loose mass of thorny sticks, lined with grass, moss, and bark strips, and placed in an exposed tree or on a telephone pole.

Range: Breeds from southern Arizona, southeastern Colorado, and western Kansas southward into Mexico. Winters in southern part of breeding range.

The Chihuahuan Raven replaces the Common Raven at lower elevations, and in the United States portion of its range is the only raven likely to be seen. More gregarious than its larger northern relative, it is often found at garbage dumps. The birds gather in noisy and conspicuous roosts. During the breeding season, however, they are not social, pairs nesting in widely spaced territories.

---

642 **Common Raven**
*Corvus corax*

Description: 21–27″ (53–69 cm). Similar to American Crow but larger, with heavier bill and wedge-shaped tail. At rest, throat appears shaggy because of long, lance-shaped feathers. Often soars like a hawk. See Chihuahuan Raven.

Voice: Deep, varied, guttural croaking; a hollow *wonk-wonk.*

Habitat: Coniferous forests and rocky coasts; in West, also in deserts and arid mountains.

Nesting: 4–7 dull green eggs, spotted with brown, in a large mass of sticks containing a cup lined with fur, moss, and lichens, placed on a cliff or in the top of a conifer.

Range: Resident from Aleutians, northern Alaska, and northern Canada south throughout western United States and to Minnesota, Great Lakes, and northern New England; in Appalachians to northwestern Georgia. Also in Eurasia and North Africa.

The Common Raven is common only in wilderness areas; despite its large size and intelligence, it is very sensitive to human persecution and was long ago driven out of settled areas by shooting and poisoning. Ravens are primarily scavengers, and around towns in the North they compete with gulls for garbage. They also raid seabird colonies, consuming many eggs and young. They regularly ride on rising air currents and frequently indulge in aerial displays, with mock fighting, tumbling, and other forms of acrobatics.

## Family Paridae
Titmice

51 species: North America, Eurasia, and Africa. Eleven species breed in North America. These familiar birds include the tame and trusting chickadees, which not only come to feeders but even take food from the hand. They are small, large-headed, sometimes crested birds that usually travel in small flocks or family groups. They are mostly hole- or cavity-nesters and will utilize birdhouses. The sexes are alike.

### 621 Black-capped Chickadee
*Parus atricapillus*

Description: 4¾–5¾" (12–15 cm). Black cap and throat, white cheeks, gray back, dull white underparts. Wing feathers narrowly and indistinctly edged with white.

Voice: A buzzy *chick-a-dee-dee-dee* or a clear, whistled *fee-bee,* the second note lower and often doubled.

Habitat: Deciduous and mixed forests, and open woodlands; suburban areas in winter.

Nesting: 6–8 brown-speckled white eggs in a cup of grass, fur, plant down, feathers, and moss, placed in a hole in a rotten tree stub excavated by the birds or in a natural cavity or bird box.

Range: Largely resident from Alaska east across Canada to Newfoundland, and south to northern California, northern New Mexico, Missouri, and northern New Jersey. Winters south to Maryland and Texas.

Flocks of this tame and inquisitive bird spend the winter making the rounds of feeders in a neighborhood, often appearing at each feeder with striking regularity. Chickadees form the nucleus of mixed flocks of woodpeckers, nuthatches, creepers, and kinglets that move through the winter woods. Occasionally they move south in very large numbers, many thousands passing through even our largest cities. In spring, chickadees disband and move into the woods to nest. They often feed upside down, clinging to the underside of twigs and branches in their search for insect eggs and larvae. Easily tamed, they soon learn to feed from the hand.

---

## 623 Carolina Chickadee
*Parus carolinensis*

Description: 4–5″ (10–13 cm). Similar to more northern Black-capped Chickadee, but feathers of folded wing usually show less white edging; lower edge of black bib more sharply defined than that of Black-capped. Best identified by voice and range.

Voice: A buzzy *chickadee-dee-dee-dee,* higher pitched and faster than that of the Black-capped Chickadee; song has 4 whistled notes, *see-dee, see-dee,* with a downward inflection, rather than the 2- or 3-noted song of the Black-capped.

Habitat: Deciduous woodlands and residential areas.

Nesting: 6–8 white eggs, lightly speckled with brown, placed in a cavity in a rotten stub or birdhouse lined with feathers, grass, and plant down.

Range: Resident from southeastern Kansas and central New Jersey south to Texas, Gulf Coast, and central Florida.

So similar are the Carolina and Black-capped chickadees that Audubon did not realize that they were different species until 1834—over a century after chickadees had been discovered by Europeans. The two species have much the same needs, and thus compete and cannot coexist during the breeding season; instead, they replace each other geographically. Like its northern relative, the Carolina Chickadee is a familiar visitor to feeders and a regular member of the mixed flocks of small birds that roam the winter woods.

622 **Boreal Chickadee**
*Parus hudsonicus*

Description: 5–5½″ (13–14 cm). Similar to Black-capped Chickadee, but crown and back brown, flanks rufous.

Voice: A husky *chick-a-dee-dee,* lazier and more nasal than call of Black-capped.

Habitat: Coniferous forests.

Nesting: 5–7 white eggs, lightly speckled with red-brown, in a cup of plant down, feathers, and moss in a natural cavity, often only a few feet from the ground.

Range: Breeds from northern Alaska east to Labrador and Newfoundland, and south to northern edge of United States. Occasionally wanders southward in winter.

Every major forest habitat in North America has its species of chickadee, and this is the one found in the great coniferous forests of Canada. Unlike the Black-capped Chickadee, this species spends most of its time in the interior of dense spruces, coming less readily to the tips of branches, and so it is much less easily observed.

616, 617 **Tufted Titmouse including "Black-crested Titmouse"**
*Parus bicolor*

Description: 6″ (15 cm). Sparrow-sized. Gray above and whitish below, with *rust-colored sides and conspicuous gray crest.* The "Black-crested Titmouse," a race found in southwestern Oklahoma and Texas, is similar but has black crest.

Voice: A whistled series of 4 to 8 notes sounding like *Peter-Peter,* repeated over and over.

Habitat: Swampy or moist woodlands, and shade trees in villages and city parks; in winter, at feeders.

Nesting: 5 or 6 brown-dotted white eggs in a tree cavity or bird box stuffed with leaves and moss.

Range: Resident from eastern Nebraska, southern Michigan, and Maine south to Texas, Gulf Coast, and central Florida.

Titmice are social birds and, especially in winter, join with small mixed flocks of chickadees, nuthatches, kinglets, creepers, and the smaller woodpeckers. Although a frequent visitor at feeders, the titmouse is not as tame or confiding as a chickadee. It often clings to the bark of trees and turns upside down to pick spiders and insects from the underside of a twig or leaf. The "Black-crested Titmouse" of Texas and Oklahoma was until recently considered a separate species.

## Family Remizidae
Verdins

10 species: North America, Eurasia, and Africa. One species breeds in North America. Verdins are very small birds with short wings, relatively long tails,

and sharply pointed bills. A few species undertake short migrations, but most are nonmigratory. All make large, elaborate nests.

518 **Verdin**
*Auriparus flaviceps*

Description: 4–4½″ (10–11 cm). Smaller than a House Sparrow. Dull gray with *yellowish head* and *rufous bend of wing.* Young birds are uniformly dull gray, without yellow head or rufous bend of wing.
Voice: A thin *tsilip!* frequently repeated.
Habitat: Brushy desert; mesquite thickets.
Nesting: 3–5 pale bluish-green eggs, spotted with brown, in a globular mass of thorny twigs lined with feathers and soft grass, and placed in a bush.
Range: Resident from California, Utah, and south-central Texas southward to northern Mexico.

These tiny desert birds, rarely seen to drink, are thought to obtain moisture from the insects they eat. They live in very arid areas, often far from water, and seem to require only brushy vegetation and a source of food. The well-insulated nest no doubt protects the eggs and the young from intense heat.

Family Sittidae
Nuthatches

25 species: North America and Eurasia. Four species breed in North America. Like the titmice, these stocky little birds are cavity-nesters. Their chief peculiarity is a habit of crawling on tree trunks head downward; with their stout toes and claws, they can progress in any direction, but their short, soft tails are not used as props like those of woodpeckers and creepers.

379 **Red-breasted Nuthatch**
*Sitta canadensis*

Description: 4½–4¾" (11–12 cm). Smaller than a sparrow. Male has blue-gray upperparts, pale rusty underparts. *Crown and line through eye black, eyebrow white.* Female similar, but crown is gray.

Voice: A tinny *yank-yank,* higher pitched and more nasal than the call of the White-breasted Nuthatch.

Habitat: Coniferous forests; more widespread during migration and winter.

Nesting: 5 or 6 white eggs, spotted with red-brown, in a cup of twigs and grass lined with softer material and placed in a tree cavity. The entrance is usually smeared with pitch, presumably to discourage predators; the pitch often gets on the birds' feathers, giving them a messy appearance.

Range: Breeds across Canada from southeastern Alaska, Manitoba, and Newfoundland south to southern California, Arizona, Great Lakes region, and northern New England, and south in Appalachians to North Carolina. Winters in breeding range and irregularly south to Gulf Coast and northern Florida.

The principal winter food of the Red-breasted Nuthatch is the seeds of conifers, and in years when the seed supply fails in the North, these birds move south in large numbers. Smaller than the White-breasted Nuthatch, they tend to forage on smaller branches and twigs, seeking small insects as well as seeds. Although the Red-breasted accepts suet, it visits feeders less frequently than its relative.

380 **White-breasted Nuthatch**
*Sitta carolinensis*

Description: 5–6" (13–15 cm). Sparrow-sized. Blue-gray above, white underparts and face, black crown. Usually seen creeping on tree trunks, often downward headfirst.

Voice: Call a nasal *yank-yank.* Song a series of low whistled notes.

Habitat: Deciduous and mixed forests.

Nesting: 5 or 6 white eggs, lightly speckled with red-brown, in a cup of twigs and grass lined with feathers and hair in a natural cavity, bird box, or hole excavated by the birds.

Range: Largely resident from British Columbia, Ontario, and Nova Scotia south to southern California, Arizona, Gulf Coast, and central Florida. Absent from most of Great Plains.

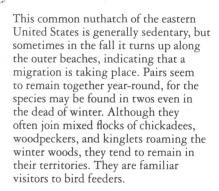

This common nuthatch of the eastern United States is generally sedentary, but sometimes in the fall it turns up along the outer beaches, indicating that a migration is taking place. Pairs seem to remain together year-round, for the species may be found in twos even in the dead of winter. Although they often join mixed flocks of chickadees, woodpeckers, and kinglets roaming the winter woods, they tend to remain in their territories. They are familiar visitors to bird feeders.

## 381 Brown-headed Nuthatch
*Sitta pusilla*

Description: 4–5″ (10–13 cm). Smaller than a sparrow. Upperparts dull blue-gray, underparts whitish. *Crown dull brown,* with whitish spot on nape.

Voice: A series of high-pitched piping notes, unlike the calls of other eastern nuthatches.

Habitat: Coniferous and mixed forests.

Nesting: 5 or 6 white eggs, heavily speckled with red-brown, in a cup of bark, grass, and feathers placed in a cavity in a dead tree or fence post, or under loose bark.

Range: Resident from Delaware, Missouri, and

eastern Texas south to Gulf Coast and central Florida.

The smallest of our eastern nuthatches, this species spends more time than the other nuthatches among terminal branches and twigs of trees. After breeding, these birds gather in flocks of a dozen or more and move through the woods along with woodpeckers and chickadees. They are quite agile and restless, flitting from one cluster of pine needles to another.

## Family Certhiidae
Creepers

7 species: Eurasia, North America, and Africa. Only the Brown Creeper is found in North America. Creepers are dull-colored birds that creep up tree trunks and probe for spiders and soft-bodied insects in the crevices of the bark, their curved bills well suited to the task. Like woodpeckers, they have stiff tail feathers that serve as a prop.

### 382 Brown Creeper
*Certhia americana*

Description: 5–5¾″ (13–14 cm). A slender, streaked, brown bird, tinged with buff on flanks; usually seen creeping up tree trunks, using its long stiff tail for support.

Voice: A high-pitched, lisping *tsee;* song a tinkling, descending warble.

Habitat: Deciduous and mixed woodlands.

Nesting: 6 or 7 white eggs, lightly speckled with brown, in a cup of bark shreds, feathers, sticks, and moss usually placed against a tree trunk behind a peeling slab of bark.

Range: Breeds from Alaska east through Ontario to Newfoundland, and southward throughout western

mountains, Great Lakes region, North Carolina, and New England. Winters in breeding range and south to Gulf Coast and Florida.

This inconspicuous bird is most often detected by its soft, lisping call as it works its way up a tree trunk, probing the bark for insects. In late winter and spring, one may sometimes hear its song—a thin, musical warble. Unlike the nuthatch, it moves only up a tree trunk; having reached the top, it flies down to the base of another tree and repeats its spiral ascent.

## Family Pycnonotidae
Bulbuls

137 species: Old World tropics. One species has been introduced into Florida. Bulbuls are generally rather dull-colored birds that travel in flocks and eat fruit or insects. Some are noisy and conspicuous, while others are very retiring and difficult to detect.

### 625 Red-whiskered Bulbul
*Pycnonotus jocosus*

Description: 8″ (20 cm). Grayish above, whitish below, with long conspicuous *black crest, red cheek patch* and undertail coverts, and black, white-tipped tail.

Voice: Various chattering notes; a whistled *queekey!*

Habitat: Residential areas, parks, and gardens.

Nesting: 2–4 pinkish-white eggs, spotted with reddish brown, in a cup of dead leaves and grass that is lined with fine roots and hair and placed in a bush or small tree.

Range: Native to Southeast Asia. Introduced and established in region around Miami, Florida.

This species has long been adapted to living in the vicinity of towns and villages in Southeast Asia, and is now successful in suburban Miami. Bulbuls are noisy, gregarious birds, usually traveling in flocks in pursuit of insects and fruit.

---

## Family Troglodytidae
Wrens

75 species: The Western Hemisphere; one wide-ranging species, the Winter Wren, also occurs in Eurasia. Nine species breed in North America. These mostly small, stocky, short-tailed birds are clad in browns, grays, and buffs. They are mainly secretive in their habits, although the familiar House Wren builds its nest in man-made birdhouses. While some wrens nest near human dwellings, others, like the Marsh Wren, which lives in cattails, construct their homes in wet places.

---

### 465 Cactus Wren
*Campylorhynchus brunneicapillus*

Description: 7–8¼″ (18–21 cm). A starling-sized wren with spotted underparts, white eyebrows, rusty crown, and white spots on outer tail feathers.

Voice: Rapid, mechanical *chug-chug-chug-chug-chug.*

Habitat: Desert thickets and cacti.

Nesting: 4 or 5 buff eggs, heavily speckled with brown. The nest, a mass of fine grass and straw, has a side entrance, is lined with feathers and hair, and is placed in the top of a thorny desert shrub or spiny cactus.

Range: Resident from southern California, southern Nevada, Utah, and western Texas southward.

It is easy to spot an area inhabited by Cactus Wrens because, like other members of the family, they build many "dummy" nests, which are never used for breeding but serve as roosting places. These nests are usually so well guarded by sharp spines that it is difficult to understand how the birds can use them without being impaled. Although their grating song is hardly musical, it is a most evocative sound for those who love the desert.

466 **Rock Wren**
*Salpinctes obsoletus*

Description: 5–6½″ (13–17 cm). A sparrow-sized wren, pale grayish brown with finely streaked breast. Outer tail feathers have whitish or pale buff tips.
Voice: A dry trill; a rhythmic series of musical notes, *chewee, chewee, chewee, chewee.*
Habitat: Rock-strewn slopes, canyons, cliffs, and dams in arid country.
Nesting: 4–6 white eggs, lightly speckled with pale brown, in a shallow nest of plant fibers and roots, lined with feathers and placed in a crevice among rocks or in a hollow stump.
Range: Breeds from interior British Columbia, Saskatchewan, and North Dakota southward in mountains. Winters north to California and Texas.

This species is found in much the same habitat as its relative the Canyon Wren but is more partial to rocky slopes, while the Canyon Wren favors sheer cliffs. The Rock Wren has the unusual habit of laying down a path of small pebbles in front of its nest; this little "pavement" often simplifies an observer's effort to locate nests.

467 **Canyon Wren**
*Catherpes mexicanus*

Description: 5½–6″ (14–15 cm). Sparrow-sized. Dark rusty above and below, with conspicuous *white throat and upper breast.*
Voice: A high clear series of descending notes, *tee-tee-tee-tee-tew-tew-tew-tew.*
Habitat: Rocky canyons and cliffs; old stone buildings.
Nesting: 4–6 white eggs, lightly speckled with reddish brown, in a shallow cup of feathers, plant down, and moss placed in a crevice among rocks or, occasionally, on a building.
Range: Resident from British Columbia, Montana, and western South Dakota southward.

Like most wrens, this bird is quite secretive, and often when one can plainly hear its musical song reverberating from the walls of a canyon, it takes a long and patient search to spot the singer, perched high up on a ledge or quietly picking its way through a clump of brush.

468 **Carolina Wren**
*Thryothorus ludovicianus*

Description: 5½″ (14 cm). Rich brown above, buff below, with *conspicuous white eyebrow.*
Voice: Loud whistled *tweedle-tweedle-tweedle* or *tea-kettle, tea-kettle, tea-kettle tea,* sung all day long in all seasons.
Habitat: Woodland thickets, ravines, and rocky slopes covered with brush.
Nesting: 5 brown-spotted whitish eggs in a feather-lined, domed stick nest with an entrance on the side. The nest is placed in stone walls, hollow tree stumps, tin cans, mail boxes, birdhouses, and even coat pockets on clotheslines.
Range: Resident in southeastern United States, north to Wisconsin and Michigan,

southern Ontario, New York, and southern New England.

These wrens do not migrate. At the northern edge of their range they increase in mild years, but a severe cold season with heavy snows will often decimate their numbers. They live in thickets and swamps, frequenting brush piles and old wooden buildings.

469 **Bewick's Wren**
*Thryomanes bewickii*

Description: 5½″ (14 cm). Gray-brown above, white below, with white eyebrow and long, fan-shaped tail tipped with white.
Voice: Loud melodious song, with the usual bubbly wren-like warble, also reminiscent of a Song Sparrow.
Habitat: Thickets, brush piles, and hedgerows in farming country; also open woodlands and scrubby areas, often near streams.
Nesting: 5–7 brown-spotted white eggs in a stick nest lined with leaves, grass, and feathers, and placed in almost any available cavity, including woodpecker holes, tin cans, coat pockets or sleeves, baskets, tool sheds, and brush piles.
Range: Breeds locally from southern British Columbia, Nebraska, southern Ontario, and southwestern Pennsylvania south to Mexico, Arkansas, and northern Gulf States. Eastern birds winter south to Gulf Coast.

Bewick's Wren was named by Audubon for Thomas Bewick (1753–1828), the English naturalist and engraver. Although this species resembles the somewhat larger Carolina Wren, it has an entirely different song and, at close range, shows white in the outer tail feathers. Bewick's Wren lives in surroundings similar to those of the Carolina Wren but generally prefers drier situations.

470 **House Wren**
*Troglodytes aedon*

Description: 4½–5¼″ (11–13 cm). A tiny bird with a short tail that is often held cocked over the back. Dusky brown above, paler below, with no distinctive markings. Winter Wren is similar but smaller, darker, with shorter tail and pale eyebrow.

Voice: A gurgling, bubbling, exuberant song, first rising, then falling.

Habitat: Residential areas, city parks, farmlands, and woodland edges.

Nesting: 5–8 white eggs, thickly speckled with brown, in a cup lined with feathers and other soft material contained within a mass of sticks and grass. The nest is placed in a natural cavity or bird box.

Range: Breeds from British Columbia east across Canada to New Brunswick, and south to southeastern Arizona, northern Texas, Tennessee, and northern Georgia. Winters north to southern California, Gulf Coast states, and Virginia. Also in tropical America.

This wren often nests in odd places such as mailboxes, flowerpots, and even the pockets of coats on clotheslines. It is a favorite with people who put out bird boxes but has the distressing habit of piercing the eggs of other birds. If House Wrens return in spring to find an old nest still in place, they usually remove it stick by stick, then proceed to rebuild, often using the very material they've just discarded. Outside the breeding season, House Wrens are shy and much less in evidence than when they are singing during the breeding season.

471 **Winter Wren**
*Troglodytes troglodytes*

Description: 4–4½″ (10–11 cm). A tiny, dark brown bird with a very short tail, dark barring on belly, and narrow pale eyebrow. See House Wren.

Voice: A high-pitched, varied, and rapid series of musical trills and chatters; call note an explosive *kit!* or *kit-kit!*

Habitat: Dense tangles and thickets in coniferous and mixed forests.

Nesting: 5–7 brown-speckled white eggs in a bulky mass of twigs and moss, with a side entrance. The nest is lined with softer material and often concealed among the upturned roots of a fallen tree.

Range: Breeds from Alaska and British Columbia east through southern Canada to Newfoundland, and south to California, northern Idaho, Great Lakes region, and southern New England; also in mountains to Georgia. Winters across much of southern United States south to southern California, Gulf Coast, and Florida. Also in Eurasia.

This wren moves like a mouse, creeping through the low, dense tangle of branches covering the forest floor. Its nest is among the hardest to find; even when an observer has narrowed the search to a few square feet, he must sometimes give up, so cleverly is the nest concealed. The Winter Wren's song, when recorded and played back at half- or quarter-speed, shows a remarkable blend of halftones and overtones all sung at the same time.

---

472 **Sedge Wren**
**"Short-billed Marsh Wren"**
*Cistothorus platensis*

Description: 4–4½" (10–11 cm). A tiny, secretive wren of grassy marshes. Buff-colored, with finely streaked crown and back. Best distinguished by voice and habitat.

Voice: A series of harsh notes, sounding like two pebbles tapping together; often heard at night.

Habitat: Grassy freshwater marshes and sedges;

also brackish marshes and wet meadows in winter.

Nesting: 5–7 white eggs in a globular mass of marsh grass with a side entrance. The nest is lined with feathers and hair that has been woven into the top of a dense stand of grass or sedge.

Range: Breeds from Saskatchewan, Manitoba, and New Brunswick south to Kansas, Missouri, and Delaware. Winters north to southern Illinois and Virginia. Very local.

The Sedge Wren is most often seen as it is flushed from grass and flies off, only to drop from view a few feet away. Its flight is distinctive, the wings vibrating stiffly as the bird seems to float over the ground. Like other wrens, it builds "dummy" nests, often hidden in dense marsh grass.

## 473 Marsh Wren
**"Long-billed Marsh Wren"**
*Cistothorus palustris*

Description: 4–5½" (10–14 cm). Smaller than a sparrow. Brown above, pale buff below, with *bold white eyebrow and white-streaked back.*

Voice: Liquid gurgling song ending in a mechanical chatter that sounds like a sewing machine.

Habitat: Freshwater and brackish marshes with cattails, reeds, bulrushes, or sedges.

Nesting: 5 or 6 pale brown eggs, speckled with dark brown, in a globular nest of reeds and cattails with a side entrance. The nest is lined with feathers and cattail down and anchored to reeds.

Range: Breeds from British Columbia, central interior Canada, Manitoba, and Nova Scotia south to Mexico, Gulf Coast, and Florida. Winters across southern tier of states on West Coast north to Washington and east to New Jersey.

The male has a number of mates, each of which builds a nest of her own. The male may also build up to half a dozen "dummy" nests, often incomplete, one of which may be used as a roost. Thus a marsh frequented by these birds often contains many nests in various stages of completion. Locating a nest with eggs or young in it can take much time, which may be one purpose of the dummy nests.

---

FAMILY MUSCICAPIDAE
**Subfamily Sylviinae**
Old World Warblers, Kinglets, and Gnatcatchers

383 species: Worldwide. Six species breed in North America. The American species include some of the smallest birds in the world. They live entirely on insects and spiders.

---

576 **Golden-crowned Kinglet**
*Regulus satrapa*

Description: 3½–4″ (9–10 cm). Tiny. Olive green above, paler below, with 2 dull-white wing bars. Eyebrow white; crown orange bordered with yellow (adult males) or solid yellow (females and young birds), *crown patch separated from white eyebrow by narrow black line.* Ruby-crowned Kinglet lacks the conspicuous face pattern.

Voice: Thin, wiry, ascending *ti-ti-ti,* followed by a tumbling chatter.

Habitat: Dense, old conifer stands; also deciduous forests and thickets in winter.

Nesting: 8 or 9 cream-colored eggs, speckled with brown, in a large mass of moss, lichens, and plant down with a small feather-lined cup at the top. The nest is generally suspended between several twigs in a densely needled conifer, less than 60′ (18 m) above ground.

Range: Breeds from Alaska to Alberta and from Manitoba to Newfoundland, and south to southern California and Southwest, to Michigan and Massachusetts, and in mountains to North Carolina. Winters from southern Canada south to southern California, Arizona, Gulf Coast, and northern Florida.

These kinglets are best known as winter visitors, often joining mixed flocks of chickadees, woodpeckers, and creepers. They seem to be entirely insectivorous and are adept at finding hibernating insects and their larvae in twigs and bark.

---

577 **Ruby-crowned Kinglet**
*Regulus calendula*

Description: 3¾–4½″ (10–11 cm). Tiny. Similar to Golden-crowned Kinglet but greener, with no face pattern except for narrow white eye ring. Males have tuft of red feathers on crown, kept concealed unless bird is aroused.

Voice: Song an excited musical chattering.

Habitat: Coniferous forests in summer; also deciduous forests and thickets in winter.

Nesting: 6–9 cream-colored eggs, lightly speckled with brown, in a large mass of moss, lichens, and plant down with a small feather-lined cup at the top.

Range: Breeds from Alaska east to Newfoundland, and south to southern California and New Mexico in West, and to Great Lakes region and northern New England in East. Winters from southern British Columbia and California across southern tier of states to southern New England.

In the northern states, this bird is scarce or absent in winter but is often seen during migration. It frequently sings on its way north, a song surprisingly loud for so tiny a bird. In the South the

Ruby-crowned Kinglet is a common winter resident, and more apt to be found in deciduous woods than the Golden-crowned. It takes a sharp eye to see the male's red crown patch, which is usually erected for a few seconds at a time when the bird is displaying aggressively. It has a characteristic habit of nervously flicking its wings.

607 **Blue-gray Gnatcatcher**
*Polioptila caerulea*

Description: 4½–5″ (11–13 cm). Smaller than a sparrow. A tiny, slender, long-tailed bird, blue-gray above and white below, with white eye ring and broad white borders on black tail. Resembles a miniature mockingbird.
Voice: Song a thin, musical warble; call note a distinctive *pzzzz* with a nasal quality.
Habitat: Open, moist woodlands and brushy streamside thickets.
Nesting: 4 or 5 pale blue, brown-spotted eggs in a small, beautifully made cup of plant down and spiderweb, decorated with flakes of lichen and fastened to a horizontal branch at almost any height above ground.
Range: Breeds from northern California, Colorado, southern Great Lakes region, southern Ontario, and New Hampshire southward. Winters north to southern California, Gulf Coast, and Carolinas.

Several species of gnatcatchers are found throughout the warmer parts of the Americas. All of them build exquisite nests, which are exceedingly difficult to find unless the adults are feeding their young; the parents are quite noisy and conspicuous, and seem to ignore intruders. These birds are extremely active, constantly flitting about through the treetops. This species apparently feeds exclusively on insects.

## Family Muscicapidae
## Subfamily Turdinae
Thrushes

310 species: Worldwide except Australia. Thirteen species breed in North America. Many members of this family are excellent singers. The best-known species in North America are the American Robin and the Eastern Bluebird. The last named, a member of a group of three species, is a hole-nester, but most others build open, cup-shaped nests. The family also includes the brown-backed, spot-breasted thrushes of the genus *Catharus,* the wheatears, and the solitaires. Young of all species have spotted breasts.

### 458 Northern Wheatear
*Oenanthe oenanthe*

Description: 5½–6″ (14–15 cm). A very rare, sparrow-sized bird of open ground. Warm brown above, buff-pink below; *bold white rump and sides of tail* contrast with black center and tip of tail, which form an inverted T.

Voice: Harsh *chak-chak!* Song is a jumble of warbling notes.

Habitat: Barren pastures and beaches in winter; nests in rocky tundra.

Nesting: 5–7 pale green eggs in a fur-lined cup of grass concealed under a rock, in a rabbit burrow, or in a crevice in a wall.

Range: Breeds in Alaska and extreme northern Canada, appearing very rarely in northern United States in fall. Winters in Eurasia and North Africa; very rarely in North America.

This Old World species has colonized North America from two directions, Siberian birds entering Alaska and European birds crossing to the eastern Canadian Arctic. Each fall they retrace their routes, wintering in Africa, where many of the 22 other species of wheatears are found. Occasionally one turns up in populated parts of North America in spring and fall. The scientific name *Oenanthe* is from the ancient Greek and means "wine-flower," alluding to the fact that these birds return to Greece in the spring just as the vineyards blossom.

## 598 Eastern Bluebird
*Sialia sialis*

Description: 7″ (17 cm). Bright blue above and on wings and tail; rusty throat and breast; white belly and undertail coverts. Female similar but duller.

Voice: Call a liquid and musical *turee* or *queedle;* song a soft melodious warble.

Habitat: Open woodlands and farmlands with scattered trees.

Nesting: 4–6 pale blue eggs in a loose cup of grasses and plant stems in natural tree cavities, old woodpecker holes, fence posts, and bird boxes.

Range: Breeds east of Rockies from southeastern Canada to Gulf of Mexico; also in mountains of southeastern Arizona and southwestern New Mexico. Winters in southern part of breeding range. Also in Mexico.

This beautiful bird is a favorite of many people and is eagerly awaited in the spring after a long cold winter. In places where bluebird nest boxes are erected and European Starlings and House Sparrows are controlled, up to six pairs of bluebirds will nest on as many acres. In the past 25 years bluebirds have become uncommon in the East for reasons not altogether clear. Competition for nest sites with European Starlings and House Sparrows is likely a critical factor. The erection of many artificial nest boxes in recent years seems to be helping to increase the population.

599 **Mountain Bluebird**
*Sialia currucoides*

Description: 7″ (18 cm). Male pure sky blue above, paler blue below, with a white abdomen; female similar, but duller and grayer.
Voice: Soft warbling notes.
Habitat: Breeds in high mountain meadows with scattered trees and bushes; in winter descends to lower elevations, where it inhabits plains and grasslands.
Nesting: 5 or 6 pale blue eggs in a nest of grass and plant fibers, placed in a natural cavity or bird box.
Range: Breeds from southern Alaska, Mackenzie, and Manitoba south to western Nebraska, New Mexico, Arizona, and southern California. Winters from British Columbia and Montana south through western United States.

This species has longer wings and a more graceful, swallow-like flight than the Eastern Bluebird. In eastern North America, it is known mainly as a winter visitor from the western plains. These birds usually travel in small parties; they search for food by hovering in the air and dropping down to pick up insects on the ground.

---

445 **Veery**
*Catharus fuscescens*

Description: 6½–7¼″ (16–18 cm). Smaller than a robin. Uniform cinnamon-brown above, with faint spotting on upper breast. Our only spotted thrush with *upperparts uniformly cinnamon.*
Voice: Song a rich, downward spiral with an ethereal quality; call note a descending *whew.*
Habitat: Moist deciduous woodlands.
Nesting: 4 blue-green eggs in a bulky cup of moss, plant fibers, and leaves, placed on the ground in a clump of grass or ferns, or a few feet above ground in a shrub.

Range: Breeds from southern British Columbia east to Newfoundland, and south to Arizona, South Dakota, Minnesota, and New Jersey, and in mountains to Georgia. Winters in tropics.

The beautiful song of the Veery sounds best at dusk, as it echoes through the deepening gloom of the forest. The bird is rather difficult to see, but it can be lured into view by an imitation of the squeaking of a bird in distress. Its diet is evenly divided between insects obtained on the ground and fruit.

---

435 **Gray-cheeked Thrush**
*Catharus minimus*

Description: 6½–8″ (17–20 cm). Dull olive-brown with pale, spotted underparts and *no rust color in plumage; sides of face tinged with gray; no eye ring.* Swainson's Thrush similar but has buff eye ring and buff, not gray, cheeks. Other spotted thrushes show rust color on upperparts or tail.

Voice: Series of thin reedy notes inflected downward at the end.

Habitat: Nests in coniferous forests, especially in dense stands of stunted spruce and balsam; widespread on migration.

Nesting: 3–5 pale blue-green eggs, finely speckled with brown, in a solidly built cup of grass reinforced with mud and placed in a low conifer.

Range: Breeds from northern Alaska across northern Canada to Newfoundland, and south to northern British Columbia, New York, and northern New England. Winters in tropics.

On migration the Gray-cheeked Thrush spends most of its time feeding quietly on the ground. While not especially shy, it is inconspicuous and easily overlooked.

## 436 Swainson's Thrush
*Catharus ustulatus*

Description: 6½–7¾" (17–20 cm). Uniformly dull olive-brown above, spotted below, with *buff eye ring and cheek.* Gray-cheeked Thrush similar, but has grayish cheeks and lacks conspicuous eye ring.

Voice: Song a series of reedy spiraling notes inflected upward.

Habitat: Coniferous forests and willow thickets.

Nesting: 3 or 4 pale green-blue eggs, finely spotted with light brown, in a well-built cup of moss and lichen lined and strengthened with twigs, leaves, and grass. The nest is generally concealed in a small forest shrub or tree.

Range: Breeds from Alaska east across Canada to Newfoundland, and south to British Columbia, Michigan, and northern New England, and in mountains to southern California, Colorado, and West Virginia. Winters in tropics.

This bird is named after the English naturalist William Swainson (1789–1855). Like the Hermit Thrush, it is a furtive, ground-dwelling bird of the northern forests. Its song, while perhaps not as beautiful as that of the Hermit Thrush, is better known to most bird-watchers because the species sings more frequently during migration.

## 437 Hermit Thrush
*Catharus guttatus*

Description: 6½–7½" (17–19 cm). Smaller than a robin. The only one of our brown, spotted thrushes with dull brown upperparts and a rusty tail. Frequently flicks its tail.

Voice: Series of clear, musical phrases, each on a different pitch, consisting of a piping introductory note and a reedy tremolo. Call note a low *tuck.*

Habitat: Coniferous and mixed forests; during migration and winter, deciduous woodlands and thickets.

Nesting: 4 blue-green eggs in a well-made cup of moss, leaves, and rootlets concealed on the ground or in a low bush in the forest.

Range: Breeds from central Alaska east to Newfoundland, and south to southern California, northern New Mexico, Wisconsin, and Virginia. Winters from Washington and southern New England southward.

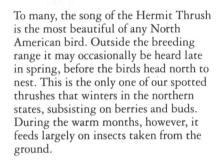

To many, the song of the Hermit Thrush is the most beautiful of any North American bird. Outside the breeding range it may occasionally be heard late in spring, before the birds head north to nest. This is the only one of our spotted thrushes that winters in the northern states, subsisting on berries and buds. During the warm months, however, it feeds largely on insects taken from the ground.

---

## 438 Wood Thrush
*Hylocichla mustelina*

Description: 8″ (20 cm). Starling-sized. Brown above, *bright rusty color on head,* and *white below with large blackish spots.* Other brown thrushes have finer spotting on breast.

Voice: A series of rich, melodious, flute-like phrases; call a sharp *pit-pit-pit-pit.*

Habitat: Moist, deciduous woodlands with a thick understory; also well-planted parks and gardens.

Nesting: 4 greenish-blue eggs in a cup of grass and twigs, reinforced with mud and lined with fine grass and rootlets, placed in a bush or sapling.

Range: Breeds from Manitoba, Ontario, and Nova Scotia south to Florida and Gulf of Mexico. Winters in tropics.

This is the most familiar of our spotted brown thrushes, and the only one that nests regularly in the vicinity of houses. The Wood Thrush has one of the most beautiful songs of any North American bird. Thoreau wrote of it: "Whenever a man hears it he is young, and Nature is in her spring; wherever he hears it, it is a new world and a free country, and the gates of heaven are not shut against him."

## 385 American Robin
*Turdus migratorius*

Description: 9–11″ (23–28 cm). Gray above, brick red below. Head and tail black in males, dull gray in females. Young birds are spotted below.

Voice: Song a series of rich caroling notes, rising and falling in pitch, *cheer-up, cheerily, cheer-up, cheerily.*

Habitat: Towns, gardens, open woodlands, and agricultural land.

Nesting: 3–5 blue-green eggs in a well-made cup of mud reinforced with grass and twigs, and lined with softer grasses. The nest is placed in a tree or on a ledge or windowsill; American Robins usually have 2 broods a season.

Range: Breeds from Alaska east across continent to Newfoundland, and south to California, Texas, Arkansas, and South Carolina. Winters north to British Columbia and Newfoundland.

Robins originally nested in forests; where they still do so they are much shyer than the robins of the dooryard. They breed only rarely in the Deep South, where they prefer large shade trees on lawns. Although considered a harbinger of spring, robins often winter in the northern states, where they frequent cedar bogs and swamps and are not usually noticed by a casual observer, except when they gather in large roosts, often containing thousands of birds.

## FAMILY MIMIDAE
Mockingbirds and Thrashers

34 species: New World. Ten species breed in North America. Included in this family are such well-known birds as the Gray Catbird, the Northern Mockingbird, and several thrashers. They are good to excellent singers, and the familiar Northern Mockingbird is a mimic of other birds. These birds are long-tailed and short-winged, and have slender, slightly to strongly curved bills.

### 612 Gray Catbird
*Dumetella carolinensis*

Description: 8–9¼" (20–23 cm). Smaller than a robin. A slender, long-tailed, *dark gray* bird with *black cap* and rusty undertail coverts.

Voice: A long, irregular succession of musical and mechanical notes and phrases; a cat-like mewing. Sometimes seems to mimic other birds.

Habitat: Thickets and brush, residential areas and gardens.

Nesting: 4 or 5 glossy blue-green eggs in a bulky mass of twigs, stems, and leaves lined with finer plant material and concealed in a dense bush or a tangle of vines.

Range: Breeds from British Columbia, Manitoba, and Nova Scotia south to Washington, Texas, and Georgia. Winters from Carolinas and Gulf Coast southward; small numbers occur regularly north to southern New England.

Formerly known simply as the "Catbird," this bird has had its name changed officially to Gray Catbird because there is an all-black species, the Black Catbird (*Melanoptila glabrirostris*), in southern Mexico. It often announces its presence by a harsh, cat-like whine issuing from a dense tangle of vegetation; the bird responds to an imitation of this call, popping suddenly into view for a better look. Catbirds are largely insectivorous, and their pleasing song has made them welcome in suburban gardens.

## 611 Northern Mockingbird
*Mimus polyglottos*

Description: 9–11″ (23–28 cm). Robin-sized. A slender, long-tailed gray bird with white patches on wings and tail.

Voice: A long series of musical and grating phrases, each repeated three or more times; often imitates other birds. Call a harsh *chack.*

Habitat: Residential areas, city parks, farmlands, open country with thickets, and desert brush.

Nesting: 3–5 blue-green eggs, spotted with brown, in a bulky cup of sticks and weed stems, placed in a bush or low tree.

Range: Breeds from northern California, central Michigan, southern Ontario, and Nova Scotia southward. Winters in southern part of range.

This bird's beautiful song is richest on warm, moonlit nights in spring, when the bird may spend hours giving amazing imitations of other species. The songs of 36 other species were recognized from the recording of one mockingbird in Massachusetts. Birds in the western part of the species' range have less musical songs and are less imitative. Mockingbirds are strongly territorial and, like a number of other birds, will attack their reflection in a window, hubcap, or mirror, at times with such vigor that they injure or kill themselves.

## 444 Sage Thrasher
*Oreoscoptes montanus*

Description: 8½″ (22 cm). Brown-gray above, buff below with conspicuous black streaks; bill strongly curved; tail relatively short with white patches in the corners; 2 white wing bars (often worn away by spring).

Voice: Continuous sweet warble without the broken-up phrases of the more familiar Brown Thrasher. The common call note is a deep *chuck.*

Habitat: Dry sagebrush plains and arid areas such as the floors of rocky canyons; winters in dense thickets and lowland scrub.

Nesting: 4 or 5 brown-blotched blue-green eggs in a stick nest lined with rootlets and grass, often with fur or feathers, and placed in a bush, usually with thorns.

Range: Breeds from southern interior British Columbia, central Idaho, and southern Montana south to southern inland California, southern Nevada, New Mexico, and western Oklahoma; also in an isolated area in southwestern Saskatchewan. Winters chiefly in southwestern states and southern Texas.

This arid-country thrasher feeds to a large extent on insects, but also on small fruits such as berries. It seems to be a cross between a thrasher and a mockingbird, but is more closely related to the latter. The flicking of its tail and its general appearance, except for the streaked underparts, recall a mockingbird, but its generally terrestrial habits, and particularly its habit of diving into a bush for cover when alarmed, are reminiscent of a thrasher. On its breeding grounds the Sage Thrasher is wary and difficult to approach, but when visiting gardens and city parks during migrations it is much tamer.

441 **Brown Thrasher**
*Toxostoma rufum*

Description: 11½″ (29 cm). Rufous-brown above, white below *with dark brown streaks*. Curved bill, long tail; yellow eye. See Long-billed Thrasher.

Voice: A variety of musical phrases, each repeated twice; call a sharp *smack!*

Habitat: Thickets, fields with scrub, and woodland borders.

Nesting: 4 or 5 pale blue, brown-dotted eggs in a large, coarsely built nest of twigs, leaves, and rootlets lined with grass. The nest is usually near the ground in a dense, often thorny bush.

Range: Breeds from southeastern Alberta, Manitoba, Ontario, and northern New England south to Gulf Coast and Florida. Winters in southern part of breeding range.

Brown Thrashers may be confused with thrushes but are larger, have longer tails, and are streaked (not spotted) below. They belong to the same family as the Mockingbird but, unlike that species, are retiring and secretive. They often feed on the ground, scattering dead leaves with their beaks as they search for insects. In recent years they have become scarce in much of their range; no one knows why.

443 **Long-billed Thrasher**
*Toxostoma longirostre*

Description: 11″ (28 cm). Jay-sized. Similar to Brown Thrasher, but darker and grayer on head and face, with longer bill, and with orange, not yellow, eye.

Voice: Song a varied series of paired phrases similar to those of the Brown Thrasher; call a low *chuck.*

Habitat: Dense tangles and thickets in both open country and wooded areas and in both moist and dry regions.

Nesting: 3 or 4 pale blue, brown-dotted eggs in a nest of twigs and leaves, lined with rootlets and placed in a dense thorn bush or cactus.

Range: Resident in south-central Texas and nearby northeastern Mexico.

This close relative of the Brown Thrasher is equally at home in dense mesquite thickets in the driest regions and in heavy bottomland forests near the Rio Grande. Many nests have been found, but details of the Long-billed Thrasher's habits remain relatively unknown. They feed extensively on insects, supplemented by fruits.

## 442 Curve-billed Thrasher
*Toxostoma curvirostre*

Description: 9½–11½″ (24–29 cm). Pale gray-brown with long tail and *strongly down-curved bill.* Breast faintly spotted; eyes yellow to orange.

Voice: Song a rapid series of musical notes and phrases; call a sharp, whistled *whit-wheet!*

Habitat: Desert brush and cactus.

Nesting: 4 pale blue-green eggs, finely speckled with brown, in a bulky cup of twigs and rootlets, placed in a dense thorny desert shrub or in a branching clump of cactus.

Range: Resident from northwestern and central Arizona, southeastern Colorado, and western Oklahoma southward.

The most characteristic dawn sound in the Texas brush country—or indeed wherever this bird occurs—is its sharp call, which sounds much like a human whistling to attract attention. Like the Cactus Wren, it builds nests that are conspicuous but hard to reach because they are placed in the center of dense, thorny desert vegetation. The curved bill is used to toss dead leaves aside during the bird's search for insects on the ground.

## FAMILY MOTACILLIDAE
Pipits and Wagtails

65 species: Primarily an Old World family; only two species breed in North America south of Alaska. These two are the widespread American Pipit and the localized Sprague's Pipit of the Great Plains. As with the similar larks, the pipits are birds of open country, inhabiting short-grass fields. Like larks, they feed and nest on the ground, walking rather than hopping. These birds are plain brown and streaked. Many bob their tails.

---

### 423 American Pipit
**"Water Pipit"**
*Anthus rubescens*

Description: 6–7″ (15–18 cm). A sparrow-sized, slender brown bird of open country. Crown and upperparts uniform brown, underparts buff with streaks; outer tail feathers white; legs usually black. Constantly bobs its tail and usually walks rather than hops. Sprague's Pipit has streaked back and yellow legs; seldom bobs its tail.

Voice: Flight song a weak and tinkling trill; call a paired, high-pitched *pip-pip.*

Habitat: Arctic and alpine tundra; during migration and winter, beaches, barren fields, agricultural land, and golf courses.

Nesting: 4 or 5 gray eggs, thickly spotted with brown and streaked with black, in a cup of grass and twigs placed on the ground in the shelter of a rock or tussock.

Range: Breeds from northern Alaska, Mackenzie, Arctic islands, and Newfoundland south in mountains to California, New Mexico, and northern New Hampshire. Winters across southern states and north to British Columbia and southern New England.

The American Pipit was formerly considered a form of the Water Pipit of the Old World. The absence of a breeding species of pipits in the open country of the eastern United States is due to the fact that until recently forests covered this area. In winter large flocks gather in open fields; when disturbed they rise in unison, wheel, turn, and resume their feeding.

424 **Sprague's Pipit**
*Anthus spragueii*

Description: 6¼–7″ (16–18 cm). Sparrow-sized. A slender-billed, streaked bird with white outer tail feathers; *yellow legs.* Rarely bobs its tail. American Pipit is similar, but has darker legs and unstreaked back; constantly bobs its tail.

Voice: Flight song, performed high in the air, is a descending series of tinkling double notes; call a series of sharp pips.

Habitat: Short-grass plains and plowed fields.

Nesting: 4 or 5 gray eggs, spotted with purple and brown, placed in a cup of grass, concealed in a tussock on the ground, and usually covered by an arch of bent grass stems.

Range: Breeds from Alberta and Manitoba south to Minnesota and Montana. Winters from southern Great Plains east to Mississippi and in Southwest.

This species was named by Audubon for Isaac Sprague (1811–1895), an artist who accompanied him on his trip up the Missouri River. An uncommon and inconspicuous bird, the first specimen was found in 1843, and it was not until 16 years later that a second bird was obtained. It is easily overlooked, slipping away through the grass or flying off quickly. Usually seen on breeding grounds, where the males put on a flight display.

## Family Bombycillidae
Waxwings

3 species: Temperate portions of the Northern Hemisphere. Two species breed in North America. These handsome, sleek, crested birds are named for the unique red, wax-like tips on the wing feathers of the adults. Waxwings are among the tamest of birds, often permitting a very close approach. They are very gregarious and often form large flocks, except in the nesting season, which is usually in late summer. They feed on both insects and berries.

---

### 450 Bohemian Waxwing
*Bombycilla garrulus*

Description: 7½–8½″ (19–22 cm). A sleek, gray-brown, crested bird. Similar to Cedar Waxwing but larger, grayer, and with conspicuous white wing patches and rusty (not white) undertail coverts.
Voice: High-pitched, lisping *seeee,* harsher and more grating than call of Cedar Waxwing.
Habitat: Open coniferous forests.
Nesting: 4–6 pale blue eggs, heavily spotted and scrawled with black, in a loose flat saucer of twigs, lichens, and grass placed in a conifer.
Range: Breeds from Alaska, Yukon, Mackenzie, Saskatchewan, and Manitoba south to central Washington, northern Idaho, and northwestern Montana. Wanders irregularly farther south and east during winter. Also in Eurasia.

This handsome bird of the North Woods is a rare visitor to the northeastern United States in winter. When it appears, often in large flocks, it feeds on berries. One hundred or more of these birds perched in the top of a leafless tree in midwinter, calling shrilly, is an unforgettable event. Highly social, Bohemian Waxwings usually move about in tight formations, descending en masse on a clump of bushes and quickly stripping them of fruit.

451 **Cedar Waxwing**
*Bombycilla cedrorum*

Description: 6½–8″ (17–20 cm). Smaller than a robin. A *sleek, crested, brown* bird with black mask, yellow tips on tail feathers, and hard red wax-like tips on secondary wing feathers. Almost always seen in flocks.
Voice: A thin lisp, *tseee.*
Habitat: Open woodlands, orchards, and residential areas.
Nesting: 4–6 blue-gray eggs, spotted with dark brown and black, in a bulky cup of twigs and grass placed in a tree in the open..
Range: Breeds from southeastern Alaska east to Newfoundland, and south to California, Illinois, and Virginia. Winters from British Columbia, Great Lakes region, and New England southward.

Waxwings spend most of the year in flocks whose movements may be quite erratic. Hundreds will suddenly appear in an area to exploit a crop of berries, only to vanish when that crop is exhausted. Since the young are fed to some extent on small fruits, waxwings tend to nest late in the summer when there is a good supply of berries. Adults store food for the young in the crop, a pouch located in the throat, and may regurgitate as many as 30 choke cherries, one at a time, into the gaping mouths of the nestlings. In summer insects are also taken, the birds hawking for them like flycatchers. These social birds have the amusing habit of passing berries or even apple blossoms from one bird to the next down a long row sitting on a branch, until one bird eats the food.

## Family Laniidae
Shrikes

74 species: Mainly Old World. Only two species live in North America, both of them migratory. These are sparrow- to robin-sized perching birds with hooked bills. They are territorial birds, inhabiting open, brushy, or wooded areas, that pursue insects or small reptiles, mammals, and birds from lookouts. They are known for impaling their prey on a thorn or pressing it into a tree crotch, often as a food cache.

### 614 Northern Shrike
*Lanius excubitor*

Description: 9–10½″ (23–27 cm). Robin-sized. Pale gray above, white below, with faint barring on underparts and *bold black mask ending at bill.* Tail black with white edges. Stout, hooked bill. Immature more brown in color. Usually seen perched in top of a tree in the open. Loggerhead Shrike is shorter-billed, with black mask that crosses forehead.

Voice: Mixture of warbles and harsh tones with a robin-like quality.

Habitat: Open woodlands and brushy swamps in summer; open grasslands with fence posts and scattered trees in winter.

Nesting: 4–6 pale gray eggs spotted with dark gray and brown. The nest is a large mass of twigs, lichens, moss, and feathers, usually in a dense conifer.

Range: Breeds from Alaska across northern Canada to Labrador Peninsula. Winters irregularly across northern tier of states south to northern California, Kansas, and Pennsylvania. Also in Old World.

Unusual among songbirds, shrikes prey on small birds and rodents, catching them with the bill and sometimes impaling them on thorns or barbed wire for storage. Like other northern birds that depend on rodent populations, the Northern Shrike's movements are cyclical, becoming more abundant in the United States when northern rodent populations are low. Sometimes they hunt from an open perch, where they sit motionless until prey appears; at other times, they hover in the air, ready to pounce on anything that moves.

615 **Loggerhead Shrike**
*Lanius ludovicianus*

Description: 8–10″ (20–25 cm). Slightly smaller than Northern Shrike, and slightly darker gray above, white below, with *black face mask extending over bill.*
Voice: Variety of harsh and musical notes and trills; a thrasher-like series of double phrases.
Habitat: Grasslands, orchards, and open areas with scattered trees; open grassy woodlands.
Nesting: 4–6 white eggs, spotted with gray and brown, in a bulky mass of twigs and grass lined with plant down and feathers and set in a thorny shrub or tree.
Range: Breeds from southern British Columbia, central Alberta, central Saskatchewan, southern Manitoba, southern Ontario, southern Quebec, and south throughout United States. Seriously declining in Northeast. Winters in southern half of breeding range.

In the southern half of North America this species is the counterpart of the Northern Shrike of the boreal regions of Alaska and Canada. In behavior and choice of habitat the two species are essentially similar, although the Loggerhead preys on insects more than its northern relative. Its flight is undulating, with alternate rapid fluttering and gliding. Since it has no talons, the Northern Shrike impales its prey—usually a small bird, mouse, or insect—on a thorn or barbed-wire fence to facilitate tearing it apart then or at a later time; hence its vernacular name "Butcher Bird."

## Family Sturnidae
Starlings

114 species. Tropical and temperate regions of the Old World. Two species have been introduced into North America. Members of this family are medium-sized songbirds with large feet and strong bills, often with brilliantly glossy black plumage. They are mainly birds of open country, although a few are adapted for living in forests. Most species are gregarious, and some form huge flocks outside the breeding season.

606, 633 **European Starling**
*Sturnus vulgaris*

Description: 7½–8½" (19–22 cm). Smaller than a robin. A short-tailed, chunky, iridescent black bird. Long, pointed bill is yellow in summer and dark in fall and early winter. Plumage flecked with white in winter. Juvenile is uniform dull gray with dark bill.

Voice: A series of discordant, musical, squeaky, and rasping notes; often imitates other birds. Call a descending *whee-ee.*

Habitat: Cities, suburban areas, farmlands, and ranches.

Nesting: 4–6 pale blue eggs in a mass of twigs, grass, and trash lined with finer plant material and feathers, and placed in a tree or building cavity.

Range: Occurs from Alaska east across southern Canada, and south to Gulf Coast and northern Mexico. Native to Eurasia, and widely introduced around the world.

Conditioned by centuries of living in settled areas in Europe, this species easily adapted to American cities after 100 birds were liberated in Central Park, New York City, in 1890. Since then it has spread over most of the continent. Its large roosts, often located on buildings, may contain tens of thousands of birds. These congregations create much noise, foul the area, and have proved difficult to drive away. Starlings are aggressive birds and compete with native species for nest cavities and food. There has been much debate regarding their economic value, but their consumption of insects seems to tip the balance in their favor.

## Family Vireonidae
Vireos

51 species: New World, mostly tropical and subtropical. Twelve species breed in North America, all in the genus *Vireo.* These small, mostly plainly colored birds inhabit woodlands and forest edges. They are usually sluggish in movement and live on insects found among the foliage and small branches. Vireos are persistent and tireless singers. They lay from three to five eggs in nests usually suspended from branches.

### 573 White-eyed Vireo
*Vireo griseus*

Description: 5″ (13 cm). Warbler-sized. Olive green above and white below with yellow flanks; *yellow "spectacles"*; white wing bars. Adult has *white eye*; immature has dark eye.

Voice: Loud, explosive series of notes, *chip-a-wheeoo-chip* or *Quick, give me a rain check!*

Habitat: Dense swampy thickets and hillsides with blackberry and briar tangles.

Nesting: 4 brown-dotted white eggs in a purse-shaped nest of bark strips and grass, lined with spider silk, moss, and lichens, and set from 3 to 6′ (1 to 2 m) up in thick undergrowth.

Range: Breeds from Nebraska, Illinois, Ohio, southeastern New York, and central New England south to eastern Texas and southern Florida. Winters from Gulf Coast and Florida southward.

While most vireos inhabit tall trees, this species is usually found in thickets, where its presence is most easily detected by its loud and distinctive song. A patient observer can usually get a good look at one by standing quietly and waiting for the bird's curiosity to bring it into view. The Brown-headed Cowbird favors this vireo's nest for its own eggs.

## 566 Bell's Vireo
*Vireo bellii*

Description: 4¾–5″ (11–13 cm). Smaller than a sparrow. Dull olive-gray above, whitish below, with faint white eye ring and fainter wing bars. White-eyed Vireo similar but larger, with yellow "spectacles" and white eyes.

Voice: Fast warbled *tweedle-deedle-dum? tweedle-deedle-dee!* with first phrase up, second phrase down.

Habitat: Dense bottomland thickets, willow scrub, and mesquite.

Nesting: 3–5 white eggs, sparsely marked with brown, in a well-made pendant cup of plant down and bark strips, placed in a dense tree or shrub.

Range: Breeds from southern California, Colorado, Dakotas, and Indiana southward. Absent from eastern third of United States. Winters in tropics.

Although like the White-eyed Vireo often victimized by cowbirds, this bird

raises relatively few of the brood parasites, simply abandoning a nest when a cowbird's egg is laid in it. The species was named by Audubon for John G. Bell (1812–1899), a New York taxidermist who accompanied him on his trip up the Missouri River in the 1840s.

## Black-capped Vireo
*Vireo atricapillus*

Description: 4½–4¾″ (11–12 cm). Smaller than a sparrow. Olive green above, white below; *crown and sides of head glossy black;* white "spectacles." Female similar, but crown and sides of head slate-gray.

Voice: Harsh and varied phrases, sometimes musical.

Habitat: Dense oak scrub and juniper thickets.

Nesting: 4 unspotted white eggs in a well-made pendant cup of plant fibers and bark strips decorated with lichens and concealed in a shrub or bush.

Range: Breeds from Kansas south through Oklahoma to central Texas. Winters in Mexico.

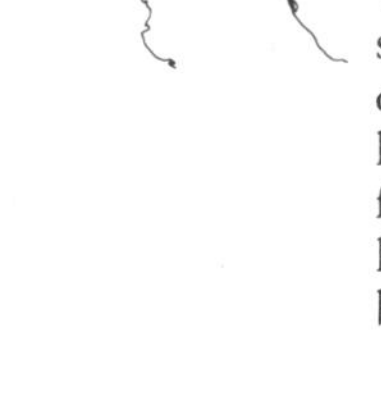

This little vireo, with its restricted range, differs from most vireos in being rather nervous and active—more like a warbler in its behavior. It is a tireless singer but is often difficult to find in the dense oak scrub. It has a titmouse-like habit of hanging upside down while foraging among twigs. In recent years it has become rare, its nesting disrupted by cowbirds.

## 568 Solitary Vireo
*Vireo solitarius*

Description: 5–6″ (13–15 cm). Sparrow-sized. Olive green above and white below, with dull yellow flanks. *Crown and sides of head slate or bluish gray,* with bold white "spectacles."

Voice: Rather slow series of sweet, slurred phrases like that of Red-eyed Vireo, but slower and more musical. Call a husky chatter.

Habitat: Coniferous and mixed forests.

Nesting: 3–5 white eggs, lightly spotted with brown, in a pendant cup of bark strips and down placed in a forked twig of a small forest tree.

Range: Breeds from British Columbia, central interior Canada, and Newfoundland south through western mountains, to Great Lakes region and southern New England, and in Appalachians to North Carolina. Winters from South Carolina and Gulf Coast southward.

This species was formerly called the "Blue-headed Vireo." Handsome and distinctively patterned, it is known to most people as a fairly common migrant, usually arriving somewhat earlier in the spring than other vireos. It is extraordinarily tame and seems to ignore humans near its nest; frequently an incubating bird will allow itself to be touched. Like other vireos, it moves slowly and deliberately through the trees, peering with head cocked to one side in search of insects.

---

## 547 Yellow-throated Vireo
*Vireo flavifrons*

Description: 6″ (15 cm). Sparrow-sized. *Bright yellow throat, breast, and "spectacles"; 2 conspicuous white wing bars,* olive green head and back, gray rump, white belly.

Voice: Similar to song of Red-eyed and Solitary vireos, but lower in pitch and with a husky or burry quality to the phrases.

Habitat: Tall deciduous trees at the edge of forests, along streams, roadsides, orchards, and parks.

Nesting: 4 brown-blotched pinkish eggs in a cup-shaped nest of lichens, mosses, and grasses decorated and lined with spiderweb silk and egg cases, and set in a forked branch well up in a tree.

Range: Breeds from Manitoba, Minnesota, Ontario, and central New England south to Gulf Coast states. Winters in tropics, with a few in southern Florida.

These handsome vireos are found mainly in open groves of tall hardwood trees. Their numbers have decreased in recent years because of the spraying of trees with toxic chemicals.

## 570 Warbling Vireo
*Vireo gilvus*

Description: 5–6″ (13–15 cm). Sparrow-sized. Similar to Red-eyed Vireo—olive green above, whitish below with no wing bars—but lacks bold face pattern, having only a narrow white eyebrow. Philadelphia Vireo also similar, but has yellow tinge to underparts and dark spot between eye and base of bill.

Voice: Drowsy, rambling warble, like song of Purple Finch but slower; ends on rising note.

Habitat: Deciduous woodlands, especially near streams; isolated groves and shade trees.

Nesting: 3 or 4 brown-spotted white eggs in a well-made pendant cup of bark strips and plant down fastened to a forked twig, usually near the top of a tall tree.

Range: Breeds from British Columbia, southern Mackenzie, Manitoba, and New Brunswick south to northern Mexico, Louisiana, and Virginia. Winters in tropics.

The best place to look for this modestly plumaged vireo is in a grove of tall shade trees on the bank of a stream. Here, in the breeding season, one may hear its rambling song and, after a careful search, spot it moving deliberately through the treetop foliage in pursuit of insects. Although still common in many areas, the Warbling Vireo has decreased considerably because of extensive spraying of elms, its favorite tree for nesting.

572 **Philadelphia Vireo**
*Vireo philadelphicus*

Description: 6″ (15 cm). Sparrow-sized. Olive above, *yellowish below*, with pale eyebrow, dark line through eye to base of bill, and no wing bars.
Voice: Like the Red-eyed Vireo but higher and slower, *See-me? Here-I-am! Up-here. See-me?*
Habitat: Open second-growth woodlands (often aspens), old clearings and burned-over areas, and thickets along streams and lakes.
Nesting: 4 brown-spotted white eggs in a cup of bark strips, grasses, and mosses lined with bits of lichen and thistledown.
Range: Breeds in southern Canada and northernmost United States. Winters in tropics.

Because this vireo was first described by John Cassin in 1842 from a specimen collected near Philadelphia, both its common and Latin names refer to Philadelphia, but it is by no means confined to that area. It is easily overlooked in spring since it does not sing much on migration; in addition, arriving chiefly during the last week in May, it is present when the foliage is already dense.

571 **Red-eyed Vireo**
*Vireo olivaceus*

Description: 5½–6½″ (14–17 cm). Sparrow-sized. Olive green above, whitish below, with *narrow white eyebrow bordered above with black. Gray crown; red eye* (eye dark in immature); no wing bars. Warbling Vireo similar, but lacks gray crown and black border over bold white eyebrow.

Voice: A series of short, musical, robin-like phrases, endlessly repeated; like that of Solitary Vireo but faster and not so musical.

Habitat: Deciduous forests, and shade trees in residential areas.

Nesting: 3 or 4 white eggs, sparsely marked with dark brown, in a thin-walled pendant cup of bark strips and plant fibers, decorated with lichen and attached to a forked twig.

Range: Breeds from British Columbia, Ontario, and the Gulf of Saint Lawrence south to Oregon, Colorado, Gulf Coast, and Florida. Winters in tropics.

This vireo is one of the most abundant birds in eastern North America. Its principal habitat, the vast broad-leaved forests, supports millions of them, often one pair per acre. A persistent singer during the breeding season, the Red-eyed Vireo utters its endless series of short phrases from dawn till dusk, even on the hottest days when other birds are silent, and may even sing while grappling with the large insects it captures.

## 569 Yellow-green Vireo
*Vireo flavoviridis*

Description: 6–7″ (15–18 cm). Sparrow-sized. Olive-green above, paler below, with yellowish tinge on back, flanks, and undertail coverts; dull gray crown; whitish eyebrow. Eye red. Similar to Red-eyed Vireo, but much yellower below, and with more indistinct markings on head.

Voice: A series of deliberate, musical phrases, more widely spaced than in song of Red-eyed Vireo.

Habitat: Streamside thickets and woodlands.

Nesting: 3 or 4 white eggs, lightly spotted with brown, in a pendant cup of plant fibers and bark strips, bound together with spiderweb and suspended from a forked branch in a bush or small sapling.

Range: Breeds from Rio Grande Valley of Texas southward. Winters in tropics.

The Yellow-green Vireo is one of the tropical members of the group of species that includes our familiar Red-eyed Vireo. Like the Red-eyed, this bird obtains its food by searching rather carefully in the foliage of trees, without the more active motions of warblers. Its song is repeated monotonously throughout the day.

---

567 **Black-whiskered Vireo**
*Vireo altiloquus*

Description: 5½″ (14 cm). Similar to the Red-eyed Vireo (olive green above, white below), but with a *dusky streak below the eye* that gives bird its name. Streak is often hard to see, and bird is best identified by voice.

Voice: Similar to that of Red-eyed Vireo but distinctly more abrupt, and in 1- to 4-note phrases, sometimes described as *Whip-Tom-Kelly.*

Habitat: Mangroves, thick scrub, and shade trees.

Nesting: 2 or 3 white eggs, with a few small scattered spots, in a nest of grass, leaves, and rootlets in the fork of a branch, usually in mangroves.

Range: Breeds in southern Florida and West Indies. Winters in tropics.

These vireos are not shy and come regularly into gardens and shade trees in Key West. They may also be seen in the dense scrub and tropical hammocks in the Upper Keys and occasionally in coconut palms and mangroves around Miami. They eat insects and, rarely, berries and other soft fruits.

## FAMILY EMBERIZIDAE
### Subfamily Parulinae
Wood Warblers

115 species: New World. Fifty-two species breed in North America. Most members of this group are brightly colored, active insect eaters. These birds are misnamed, however, as the vast majority produce nothing more than buzzy, insect-like songs, hardly what could be called a warble. In spring, warblers are the delight of bird-watchers, with their distinctive patterns and bright colors. In autumn, however, many are in dull plumage; known as the "confusing fall warblers," they then become difficult to identify.

---

508 **Bachman's Warbler**
*Vermivora bachmanii*

Description: 4½" (11 cm). Male is olive green above and bright yellow below, with yellow forehead and cheeks; *black cap and large throat patch.* Female has gray cap, lacks black throat, and is duller in color. Male Hooded Warbler has black cap and throat joined into a hood.

Voice: Buzzy song is a cross between those of Worm-eating Warbler and Northern Parula.

Habitat: Densely wooded swamps and wet thickets in heavy forests.

Nesting: 3 or 4 white eggs in a nest made of plant stems and leaves, lined with fine fibers and placed low in shrubs and vines.

Range: Very local and rare in southeastern United States. Historically nested mainly in South Carolina, Alabama, Arkansas, and Missouri. Winters in West Indies.

By far the rarest and least known of North American warblers, since it inhabits impenetrable swamps, Bachman's is more often heard than seen. For the past several decades it has been something of a mystery; placed on the endangered list, it is undoubtedly close to extinction. This warbler was named for Dr. John Bachman (1790–1874), friend and associate of Audubon.

## 505 Blue-winged Warbler
*Vermivora pinus*

Description: 4½″ (11 cm). Sexes similar, *mostly bright yellow with blue-gray wings, 2 white wing bars,* and black line through eye. Greenish back and tail.

Voice: Insect-like buzzy song, which sounds like a tired sigh, *seee-bzzz,* the *bzzz* pitched lower.

Habitat: Abandoned fields and pastures grown up to saplings; forest clearings and edges with clumps of catbrier, blackberry, and various bushes and young trees.

Nesting: 5 brown-dotted white eggs in a grass-lined cup of dead leaves and fibers, placed on or very near the ground in thick undergrowth.

Range: Breeds from Nebraska, central Iowa, southern Wisconsin, southern Ontario, and central New England south through east-central and Atlantic Coast states to northern Georgia. Winters in tropics.

This warbler perches motionless for minutes at a time when uttering its song. It frequently hybridizes with its close relative the Golden-winged Warbler. Where the ranges of the two species overlap, the Blue-winged is crowding out the Golden-winged.

## 519 Golden-winged Warbler
*Vermivora chrysoptera*

Description: 4½″ (11 cm). Male gray above, white below, with *black mask* and throat; white eyebrow and "mustache"; *yellow crown and wing patch.* Female similar, but has gray mask and throat.

Voice: Slow, drawled, insect-like song resembling that of Blue-winged but longer, *seee-bzzz, bzzz,* with first note higher.

Habitat: Abandoned fields and pastures grown to saplings, usually in drier situations than Blue-winged.

Nesting: 5 purplish-spotted white eggs in a cup of dead leaves and fibers set on or near the ground in thick vegetation.

Range: Breeds from southern Manitoba and New Hampshire south to New Jersey and Iowa, and in mountains to Georgia. Winters from southern Mexico to northern South America.

Where the breeding ranges of this species and the Blue-winged Warbler overlap, the two frequently hybridize; the offspring of these crosses show various combinations of the characteristics of the parent species and have been called "Brewster's Warbler" and "Lawrence's Warbler." The fact that these two species interbreed shows that they are closely related, and suggests that the striking differences between them have evolved during the last few tens of thousands of years.

## 525 Tennessee Warbler
*Vermivora peregrina*

Description: 5″ (13 cm). In spring, male greenish above, white below, with gray cap, white line over eye, dusky line through eye. In fall, olive above, yellowish below.

Voice: A sharp, staccato *di-dit-di-dit-swit-swit-swit-chip-chip-chip-chip-chip,* fastest at the end; song usually has 3 distinct segments.

Habitat: Open mixed woodlands in the breeding season; in trees and bushes during migration.

Nesting: 5 or 6 brown-spotted white eggs in a nest lined with fine grasses, placed on the ground and usually well hidden under a shrub or in a moss clump under a tussock.

Range: Breeds from Yukon east across Canada to Labrador, and south to British Columbia, Wisconsin, southern Ontario, and Maine. Winters in tropics.

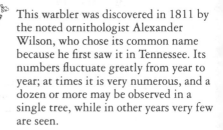

This warbler was discovered in 1811 by the noted ornithologist Alexander Wilson, who chose its common name because he first saw it in Tennessee. Its numbers fluctuate greatly from year to year; at times it is very numerous, and a dozen or more may be observed in a single tree, while in other years very few are seen.

## 527 Orange-crowned Warbler
*Vermivora celata*

Description: 4½–5½" (11–14 cm). *Olive green above* with orange crown feathers, which usually remain hidden. Olive-yellow underparts with very faint breast streaking. *No eye ring or wing bars.*

Voice: Song is a simple trill going up or down the scale toward the end. Call a sharp *stik.*

Habitat: Forest edges, especially in low deciduous growth, burns, clearings, and thickets. During migration often seen in riverside willows and in scrub-oak chaparral.

Nesting: 4–6 white eggs, with reddish or lavender spots often concentrated around the large end, in a rather large nest of grass and other plant fibers that is lined with fur or feathers. Nest is usually placed on the ground or in a low shrub.

Range: Breeds from Alaska east to Quebec and Labrador, and south to California,

Arizona, and New Mexico. Winters from southern United States into tropics.

While the Orange-crowned Warbler is a common bird in the West and in winter along the Gulf Coast, in most of the East it is a rather rare migrant. It is slightly more numerous in the fall, when the birds—mostly immatures—show a fondness for stands of goldenrod and generally forage close to the ground.

---

522 **Nashville Warbler**
*Vermivora ruficapilla*

Description: 4–5″ (10–13 cm). Olive green above, bright yellow below, with *top and sides of head gray, narrow white eye ring,* and inconspicuous patch of rust on crown. Differs from Mourning Warbler in having *yellow throat,* not gray or black.

Voice: A loud, ringing *teebit-teebit-teebit chipper-chipper-chipper-chipper;* usually has 2 distinct segments.

Habitat: Woodland edges; thickets in open mixed forests or brushy borders of swamps.

Nesting: 4 or 5 white eggs, speckled with brown, in a cup of grasses, leaves, and roots lined with pine needles and fine grass. Nest concealed on the ground in the base of a bush or a tussock of grass.

Range: Breeds from British Columbia and northwestern Montana south to central California and central Idaho; and from Manitoba, Quebec, and Nova Scotia south to Minnesota, northern West Virginia, and western Maryland. Winters south of U.S.–Mexico border.

This warbler has benefited from the arrival of settlers and the clearing of forests. It breeds most successfully in brushy, overgrown pastures, a habitat that has become more widespread with the decline of farming in the Northeast. As these pastures become second-growth woodland and the ground loses its cover of brush, the Nashville Warbler will probably become less abundant.

520, 521 **Northern Parula**
*Parula americana*

Description: 4½″ (11 cm). A small warbler; blue above with yellow-green "saddle" on its back, yellow throat and breast, and white belly; 2 white wing bars. Male has orange-brown chest band.

Voice: 1 or more rising buzzy notes dropping abruptly at the end, *bzzzzz-zip* or *bz-bz-bz-zip.*

Habitat: Breeds in wet, chiefly coniferous woods, in swamps, and along lakes and ponds; more widespread during migration.

Nesting: 4 or 5 brown-spotted white eggs in a woven basket-shaped nest of grass, bark, and vegetable fibers—neatly hidden in Spanish moss in the South, in "beard moss" or *Usnea* lichen in the North.

Range: Breeds from southeastern Canada to Gulf Coast. Winters from southern Florida southward into tropics.

This species is almost entirely dependent upon either Spanish moss or "beard moss" for nest sites. Although they breed mostly in coniferous forests in the North, during migration these birds also frequent deciduous trees and shrubs. In spring they are seen in large numbers along roadsides and in parks, yards, orchards, and gardens as well as woods.

500 **Tropical Parula**
*Parula pitiayumi*

Description: 4–5″ (10–13 cm). A small, bluish-backed warbler with bright yellow underparts, 2 white wing bars, and patch of olive green in middle of back. Male has orange wash on breast.

Northern Parula similar, but male has orange-brown breast band.

Voice: A buzzy, ascending trill, *zzzzzzzzzz-up.*

Habitat: River-bottom woodlands and thickets.

Nesting: 3 or 4 white eggs, spotted with brown, in a cup built into a mass of hanging moss, usually along a stream.

Range: Breeds in Rio Grande Valley of Texas. A few winter in Texas, but most do so in Mexico. Also in tropics.

This species has become quite scarce along the Rio Grande, the only part of the United States in which it nests, due to parasitism by cowbirds, the disappearance of Spanish moss, and the use of pesticides. During a period in the 1960s it apparently did not nest north of the U.S.–Mexico border at all, but now a few pairs breed in certain tracts of river-bottom woods.

504 **Yellow Warbler**
*Dendroica petechia*

Description: 4½–5″ (11–13 cm). Bright yellow with light olive green tinge on back. Male has fine rusty streaks on breast. The only largely yellow warbler with *yellow spots in tail* (not white).

Voice: Song a bright, musical *sweet-sweet-sweet, sweeter-than-sweet.* Call a sharp *chip.*

Habitat: Moist thickets, especially along streams and in swampy areas; gardens.

Nesting: 4 or 5 pale blue eggs, thickly spotted with brown, in a well-made cup of bark, plant fibers, and down, placed in an upright fork in a small sapling.

Range: Breeds across much of North America, from Alaska east to Newfoundland, and south to southern California, northern Oklahoma, and northern Georgia; also local in southern Florida. Winters in tropics.

This is one of the most widespread of our warblers, showing great

geographical variation. In the tropical parts of its breeding range this bird nests mainly in mangrove swamps, and there it may have a chestnut head or crown patch. In temperate North America the Yellow Warbler is one of the principal victims of the cowbird, which lays its eggs in the nests of other birds. The warbler often responds to the unwanted egg by burying it, along with some of its own eggs, under a new nest lining. Occasionally a nest is found with up to six layers, each containing one or more cowbird eggs.

523, 531 **Chestnut-sided Warbler**
*Dendroica pensylvanica*

Description: 5″ (13 cm). Sexes similar: yellow-green crown; *long chestnut line on sides; white underparts;* streaked back. Immatures uniform yellow-green above, dull whitish below, with white eye ring and yellow wing bars.

Voice: Rich and musical with an emphatic ending, sometimes interpreted as *very very pleased to meet cha!*

Habitat: Young, open, second-growth woodlands and scrub.

Nesting: 4 brown-spotted white eggs in a grass-and-bark nest lined with hair and rootlets, a few feet (about a meter) off the ground in a small tree or bush.

Range: Breeds from south-central Canada, east to Nova Scotia, south to east-central United States and in Appalachian Mountains. Winters in tropics.

This attractive bird was rare in the days of Audubon and Wilson, who seldom saw it and knew little about its habits. It has increased tremendously as abandoned pastures in the northern states have grown up in dense thickets, a vast new habitat unavailable when the land was covered with virgin forest.

513 **Magnolia Warbler**
*Dendroica magnolia*

Description: 5″ (13 cm). Male bright yellow below with heavy black streaks, black facial patch, large white wing patch, and yellow rump. Female and immature birds similar but duller. Broad white patches on sides of tail in all plumages.
Voice: Song a rising *weeta-weeta-weeteo.* Call note is *tslip.*
Habitat: Breeds in open stands of young spruce and fir. During migration, almost any place where there are shrubs or trees.
Nesting: 4 brown-spotted white eggs in a shallow twig-and-grass nest lined with rootlets.
Range: Breeds from British Columbia across central Canada to northeastern United States, and in Appalachian Mountains south to Virginia. Winters in tropics.

This attractive warbler got its name from the first specimen obtained by the famous ornithologist Alexander Wilson among some magnolia trees in Mississippi in the early 1800s. It actually breeds in conifers in the North, but the name has persisted. The Magnolia is one of our most numerous warblers and on certain spring days during migration the trees seem to be filled with the birds. They also regularly forage near the ground in low bushes.

510, 574 **Cape May Warbler**
*Dendroica tigrina*

Description: 5″ (13 cm). In breeding plumage, male yellow below with *conspicuous chestnut cheek patch; yellow neck patch;* white wing patch; yellow rump; heavy black streaks on underparts. Female much duller, with greenish-yellow patch on neck.
Voice: Song is 4 or more high thin notes without change in pitch or volume, *seet-seet-seet-seet.*
Habitat: Open spruce forests; during migration,

evergreen or deciduous woodlands and often parks or suburban yards.

Nesting: 4 brown-spotted white eggs in a bulky, compact, twig-and-moss nest lined with grass, fur, and feathers.

Range: Breeds from southern Mackenzie, Manitoba, Ontario, and Quebec south to North Dakota, Michigan, northern New York, Maine, and Nova Scotia. Winters in southern Florida and West Indies.

This warbler gets its name from the fact that the first specimen was collected at Cape May, New Jersey, where it is sometimes a common migrant. During migration these birds show a curious attraction to ornamental spruces.

---

600, 610 **Black-throated Blue Warbler**
*Dendroica caerulescens*

Description: 5″ (13 cm). Male blue-gray above, white below, with black face, throat, and sides; female dull olive green, with narrow white eyebrow and usually a small, square, white wing patch.

Voice: Song a husky, rising *zwee-zwee-zwee.*

Habitat: Mixed deciduous and evergreen woodlands with thick undergrowth, especially mountain laurel.

Nesting: 4 brown-spotted white eggs in a nest made of leaves and grass, lined with cobwebs and hair and set near the ground in a shrub or a young tree.

Range: Breeds from western Ontario east to southern Quebec and Nova Scotia; south to Minnesota, Great Lakes, and Connecticut; and in mountains to northern Georgia. Winters in Gulf Coast states (irregularly) and Greater Antilles.

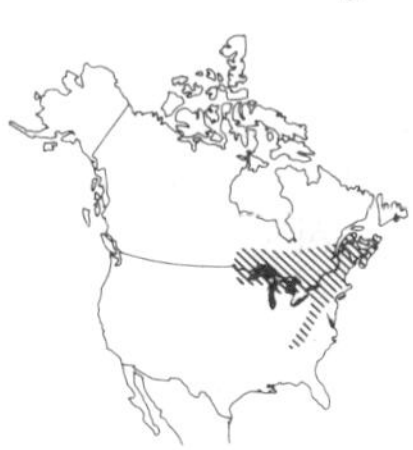

The male is one of the easier warblers to identify since it retains its strikingly patterned plumage year-round. These warblers are among the tamest and most trusting of this family. If an observer moves very deliberately, the bird may be approached to within a few feet (about a meter).

459, 517 **Yellow-rumped Warbler including "Myrtle Warbler" and "Audubon's Warbler"**
*Dendroica coronata*

Description: 5–6″ (13–15 cm). Breeding male dull bluish above, streaked with black; breast and flanks blackish. *Rump, crown, and small area at sides of breast yellow.* Eastern male ("Myrtle Warbler") has white throat, 2 white wing bars. Western male ("Audubon's Warbler") has yellow throat, large white patch in folded wing. Females, fall males, and young are streaked gray-brown, but always have yellow rump and white spots in tail.

Voice: A thin, buzzy warble; a sharp *chek!*

Habitat: Coniferous and mixed forests; widespread during migration and winter.

Nesting: 4 or 5 white eggs, spotted and blotched with brown, in a bulky nest of twigs, rootlets, and grass, lined with hair and feathers and placed in a conifer.

Range: Breeds from northern Alaska, northern Manitoba, central Quebec, and Newfoundland south in West to northern Mexico and in East to Michigan, northern New York, Massachusetts, and Maine. Winters from southern part of breeding range southward into tropics.

Until recently, the eastern and western populations of the Yellow-rumped Warbler were thought to be two distinct species, respectively the "Myrtle Warbler" and "Audubon's Warbler." However, it has been found that in the narrow zone where the ranges of the two come together, the birds hybridize freely. In the East, the "Myrtle Warbler" is an abundant migrant, and the only warbler that regularly spends the winter in the northern states.

516 **Black-throated Green Warbler**
*Dendroica virens*

Description: 5″ (13 cm). Crown and upperparts olive green, *throat and sides of breast black, face yellow.* Female similar but duller.
Voice: Thin, buzzy, lazy *zeer, zeer, zeer, zeer, zee?* or faster *zee-zee-zee-zoo-zee.*
Habitat: Open stands of hemlock or pine; during migration, a variety of habitats.
Nesting: 4 or 5 brown-spotted white eggs in a cup of grass, moss, and plant fibers, lined with hair and feathers and placed in the branches of a conifer.
Range: Breeds from eastern British Columbia, Ontario, and Newfoundland south to Alberta, Minnesota, Ohio, northern New Jersey, and in mountains to Georgia. Winters from Florida and Texas southward.

The Black-throated Green is one of the most commonly seen warblers during migration; at this season it feeds at any height above the ground, but where the trees are tall it spends most of its time among the highest branches. This bird's distinctive song is one of the easiest of warbler songs to learn.

534 **Golden-cheeked Warbler**
*Dendroica chrysoparia*

Description: 4½–5″ (11–13 cm). Male black, with 2 white wing bars, white belly, and *conspicuous yellow face.* Female similar, but back olive green with dark streaks.
Voice: A buzzy *zee, zoo, zeedee, zeep.*
Habitat: Rocky hillsides covered with juniper.
Nesting: 4 white eggs, finely dotted with brown, in a cup of bark strips, grass, and cobwebs, placed in a juniper.

Range: Breeds in south-central Texas. Winters south of U.S.–Mexico border.

This relative of the Black-throated Green Warbler of the East breeds only in Texas in juniper woodlands on the Edwards Plateau and in a small area near Dallas. Even in this restricted range the birds are localized, and the small population is being steadily reduced by habitat destruction and the depredations of cowbirds.

## 515 Blackburnian Warbler
*Dendroica fusca*

Description: 5″ (13 cm). Breeding male black and white with *vivid orange throat, crown patch, and eyebrow; and large white wing patch;* female similar, but has yellow throat. Back of both sexes boldly striped. Immature male similar to female.

Voice: Very thin and wiry, increasing in speed and rising to the limit of hearing, *sleet-sleet-sleet-sleet-sleetee-sleeeee.* Also *tiddly-tiddly-tiddly-tiddly* at same speed and pitch.

Habitat: Most numerous in mixed forests of hemlock, spruce, and various hardwoods, usually ranging high in trees.

Nesting: 4 brown-spotted white eggs in a twig nest lined with lichens, mosses, and hair, usually placed high in a large conifer.

Range: Breeds from Saskatchewan east to Nova Scotia, south to Great Lakes, southern New England, and in mountains to northern Georgia. Winters in tropics.

Blackburnian Warblers are usually found high in trees, even during migration, and are not readily noticed in the dense foliage unless their high-pitched song announces their presence. At times they may be detected at the ends of branches, picking among leaves for bugs or caterpillars.

533 **Yellow-throated Warbler**
*Dendroica dominica*

Description: 5″ (13 cm). Gray, unstreaked upperparts, *bright yellow throat,* white belly, *black-and-white facial pattern,* heavy black streaks on sides. Sexes alike.

Voice: A series of clear ringing notes descending in pitch and increasing in speed, rising abruptly at the end, *teeew-teeew-teeew-teeew-tew-tew-twi.*

Habitat: Forests of pine, cypress, sycamore, and oak, in both swampy places and dry uplands.

Nesting: 4 purple-spotted greenish eggs in a nest of grass and bark strips lined with hair and feathers, often set in clumps of Spanish moss or among pine needles.

Range: Breeds from Illinois, Ohio, and New Jersey south to Missouri, Texas, Gulf Coast, and northern Florida. Winters from Gulf Coast states southward.

This attractive warbler is usually found in live oaks draped with Spanish moss or in longleaf pines. It often creeps over the branches of the trunk like a Black-and-White Warbler. Occasionally it may stray, and even breed, as far north of its usual range as New York and southern New England.

537 **Pine Warbler**
*Dendroica pinus*

Description: 5½″ (14 cm). Unstreaked olive above, with yellow throat and breast; blurry streaking below; white belly; inconspicuous eye stripe; 2 white wing bars. Female and immature similar but duller; often lack yellowish color on breast.

Voice: Musical and somewhat melancholy, a soft, sweet version of the trill of the Chipping Sparrow.

Habitat: Pine forests.

Nesting: 4 brown-spotted white eggs in a

compact nest well concealed among pine needles near the tip of a horizontal branch, usually higher than 20′ (6 m).

Range: Breeds from southeastern Manitoba, southern Ontario, and Maine south to eastern Texas, Gulf Coast, and Florida. Winters in southern states, occasionally north to New England.

No bird is more aptly named: it nests exclusively in pine trees, spends much of its life there, and only during migration is found in shrubbery or the deciduous growth of parks and gardens. The Pine Warbler is relatively rare and local inland in the North.

## 536 Kirtland's Warbler
*Dendroica kirtlandii*

Description: 6″ (15 cm). A large warbler, gray above with black streaks; yellow below with black streaks on sides; black cheeks with conspicuous white eye ring. Female similar but duller. *Bobs its tail.*

Voice: Low pitched, loud, bubbling, and rising at the end.

Habitat: Dense stands of young jack pines; in winter, also other low scrub.

Nesting: 4 brown-dotted white eggs in a nest composed of bark strips and vegetable fibers, lined with grass and pine needles and sunk in the ground.

Range: Breeds only in north-central Michigan. Winters in Bahamas.

This warbler is noted for its extremely limited range. During the breeding season it is confined to dense stands of young jack pines that spring up after forest fires. Once such stands reach about 20 feet (6 meters), the birds abandon them. Even in winter Kirtland's Warbler inhabits low scrub, although not always pines. The U.S. government has recently established a sanctuary where controlled burning will attempt to maintain the required habitat of this rare bird.

512 **Prairie Warbler**
*Dendroica discolor*

Description: 5″ (13 cm). Olive above, *bright yellow below, with black spots and streaks along sides; male has chestnut streaks on back.* Female and immature have fewer streaks. Bobs its tail vigorously.

Voice: Buzzy *zee-zee-zee,* up to 10 rapidly ascending notes.

Habitat: Not found on prairies. In the North, mixed pine-oak barrens, old pastures, and hillsides with scattered red cedars; in the South, open scrub; in extreme southern Florida, mangrove swamps.

Nesting: 4 brown-spotted white eggs in a nest of grass and leaves lined with hair and feathers, usually set low in a bush or small tree.

Range: Breeds from eastern Nebraska, central Wisconsin, southern Ontario, and central New England south to Oklahoma, Gulf Coast, and Florida; local in many areas. Winters in southern Florida and in tropics.

This species avoids thick woods and has benefited greatly from the cutting and burning of the forests, which favors the younger seedlings and smaller bushes that sprout after fires. Like the Palm Warbler, it forages in low undergrowth, rarely ascending higher than 10 feet (3 meters).

535 **Palm Warbler**
*Dendroica palmarum*

Description: 5½″ (14 cm). An olive-drab, streaked, ground-feeding warbler with bright olive rump, bright yellow undertail coverts, and *distinctive habit of wagging its tail.*

Underparts vary from yellow to whitish buff, depending on age and geography; adults in spring have *rufous cap.*

Voice: Weak dry trill, like that of Chipping Sparrow but slower.

Habitat: In summer, bogs in the North; during migration, open places, especially weedy fields and borders of marshes.

Nesting: 4 or 5 brown-speckled white eggs in a grass nest fashioned with shreds of bark and lined with feathers and rootlets. Nest is placed on the ground in a grass clump, often at the base of a small tree or bush.

Range: Breeds from west-central Canada east to Labrador and Newfoundland, and south to extreme northern portions of United States. Winters from southeastern United States southward.

The Palm Warbler is one of the first warblers to arrive in the spring, and at this season is commonly found feeding quietly on the ground, sometimes with flocks of sparrows. It is unusual among warblers of the genus *Dendroica* in nesting on the ground; the only other species that does this is the rare Kirtland's Warbler.

---

526, 532 **Bay-breasted Warbler**
*Dendroica castanea*

Description: 5½″ (14 cm). In breeding plumage, male has chestnut cap, throat, and sides; blackish face; conspicuous pale buff patch on side of neck. Upperparts streaked. Females, fall males, and immatures are olive above, with 2 white wing bars; similar to fall Blackpoll Warblers, but with dark legs and often a trace of rust color on flanks.

Voice: A high thin *teesi-teesi-teesi-teesi,* without change in pitch or volume.

Habitat: Breeds in open spruce forests. During migration, frequents deciduous trees as well.

Nesting: 5 white eggs, with brown markings, in a loosely built, hair-lined nest of twigs, grass, and needles set in a conifer as much as 50′ (15 m) above ground.

Range: Breeds from northeastern British Columbia east to Maritime Provinces and south to northern Great Lakes region and northern New England. Winters in tropics.

This warbler, like the Cape May and Tennessee warblers, increases in numbers during years of spruce budworm outbreaks in its breeding areas; the excess of food means the warblers are able to produce more young. A handsome bird, it is eagerly sought by enthusiasts during the warbler migrations in middle and late May.

## 538, 618 Blackpoll Warbler
*Dendroica striata*

Description: 5½″ (14 cm). Breeding male gray streaked above, with *black cap*, white cheeks and underparts, blackish streaks on sides. Female and nonbreeding male greenish above with vague streaking, yellowish green below. *Feet usually flesh-colored.* See Bay-breasted Warbler.

Voice: Rapid series of high lisping notes all on one pitch, increasing and then decreasing in volume, *seet-seet-seet-seet-seet-seet-seet-seet.*

Habitat: Breeds in coniferous forests. During migration, found chiefly in tall trees.

Nesting: 4 or 5 brown-spotted white eggs in a twig-and-grass nest often lined with feathers and usually placed in a small evergreen tree.

Range: Breeds from Alaska and northern Canada to central Canada and northern New England. Winters in tropics.

The Blackpoll is one of the most abundant warblers in the East during migration and has an enormous breeding range in the northern part of the continent. During migration in late

May, and again in September and early October, dozens may be seen in a single day. Like all wood warblers, these birds migrate at night; sometimes large numbers, attracted to bright lights on overcast or stormy nights, collide with such obstacles as lighthouses, television towers, and tall buildings.

**601 Cerulean Warbler**
*Dendroica cerulea*

Description: 4½″ (11 cm). Male has *sky-blue head and back; black band across white breast.* Female is dull blue-gray above and whitish below, and lacks breast band.
Voice: Series of short buzzy notes, followed by a higher-pitched buzz.
Habitat: Open woodlands, often near streams and rivers.
Nesting: 4 brown-spotted whitish eggs in a nest of plant fibers lined with grass, moss, and hair, and placed high in a deciduous tree, generally near the end of a branch.
Range: Breeds from southeastern Minnesota, southern Ontario, and western New England south to Texas, Louisiana, and northern Gulf Coast states. Winters in tropics.

This species has a discontinuous range, occurring here and there in rather loose colonies. It is usually found high in the treetops, where it is difficult to see in the thick foliage.

**619 Black-and-White Warbler**
*Mniotilta varia*

Description: 5″ (13 cm). *Black and white stripes, including crown.* Male has black throat; female's throat white. *Creeps on tree trunks.*
Voice: A thin, high-pitched, monotonous *weesy-weesy-weesy-weesy,* like a squeaky wheelbarrow.

Habitat: Primary and secondary forests, chiefly deciduous. During migration, parks, gardens, and lawn areas with trees and shrubs.

Nesting: 4 or 5 purple-spotted white eggs in a ground nest composed of leaves, grass, and rootlets, and lined with hair and fern down. Nest is set at the base of a tree, stump, or rock.

Range: Breeds from southern Mackenzie, northern Alberta, and central Manitoba east to Newfoundland, and south to southern United States east of Rockies. Winters from southern parts of Gulf Coast states southward.

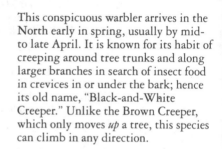

This conspicuous warbler arrives in the North early in spring, usually by mid- to late April. It is known for its habit of creeping around tree trunks and along larger branches in search of insect food in crevices in or under the bark; hence its old name, "Black-and-White Creeper." Unlike the Brown Creeper, which only moves *up* a tree, this species can climb in any direction.

530, 629 **American Redstart**
*Setophaga ruticilla*

Description: 4½–5½" (11–14 cm). Male black with bright orange patches on wings and tail; white belly. Females and young birds dull olive-brown above, white below, with yellow wing and tail patches.

Voice: 5 or 6 high-pitched notes or 2-note phrases, ending with an upward or downward inflection, *chewy-chewy-chewy, chew-chew-chew.*

Habitat: Second-growth woodlands; thickets with saplings.

Nesting: 4 brown-speckled, dull-white eggs in a well-made cup of grass, bark shreds, plant fibers, and spiderweb lined with fine grass and hair. Nest is placed in a sapling or next to the trunk of a tree.

Range: Breeds from southeastern Alaska east to

central Manitoba, Quebec, and Newfoundland, and south to northern California, Colorado, Oklahoma, northern Louisiana, and South Carolina. Winters in California, Texas, and Florida, and in tropics.

This is one of the most abundant warblers in North America, because its favored habitat, second-growth woodland, covers such vast areas of the continent. The American Redstart has a distinctive habit of dropping down suddenly in pursuit of a flying insect, then fanning its brightly marked tail from side to side. Only after a full year do males acquire the black-and-orange adult plumage, so it is not unusual to find what appears to be a female singing and displaying like a male.

## 506 Prothonotary Warbler
*Protonotaria citrea*

Description: 5½″ (14 cm). Male *golden-orange with blue-gray wings;* no wing bars; large white spots in tail. Female similar but duller.

Voice: Song a ringing *sweet-sweet-sweet-sweet-sweet-sweet-sweet;* also a canary-like flight song. Call a loud, metallic *chip.*

Habitat: Wooded swamps, flooded bottomland forests, and streams with dead trees.

Nesting: 6 creamy-white, purple-spotted eggs in a tree cavity, hole in a stump, birdhouse, or other man-made structure, such as a mailbox. The hole is stuffed with mosses to form a nest cup.

Range: Breeds mainly in southeastern states north to Minnesota, Michigan, and New York. Winters in tropics.

This is one of the characteristic birds of the southern swamplands, where its bright plumage is conspicuous in the gloomy, cypress-lined bayous. It is unusual among warblers in that it nests in holes in trees; this may be an adaptation to a habitat where such holes are numerous but where dense bushes—the usual warbler nesting sites—are scarce.

460 **Worm-eating Warbler**
*Helmitheros vermivorus*

Description: 5½″ (14 cm). Sparrow-sized. Plain brownish above and below, with conspicuous *dark and light crown stripes.* Sexes look alike.

Voice: Song like that of Chipping Sparrow, but faster, buzzy, and more insect-like.

Habitat: Chiefly dry wooded hillsides.

Nesting: 4 or 5 brown-spotted white eggs in a ground nest of dead leaves lined with moss.

Range: Breeds from southeastern Iowa, Ohio, New York, and southern New England south to northeastern Texas, central Gulf Coast states, and eastern North Carolina. Winters in tropics.

The Worm-eating Warbler spends much of its time on or near the ground, quietly searching for its insect prey in leaf litter and low vegetation. A singing male, however, often perches rather high up in a forest tree, where its habit of sitting motionless for long periods of time makes it very difficult to spot. The name "Worm-eating" reflects the bird's fondness for the small larvae of moths.

461 **Swainson's Warbler**
*Limnothlypis swainsonii*

Description: 5″ (13 cm). A plain warbler, olive-brown above and whitish beneath, with rufous cap and whitish line over eye.

Voice: 3 or 4 clear notes followed by several rapid descending notes, described as *whee-whee-whee-whip-poor-will;* similar to song of Louisiana Waterthrush.

Habitat: Wooded swamps and southern canebrakes; also rhododendron thickets in the mountains.

Nesting: 3 bluish-white eggs in a loose, bulky nest of vegetable fibers, rootlets, and dead leaves, placed in a dense bush or vine.

Range: Breeds from northeastern Oklahoma, southern Illinois, southern Virginia, and southern Delaware south to southeastern United States. Winters in tropics.

This dull-colored warbler is shy and retiring, dwelling in remote, often impenetrable swamps and cane thickets. If not for its song—like that of a Louisiana Waterthrush—it would frequently be overlooked. It is named after William Swainson, an early-19th-century British naturalist.

## 446 Ovenbird
*Seiurus aurocapillus*

Description: 6″ (15 cm). A terrestrial, thrush-like warbler. Olive green above, white below with dark streaks; conspicuous eye ring; *orange-brown crown bordered with black stripes;* pinkish legs.

Voice: Loud staccato song—*teacher, teacher, teacher*—with geographical variation in emphasis. Flight song, often given at night, is bubbling and exuberant series of jumbled notes ending with the familiar *teacher, teacher.*

Habitat: Mature, dry forests with little undergrowth.

Nesting: 4 or 5 brown-spotted white eggs in a domed or oven-shaped nest of dead leaves and plant fibers, lined with grass. Nest is placed on the ground, with a side entrance.

Range: Breeds from west-central Canada east to Maritimes, and south to northern Gulf Coast states, and South Carolina. Winters from Gulf Coast and Florida to South America.

This warbler gets its name from its peculiar ground nest, which resembles a miniature Dutch oven. A male frequently has more than one mate (as many as three in one instance); it also has been observed that two males, as well as the female, may feed the young.

439 **Northern Waterthrush**
*Seiurus noveboracensis*

Description: 6″ (15 cm). A terrestrial, thrush-like warbler. Olive-brown above, pale yellowish below with black streaks; *narrow, yellowish-white eyebrow; streaked yellowish throat. Frequently bobs tail.* See Louisiana Waterthrush.

Voice: Song *chee-chee-chee, chip-chip-chip-chew-chew-chew*, loud and ringing, speeding up at the end. Call a sharp *chink.*

Habitat: Cool bogs, wooded swamps, and lakeshores in the breeding season; almost any wooded habitat during migration.

Nesting: 4 or 5 creamy-white eggs, with brown blotches, in a nest of moss set in a bank, at the base of a trunk, or among the roots of an overturned tree.

Range: Breeds from Alaska and much of Canada south to northern United States. Winters in tropics.

This warbler is called a waterthrush because of its superficial resemblance to a thrush and its fondness for water. Like its relative the Ovenbird, it walks rather than hops. This species is among the first to move south during the fall migration, and southern migrants are regularly reported by the middle of July or earlier. One individual banded on Long Island during a southbound flight was recovered the following winter in Venezuela and, remarkably, was trapped a year later at the same place in Venezuela.

440 **Louisiana Waterthrush**
*Seiurus motacilla*

Description: 6½″ (17 cm). A terrestrial, thrush-like warbler. Dark olive-brown above, white and streaked below. *Frequently bobs tail.* Similar to Northern Waterthrush, but *throat unstreaked* and *eyebrow longer, broader, and whiter.*

Voice: Song is 3 clear notes followed by a descending jumble.

Habitat: Swift-moving brooks on hillsides; where Northern Waterthrush is absent, occurs in river swamps and along sluggish streams.

Nesting: 5 brown-blotched white eggs in a grass-lined nest of dead leaves and moss set under the overhang of a stream bank, in a stump cavity, or among exposed tree roots.

Range: Breeds from Minnesota, southern Ontario and central New England south to Texas and Georgia. Winters in tropics.

This bird is very similar to the Northern Waterthrush; the waterthrushes were confused by early American ornithologists, who at one time thought there were three species. During spring migration, this species arrives much earlier than the Northern. Where the two species breed together, the Northern prefers bogs and swamps, while the Louisiana prefers rushing streams and clear brooks.

514 **Kentucky Warbler**
*Oporornis formosus*

Description: 5½″ (14 cm). Olive green above, bright yellow below; *black forecrown, lores, and sides of throat; bright yellow "spectacles."* No wing bars. Sexes similar.

Voice: Loud, penetrating, rich *tur-dle, tur-dle, tur-dle, tur-dle,* reminiscent of song of Carolina Wren.

Habitat: Low, moist, rich woodlands with luxuriant undergrowth; often ravines.
Nesting: 4 or 5 brown-spotted white eggs in a nest of dead leaves lined with grass, hair, and rootlets, placed on or near the ground.
Range: Breeds from Iowa and Indiana east to New Jersey, and south to southeastern United States. Winters in tropics.

Named for the state where it was discovered in 1811 by Alexander Wilson, father of American ornithology, this bird is actually no more common in Kentucky than elsewhere in its range. Usually heard before it is seen, the rather secretive Kentucky Warbler remains hidden, especially in ravines with thick vegetation and running streams.

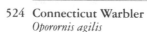

524 **Connecticut Warbler**
*Oporornis agilis*

Description: 5½″ (14 cm). Olive green above, dull yellow below; head, throat, and upper breast gray in males and dull brownish in females. Has conspicuous, *unbroken white eye ring.* No wing bars. Mourning Warbler similar but has faint, broken eye ring.
Voice: A loud, ringing *beecher-beecher-beecher-beecher* or *chippy-chipper-chippy-chipper.*
Habitat: Open larch-spruce bogs; during migration, low wet woods and damp thickets.
Nesting: 4 or 5 whitish eggs, blotched with brown, in a nest of grass concealed in a clump of moss.
Range: Breeds from eastern British Columbia east through central Canada to western Quebec, and south to northern Minnesota, Wisconsin, and Michigan. Winters in tropics.

Named for its place of discovery, this species is only an uncommon migrant in

Connecticut. The bird is seldom seen except by observers who know where to look. During spring migration, it feeds close to the ground in dense swampy woods; in the fall, it occurs most often in woodland edges where the growth is rank.

528 **Mourning Warbler**
*Oporornis philadelphia*

Description: 5½″ (14 cm). Similar to Connecticut Warbler—olive above and bright yellow below with a gray hood; no eye ring. Male has *black patch below throat;* female has gray throat. Immatures usually have faint, broken eye ring.

Voice: Loud, ringing, musical song, *teedle-teedle, turtle-turtle,* the last pair of notes lower.

Habitat: Dense thickets of blackberries and briars in forest clearings; also wet woods with thick undergrowth.

Nesting: 4 brown-spotted white eggs in a nest of fibers and leaves, lined with grass and hair, on or near the ground.

Range: Breeds from Alberta to Newfoundland and south to North Dakota and northern New England, and in mountains to Virginia. Winters in tropics.

This warbler supposedly gets its vernacular name from the black crepe-like patch on the breast of the male, which suggests a symbol of mourning. The scientific species name, *philadelphia,* derives from the city where Alexander Wilson discovered the bird in 1810. It is actually less common in Philadelphia than in many other places. Like other warblers of the genus *Oporornis,* the Mourning Warbler is often heard before it is seen.

543, 544 **Common Yellowthroat**
*Geothlypis trichas*

Description: 4½–6″ (11–15 cm). Olive-brown above, *bright yellow on throat and upper breast.* Male has *bold black mask,* bordered above with white. Females and young males lack face mask, but may be recognized by bright yellow throat and wren-like behavior.

Voice: Loud, fast *witchity-witchity-witchity-witchity-wit* or *which-is-it, which-is-it, which-is-it*. Call a sharp *chip.*

Habitat: Moist thickets and grassy marshes.

Nesting: 3–5 white eggs, with brown and black spots, in a loose mass of grass, sedge, and bark lined with rootlets, hair, and fine grass. Nest is concealed on or near the ground in a dense clump of weeds or grass.

Range: Breeds from Alaska east across southern half of Canada to Newfoundland, and south throughout United States. Winters in southern states and in tropics.

A small bird with a yellow throat, skulking in the grass or weeds of a marshy spot, is almost certainly a Common Yellowthroat, whose cheerful song is well known. At the height of the breeding season, the males perform an attractive flight display, mounting into the air while uttering a jumble of high-pitched notes, then bouncing back into the grass while giving the usual song. The bird is the northernmost member of a group of yellowthroat species that occurs as far south as Argentina.

509 **Hooded Warbler**
*Wilsonia citrina*

Description: 5½″ (14 cm). Olive above, yellow below. Male has yellow face, *black hood* and black throat. Female lacks hood or has only a trace of it. Both sexes have *white tail spots.* See Bachman's Warbler.

Voice: Clear, ringing *tawee-tawee-tawee-tee-o.*
Habitat: Mature, moist forests with luxuriant undergrowth, especially in ravines; also in wooded swamps.
Nesting: 3 or 4 creamy-white, brown-spotted eggs in a grass-lined nest of dead leaves and plant fibers, placed low in a small tree or shrub.
Range: Breeds from Iowa, Michigan, and southern New England south to Gulf Coast and northern Florida. Winters in tropics.

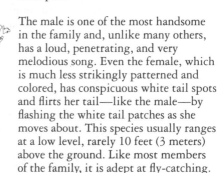

The male is one of the most handsome in the family and, unlike many others, has a loud, penetrating, and very melodious song. Even the female, which is much less strikingly patterned and colored, has conspicuous white tail spots and flirts her tail—like the male—by flashing the white tail patches as she moves about. This species usually ranges at a low level, rarely 10 feet (3 meters) above the ground. Like most members of the family, it is adept at fly-catching.

507 **Wilson's Warbler**
*Wilsonia pusilla*

Description: 4½–5″ (11–13 cm). Adult male olive green above and yellow below, with *black crown patch*. Most females and all young birds lack black crown and may be distinguished from other olive green warblers with yellow underparts by lack of wing bars, streaks, tail spots, or other markings.
Voice: A rapid, staccato series of *chips,* which drop in pitch at the end.
Habitat: Moist thickets in woodlands and along streams; alder and willow thickets and bogs.
Nesting: 4 or 5 brown-spotted white eggs in a bulky mass of leaves, rootlets, and moss lined with hair and fine plant materials, concealed on the ground in a dense clump of weeds or sedge.

Range: Breeds from Alaska east across Canada to Newfoundland, and south to southern California, New Mexico, central Ontario, and Nova Scotia. Winters in tropics.

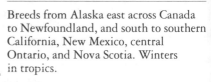

Seen briefly during migration, Wilson's Warbler is seldom found more than a dozen feet (3 or 4 meters) from the ground. It is an active bird and, like a flycatcher, spends much time darting after small flying insects. It is named for Scottish-American ornithologist and artist Alexander Wilson (1766–1813).

---

511 **Canada Warbler**
*Wilsonia canadensis*

Description: 5″ (13 cm). Solid gray above, without wing bars, yellow below; yellow "spectacles"; *black-spotted "necklace" on breast.* Female similar but duller, with only a trace of necklace.
Voice: A rapid, sputtering warble.
Habitat: Cool, moist woodlands that are nearly mature and have much undergrowth.
Nesting: 4 brown-spotted white eggs in a nest of dried leaves and grass, on or near the ground at the base of a stump or in a fern clump.
Range: Breeds from southern Canada to northern United States east of Rockies, and in mountains to northern Georgia. Winters in tropics.

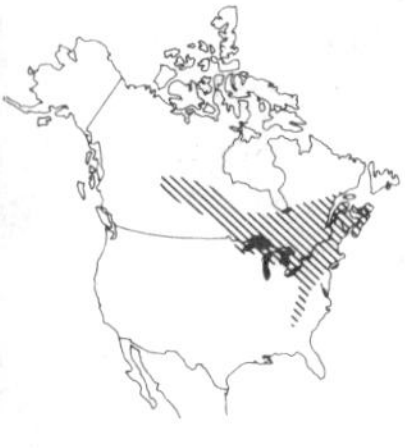

This warbler received its name from its discovery in Canada, although it is certainly not confined to Canada, even in the breeding season. It ordinarily ranges at low levels, usually from the ground to 6 feet (nearly 2 meters) up. Like several other warblers, it is adept at fly-catching, conspicuously flitting from bush to bush. Flying insects form a great portion of its diet, but it also captures spiders and insect larvae.

529 **Yellow-breasted Chat**
*Icteria virens*

Description: 6½–7½" (17–19 cm). Larger than a sparrow. Olive green above, with bright yellow breast and white abdomen. *Stout black bill;* black face mask bordered above and below with white; *white "spectacles."* Long tail.

Voice: A series of widely spaced croaks, whistles, and short repeated phrases, very unlike a typical warbler's song. Often sings at night. At times it performs a musical display flight, flopping awkwardly up and down with legs dangling while singing.

Habitat: Dense thickets and brush, often with thorns; streamside tangles and dry brushy hillsides.

Nesting: 4 or 5 brown-spotted white eggs in a bulky mass of bark, grass, and leaves, lined with finer grass and concealed in a dense bush.

Range: Breeds from southern British Columbia east to Massachusetts (rare), and south to California, Gulf Coast, and Florida. Winters in tropics.

The Yellow-breasted Chat is an atypical wood warbler. Its large size and stout bill, long tail, and distinctive display flight—the bird hovers with slow, deep-flapping wings and dangling feet—make it seem more like a mockingbird or a thrasher. Since it prefers brushy tangles and is relatively shy, this bird is more often heard than seen.

## Family Emberizidae
## Subfamily Thraupinae
Tanagers

241 species: Chiefly tropical America; only five species—one of them introduced—breed in North America north of Mexico. These brightly colored, stout-billed birds are mainly forest

inhabitants and chiefly insectivorous, but they also eat small fruits. They occur in our area in the warmer months and spend the winter well within the tropics.

---

488, 496 **Summer Tanager**
*Piranga rubra*

Description: 7–8″ (18–20 cm). Smaller than a robin. Male solid rose-red with *pale bill.* Female pale olive green above, dull yellow below. Male Northern Cardinal has black face, conical red bill, and crest; male Scarlet Tanager has black wings and tail.

Voice: Song like an American Robin's, but softer and sweeter, and not as hoarse as Scarlet Tanager's. Call a distinctive rattling *chick-tucky-tuck.*

Habitat: Open woodlands and shade trees.

Nesting: 3 or 4 blue-green eggs, spotted with brown, in a shallow, flimsy cup near the end of a horizontal branch, 10 to 20′ (3 to 6 m) above ground.

Range: Breeds from southern California, Nevada, Nebraska, and New Jersey south to Gulf Coast and northern Mexico. Winters in tropics.

Each major forest region of North America has its species of tanager; this one is found in dry oak and mixed forests of the southern states. Despite their bright colors, the males are difficult to detect in the dense foliage. On their breeding grounds the birds are most easily located by their calls, which they utter persistently throughout the day. A major part of the diet during the summer consists of flying insects captured in the air.

489, 549 **Scarlet Tanager**
*Piranga olivacea*

Description: 7½" (19 cm). In breeding plumage, male *brilliant scarlet with black wings and tail.* In nonbreeding plumage, female and male olive green; *male has black wings.*

Voice: Song a hurried, burry, repetitive warble, somewhat like that of a robin. Call note an emphatic, nasal *chip-bang.*

Habitat: Chiefly mature woodlands, especially oak and pine.

Nesting: 3 or 4 brown-spotted greenish eggs in a shallow nest of twigs and stems lined with grass and placed on a horizontal branch.

Range: Breeds from extreme southeastern Canada to east-central United States. Winters in tropics.

The brilliantly colored male Scarlet Tanager gleams in the sunlight but is often difficult to see in thick foliage, especially if the bird is motionless or moving slowly from branch to branch high up in the tree canopy. It is conspicuous only when perched on a dead tree limb or when feeding on the ground during a cold, rainy spell. During late summer or early autumn, some of the males may show a patchwork plumage of red and green as they undergo a molt to olive green, except for their wings and tails, which remain black throughout the winter.

495, 550 **Western Tanager**
*Piranga ludoviciana*

Description: 6–7½″ (15–19 cm). Adult male has *brilliant red head, bright yellow body, with black back, wings, and tail.* 2 wing bars; smaller uppermost bar yellow, lower white. Female yellow-green above, yellow below; wing bars similar to male's.

Voice: Song is robin-like in its short fluty phrases rendered with a pause between phrases, but the quality is much hoarser. Call a dry *pit-r-ick.*

Habitat: Open coniferous forests.

Nesting: 3–5 speckled bluish-green eggs in a frail, shallow saucer nest of woven rootlets, weed stalks, and bark strips. Nest is "saddled" in the fork of a horizontal branch of Douglas fir, spruce, pine, or (occasionally) oak, usually at a low elevation.

Range: Breeds from southern Alaska and Mackenzie southward. Winters in tropics. Rarely wanders east to Atlantic Coast.

This western relative of the Scarlet and Summer tanagers occasionally turns up at feeders in the East, where it is easily recognized by its two wing bars. In the West this bird spends most of its time feeding deliberately in the tops of dense forest trees, making it difficult to see despite its bright colors. It feeds on insects and, like other tanagers, supplements its diet with fruit.

595 **Blue-gray Tanager**
*Thraupis episcopus*

Description: 7″ (18 cm). Larger than a House Sparrow. Pale blue, darker on wings and tail; bend of wing whitish.

Voice: Song weak and squeaky, consisting of short irregular phrases.

Habitat: Residential areas and parks with shade trees.

Nesting: 1 or 2 grayish eggs, spotted with brown, in an open cup of dead leaves and grass, placed high in a broad-leaved tree.

Range: Native to tropical forests of Central and South America. Introduced in Miami, Florida.

Like many tropical tanagers, these brightly colored birds travel in small flocks in search of insects and fruit. Such flocks include mated pairs regardless of the time of year, for Blue-gray Tanagers remain mated for life.

---

## Family Emberizidae
**Subfamily Cardinalinae**
Cardinals, Grosbeaks, and Allies

39 species: Chiefly tropical America. Ten species occur in North America. These mainly bright-colored birds have conical bills that are adapted for crushing seeds. Some are nonmigratory and strongly territorial year-round, while others migrate back to the tropics at the end of the breeding season.

---

485, 609 **Northern Cardinal**
*Cardinalis cardinalis*

Description: 8–9″ (20–23 cm). Male bright red with *crest,* black face, *stout red bill.* Female buff-brown, tinged with red on crest, wings, and tail.

Voice: Rich *what-cheer, cheer, cheer; purty-purty-purty-purty or sweet-sweet-sweet-sweet.* Also a metallic *chip.*

Habitat: Woodland edges, thickets, brushy swamps, and gardens.

Nesting: 3 or 4 pale green eggs, spotted with red-brown, in a deep cup of twigs, leaves, and plant fibers concealed in a thicket.

Range: Resident in eastern United States and

southern Canada (locally) south to Gulf Coast, and from southern California, Arizona, and southern Texas southward.

This species, named after the red robes worn by Roman Catholic cardinals, has extended its range northward into southern Canada in recent decades. Cardinals are aggressive birds that occupy territories year-round. Both sexes are accomplished songsters and may be heard at any time of year, rather than just in the spring when most other birds are singing. Seeds form a main part of the diet, although insects are eaten in the breeding season. These birds often come to feeders in winter.

608 **Pyrrhuloxia**
*Cardinalis sinuatus*

Description: 7½–8½″ (19–22 cm). Male gray with rose-red breast, crest, wings, and tail. Female similar but paler, and lacks red on breast. Stubby, parrot-like *yellow bill.*

Voice: A series of whistled notes, similar to Northern Cardinal but thinner and shorter.

Habitat: Desert brush, especially along streambeds.

Nesting: 3 or 4 white eggs, lightly speckled with brown, in a loosely built cup of grass, twigs, and bark strips concealed in a dense, thorny bush.

Range: Resident from Arizona, southern New Mexico, and southern Texas southward.

Also called the "Gray Cardinal," the Pyrrhuloxia is similar to the Northern Cardinal in most respects except that it is often found in flocks after the breeding season. Partial to mesquite thickets, these birds use their strong bills to crush the mesquite beans. Although shy and difficult to detect in their dense habitat, they respond to squeaking noises made by an observer.

455, 624 **Rose-breasted Grosbeak**
*Pheucticus ludovicianus*

Description: 8″ (20 cm). Starling-sized. Heavy pinkish-white bill. Male black and white with a conspicuous *rose-red patch on breast and underwings.* Female white above and below with heavy brown streaking; prominent white eyebrow.
Voice: Distinctive call note a sharp, penetrating, metallic *eek-eek.* Song is like that of an American Robin, but softer and more melodious.
Habitat: Moist woodlands adjacent to open fields with tall shrubs; also old and overgrown orchards.
Nesting: 4 or 5 purple-spotted whitish eggs in a loosely made nest of twigs, grass, and plant fibers set in a low branch of a tree.
Range: Breeds from northeastern British Columbia, southern Manitoba, and Nova Scotia south to southern Alberta, central North Dakota, central Oklahoma, and New Jersey, and in mountains as far south as northern Georgia. Winters in tropics.

This handsome grosbeak is one of the most conspicuous birds before the foliage comes into full leaf in early May. It is beneficial to farmers, consuming many potato beetles and larvae as well as weed seeds, wild fruits, and buds.

383, 457 **Black-headed Grosbeak**
*Pheucticus melanocephalus*

Description: 7½″ (19 cm). Starling-sized. Heavy pinkish-white bill. Male has black head; *tawny-orange breast,* yellow belly, and *tawny back with black streaking;* black wings and tail have conspicuous white patches. Female has white eyebrows and pale buff underparts; very finely streaked breast.
Voice: Rich warble similar to that of a robin, but softer, sweeter, and faster. Call note

an emphatic sharp *tick,* slightly metallic in tone.

Habitat: Open, deciduous woodlands near water, such as river bottoms, lakeshores, and swampy places with a mixture of trees and shrubs.

Nesting: 3 or 4 greenish eggs, spotted with brown, in a loosely built stick nest lined with rootlets, grasses, and leaves, and placed among the dense foliage of an outer tree limb.

Range: Breeds from southwestern Canada east to western North Dakota and Nebraska and south to mountains of Mexico; winters in Mexico. Occasionally appears at feeders in East.

Like the Rose-breasted Grosbeak, the males of this species, despite their bright colors, share incubation with the females. However, they are not conspicuously marked above; the brightest coloration is on the breast and belly, which is concealed as they incubate. Their food is quite varied. Heavy seeds are easily cracked open with their huge beaks; although sometimes they pose a problem in fruit orchards, Black-headed Grosbeaks also consume harmful insects and are highly valuable to farmers.

---

456, 592 **Blue Grosbeak**
*Guiraca caerulea*

Description: 6–7½″ (15–19 cm). Slightly larger than a House Sparrow. Male dark blue with *2 chestnut wing bars* and stout, dark bill. Female dark buff-brown with 2 buff wing bars. Indigo Bunting similar, but is smaller, lacks wing bars, and is not as rust-colored.

Voice: Sweet, jumbled warble. Also a metallic *klink.*

Habitat: Brushy, moist pastures and roadside thickets.

Nesting: 3 or 4 pale blue eggs in a loose cup of

grass, weed stems, and leaves concealed in a clump of weeds.

Range: Breeds from California east through Colorado, Missouri, southern Illinois, and New Jersey southward. Winters in tropics.

This grosbeak is the only North American member of a genus of tropical birds common in parts of South America. Each fall these birds gather in large flocks and visit sorghum fields in search of insects and seeds.

593 **Lazuli Bunting**
*Passerina amoena*

Description: 5–5¼″ (13–14 cm). Sparrow-sized. Male bright blue with pale cinnamon breast, white belly and wing bars. Female dull brown, lighter below, with 2 pale wing bars. Female Indigo Bunting similar, but lacks conspicuous wing bars.

Voice: A high-pitched, excited series of warbled phrases, the first notes usually repeated, descending the scale and ascending again at the end; similar to song of Indigo Bunting, but phrases less distinct and only the first phrases repeated.

Habitat: Dry, brushy ravines and slopes; cleared areas and weedy pastures.

Nesting: 3 or 4 pale blue eggs in a loose cup of grass and rootlets in a bush.

Range: Breeds from British Columbia, Saskatchewan, and North Dakota south through western United States to southern California, northern New Mexico, western Oklahoma, and eastern Nebraska. Winters south of U.S.–Mexico border.

This western relative of the Indigo Bunting has increased in numbers with the cutting of western forests and their replacement by brush. The two species hybridize sparingly where their ranges overlap, but because this hybridization has not become more widespread the two birds are still considered separate species.

430, 594 **Indigo Bunting**
*Passerina cyanea*

Description: 5½″ (14 cm). Sparrow-sized. *In bright sunlight male brilliant turquoise blue,* otherwise looks black; wings and tail darker. Female drab brown, paler beneath.

Voice: Rapid, excited warble, each note or phrase given twice.

Habitat: Brushy slopes, abandoned farmland, old pastures and fields grown to scrub, woodland clearings, and forest edges adjacent to fields.

Nesting: 3 or 4 pale blue eggs in a compact woven cup of leaves and grass placed in a sapling or bush in relatively thick vegetation and within a few feet of the ground.

Range: Breeds from southeastern Saskatchewan east to New Brunswick, and south to central Arizona, central Texas, Gulf Coast, and northern Florida. Winters in southern Florida and tropics.

Indigo Buntings have no blue pigment; they are actually black, but the diffraction of light through the structure of the feathers makes them appear blue. These attractive birds are also found in rural roadside thickets and along the right-of-way of railroads, where woodlands meet open areas. They are beneficial to farmers and fruit growers, consuming many insect pests and weed seeds.

603 **Varied Bunting**
*Passerina versicolor*

Description: 4½–5½" (11–14 cm). Sparrow-sized. Male dark purple-blue, with dull red patch on nape; looks all black at a distance. Female dull gray-brown *without distinctive markings.* Female Indigo Bunting is browner, with suggestion of wing bars.

Voice: A series of sweet notes, similar to song of Indigo Bunting but thinner.

Habitat: Dense desert brush, especially along streambeds.

Nesting: 3 or 4 pale blue eggs in a deep cup of grass, twigs, and bark strips placed in a dense thicket.

Range: Resident in southern Arizona, southern New Mexico, and southern Texas.

This primarily Mexican species reaches the southernmost parts of the United States. It is unevenly distributed and inconspicuous, so very little is known about it. The birds spend most of their time concealed in dense desert brush, coming into view only when the male sings from the top of a bush. They probably feed primarily on weed seeds.

584, 602 **Painted Bunting**
*Passerina ciris*

Description: 5½" (14 cm). Sparrow-sized. Perhaps North America's most colorful bird: Male has bright red underparts and rump, green back, blue head, and red eye ring; female bright green all over, paler below.

Voice: Loud, clear, and variable song consisting of a series of high-pitched musical notes reminiscent of that of Indigo Bunting; call a sharp, metallic *tsick.*

Habitat: Brushy tangles, hedgerows, briar patches, woodland edges, and swampy thickets.

Nesting: 3 or 4 white eggs, marked with reddish-brown dots, in a cup of compactly woven grass stems, rootlets, and bark strips. Nest is lined with moss and hair, and placed near the ground in the fork of a bush or small tree.

Range: Breeds from Missouri south to southern New Mexico and southern Alabama; along Atlantic Coast from North Carolina south to Florida. Winters from the Gulf Coast states southward.

This gaudy bird is one of the most beautiful in North America. Its brilliant plumage made it a popular cage bird until it came under federal protection; it is still sold in the markets of Mexico and the West Indies. Despite its vivid coloration, however, it is often difficult to see as it skulks among dense thickets, although in Florida, at least, it often comes to feeding stations. Its other well-known name is "Nonpareil," meaning "without equal." This species, common in parts of the Deep South, raises as many as three broods each year. The female is one of the few bright green birds in North America.

## 390 Dickcissel
*Spiza americana*

Description: 6″ (15 cm). Male like *miniature meadowlark* (yellow breast with black V), but has heavy bill and *chestnut wing patch.* Female much like female House Sparrow, but with narrow streaks along sides, and yellowish throat and breast.

Voice: Song sounds like *dick-dick-cissel,* the first two notes being sharp sounds followed by a buzzy, almost hissed *cissel;* repeated over and over again from a conspicuous perch on a fence, bush, or weed. Call a distinctive buzzy note, often given in flight.

Habitat: Open country in grain or hay fields and in weed patches.

Nesting: 4 or 5 pale blue eggs in a cup of plant

stems and grass set on or near the ground, often in alfalfa and clover fields.

Range: Breeds from eastern Montana and Great Lakes region south to Texas and Gulf Coast, locally farther east. Winters mainly in tropics.

Formerly common in farming regions of the eastern states, especially on the Atlantic coastal plain, the Dickcissel disappeared from that region by the middle of the last century and is now most numerous in the Midwest. It appears in small numbers on the East Coast during the fall migration and rarely but regularly in winter at feeders, often with House Sparrows.

## Family Emberizidae
### Subfamily Emberizinae
New World Sparrows and Allies

279 species: Worldwide except the Australian region. Fifty-two species breed in North America. They range from the small, streaked sparrows to the larger towhees, and include the juncos, the longspurs, and the Snow and McKay's buntings. All have conical bills, which they use to crush seeds. Most species also eat insects, especially during the summer when there are young to be raised.

### 401 Olive Sparrow
*Arremonops rufivirgatus*

Description: 5¾″ (15 cm). Unstreaked, dull olive green, with *brown head stripes,* buff breast, and whitish belly; no wing bars; like a small edition of the Green-tailed Towhee.

Voice: Series of musical *chips,* becoming more rapid at the end.

Habitat: Brushy areas, woodland borders and clearings, and overgrown fields.

Nesting: 4 white eggs in a domed nest made of twigs, grass, and leaves, placed low in a shrub or cactus.

Range: Resident in lower Rio Grande Valley of Texas.

Flitting from shrub to shrub and crawling about the undergrowth, this unobtrusive, drab little bird is seldom seen out in the open. Nevertheless, it is not shy and may be readily observed when it sings from an exposed perch or engages in nesting activities. It feeds on seeds, small larvae, and grubs.

## 578 Green-tailed Towhee
*Pipilo chlorurus*

Description: 6¼–7″ (16–18 cm). A ground-dwelling species, smaller than the other towhees. *Rufous cap, olive green above,* with white throat and belly, gray breast. White lores and dark "mustache" stripe. Yellow wing linings. Sexes similar.

Voice: Song a loud, lively series of slurred notes and short, buzzy trills. Call a short nasal *mew.*

Habitat: Sagebrush, mountain chaparral, piñon-juniper stands, and thickets bordering alpine meadows.

Nesting: 4 heavily spotted white eggs in a loosely built nest placed on the ground or in low, protected sites such as chaparral, juniper, and yucca.

Range: Breeds from central Oregon south through mountains to southern California and Great Basin to southeastern New Mexico. Winters at lower elevations and south to southern Arizona and central and southern Texas.

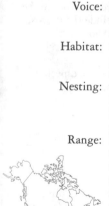

This shy bird hops and scratches for food under low cover, flicking its tail and raising its rufous cap into a crest. It prefers low scrub and frequents brushy openings in boreal forests on western mountains, as well as sagebrush habitats.

384, 474 **Rufous-sided Towhee**
*Pipilo erythrophthalmus*

Description: 7–8½″ (17–22 cm). Male has black head and upperparts, white underparts; bright rufous patches on flanks. Female is similar, but warm brown where male is black. Western birds have spotted upperparts.

Voice: Song a cheerful *drink-your-tea,* second note lower, third note higher. Call a clear *to-wheee?* and *chewink.*

Habitat: Thickets and brushy woodland edges.

Nesting: 3–6 white eggs, lightly spotted with red-brown, in a loose cup of weed stems, grass, and bark placed on or near the ground in dense cover.

Range: Breeds from British Columbia east to Maine, and south to California, Southwest, Louisiana, Florida, and Guatemala. Winters south from southern British Columbia, Nebraska, and southern New England.

The name "Towhee," an imitation of this bird's call note, was given in 1731 by the naturalist and bird artist Mark Catesby, who encountered it in the Carolinas. Few birds show as much geographical variation in voice; the calls of birds in the West bear little resemblance to those in the East. The birds vary greatly in appearance as well, and until recently the eastern "Red-eyed Towhee" and the western "Spotted Towhee" were thought to be distinct species. They interbreed where they come in contact, however, and are now considered the same species. Towhees often feed on the ground, scratching noisily in the dry leaves.

400 **Bachman's Sparrow**
*Aimophila aestivalis*

Description: 6″ (15 cm). A dull-colored nondescript bird, streaked above, plain below, with *buff breast.*
Voice: Clear, sweet whistle followed by a trill on a different pitch.
Habitat: Dry open pine or oak woods with a scattering of scrub; overgrown weedy fields and pastures.
Nesting: 4 white eggs in a domed nest made of plant fibers and placed on the ground in a grass clump or at the base of a bush or palmetto; nest has entrance on the side.
Range: Southeastern United States, breeding north to Illinois, Indiana, Ohio, and Pennsylvania, but very local. Winters chiefly in southern Atlantic and Gulf Coast states.

In the southern parts of this bird's range, its older name, "Pine-woods Sparrow," is more appropriate since it dwells in open stretches of pines with grass and scattered shrubs for ground cover. Farther north it is also commonly found in abandoned fields and pastures. Bachman's Sparrow spends much of the time feeding on the ground, where it is hard to see except when it mounts a bush or weed stalk to sing. Like many other sparrows, it feeds on insects such as crickets and beetles, and on seeds of grasses and sedges. The bird was named by Audubon for his close friend Dr. John Bachman (1790–1874), who discovered the species in South Carolina.

418 **Botteri's Sparrow**
*Aimophila botterii*

Description: 5¼–6 ¼″ (13–16 cm). Similar to Cassin's Sparrow, but more slender, browner, less boldly streaked on upperparts, with a more conspicuous eyebrow, and slightly less conical bill.

Voice: Song consists of several short trills often introduced by a couple of *clips* and *che-licks,* but is variable.
Habitat: Open arid country such as grasslands, savannas, or desert-scrub areas.
Nesting: 2–5 white eggs. Apparently builds nests on the ground, but little else is known about its breeding habits.
Range: Breeds in southeastern Arizona and southern Texas. Winters south of the U.S.–Mexico border.

Botteri's Sparrow is an entirely terrestrial bird that lives and feeds on the ground and hides in thick vegetation. It is best distinguished from the similar Cassin's Sparrow by its song.

402 **Cassin's Sparrow**
*Aimophila cassinii*

Description: 5¼–5¾″ (13–15 cm). Fine brown streaking on *grayish-brown head and back;* dingy buff unstreaked underparts, with faint streaking on lower flanks occasionally visible. Sexes look alike. Young streaked on breast as well. See Botteri's Sparrow.
Voice: 4 loud, melodious, clear whistles, uttered from the top of tall grass and also in flight. Second note is prolonged and quavering; third note is lowest.
Habitat: Semidesert; arid uplands such as those with yuccas and tall grass.
Nesting: 3 or 4 white eggs in a deep, almost tunnel-like cup on the ground, or at the base of a bush or cactus.
Range: Breeds from southern Arizona and southwestern Kansas south to southern New Mexico and western and southern Texas; also in Mexico. Winters in southern part of breeding range.

This bird is very secretive except when the male is on its breeding grounds. There it steadily proclaims its territory with its flight song, which is similar to a lark's. Rival males often hold song duels from atop grass stems just 20 feet (6 meters) apart. After breeding, the Great Plains population is believed to migrate southwestward into the grassy deserts of Arizona and Mexico.

## 404 Rufous-crowned Sparrow
*Aimophila ruficeps*

Description: 5–6″ (13–15 cm). *Rufous crown with darker rufous eye stripe* on gray head; conspicuous black "whisker" mark. Mantle gray with rufous-brown streaks; underparts unstreaked gray. Juveniles have buff breast with faint streaking and little, if any, rufous marking.

Voice: Song is a rapid, pleasing jumble of notes, recalling that of the House Wren, but with "sparrow quality." Distinctive call is a down-slurred *dear dear dear,* and a thin plaintive *tseeee.*

Habitat: Open oak woodlands; treeless dry uplands with grassy vegetation and bushes, often near rocky outcrops.

Nesting: 3–5 white or slightly bluish eggs in a neat nest of plant fiber and grasses placed on or near the ground.

Range: Mainly resident from California, southern Arizona, and southern New Mexico east to Texas and central Oklahoma.

The Rufous-crowned Sparrow is a secretive bird. In spring the male sings in the early morning from the tops of boulders, but otherwise is usually on the ground. If disturbed, the bird will fly to a nearby rock for a short survey, then return to the grass.

422 **American Tree Sparrow**
*Spizella arborea*

Description: 5½–6½″ (14–17 cm). Gray head with rufous crown and ear stripe; streaked brown above; 2 prominent wing bags; plain gray below with *dark spot in center of breast.* Similar to Field Sparrow, but larger and without white eye ring or pink bill.

Voice: 1 or 2 clear notes followed by a sweet, rapid warble. Winter feeding call a silvery *tsee-ler.*

Habitat: Arctic willow and birch thickets; fields, weedy woodland edges, and roadside thickets in winter.

Nesting: 4 or 5 pale blue eggs, speckled with brown, in a bulky, well-insulated cup of bark strips and weed stems, lined with feathers and hair and concealed in low tundra vegetation.

Range: Breeds from Alaska east across northern Canada, and south to northern British Columbia, central Quebec, and Newfoundland. Winters regularly south to California, Arkansas, and Carolinas.

This northern species is a winter visitor to the continental United States. Unlike northern finches such as Pine Siskins and crossbills, its numbers seem to depend on weather, not on the food supply—the birds are less numerous in mild winters. They roam the snow-covered landscape in flocks, uttering tinkling calls and often visiting feeders.

420 **Chipping Sparrow**
*Spizella passerina*

Description: 5–5½″ (13–14 cm). A small sparrow. Upperparts brown, streaked with black; underparts, sides of face, and rump gray; *crown chestnut; eyebrow white,* with thin black line through eye. Young birds have streaked crown, buff eyebrow, and duller underparts.

Voice: Thin musical trill, all on one note like a sewing machine.

Habitat: Grassy woodland edges, gardens, city parks, brushy pastures, and lawns.

Nesting: 3–5 pale blue eggs, lightly spotted with brown, in a solid cup of grass and stems, almost always lined with hair; nest is placed in shrubbery or in a tangle of vines.

Range: Breeds from Yukon east through Manitoba to Newfoundland, and south to California, Texas, and northern Florida. Winters along southern border of United States into Mexico.

The Chipping Sparrow's habit of lining its nest with hair has earned it the name "Hairbird." The birds formerly utilized horsehair, but with the decline in the use of horses they take any hair available and will even pluck strands from the coat of a sleeping dog. Originally inhabitants of natural clearings and brushy forest borders, they are now found in gardens and suburban areas and have become familiar songbirds. During most of the year they feed on the ground, but in the breeding season males always sing from an elevated perch. Their food consists mainly of seeds, though in summer the adults and the young feed on insects.

---

## 406 Clay-colored Sparrow
*Spizella pallida*

Description: 5–5½″ (13–14 cm). A small sparrow with streaked crown and buffy upperparts and *clear gray breast;* similar to an immature Chipping Sparrow but brighter, with rump brownish buff instead of lead-gray; sides of neck gray; buff cheek patch bordered above and below with black. Grasshopper Sparrow has buff underparts.

Voice: Series of 4 or 5 toneless, insect-like buzzes.

Habitat: Brushy grasslands and prairies.

Nesting: 3–5 pale blue eggs, spotted with dark brown, in a bulky cup of hair-lined grass, placed in a bush or clump of weeds up to 6′ (2 m) above the ground.

Range: Breeds from north-central Canada and Great Lakes region south to Colorado and Michigan. Winters north to southern Texas.

This western relative of the Chipping Sparrow has been gradually extending its range eastward and now breeds in the eastern Great Lakes region. Each spring and fall a few individuals, most of them immatures, appear on the Eastern Seaboard, where they can be difficult to distinguish from immature Chipping Sparrows, with which they often associate.

407 **Field Sparrow**
*Spizella pusilla*

Description: 5¼″ (13 cm). The combination of *bright pink bill, rufous cap, white eye ring,* and unstreaked buff breast distinguishes this bird from other sparrows.

Voice: A series of soft plaintive notes, all on the same pitch, accelerating to a trill at the end.

Habitat: Abandoned fields and pastures grown to weeds, scattered bushes, and small saplings.

Nesting: 4 brown-spotted pale green eggs in a woven cup-shaped nest of grass, lined with rootlets or fine grass and set on or near the ground.

Range: Breeds from northern North Dakota east to central New England, and south to Georgia, Mississippi, Louisiana, central Texas, and western Colorado. Winters south to Gulf of Mexico and northeastern Mexico.

When farms and pastures become overgrown with weeds and bushes, birds such as Field Sparrows and Indigo Buntings move in and nest. Although shyer than its close relative the Chipping Sparrow—and thus more difficult to observe—the Field Sparrow may be studied at leisure when it sings its sweet plaintive song from a conspicuous perch atop a bush or fence post. During fall migration it may be seen among flocks of mixed sparrows.

## 405 Vesper Sparrow
*Pooecetes gramineus*

Description: 5–6½″ (13–17 cm). A grayish, streaked sparrow with *white outer tail feathers, narrow white eye ring,* and small patch of chestnut on bend of wing.

Voice: Song a slow series of 4 clear musical notes, the last 2 higher, ending in a descending series of trills, sometimes rendered as *come-come-where-where-all-together-down-the-hill.*

Habitat: Fields, pastures, and roadsides in farming country.

Nesting: 4–6 white eggs, heavily spotted with brown, in a well-made cup of grass and rootlets concealed in grass on the ground.

Range: Breeds from British Columbia east across southern Canada, and south to central California, Texas, Tennessee, and western North Carolina. Winters north to central California, Oklahoma, New Jersey, and Long Island.

The rich, musical song of this sparrow is a most distinctive sound on rolling farmlands. Long known as the "Bay-winged Bunting," the bird was given the pleasing if somewhat inappropriate name "Vesper Sparrow" by the naturalist John Burroughs, who thought the song sounded more melodious in the evening. The bird is usually found on the ground but often mounts to an exposed perch to sing.

## 398 Lark Sparrow
*Chondestes grammacus*

Description: 5½–6½″ (14–17 cm). Head boldly patterned with black, chestnut, and white; streaked above; white below with black spot in center of breast. Tail black with white edges.

Voice: Alternating buzzes and melodious trills.

Habitat: Grasslands with scattered bushes and trees; open country generally in winter.

Nesting: 3–5 white eggs, heavily spotted with dark brown and black, in a well-made cup of grass and plant stems on the ground or in a bush.

Range: Breeds from British Columbia, Saskatchewan, and northern Minnesota south to California, northern Mexico, Louisiana, and Alabama. Winters from southern California to Florida and southward.

The easiest way to find Lark Sparrows is to drive through grasslands and watch for the birds to fly up into trees along the road. The nests of Northern Mockingbirds have been found with both their own and Lark Sparrow eggs in them, but it is not clear whether the sparrows have taken over an abandoned nest or have driven away the original occupants; since mockingbirds are very aggressive, the latter seems unlikely.

## 397 Black-throated Sparrow
*Amphispiza bilineata*

Description: 5¼″ (13 cm). Gray above, white below, with striking black throat and breast; 2 conspicuous white stripes on sides of head, 1 above and 1 below the eye. Sexes alike.

Voice: 2 clear notes followed by a buzzy trill.

Habitat: Desert with cacti, mesquite, and creosote bushes, and also sagebrush; partial to rocky places.

Nesting: 4 white eggs in a loosely built nest of

bark strips, grass, and stems, lined with wool, hair, or feathers and placed in a thorny bush.

Range: Breeds from northeastern California, southwestern Wyoming, and southeastern Colorado southward. Winters north to desert regions of southern United States.

This handsome sparrow of the arid Southwest is well named. Its alternate name, "Desert Sparrow," is also apt, for despite its vivid markings, it is often difficult to detect among the rocks and scrub, especially when not moving about. However, it may be observed when it mounts a bush or rock to sing its pleasant song. The Black-throated Sparrow can go for long periods without water, obtaining necessary moisture from the plants and insects that are its principal diet during the summer months.

---

626 **Lark Bunting**
*Calamospiza melanocorys*

Description: 6–7½" (15–19 cm). Breeding *male black, with large white wing patch.* Female, immature, and winter male streaked sandy buff above, white below; white eye line, faint "mustache" stripe; *white wing patch* (not always visible); rounded, white-tipped tail feathers.

Voice: A canary-like song with loud bubbling sequences and trills, interspersed with harsher notes. Call a 2-note whistle.

Habitat: Dry plains and prairies; open sagebrush.

Nesting: 4 or 5 light blue eggs in a loose grass nest, placed in a scrape with rim flush with the ground; nest often protected by weedy patch.

Range: Breeds on prairies of south-central Canada and central United States. Winters southward into Mexico.

Lark Buntings are usually seen in large flocks feeding along roadsides. On the

breeding grounds they are quite gregarious, several pairs crowding into a few acres of suitable habitat. Since there are few elevated song perches in their grassland breeding area, males advertise their presence with a conspicuous song flight. Often one can see several singing males in the air at one time, providing watchers an easy way to locate a nesting colony. Like many seed-eating birds, they supplement their summer diet with insects.

411, 412 **Savannah Sparrow including "Ipswich Sparrow"**
*Passerculus sandwichensis*

Description: 4½–6″ (11–15 cm). Pale and streaked, with yellowish eyebrow and pinkish legs. Tail notched; other grassland sparrows have shorter, more pointed tails.

Voice: Song a high-pitched, buzzy *tsip-tsip-tsip-se-e-e-srr.*

Habitat: Fields, prairies, salt marshes, and grassy dunes.

Nesting: 4–6 pale blue-green eggs, variably spotted and speckled with dark brown, in a cup of grass lined with finer plant material and hair.

Range: Breeds from Alaska east across Canada, and south to New Jersey, Missouri, and northern Mexico. Winters regularly north to southeastern Alaska and Massachusetts.

This most abundant and familiar of the grass sparrows shows a great deal of color variation over its wide range. One large and pale form that breeds at Sable Island, Nova Scotia, was until recently considered a separate species, the "Ipswich Sparrow." Savannah Sparrows are able runners; once discovered, they drop into the grass and dart away. In the fall they migrate southward in huge numbers and may then be found almost anywhere, even in city parks.

413 **Baird's Sparrow**
*Ammodramus bairdii*

Description: 5–5½″ (13–14 cm). A pale, streaked sparrow, whitish below; breast crossed by a band of narrow black streaks; *crown stripe bright ocher.*
Voice: 3 short notes followed by a musical trill on a lower pitch.
Habitat: Dry upland prairies.
Nesting: 3–5 white eggs, blotched and scrawled with dark brown, in a cup of weed stems and grass, concealed in grass or weeds on the ground.
Range: Breeds from Saskatchewan and Manitoba south to Montana and Minnesota. Winters in Texas, Arizona, and northern Mexico.

This elegant grass sparrow was first described in 1844 by Audubon, who named it after Spencer F. Baird, 19th-century ornithologist and Secretary of the Smithsonian Institution. The total population of Baird's Sparrows is small, and once they leave the breeding grounds they are difficult to find. Even on the breeding grounds, one must search hard for the habitat that suits them, but a few singing males usually can be found there, often perched on the tips of weed stalks.

414 **Grasshopper Sparrow**
*Ammodramus savannarum*

Description: 4½–5″ (11–13 cm). A small chunky grassland sparrow with *clear buff breast* and dark rufous upperparts with a scaly pattern; pale central stripe on crown. Tail short and pointed.
Voice: A high-pitched, insect-like *kip-kip-kip, zeeee,* usually uttered from the top of a weed stalk.
Habitat: Open grassy and weedy meadows, pastures, and plains.
Nesting: 4 or 5 white eggs, speckled with red-

brown, in a cup of grass (often domed) lined with rootlets and hair.

Range: Breeds from British Columbia, Manitoba, and New Hampshire south to Florida (rare), West Indies, and Mexico. Winters north to California, Texas, and North Carolina.

This elusive sparrow—named for its buzzy song—is sensitive to subtle changes in its habitat. As soon as a weedy field becomes overgrown or trees have filled in an abandoned pasture, the Grasshopper Sparrow no longer uses the site for breeding. In some parts of the country it chooses different habitats, such as palmetto grasslands in Florida. Less of a seed-eater than our other grass sparrows, it feeds largely on insects.

415 **Henslow's Sparrow**
*Ammodramus henslowii*

Description: 5″ (13 cm). Dull olive green head, reddish-brown wings, and streaked breast and flanks.

Voice: Explosive 2-note sneeze, *tsi-lick.*

Habitat: Moist or dry grasslands with scattered weeds and small shrubs.

Nesting: 4 brown-spotted whitish eggs in a woven grass nest on the ground, usually in a grass clump.

Range: Breeds (locally) from Minnesota, southern Ontario, and central New York (rarely New England) south to Kansas, Illinois, and North Carolina. Winters in Gulf Coast states, northern Florida, and along Atlantic Coast to South Carolina.

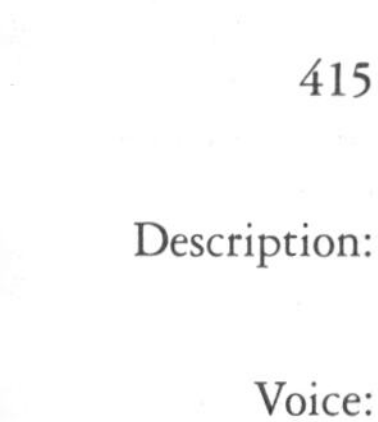

This sparrow is secretive and mouse-like, skulking low in the grass. It relies on running rather than flying, and is seldom observed unless perched atop a weed stalk uttering its insect-like "song." These birds are sometimes found in loose colonies of up to a dozen pairs, but one to three pairs are more common. Curiously, Henslow's Sparrows may be present in a certain locality and absent from a seemingly similar habitat not far away. The bird was named for John Henslow, a prominent early-19th-century English botanist.

416 **Le Conte's Sparrow**
*Ammodramus leconteii*

Description: 5″ (13 cm). Similar to the interior Canadian race of the Sharp-tailed Sparrow, but crown stripe is white instead of gray; *wide reddish collar* on nape and upper back.
Voice: 2 very thin, insect-like hisses.
Habitat: Moist grasslands and boggy meadows; also dry fields in winter.
Nesting: 4 brown-spotted whitish eggs in a grass cup lined with hair and set on the ground, usually in a grass clump.
Range: Breeds from Mackenzie and central Quebec south to northern Montana, Minnesota, and northern Michigan. Winters in southeastern states.

This elusive bird keeps to the thick grass like all grass-loving sparrows except when it mounts an exposed perch to sing. It is almost impossible to flush, for it prefers running to flying. Common in the prairie regions of west-central Canada, it inhabits the drier grass borders of rush-grown marshes. It was named for Major John Le Conte of Georgia, an early American naturalist (1818–1891).

417 **Sharp-tailed Sparrow**
*Ammodramus caudacutus*

Description: 5½″ (14 cm). The combination of dark cap, gray ear patch, and bright orange-buff triangular area on the face distinguishes this species from the only other salt-marsh sparrow, the Seaside Sparrow. Inland population ("Nelson's Sharp-tailed Sparrow") is more richly colored than coastal birds.

Voice: A dry, insect-like *kip-kip-zeeeee.*

Habitat: Along the coast, in drier, grassy portions of salt marshes and inland to grassy, freshwater marshes.

Nesting: 4 or 5 brown-dotted pale blue eggs in a loosely woven cup of grass set in a tussock above the high-tide line or locally in freshwater marsh grass.

Range: Breeds in disjunct colonies in interior Canada; also along coast from Nova Scotia to North Carolina. Winters chiefly on southern Atlantic and Gulf coasts.

These birds spend most of their lives in dense, coarse marsh grass; by the end of the breeding season their plumage is so badly worn that little of the distinctive pattern remains visible. Indeed, there are few birds more unprepossessing than a threadbare Sharp-tailed Sparrow in August. A month later, however, when they have acquired a fresh coat of feathers, they are among our most attractive sparrows.

## 403 Seaside Sparrow including "Cape Sable Seaside Sparrow"

*Ammodramus maritimus*

Description: 6″ (15 cm). A dark, gray-streaked salt-marsh sparrow with dull yellow "mustache" and dull yellow spot in front of the eye.

Voice: 2 short, sharp notes followed by a buzzy *zeeee.*

Habitat: Exclusively grassy salt marshes, favoring the wetter portions.

Nesting: 4 or 5 white eggs, with brown blotches, in a woven grass nest placed in a grass tussock above the high-tide line.

Range: Breeds in salt marshes of Atlantic and

Gulf coasts from southern New England to Florida and Texas. Winters in southern portions of this range.

This is literally a seaside bird; few other sparrows have so restricted a habitat. Favoring the wetter sections of salt marshes, it feeds much less on seeds than other sparrows do, but eats tiny young crabs, snails, and other small marine animals along the tidal creeks of salt meadows. Like all birds living near the ground in grass, the Seaside Sparrow is difficult to detect until it is almost underfoot, whereupon it flushes, flies for a short distance, drops down into the thick grass, and runs along like a mouse. The best opportunity to view one is when it is singing atop a grass stem or small shrub. Two distinctively plumaged populations of this bird in Florida were once considered separate species, called the "Dusky Seaside Sparrow" and the "Cape Sable Seaside Sparrow." The former is now extinct.

419 **Fox Sparrow**
*Passerella iliaca*

Description: 6–7½" (15–19 cm). Larger and heavier than a House Sparrow. Upperparts boldly striped with *rich rufous;* underparts white, heavily spotted with rufous. Sides of head gray with rufous stripes. *Tail bright rufous.*

Voice: Loud, short, melodious warble.

Habitat: Coniferous forest undergrowth in summer; dense woodland thickets, weedy pastures, and brushy roadsides in winter.

Nesting: 4 or 5 pale green eggs, densely spotted with red-brown, in a thick-walled cup of leaves in grass and moss, concealed in vegetation on or near the ground.

Range: Breeds from Aleutians and mainland Alaska east to northern Quebec and Maritimes, and south to southern

California, Colorado, and New Brunswick. Winters south from British Columbia, across southern United States, and locally farther north.

Away from the breeding grounds, Fox Sparrows are most conspicuous during spring migration, when one frequently hears their rich, melodious song coming from brushy thickets and roadsides. They scratch in leaves for food and often make so much noise that one expects to find a larger animal. Western birds tend to be more dusky brown or slate-colored, and they bear little resemblance to the "fox-colored" eastern birds.

## 408 Song Sparrow
*Melospiza melodia*

Description: 5–7″ (13–17 cm). A common sparrow with heavily streaked underparts and *large central spot on breast* (sometimes lacking in juveniles). *Pumps tail in flight.*

Voice: Song consists of 3 short notes followed by a varied trill, sometimes interpreted as *Madge-Madge-Madge, put-on-your-tea-kettle-ettle-ettle.*

Habitat: Thickets, pastures, undergrowth in gardens, and city parks.

Nesting: 3–6 brown-spotted pale green eggs in a well-made cup of grass and leaves, often lined with hair and concealed in weeds on the ground or in a low bush.

Range: Breeds from Aleutians and mainland Alaska east to Newfoundland, and south to California, North Dakota, and Carolinas. Winters from southern Canada to Gulf Coast and Mexico.

Probably the best known of our native sparrows, this bird is found almost everywhere in North America. Over its vast range the species shows a great deal of geographical variation. In Alaska and the Aleutian Islands the birds are large, dark, and long-billed; it is hard to believe they are the same species as the familiar bird of our lawns and parks.

## 409 Lincoln's Sparrow
*Melospiza lincolnii*

Description: 5–6″ (13–15 cm). Gray crown has 2 rusty stripes; gray eyebrow. *Upper breast has buff band finely streaked with black.* Similar to Song Sparrow, but more finely streaked and *shyer.*

Voice: A rich, gurgling, wren-like song rising in the middle and dropping abruptly at the end.

Habitat: Brushy bogs, or willow or alder thickets; winters in woodland thickets and brushy pastures.

Nesting: 4 or 5 pale green eggs, heavily spotted with brown, in a cup of grass well concealed in forest undergrowth.

Range: Breeds from Alaska across Canada, and south to California, northern New Mexico, and northern New England. Winters across southern tier of United States.

This unobtrusive bird of the northern bogs was first described by Audubon in 1834 from a specimen he collected in Quebec, and he named the bird for Robert Lincoln, a companion on his trip to Labrador. Although not uncommon during migration, Lincoln's Sparrow is seldom noticed because of its shyness and its resemblance to the Song Sparrow.

## 410 Swamp Sparrow
*Melospiza georgiana*

Description: 5″ (13 cm). A chunky *dark* sparrow with unstreaked underparts, *bright rufous cap, and rusty wings;* dark brown back and tail; gray face and breast; white throat. White-throated Sparrow has striped crown and whiter throat, and lacks rusty coloration on wings.

Voice: Sweet, musical trill, all on one note.

Habitat: Freshwater marshes and open wooded swamps; during migration with other sparrows, weedy fields, parks, and brush piles.

Nesting: 4 or 5 blue-green eggs, with brown blotches, in a grassy cup on the ground, well hidden in dense tussocks or marsh vegetation.

Range: Breeds from Mackenzie east to Newfoundland, and south to northern Missouri, Ohio, Maryland, and Delaware. Winters north to Nebraska, southern Great Lakes region, and southern New England.

A bird of the wetlands during the breeding season, the Swamp Sparrow appears in a variety of other habitats during migration and in winter. It is rather shy, but responds readily to any squeaking noise, and can usually be lured into view by a patient observer. It is never seen in large flocks like the White-throated and White-crowned sparrows, but is usually found singly, foraging on the ground in rather dense cover.

## 393 White-throated Sparrow
*Zonotrichia albicollis*

Description: 6–7″ (15–18 cm). Upperparts streaked, underparts clear gray. There are 2 color forms, 1 with black and white head stripes, 1 with tan and black head stripes. Both have *sharply defined white throat patch; dark bill.* Females and young birds duller. White-crowned Sparrow similar, but lacks white throat patch and is slimmer, with pink bill.

Voice: Song a clear, whistled *Poor Sam Peabody, Peabody, Peabody,* or *Sweet Sweet Canada, Canada, Canada.* The latter rendition is perhaps more appropriate, since most of these birds breed in Canada.

Habitat: Brushy undergrowth in coniferous woodlands. Winters in brushy woodlands, pastures, and suburban areas.

Nesting: 4 or 5 pale green eggs, heavily spotted with brown, in a cup of grass, rootlets, and moss, on or near the ground in forest undergrowth.

Range: Breeds from Mackenzie, central Quebec, and Newfoundland south to North Dakota, Wisconsin, and Pennsylvania. Winters in much of eastern United States and in small numbers in southwestern states.

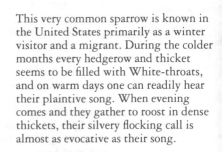

This very common sparrow is known in the United States primarily as a winter visitor and a migrant. During the colder months every hedgerow and thicket seems to be filled with White-throats, and on warm days one can readily hear their plaintive song. When evening comes and they gather to roost in dense thickets, their silvery flocking call is almost as evocative as their song.

## 394 White-crowned Sparrow
*Zonotrichia leucophrys*

Description: 6–7½″ (15–19 cm). Similar to White-throated Sparrow, but more slender and without white throat, and generally with a more erect posture. *Crown has bold black-and-white stripes.* Upperparts streaked, underparts clear pearly gray. *Pink bill.* Young birds similar, but crown stripes buff and dark brown, underparts washed with dull buff.

Voice: A short series of clear whistles followed by buzzy notes.

Habitat: Nests in dense brush, especially where near open grasslands; winters in open woods and gardens.

Nesting: 3–5 pale green eggs, thickly spotted with brown, in a bulky cup of bark strips, grass, and twigs lined with grass and hair, on or near the ground.

Range: Breeds from Alaska and Manitoba east to Labrador and Newfoundland, and south in western mountains to northern New Mexico and central California. Winters north to southeastern Alaska, Idaho, Kansas, Kentucky, and Maryland.

The handsome White-crown is a favorite not only of bird-watchers but of laboratory scientists. Much of what we know about the physiology of bird migration has been learned from laboratory experiments with this species. In the East, these birds are much less numerous than White-throated Sparrows, but flocks of White-throats often contain a few of these slender, elegant birds. Much of their feeding is done on the ground but, like White-throats, they will respond to a squeaking noise made by an observer by popping up to the top of a bush.

---

395 **Harris' Sparrow**
*Zonotrichia querula*

Description: 7½" (19 cm). Adult has *black crown, throat, and chest;* pink bill; gray face; brown back, wings, and tail; and *white abdomen with spotted or streaked sides.* Immatures have buff faces and lack solid black crown, throat, and breast.

Voice: Series of clear high notes followed by another series, each on a different pitch.

Habitat: Breeds in mossy bogs and scrub forests, migrates through the prairie regions, and winters in dense river-bottom thickets, woodland borders, clearings, and brush piles.

Nesting: 3–5 brown-blotched pale green eggs in a plant-fiber-and-leaf nest, lined with grass and placed on the ground at the base of a bush or in a stunted spruce tree.

Range: Breeds in northern Canada west of Hudson Bay south to northern Manitoba. Winters in interior from

Iowa and Nebraska south to Texas and Louisiana.

These large, handsome sparrows are favorites at eastern feeders since they rarely stray so far from their normal Midwestern range. They vigorously scratch in the leaves and soil for food, and eat weed seeds, flower buds and blossoms, small fruits such as berries, and a great variety of insects, spiders, and snails. They were named by Audubon for Edward Harris (1799–1863), who accompanied him on his western trip in 1843.

388, 613 **Dark-eyed Junco including "Slate-colored Junco," "White-winged Junco," and "Oregon Junco"**
*Junco hyemalis*

Description: 5–6½″ (13–16 cm). Sparrow-sized. Variable, but generally slate-gray or gray-brown above, with white abdomen sharply demarcated from gray of breast. White along sides of tail shows in flight. Pink bill. Some birds have buff flanks. Birds of the dominant western form, the "Oregon Junco," have black hoods and rufous backs. The form breeding in the Black Hills, the "White-winged Junco," has white wing bars and more white in the tail.

Voice: Trill like that of Chipping Sparrow, but slower and with a more musical, tinkling quality. Also a soft twittering.

Habitat: Coniferous or mixed forests; winters in fields, gardens, city parks, and roadside thickets.

Nesting: 3–6 brown-spotted pale green or blue eggs in a deep, well-made cup of grass, moss, and strips of bark, well concealed on or near the ground in vegetation in a bank or on the forest floor.

Range: Breeds from Alaska east across Canada to Newfoundland, and south to

mountains in Mexico and Georgia. Winters south to Gulf Coast and northern Mexico.

Until recently the many geographical forms of this bird were considered separate species, but since they interbreed wherever their ranges meet, they are now considered one species. The eastern form, formerly called the "Slate-colored Junco," is the only one usually encountered in the eastern states. Occasionally, however, black-headed, rusty-flanked western birds, "Oregon Juncos," may also be seen. Juncos are among the most common of our winter birds, often visiting feeders.

427 **McCown's Longspur**
*Calcarius mccownii*

Description: 5¾–6″ (15 cm). Sparrow-sized. Breeding male streaked above with black crown, whitish face, and black "mustache"; gray below with bold black band across breast. Female and winter male duller and more streaked; best identified by tail pattern, which is largely white with central pair of tail feathers black and narrow black band at tip.

Voice: Dry rattle; also a clear sweet warble given during a fluttering flight with wings raised high over back.

Habitat: Arid plains.

Nesting: 3 or 4 pale green eggs, spotted with dark brown and black, in a hollow scrape lined with fine grass and hair, on open ground.

Range: Breeds from Alberta and southwestern Manitoba south to Dakotas, Wyoming, and Colorado. Winters from Nebraska and Colorado southward.

This longspur nests in higher and more arid short-grass plains than does the Chestnut-collared Longspur, and so has

been less affected by plowing of the prairie. They so dislike moisture that in wet seasons they may abandon areas where they normally are abundant. In summer they feed chiefly on grasshoppers, but in fall and winter, when they gather in large flocks with other longspurs and with Horned Larks, they prefer seeds. In winter plumage they can be difficult to distinguish from the other longspurs, but close up they are easily identified by their stouter bill.

---

391, 428 **Lapland Longspur**
*Calcarius lapponicus*

Description: 6–7″ (15–18 cm). Sparrow-sized. The only longspur in most of the East. Breeding male has black face, crown, and upper breast; chestnut nape; streaked above, white below with streaked flanks. Female and winter male dull and without bold pattern; best identified by largely black tail with white outermost tail feathers. Smith's Longspur has similar tail, but is always buff above and below, and usually shows small white wing patch.

Voice: Rattling call. Flight song is sweet and bubbling.

Habitat: Arctic tundra; winters in open windswept fields and on grassy coastal dunes. Often found in parking lots along the coast in winter.

Nesting: 4 or 5 pale olive green eggs, heavily spotted with brown and purple, in a grass-lined hollow in the ground that is concealed under a clump of grass or a dwarf birch.

Range: Breeds from Aleutians, Alaska, and Arctic islands to northern Quebec. Winters regularly to California, Texas, and New York. Also in northern Eurasia.

This species is the only one of four longspurs that is found in both hemispheres. Like other longspurs, it is almost invisible on the ground; often a whole flock will dart into the air at an observer's feet, only to disappear again when they land on bare ground a few hundred yards away.

## 426 Smith's Longspur
*Calcarius pictus*

Description: 5¾–6½" (15–17 cm). Sparrow-sized. Breeding male streaked dark brown and buff above, clear warm buff below; bold black-and-white head pattern. Small white wing patch most evident in flight; tail black, with white outer feathers. Females and winter males duller and without head pattern, but always more buff-colored than other longspurs.

Voice: Dry rattle, like a finger running along the teeth of a comb.

Habitat: Arctic tundra and forest edges; winters on open grassy plains.

Nesting: 3–5 pale brown eggs, spotted with darker brown, placed in a grass-walled hollow lined with plant down and feathers concealed under a clump of grass or a dwarf willow.

Range: Breeds from northern Alaska across northern Canada to Hudson Bay. Winters from Nebraska south to Texas.

Longspur identification is difficult in the Midwest, where all four species winter, but this species, clad in warm buff year-round, can be told at a glance. At times they are found in huge flocks moving over the dry winter grasslands in search of seeds, uttering a distinctive clinking call. On the Arctic tundra they seem to prefer drier, more elevated areas than does the Lapland Longspur.

392 **Chestnut-collared Longspur**
*Calcarius ornatus*

Description: 5½–6½" (14–17 cm). Sparrow-sized. Similar to Lapland Longspur, but breeding male has *wholly black underparts* and some white on face. Tail of female and winter male similar to that of Lapland Longspur, but with *more white at sides.*

Voice: Soft, sweet, and tumbling, somewhat like that of Western Meadowlark; also a hard *ji-jiv* in flight.

Habitat: Dry elevated prairies and short-grass plains.

Nesting: 3–5 pale green eggs, spotted with brown and lavender, in a grass-lined hollow under a clump of grass.

Range: Breeds from Alberta and Manitoba south to Minnesota and Wyoming. Winters from Colorado and Kansas south to Texas and northern Mexico.

The upland prairies favored by the Chestnut-collared Longspur for nesting have been extensively planted in wheat, so these birds are much less numerous than in the past. They need only a small area, however, and often several pairs will crowd into a patch of land or even the narrow strips of unplowed grassland along highways. Here the males can be seen singing from the tops of fence posts, rocks, or tall weed stalks.

---

429, 620 **Snow Bunting**
*Plectrophenax nivalis*

Description: 6–7¼" (15–18 cm). Sparrow-sized. Breeding male has black back with *much white* on head, underparts, wings, and tail. Female similar, but duller. Winter birds have brown on crown and upperparts, have duller underparts, but still show much white in wings.

Voice: Clear whistle or soft buzzy note. Song a sweet warble.

Habitat: Arctic tundra. Winters on windswept grasslands and beaches.

Nesting: 4–6 white eggs, with red-brown spots in a ring around the larger end, placed in a cup of grass lined with fur and feathers and concealed among rocks or in tundra vegetation.

Range: Breeds from Aleutians, Alaska and Arctic islands south to northern Quebec. Winters regularly across southern Canada and northern United States. Also in Eurasia.

This circumpolar bird, often called the "Snowflake," breeds farther north than almost any other land bird. In severe winters large flocks descend to our northern states, where they favor the most barren places. They occasionally can be found at beach parking lots in the dead of winter searching for weed seeds.

---

**FAMILY EMBERIZIDAE**
**Subfamily Icterinae**
New World Blackbirds and Allies

95 species: This exclusively American family contains such familiar species as the Bobolink, meadowlarks, orioles, grackles, and cowbirds, as well as the many blackbirds. Twenty-three species breed in North America. Members of this family are diverse in appearance, nesting habits, and habitat. The orioles are master nest builders, weaving bag-like, hanging nests. The Bobolink and meadowlarks are ground-nesters, while the cowbirds are nest parasites.

---

425, 628 **Bobolink**
*Dolichonyx oryzivorus*

Description: 6–8″ (15–20 cm). Breeding male largely black with *white rump* and back, *dull yellow nape.* Female and winter male rich buff-yellow, streaked on back and crown. *Short, finch-like bill.* Female Red-winged Blackbird darker and less buffy, and has longer bill.

Voice: Flight song a series of joyous bubbling, tumbling, gurgling phrases with each note on a different pitch. Call a soft *pink,* often heard on migration.

Habitat: Prairies and meadows; marshes during migration.

Nesting: 4–7 gray eggs, spotted with red-brown and purple; nest is a poorly made but well-concealed cup of grass, stems, and rootlets placed on the ground in a field.

Range: Breeds from British Columbia east to Newfoundland, and south to northern California, Colorado, and Pennsylvania. Winters in southern South America.

Originally the Bobolink was probably confined to the central grasslands, but with the settling of the Northeast it quickly spread into New England. Now, with farms abandoned and the land returning to forest, the species is declining. Each fall, migrant Bobolinks gather in large numbers in southern rice fields, where their habit of eating grain has earned them the name "Ricebird."

432, 634 **Red-winged Blackbird**
*Agelaius phoeniceus*

Description: 7–9 ½″ (18–24 cm). Smaller than a robin. Male black with *bright red shoulder patches.* Female and young heavily streaked with dusky brown.

Voice: A rich, musical *o-ka-leeee!*

Habitat: Marshes, swamps, and wet and dry meadows; pastures.

Nesting: 3–5 pale blue eggs, spotted and scrawled with dark brown and purple. Nest is a well-made cup of marsh grass or reeds attached to growing marsh vegetation or built in a bush in a marsh.

Range: Breeds from Alaska southeast across

Canada to Newfoundland, and south to northern Baja California, central Mexico, Gulf Coast, and Florida. Winters regularly north to British Columbia, Great Lakes, and Pennsylvania.

Although primarily a marsh bird, the Red-winged Blackbird will nest near virtually any body of water and occasionally breeds in upland pastures. Each pair raises two or three broods a season, building a new nest for each clutch. After the breeding season, the birds gather with other blackbirds in flocks sometimes numbering in the hundreds of thousands, or even millions, and have come to be viewed as a health hazard.

498 **Eastern Meadowlark**
*Sturnella magna*

Description: 9–11″ (23–28 cm). Robin-sized. A stocky, brown-streaked bird with *white-edged tail; bright yellow throat and breast. Breast crossed by a black V.* Western Meadowlark very similar, but paler above, and yellow of throat extends onto cheeks; best distinguished by voice.
Voice: Clear, mellow whistle, *see-you, see-yeeeer;* also a loud rattling alarm note.
Habitat: Meadows, pastures, and prairies; during migration, in open country generally.
Nesting: 3–7 white eggs, spotted with brown and dull lavender, in a partly domed structure of grass concealed in a depression in a meadow.
Range: Breeds from southeastern Canada south throughout eastern United States, west to Nebraska, Texas, and Arizona. Winters in most of breeding range.

One of the best-known birds of American farmlands, the Eastern Meadowlark usually delivers its cheerful song from a conspicuous perch.

Meadowlarks are often polygamous; more than one female may be found nesting in the territory of a single male. Because the birds often breed in hay fields, their nests may be destroyed by mowing; unless the season is well advanced, they normally nest again. During migration and winter Eastern Meadowlarks band together in groups of up to a dozen birds and can be found in almost any open grassy area.

---

499 **Western Meadowlark**
*Sturnella neglecta*

Description: 8½–11″ (22–28 cm). Robin-sized. Streaked brown above, bright yellow below, with bold black V on breast. Very similar to Eastern Meadowlark, but *upperparts paler, and yellow of throat extends onto cheeks.* Best identified by voice.

Voice: Rich, flute-like jumble of gurgling notes, usually descending the scale; very different from the Eastern Meadowlark's series of simple, plaintive whistles.

Habitat: Meadows, plains, and prairies.

Nesting: 3–7 white eggs, with dark brown and purple spots, in a domed cup of grass and weed stems concealed in grass or weeds.

Range: Breeds from British Columbia, Manitoba, northern Michigan, and northwestern Ohio south to Missouri, central Texas, and northern Mexico. Has spread eastward in recent years. Winters north to southern British Columbia, Utah, and Arkansas.

The clearing of eastern North American forests has caused this bird to extend its range eastward beyond the Great Lakes, where it has occasionally interbred with the Eastern Meadowlark. The two species are so similar that it was not until 1844 that Audubon noticed the difference and named the western bird *neglecta* because it had been overlooked for so long. The song of the Western Meadowlark is often heard on movie sound tracks even when the setting is far from the bird's range.

434, 497 **Yellow-headed Blackbird**
*Xanthocephalus xanthocephalus*

Description: 8–11″ (20–28 cm). Robin-sized. Male much larger than female; *head, neck, and upper breast of male bright yellow; blackish elsewhere;* conspicuous white markings on wings. Female duller and lighter; yellow on chest, throat, and face; no white wing marks.

Voice: Harsh, incessant *oka-wee-wee* and *kruck* calls, coming from many individuals in a colony, blend into a loud, wavering chorus.

Habitat: Freshwater marshes.

Nesting: 3–5 brown-speckled whitish eggs in a basket woven around several strong stalks. Nests in colonies.

Range: Breeds from central British Columbia, northern Alberta, and Wisconsin south to southern California, northern New Mexico, and Illinois. Winters mainly in Southwest and Mexico.

In spring, visiting a Yellow-headed Blackbird colony in a marsh or slough is an exciting experience. The surrounding water provides safety but often limits the nesting habitat; crowding is thus inevitable. Some males are always in display flight, with head stooped, feet and tail drooped, wings beating in a slow, accentuated way. Some quarrel with neighbors over boundaries while others fly out to feed. Approaching predators are mobbed by clouds of Yellow-headed Blackbirds and neighboring Red-wings, which nest in the drier stands of cattails.

433, 635 **Rusty Blackbird**
*Euphagus carolinus*

Description: 9″ (23 cm). In spring, males are black, with bluish and greenish iridescence; females are dark gray. In fall, much more rust-brown, especially head, breast, and back. *Conspicuous pale yellow eyes in both sexes.*

Voice: Like the squeaks of a rusty gate; call note a sharp *check.*

Habitat: Wooded swamps and damp woods with pools during migration; boreal bogs in the breeding season.

Nesting: 4 or 5 blue-green eggs, with brown blotches, in a bulky stick nest lined with grass, moss, and lichens, and set in a dense shrub or low tree near or over water.

Range: Breeds from Alaska and across northern Canada to southern Canada, northern New York, and northern New England. Winters from southeastern South Dakota and southern New England south to Gulf Coast.

The Rusty Blackbird is most often seen during migration, when small parties may be found walking about on the floor of swampy woods, turning over dead leaves in search of insects. They seldom occur in very large flocks, and do not as a rule associate with Red-winged Blackbirds and grackles.

---

431, 636 **Brewer's Blackbird**
*Euphagus cyanocephalus*

Description: 8–10″ (20–25 cm). Robin-sized. Male solid black with purplish-blue iridescent head and yellow eyes. Female gray with dark eyes. Similar to Rusty Blackbird, but male Rusty has faint green reflections on head; female Rusty has yellow eyes.

Voice: Gurgles, squawks, and whistles.

Habitat: Prairies, fields, and farmyards.

Nesting: 3–5 gray eggs, with dark brown spots, in a nest of coarse grass and twigs reinforced with mud and lined with fine grass and hair, placed on the ground or in a tree. Nests in loose colonies of up to 30 pairs.

Range: Breeds from British Columbia, Manitoba, and Ontario south to southern California, New Mexico, and Texas. Winters north to British Columbia and Carolinas.

This blackbird, named for 19th-century ornithologist Thomas M. Brewer of Boston, is best known as a winter visitor to stockyards and farms, where it feeds on spilled grain. It also takes insects that are stirred up by livestock and plows. Brewer's Blackbirds nest in hay fields, but the young are usually fledged before the hay is harvested. During breeding season, the male has an elaborate display that includes fluffing out the feathers, making the wing quiver, cocking the tail, and pointing the bill upward.

631 **Great-tailed Grackle**
*Quiscalus mexicanus*

Description: Male, 16–17″ (41–43 cm); female, 12–13″ (30–33 cm). Tail very long and keel-shaped. Male black, with *iridescent purple on back and breast.* Female smaller; brown with pale breast. *Eyes always yellow.* Common Grackle smaller; female lacks pale breast. Boat-tailed Grackle of salt marshes very similar, but males are iridescent blue or blue-green and often have brown eyes. Best distinguished by calls.

Voice: Variety of whistles, clucks, and hissing notes.

Habitat: Farmlands with scattered trees and thickets.

Nesting: 3 or 4 pale blue eggs, spotted and scrawled with brown and purple, placed in a bulky nest of sticks, grass, and mud in a tree. Nests in loose colonies.

Range: Resident in California, Colorado, Kansas, and western Louisiana southward.

Where Great-tailed and Boat-tailed grackles occur together, the Great-tailed tends to avoid salt marshes, the chief habitat of the Boat-tailed. Occasionally, however, the two may nest very near one another, and on rare occasions the species have been known to hybridize. The Great-tail seems to be extending its range eastward but has not yet reached Florida.

480, 630 **Boat-tailed Grackle**
*Quiscalus major*

Description: Males 16–17″ (41–43 cm); females 12–13″ (30–33 cm). Tail very long and keel-shaped. Male black, *iridescent blue on back and breast; yellow or brown eyes.* Female smaller, brown with paler breast. Common Grackle smaller; female lacks paler breast. Great-tailed Grackle of western Louisiana and Texas has iridescent purple back and breast, and always has yellow eyes.

Voice: Harsh *jeeb-jeeb-jeeb-jeeb,* unlike the whistles and clucks of the Great-tailed Grackle.

Habitat: Marshes along the coast; in Florida, also on farmlands.

Nesting: 3 or 4 pale blue eggs, spotted and scrawled with brown and purple, in a bulky cup of grass, mud, and decayed vegetation placed from 2 to 10′ (60 cm to 3 m) up in marsh grass or bushes.

Range: Resident along coasts from New Jersey south and west to Louisiana; also inland in peninsular Florida.

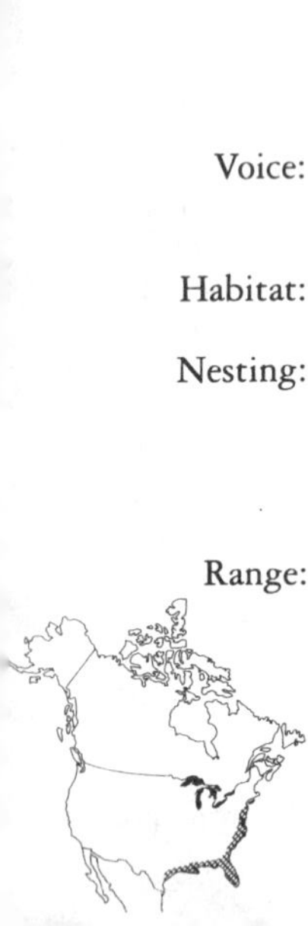

This species and its close relative the Great-tailed Grackle were thought to be a single species until it was found that both nest in southwestern Louisiana without interbreeding.

479, 632 **Common Grackle**
*Quiscalus quiscula*

Description: 12″ (30 cm). Jay-sized. *Long, wedge-shaped tail* displaying longitudinal ridge or keel when in flight. Appears all black at a distance but is actually highly iridescent, with colors varying from blue to purple to green to bronze, depending on the light. Bright yellow eyes. Female duller and somewhat smaller than male.

Voice: Clucks; high-pitched, rising screech like a rusty hinge.

Habitat: Lawns, parks, fields, open woodlands.

Nesting: 5 pale blue eggs, with black scrawls, in a bulky stick nest lined with grass, placed anywhere from low in a bush to high in a tree. Some birds nest in colonies, breeding most often in tall evergreens.

Range: Breeds from northern Alberta, central Ontario, and Newfoundland, south to Gulf Coast states east of Rockies, but expanding into Idaho and Washington in Northwest. Winters north to Kansas, southern Great Lakes region, and New England.

These familiar birds arrive from the South early in spring and depart late in fall. In some northern areas they congregate by the thousands during migration as well as in winter roosts. Their diet is extremely varied, including insects, crayfish, frogs, mice, nestling birds, and eggs as well as grains and wild fruits. At feeders they are especially attracted to cracked corn. They are most numerous near dwellings and even raid litter baskets at public beaches.

637, 638 **Bronzed Cowbird**
**"Red-eyed Cowbird"**
*Molothrus aeneus*

Description: 8½" (22 cm). Male bronze-black with bluish-black wings and tail. Prominent red eye can be seen at close range. Female similar but duller. Brown-headed Cowbird smaller, with distinctive brown head.

Voice: Wheezy and guttural whistling notes, and various squeaks and squeals.

Habitat: Pastures, roadside thickets, ranches, open country generally; also parks and orchards.

Nesting: 1–3 blue-green eggs laid in other birds' nests, particularly nests of orioles, tanagers, flycatchers, buntings, and grosbeaks, more rarely thrashers and thrushes.

Range: Breeds in southern Arizona, New Mexico, and south-central Texas. Withdraws southward from much of Arizona during winter.

During courtship both sexes, but especially males, erect their neck feathers into a ruff. The males bow and jump up and down, whistling unmusical squeaky calls. Like their close relatives the Brown-headed Cowbirds, these birds follow livestock, especially cattle, snapping up insects flushed from the grass. They alight on the backs and necks of livestock to feed on ticks. Cowbirds also feed extensively on seeds and grain. During the colder months these birds form enormous flocks and move around the countryside with other species of blackbirds.

639 **Shiny Cowbird**
*Molothrus bonariensis*

Description: 7–8" (18–20 cm). Male purplish black glossed with blue above, shining purplish black below. Female grayish brown, paler below. Bill large, conical, and black. Eyes dark.

Voice: Song a melodious warble. A variety of harsh metallic call notes.

Habitat: Open country and farmlands.

Nesting: 1–3 heavily spotted white eggs, laid in the nests of other species.

Range: A recent invader from West Indies. Has been recorded in a number of southeastern states.

During the present century, this species has spread from South America through the West Indies, and now seems poised to add at least the southeastern states to its range. If it succeeds, it could pose an additional threat to our native songbirds, for cowbirds are brood parasites.

477, 478 **Brown-headed Cowbird**
*Molothrus ater*

Description: 6–8″ (15–20 cm). Male black with glossy brown head; female plain gray-brown. Both have finch-like bill.

Voice: Squeaky gurgle. Call is *check* or a rattle.

Habitat: Agricultural land, fields, woodland edges, and suburban areas.

Nesting: 4 or 5 white eggs, lightly speckled with brown, laid one at a time in the nests of other songbirds.

Range: Breeds from British Columbia, central Saskatchewan, central Ontario, Quebec, and Newfoundland southward throughout United States except extreme Southeast and Florida. Winters in central and southern part of breeding range as well as in Florida.

Cowbirds are brood parasites, laying their eggs in the nests of other birds and leaving them to the care of foster parents. Unlike parasitic Old World cuckoos, which lay eggs closely resembling those of a host species, cowbirds lay eggs in the nests of more than 200 other species, most smaller than themselves. Some host species eject the unwanted egg, others lay down a new nest lining over it, but most rear the young cowbird as one of their own. The young cowbird grows quickly at the expense of the young of the host, pushing them out of the nest or taking most of the food. It has been suggested that cowbirds became parasitic because they followed roving herds of bison and had no time to stop to nest.

---

387, 546 **Orchard Oriole**
*Icterus spurius*

Description: 7″ (18 cm). Bluebird-sized. Adult male has *chestnut body* and *black head, back, wings, and tail.* Female yellow-green; immature male similar to female, but has *black throat.*

Voice: A rapid musical warble, somewhat like that of Purple Finch, but not as rich in quality.

Habitat: Orchards, shade trees in parks and gardens, and scattered trees along lakes and streams.

Nesting: 4–6 whitish eggs, with purple scrawls, in a woven, pouch-shaped nest of vegetable fibers and grass, suspended from the forked branch of a tree or bush.

Range: Breeds from Manitoba, Wisconsin, Michigan, Ontario, New York, and central New England south to southern United States and west to Dakotas, Nebraska, Colorado, and Texas. Winters in tropics.

Southeastern Louisiana seems to be the heart of this oriole's nesting range since the highest densities have been recorded there. At one locality there were nearly 20 nests in a single live oak, and at another locality 114 nests were found on a seven-acre tract, with 80 in oaks.

491 **Hooded Oriole**
*Icterus cucullatus*

Description: 7–7¾″ (18–20 cm). Male *orange,* with black wings crossed with 2 white bars; black tail, and *black throat and upper breast.* Bill thin and curved; tail long and graduated. Female olive-gray above, olive-yellow below, with 2 white wing bars. Yearling male looks like female, but has black throat. See Altamira Oriole.

Voice: Series of whistles, chatters, and warbles.

Habitat: Originally streamside growth, but has adapted to tree plantations, city parks, and suburban areas with palm or eucalyptus trees and shrubbery.

Nesting: 3–5 white eggs, blotched with dark brown and purple, in a basket of plant fibers with entrance at top, hanging from palm fronds or the branches of eucalyptus or other trees.

Range: Breeds from central California, Nevada, central Arizona, southern New Mexico, and southern Texas southward. A few winter in southern California and southern Texas.

Probably the most common breeding orioles in southern Texas, these trusting birds often visit ranches and suburban areas for food. They are largely insectivorous but take fruit when it is available. This species is heavily parasitized by the Bronzed Cowbird. Most Hooded Oriole nests contain one or more eggs of this brood parasite.

494 **Spot-breasted Oriole**
*Icterus pectoralis*

Description: 8″ (20 cm). Bright orange with black throat, wings, and tail; white patches on wings; *black spots on sides of breast.*

Voice: Like that of other orioles—loud, varied, and continuous.

Habitat: Open country with scattered trees, orchards, gardens, and parks.
Nesting: 4 whitish eggs, with black scrawls, in a woven basket nest of palm fibers or other vegetable matter.
Range: Resident from southern Mexico to northern Costa Rica. Introduced around Miami, Florida.

This handsome oriole, a native of Mexico, was first reported in the Miami area in 1949, where it was probably introduced from escaped captives. It has since been found in Florida from Homestead to Fort Lauderdale and appears to be thriving.

---

492 **Altamira Oriole**
**"Lichtenstein's Oriole"**
*Icterus gularis*

Description: 9″ (23 cm). Robin-sized. Bright orange-yellow with black face and throat, upper back, wings, and tail. Similar to Hooded Oriole but larger, with heavier bill and *orange-yellow shoulders*. Male and female look alike.
Voice: Series of loud whistles and harsh chatters.
Habitat: Forest and scattered groves of tall trees, especially near water.
Nesting: 3 or 4 purple-streaked whitish eggs, often in a cylindrical or bag-shaped nest up to 2′ (about 60 cm) long, woven of tough fibers and suspended from a branch.
Range: Resident in Rio Grande Valley of extreme southern Texas.

The best places to see this very local species north of the Mexican border are the Brownsville region and the Santa Ana Wildlife Refuge. Although mainly found in the dense foliage of tall forest trees, the Altamira Oriole builds a conspicuous nest suspended far out on a slender, drooping limb, safe from most predators. It varies a diet of insects and spiders with fruits such as figs and berries.

---

502 **Audubon's Oriole**
**"Black-headed Oriole"**
*Icterus graduacauda*

Description: 9″ (23 cm). Robin-sized. Male *greenish yellow with black head,* wings, and tail. Females slightly duller and smaller. Immatures lack black on head.

Voice: 3-syllable warble, one of the sweetest, most melodious songs of any oriole.

Habitat: Wet thickets in woodlands, forest openings, and tangles near water.

Nesting: 4 whitish eggs, with black scrawls, in a woven and partly hanging nest made of fresh green grass. Nests are often found in mesquite; less often in hackberry, ebony, persimmon, and other trees.

Range: Resident from southern Texas to northern Guatemala.

This oriole appears to be the least known of the family in the United States, probably due to its retiring habits. It keeps well within foliage or under the forest canopy. It feeds extensively on wild fruits, especially hackberries. In Texas and Mexico these birds travel in pairs, even outside the nesting season.

---

386, 493, 545 **Northern Oriole**
**including "Baltimore Oriole"**
**and "Bullock's Oriole"**
*Icterus galbula*

Description: 7–8½″ (18–22 cm). Eastern male, formerly "Baltimore Oriole," has black head, back, wings, and tail; orange breast, rump, and shoulder patch. Eastern female olive-brown with dull yellow-orange underparts; 2 dull-white wing bars. Western male, formerly "Bullock's Oriole," similar to eastern male, but has orange cheeks and eyebrow and large white wing patch. Western female has whitish underparts.

Voice: Clear and flute-like whistled single or double notes in short, distinct phrases with much individual variation.

Habitat: Deciduous woodlands and shade trees. Before the tree's decline, the American elm was a favorite nesting site for the eastern bird.

Nesting: 4–6 grayish eggs, spotted and scrawled with dark brown and black. Nest a well-woven pendant bag of plant fibers, bark, and string suspended from tip of a branch.

Range: Breeds from British Columbia east to Nova Scotia, and south throughout most of United States. Winters in tropics.

For many decades the western populations of this bird ("Bullock's Oriole") were thought to be a separate species from the eastern populations, which were called the "Baltimore Oriole." When trees were planted on the Great Plains, the two forms extended their ranges and met. Despite the differences in their appearance, it was found that they interbreed, and most birds in the central plains are hybrids, so the birds were combined into a single species. Now it seems that in some places the birds are choosing mates of their own type; soon these birds may be considered separate species again.

## FAMILY FRINGILLIDAE
Finches

145 species: Worldwide. Sixteen species breed in North America. These are small to medium-sized birds with conical bills and often brightly colored plumage. Some species wear various shades of red, while others are yellow.

Outside the nesting season they are sociable, and often travel in flocks. Many nest in northern areas, entering the United States in large numbers only when their usual food supply fails them.

453, 482 **Pine Grosbeak**
*Pinicola enucleator*

Description: 8–10″ (20–25 cm). A large plump finch. Stubby, strongly curved black bill. *Male has dull rose-red body,* with dark streaking on back, dark wings with 2 white wing bars; dusky, notched tail. *Juvenile male dull pinkish red* on head and rump, with gray body. Females similar to first-year males in pattern, with *dull mustard head* and rump markings.

Voice: A 3-note whistle similar to that of Greater Yellowlegs.

Habitat: Coniferous forests.

Nesting: 2–5 pale blue-green, blotched eggs in a bulky nest of grasses, rootlets, and moss lined with hair; nest placed low in a coniferous tree, usually no more than 10 to 12′ (3 to 4 m) from the ground.

Range: Breeds from Alaska east to Newfoundland and Nova Scotia, and south in western mountains to California and Arizona. Winters south to Dakotas and New York, occasionally farther. Also in Eurasia.

Largest of the northern finches, the Pine Grosbeak is less common than the Pine Siskin or the redpolls. When these birds do appear their preference for the seeds and fruit of trees such as mountain ash and cedar makes them more conspicuous than their smaller relatives. They are very tame and slow moving, allowing close approach. On their northern breeding grounds they avoid unbroken forests and frequent mainly brushy clearings and forest edges.

463, 484 **Purple Finch**
*Carpodacus purpureus*

Description: 5½–6½″ (14–17 cm). Sparrow-sized, but with a thicker bill. *Male dull rosy-red,* more raspberry than purple, *especially on head and rump.* Female and young heavily streaked with dull brown and have *bold, pale eyebrow.* Similar to House Finch but duller, with red coloration not concentrated on crown and breast. Female House Finch more finely streaked and lacks line over eye.

Voice: Rich musical warble. Call a distinctive *tick* as it flies.

Habitat: Mixed and coniferous woodlands; ornamental conifers in gardens.

Nesting: 4 or 5 blue-green eggs, spotted at the larger end with dark brown, in a well-made cup of grasses and twigs, often lined with hair and placed in a conifer.

Range: Breeds from British Columbia east to Newfoundland, southward in western mountains to California and from eastern Minnesota to West Virginia. Winters south to U.S.–Mexico border.

Purple Finches are numerous and conspicuous during spring migration; for a few weeks each year one can hear the rich, spirited song of the brightly colored males. In winter they visit feeding stations in large numbers, showing a fondness for sunflower seeds.

462, 483 **House Finch**
*Carpodacus mexicanus*

Description: 5–6″ (13–15 cm). Sparrow-sized. Male streaked brown with bright red breast, forehead, eyebrow, and rump. Female lacks red; similar to female Purple Finch, but more finely streaked and without contrasting stripes on face. Immature male often orangish or yellowish on head and breast, rather than red.

Voice: Clear warble like that of Purple Finch, but weaker and less musical; ends with *zeee.* Sings from a high tree, antenna, or similar post for long periods. Call a *chirp.*

Habitat: Cities and residential areas in East; also desert brush in Texas and Far West.

Nesting: 4 or 5 pale blue eggs, lightly spotted with black, in a well-made cup of grass in a bush, thicket, or natural cavity, or on a building.

Range: This western species occurred naturally east to Nebraska and Texas. Introduced in the East, it is now established in much of the eastern half of the continent.

The eastern population of this species is descended from cage birds released near New York City in the 1940s. For years the birds barely survived on Long Island, but they then spread in suburban areas. In the late 1960s and 1970s they finally established themselves in urban New York, where their musical song and bright colors add a cheerful touch. The eating habits of these city birds are not well known, but they probably subsist on the berries of ornamental shrubs and on food put out for the more abundant House Sparrows.

## 486 Red Crossbill
*Loxia curvirostra*

Description: 5¼–6½" (13–17 cm). Sparrow-sized. *Mandibles crossed* at tips. Male dusky brick red. Female gray tinged with dull green, brightest on rump. White-winged Crossbill has 2 white wing bars.

Voice: Song *chipa-chipa-chipa, chee-chee-chee-chee;* also a sharp *kip-kip-kip.*

Habitat: Coniferous forests; visits ornamental evergreens in winter.

Nesting: 3 or 4 pale blue-green eggs, lightly spotted with brown, in a shallow saucer of bark strips, grass, and roots lined with moss and plant down and placed near the end of a conifer branch.

Range: Breeds from southern Alaska, Manitoba, Quebec, and Newfoundland south in West to northern Nicaragua; in eastern United States to Wisconsin and North Carolina (mountains). Winters irregularly south to Gulf Coast. Also in Eurasia.

These birds are sporadic visitors in winter, appearing in large numbers, then not appearing for several years. Such winter flocks often travel great distances; many of the birds that visit New England come all the way from the Rocky Mountains. Crossbills feed exclusively on conifer seeds, the crossed mandibles enabling them to extract seeds from the cones. Because their chosen food is available in winter, they commonly begin nesting as early as January, but they have been found nesting in every month of the year.

---

## 487 White-winged Crossbill
*Loxia leucoptera*

Description: 6–6½″ (15–17 cm). Size of a medium-sized sparrow. *Mandibles crossed* at tips. Male raspberry-pink; females grayer, without pink. Both sexes have 2 white wing bars.

Voice: Like that of Red Crossbill but a softer *chiff-chiff-chiff.* Song a series of sweet, canary-like warbles and trills.

Habitat: Coniferous forests.

Nesting: 2–4 pale blue eggs, spotted with dark brown, laid in a shallow saucer of bark strips, grass, and roots lined with moss and plant down, placed near end of a conifer branch.

Range: Breeds from Alaska and northern Quebec south to Newfoundland and British Columbia. In winter, south to Carolinas and Oregon. Also in Eurasia.

Like the Red Crossbills, these birds use their crossed mandibles to extract seeds from the cones of pines and spruces. Their winter wanderings depend largely on the supply of conifer seeds; in years when seeds are abundant in the northern forests the birds tend to remain there. When the supply fails they come south in large numbers and may often be seen in quiet flocks, clinging to clusters of cones like little parrots. Their travels sometimes take them far to the south of their breeding range, and the species has managed to establish itself in the pine forests of Hispaniola in the West Indies.

481 **Common Redpoll**
*Carduelis flammea*

Description: 5–5½″ (13–14 cm). Smaller than a sparrow. Pale, brown-streaked, with *bright red cap* and black chin. Male has pink breast.

Voice: Twittering trill; call a soft rattle.

Habitat: Tundra and dwarf arctic birch in summer; brushy pastures, open thickets, and weedy fields in winter.

Nesting: 4–6 pale green eggs, spotted with red-brown, in a well-made cup of grass, moss, and twigs lined with plant down, and placed in a low willow or birch.

Range: Breeds from Alaska and northern Quebec south to British Columbia, Newfoundland, and Magdalen Islands. Winters irregularly south to California, Oklahoma, and Carolinas. Also in Eurasia.

A stand of winter weeds visited by a flock of these energetic little birds is a scene of feverish activity as they tear dried flower stalks apart and rush to the ground to pick up the seeds. They spend much time on the ground, often in dense stands of weeds, and are therefore easier to overlook than the more arboreal goldfinches and Pine Siskins.

Tame and trusting, they allow close approach; unfortunately this trait often causes them to fall prey to predators.

**Hoary Redpoll**
*Carduelis hornemanni*

Description: 4½–5½″ (11–14 cm). Smaller than a sparrow. Similar to Common Redpoll but slightly paler, with smaller bill and unstreaked rump and undertail coverts.

Voice: Series of metallic *chips* given in flight; soft twittering calls when feeding on ground. Calls sharper than those of Common Redpoll.

Habitat: Weedy pastures and roadsides in winter, tundra in summer.

Nesting: 5 or 6 pale blue eggs, lightly spotted with brown, in a feather-lined cup of grass and shreds of bark, concealed under a rock or a clump of tundra vegetation.

Range: Breeds along coasts of Arctic Ocean, wandering southward in winter to much of Canada and northern United States.

The Hoary Redpoll is generally found farther north and on more open tundra than the Common Redpoll. The two have at times been considered a single species, but they are now known to nest side by side, without interbreeding, in parts of Canada and Alaska.

464 **Pine Siskin**
*Carduelis pinus*

Description: 4½–5″ (11–13 cm). Dark streaked finch, with notched tail and small patches of yellow in wings and tail. Usually seen in flocks, which have distinctive flight pattern: Birds alternately bunch up and disperse in undulating flight.

Voice: Distinctive rising *bzzzzzt.* Song like that of a hoarse goldfinch.

Habitat: Coniferous and mixed woodlands, alder thickets, and brushy pastures.

Nesting: 3 or 4 pale green eggs, lightly speckled with dark brown and black, in a shallow saucer of bark, twigs, and moss lined with plant down and feathers, placed in a conifer.

Range: Breeds from southern Alaska, Mackenzie, Quebec, and Newfoundland south to California, Arizona, New Mexico, Texas, Great Lakes region, and northern New England. In winter wanders southward throughout United States.

The Pine Siskin is another of the northern finches whose winter visits to the United States occur mainly in years when the seed crop has failed in the boreal forests. In some years large flocks may appear as far south as Florida. Their principal foods are the seeds of hemlocks, alders, birches, and cedars. Like most northern finches, they are also fond of salt, and can be found along highways that have been salted to melt snow.

539 **Lesser Goldfinch**
*Carduelis psaltria*

Description: 3½–4″ (9–10 cm). Male has *black back* and black crown, white markings on black wing and tail, with *bright yellow underparts.* Female similar to American Goldfinch but smaller, with *dark rump.* Immature similar to female, but with greener underparts.

Voice: Song a rapid medley of twittering notes. Calls include plaintive *tee-yee?* and *cheeo?*

Habitat: Oak savannas, woodlands, suburban gardens.

Nesting: 4–5 pale blue eggs in a twiggy nest, placed in a bush or low tree.

Range: Resident from Washington, Oregon, and northern Nevada east to northern Colorado and Texas.

Lesser Goldfinches feed on dandelion seeds and raise their young on soft unripe seeds. They adjust the time and place of their breeding to the presence of this staple food. Their Old World cousins, the Pine Siskins, goldfinches, serins, and canaries, have been kept as cage birds for centuries, the males singing incessantly all year except during the molt period.

503, 548 **American Goldfinch**
*Carduelis tristis*

Description: 4½–5″ (11–13 cm). Smaller than a sparrow. Breeding male *bright yellow* with white rump, *black forehead, white edges on black wings and tail,* and yellow at bend of wing. Female and winter male duller and grayer, with black wings, tail, and white wing bars. Travels in flocks; undulating flight.

Voice: Bright *per-chick-o-ree,* also rendered as *potato-chips,* delivered in flight and coinciding with each undulation.

Habitat: Brushy thickets, weedy grasslands, and nearby trees.

Nesting: 4 or 5 pale blue eggs in a well-made cup of grass, bark strips, and plant down placed in the upright fork of a small sapling or shrub.

Range: Breeds from southern British Columbia east to Newfoundland, and south to California, Utah, southern Colorado, central Oklahoma, Arkansas, and Carolinas. Winters in much of United States.

This familiar and common species is often called the "Wild Canary." Since the birds' main food is seeds, nesting does not begin until midsummer or late summer, when weed seeds are available. Thus goldfinches remain in flocks until well past the time when other species have formed pairs and are nesting. Because they nest so late, only a single brood is raised each season. In the winter they gather in large flocks, often with other finches such as redpolls and Pine Siskins.

454, 501 **Evening Grosbeak**
*Coccothraustes vespertinus*

Description: 7½–8½" (19–21 cm). Starling-sized, stocky finch with very large, *pale greenish or yellowish conical bill.* Male has brown head shading to *yellow on lower back,* rump, and underparts; bright yellow forehead and eyebrow; *bold white wing patches.* Female similar but grayer.

Voice: Song a series of short, musical whistles. Call note similar to chirp of House Sparrow, but louder and more ringing.

Habitat: Nests in coniferous forests; visits deciduous woodlands and suburban areas in winter.

Nesting: 3 or 4 pale blue-green eggs, lightly speckled with dark brown, gray, and olive, in a shallow, loose cup of twigs lined with rootlets and placed in a conifer.

Range: Breeds from British Columbia east to Nova Scotia, and south to northern New England, Minnesota, Mexico (in mountains), and California. Winters south to southern California, Texas, and South Carolina.

This grosbeak formerly bred no farther east than Minnesota, but food available at bird feeders may have enabled more birds to survive the winter, and the species now breeds east to the Atlantic. Like most of the northern finches, however, these birds are more numerous in some years than in others. In winter they feed in flocks mainly on the seeds of box elders or, at feeders, on sunflower seeds. In spring the outer coating of the bill peels off, exposing the blue-green color beneath.

**Family Passeridae**
Old World Sparrows

37 species: Widespread in the Old World, especially in Africa. Represented in North America by only two species, both of them introduced. These are finch-like birds, with stout conical bills and short legs. They are highly gregarious, and often roost in large flocks.

---

396, 399 **House Sparrow**
*Passer domesticus*

Description: 5–6½″ (13–17 cm). Male has *black throat,* white cheeks, and chestnut nape; gray crown and rump. Female and young are streaked dull brown above, dingy white below, with pale eyebrow.
Voice: Shrill, monotonous, noisy chirping.
Habitat: Cities, towns, and agricultural areas.
Nesting: 5 or 6 white eggs, lightly speckled with brown, in a loose mass of grass, feathers, strips of paper, string, and similar debris placed in a man-made or natural cavity. 2 to 3 broods a season. Sometimes builds a globular nest in a tree.
Range: Introduced and resident throughout temperate North America. Native to Eurasia and North Africa, and introduced on all continents and many islands.

Wherever this species occurs it is intimately associated with man, as its scientific name *domesticus* suggests. The entire North American population is descended from a few birds released in New York City's Central Park in 1850. These birds found an unoccupied niche—the many towns and farms of the settled parts of the country—and quickly multiplied. As so often happens, introduced species can become a problem, and the House Sparrow is no exception. Because they compete for food and nest sites, some native species have suffered. Although they consume insects and weed seeds, they may do considerable damage to crops.

421 **Eurasian Tree Sparrow**
*Passer montanus*

Description: 6″ (15 cm). Streaked brown above, dull white below. *Crown chocolate brown,* throat black, *cheek white with prominent black spot.* Sexes alike. Male House Sparrow similar, but has gray crown and lacks black spot on cheek.
Voice: Loud chirping, similar to that of House Sparrow.
Habitat: City parks, suburban areas, and farmland.
Nesting: 5 brown-spotted buff eggs in a tree cavity, bird box, or hole in a wall.
Range: Introduced around St. Louis, Missouri, in 1870. Native to Europe and much of Asia.

This introduced species differs from its relative, the House Sparrow, in that the sexes are alike. It is much less aggressive and quarrelsome, and it is more gregarious, often assembling in larger flocks. Altogether, the Eurasian Tree Sparrow is a more attractive bird, both in appearance and behavior. These birds sometimes visit grainfields and feed on corn, oats, and wheat, but they also consume many injurious weed seeds and, to a lesser extent, insects.

# LIST OF ACCIDENTAL SPECIES

Accidental species are rare birds that do not breed regularly or occur annually in North America, but whose presence has been accepted by the American Ornithologists' Union. The following list includes only those species that have been either collected or photographed in the area covered by this guide at least once and that have been accepted by the American Ornithologists' Union; species that have been observed but never collected or photographed are not included. The list is broken down into the five following categories, based on the regions they come from:

*Oceanic:* Coming mainly from the southern oceans and usually but not always driven to our shores by tropical storms.

*Old World:* Coming mainly from western Europe or eastern Asia, and occurring mainly along the East Coast.

*Caribbean:* Coming from the West Indies and various small islands throughout the Caribbean Sea, and found in our area mainly in southern Florida and along the Gulf Coast.

*Central American:* Species that wander north into extreme southern Texas.

*South American:* Several South American species that have wandered to eastern North America, usually along the Atlantic and Gulf coasts.

Oceanic

Black-browed Albatross, *Diomedea melanophris*
Yellow-nosed Albatross, *Diomedea chlororhynchos*
Black-capped Petrel, *Pterodroma hasitata*
Mottled Petrel, *Pterodroma inexpectata*
South Trinidad Petrel, *Pterodroma arminjoniana*
Little Shearwater, *Puffinus assimilis*
White-faced Storm-Petrel, *Pelagodroma marina*
British Storm-Petrel, *Hydrobates pelagicus*
Band-rumped Storm-Petrel, *Oceanodroma castro*
Red-billed Tropicbird, *Phaethon aethereus*
Red-footed Booby, *Sula sula*
Lesser Frigatebird, *Fregata ariel*

Old World

Little Egret, *Egretta garzetta*
Western Reef-Heron, *Egretta gularis*
Pink-footed Goose, *Anser brachyrhynchus*
Smew, *Mergus albellus*
Common Buzzard, *Buteo buteo*
White-tailed Eagle, *Haliaeetus albicilla*
Eurasian Kestrel, *Falco tinnunculus*
Corn Crake, *Crex crex*
Paint-billed Crake, *Neocrex erythrops*
Spotted Rail, *Pardirallus maculatus*
Eurasian Coot, *Fulica atra*
Common Crane, *Grus grus*
Eurasian Lapwing, *Vanellus vanellus*
Greater Golden-Plover, *Pluvialis apricaria*
Common Ringed Plover, *Charadrius hiaticula*
Spotted Redshank, *Tringa erythropus*
Wood Sandpiper, *Tringa glareola*
Slender-billed Curlew, *Numenius tenuirostris*
Eurasian Curlew, *Numenius arquata*
Black-tailed Godwit, *Limosa limosa*
Jack Snipe, *Lymnocryptes minimus*
Eurasian Woodcock, *Scolopax rusticola*
Large-billed Tern, *Phaetusa simplex*
White-winged Tern, *Chlidonias leucopterus*
Common Cuckoo, *Cuculus canorus*

Fieldfare, *Turdus pilaris*
Redwing, *Turdus iliacus*
Brambling, *Fringilla montifringilla*

Caribbean

White-cheeked Pintail, *Anas bahamensis*
Caribbean Coot, *Fulica caribaea*
Scaly-naped Pigeon, *Columba squamosa*
Zenaida Dove, *Zenaida aurita*
Ruddy Quail-Dove, *Geotrygon montana*
Key West Quail-Dove, *Geotrygon chrysia*
Antillean Palm Swift, *Tachornis phoenicobia*
Antillean Crested Hummingbird, *Orthorhynchus cristatus*
Cuban Emerald, *Chlorostildon ricordii*
Bahama Woodstar, *Calliphlox evelynae*
La Sagra's Flycatcher, *Myiarchus sagrae*
Stolid Flycatcher, *Myiarchus stolidus*
Loggerhead Kingbird, *Tyrannus caudiifasciatus*
Cuban Martin, *Progne cryptoleuca*
Bahama Swallow, *Callichelidon cyaneoviridis*
Bahama Mockingbird, *Mimus gundlachii*
Thick-billed Vireo, *Vireo crassirostris*
Gray-crowned Yellowthroat, *Geothlypis poliocephalus*
Bananaquit, *Coereba flaveola*
Black-faced Grassquit, *Tiaris bicolor*
Tawny-shouldered Blackbird, *Agelaius humeralis*

Central American

Jabiru, *Jabiru mycteria*
Hook-billed Kite, *Chondrohierax uncinatus*
Roadside Hawk, *Buteo magnirostris*
Double-striped Thick-knee, *Burhinus bistriatus*
Ruddy Ground Dove, *Columbina talpacoti*
Red-crowned Parrot, *Amazona viridigenalis*
Mottled Owl, *Ciccaba virgata*
White-collared Swift, *Streptoprocne zonaris*
Gray-breasted Martin, *Progne chalybea*
Clay-colored Robin, *Turdus grayi*
Rufous-backed Robin, *Turdus rufopalliatus*

| | |
|---|---|
| | Crescent-chested Warbler, *Parula superciliosa* |
| | Crimson-collared Grosbeak, *Rhodothraupis celaeno* |
| | Blue Bunting, *Cyanocompsa parellina* |
| | Orange-breasted Bunting, *Passerina leclancherii* |
| | White-collared Seedeater, *Sporophila torqueola* |
| South American | Scarlet Ibis, *Eudocimus ruber* |
| | Band-tailed Gull, *Larus belcheri* |
| | Variegated Flycatcher, *Empidonomus varius* |
| | Fork-tailed Flycatcher, *Muscivora tyrannus* |
| | Southern Martin, *Progne elegans* |

# BIRD-WATCHING

Bird-watching, or birding, is a hobby that can be made as inexpensive or as costly as one wishes. One can even begin without purchasing anything except a field guide, relying on eyes and on memory. But sooner or later a birder will want to buy that most basic piece of equipment, a pair of binoculars.

In selecting binoculars, a major consideration is weight; a lightweight pair is better for hours of continuous use than a heavier one. Choose a pair with an adjustable right eyepiece and central focusing; this will permit you to adjust the focus quickly from a nearby sparrow to a distant soaring hawk. In general, the best magnification will depend on how steadily you can hold your field glasses. Seven- or eight-power glasses will provide adequate magnification, but after years of experience, and if you are very steady-handed, you may be able to use a pair of ten-power glasses. To ensure adequate light, the objective (front) lens should have a diameter in millimeters of at least five times the magnification. Thus, a seven-power binocular should have an objective lens diameter of not less than 35 millimeters (7 × 35), an eight-power pair should have an objective diameter of 40 millimeters (8 × 40), and so on. A pair of binoculars with an objective wider than this ratio will let in more light. This may be useful in a dimly lit forest, but on an open, strongly illuminated beach there may be too much glare to allow you to see the birds well. Then, too, glasses with wider objectives are generally heavier than those of the same power with a smaller objective. The best advice on binoculars is to buy the best you can afford. Binoculars suitable for brief use at the opera or racetrack may cause eyestrain and fatigue when used for hours at a time under the varying conditions of an all-day field trip.

Most experienced birders also purchase a telescope, which, if mounted on a sturdy tripod or gunstock, is an excellent way to view and identify distant shorebirds and water birds. Many of the considerations that apply to binoculars apply here. Choose a good telescope, one that will last for years. A suitable telescope may have adjustable eyepieces, offering various magnifications such as 15-, 20-, 40-, and 60-power. At higher magnifications—above about 30-power—one may have trouble with vibrations caused by the wind or with distortion of the image by shimmering heat waves.

Another useful piece of equipment is a pocket notebook. It is wise to jot down a description of unfamiliar birds immediately after observing them. Not only will this enable you to remember critical field marks, but it will train you to notice small but important details that might otherwise be overlooked. You might also record other observations, such as numbers of birds seen, dates of their arrival and departure, peak numbers of migrants, and interesting behavioral or ecological details.

Sooner or later you may want to preserve these notes in a more permanent form, using larger, bound notebooks or a system of file cards. Notes can be grouped according to date, locality, or species, or by whatever arrangement best suits your needs and purposes. A gradually increasing store of notes is a valuable record not only of past field trips, but of your own steadily growing knowledge of birds.

# GLOSSARY

**Accidental** A species that has appeared in a given area only a very few times and whose normal range is in another area. Also used as an adjective.

**Auriculars** Feathers covering the ear opening and the area immediately around it; often distinctively colored. Also called ear coverts.

**Boreal forest** The belt of coniferous forest stretching from Alaska to Newfoundland and across northern Eurasia; also called the taiga.

**Breeding plumage** A coat of feathers worn by many birds during the breeding season; often more brightly colored than the winter plumage.

**Casual** A species that has appeared in a given area somewhat more frequently than an accidental, but whose normal range is in another area. Also used as an adjective.

**Cere** A fleshy, featherless area surrounding the nostrils of hawks, falcons, pigeons, and a few other groups of birds.

**Circumpolar** Of or inhabiting the Arctic (or Antarctic) regions in both the Eastern and Western hemispheres.

**Clutch** A set of eggs laid by one bird.

**Colonial** Nesting in groups (or colonies) rather than in isolated pairs.

**Cosmopolitan** Worldwide in distribution, or at least occurring in all continents except Antarctica.

**Coverts** Small feathers that overlie or cover the bases of the large flight feathers of the wings and tail, or that cover a particular area or structure (e.g., ear coverts).

**Crest** A tuft of elongated feathers on the crown or nape.

**Crown** The top of the head.

**Cryptic** Serving to conceal.

**Eclipse plumage** A dull-colored coat of feathers acquired immediately after the breeding season by most ducks and worn for a few weeks; it is followed in males by a more brightly colored plumage.

**Ecosystem** An ecological unit consisting of interrelationships between animals, plants, and the physical environment.

**Eyebrow** A conspicuous stripe of color above, but not through, the eye.

**Eye stripe** A stripe that runs horizontally from the base of the bill through the eye; also called the eye line.

**Field mark** A characteristic of color, pattern, or structure useful in distinguishing a species in the field.

**Flight feathers** The long, stiff feathers of the wings and tail, used during flight. The flight feathers of the wings are divided into primaries, secondaries, and tertials. See also Rectrix.

**Frontal shield** A fleshy, featherless, and often brightly colored area on the forehead of jacanas, moorhens, gallinules, and a few other birds.

Gorget A patch of brilliantly colored feathers on the chin or throat of certain birds, such as male hummingbirds.

Immature A young bird no longer under parental care but not yet wearing an adult plumage.

Juvenile (*adj.* juvenal) A bird wearing its first coat of feathers, often molted into a first-winter plumage within a few weeks after the bird leaves the nest.

Lek A place where males of some species of birds, such as certain grouse and the European Ruff, gather and perform courtship displays in a group, rather than courting females individually and in isolation from one another; females visit a lek to mate but generally build their nests elsewhere.

Local Occurring in relatively small, restricted areas within the range, rather than commonly and widespread throughout the range. Birds whose occurrence is local usually have highly specialized habitat requirements.

Lore (*pl.* lores) The small area between the eye and the base of the bill, sometimes distinctively colored.

Mandible One of the two parts of a bird's bill, termed the upper mandible and the lower mandible.

Mantle A term used to describe the back of a bird together with the upper surface of the wings when these areas are of one color.

Molt The process of shedding and replacing feathers; usually occurs after breeding but before the autumn migration. In many species there is another molt in spring or late winter.

Morph One or more distinctive plumages seen in certain species; see Phase.

Mustache A colored streak running from the base of the bill back along the side of the throat.

Naris (*pl.* nares) The external nostril; in birds located near the base of the upper mandible.

Pelagic Of or inhabiting the open ocean.

Phase One or more distinctive plumages seen in certain species, such as the Eastern Screech-Owl and some hawks and herons, irrespective of age, sex, or season. Also called a morph.

Plume A feather that is larger, longer, or of a different color than the feathers around it, generally used in displays.

Primaries The outermost and longest flight feathers on a bird's wing. Primaries vary in number from 9 to 11 per wing, but always occur in a fixed number in any particular species.

Race A geographical population of a species that is different in appearance from other populations; a subspecies.

Range The geographical area or areas normally inhabited by a species.

Raptor A bird of prey.

Rectrix (*pl.* rectrices) One of the long flight feathers of the tail.

Resident Remaining in one place all year; nonmigratory.

Riparian Of or inhabiting the banks of rivers or streams.

Scapulars A group of feathers along the side of the back and overlapping the folded wing.

**Scrape** A shallow depression on the ground made by a bird to serve as a nest.

**Secondaries** The large flight feathers located in a series along the rear edge of the wing, immediately inward from the primaries.

**Shoulder** The point where the wing meets the body, as in the Red-shouldered Hawk. The term is also loosely applied to the bend of the wing when this area is distinctively colored, as it is in the Red-winged Blackbird.

**Spatulate** Spoon-shaped or shovel-shaped; used to describe the bills of certain birds, such as the Roseate Spoonbill and Northern Shoveler.

**Speculum** A distinctively colored area on the wing of a bird, especially the metallic patch on the secondaries of some ducks.

**Subalpine** Of or pertaining to the stunted forest or other vegetation immediately below the treeless, barren alpine zone on high mountains.

**Subspecies** A geographical population of a species that is different in appearance from other populations of that species; also called a race.

**Taiga** The belt of coniferous forest covering the northern part of North America and Eurasia; also called the boreal forest.

**Tarsus** The lower, usually featherless part of a bird's leg.

**Territory** An area defended by the male, by both members of a pair, or by an unmated bird.

**Tertials** The innermost flight feathers on a bird's wing, immediately adjacent to the body. They are often regarded simply as the innermost secondaries. Also called tertiaries.

**Window** A translucent area in the wing of certain birds such as the Red-shouldered Hawk, visible from below in flight.

**Wing bar** A crosswise stripe on the folded wing, formed by the tips of the wing coverts.

**Wing stripe** A conspicuous stripe running the length of the open wing.

**Winter plumage** A coat of feathers worn by many birds during the nonbreeding season, and often less brightly colored than the breeding plumage.

# CONSERVATION STATUS OF EASTERN BIRDS

Federal laws in the United States and Canada prohibit the taking or molesting of birds or their nests, eggs, or young, other than those species that damage property or agriculture or that are covered by hunting regulations. In addition, rare or endangered species are protected by special measures and by bird management agencies. Increasingly, states are also passing conservation measures and are studying the status of their bird populations with the aim of protecting this precious natural heritage. In our species accounts we have noted those birds that have a special conservation status. But it should be understood that the status of birds changes and that they may be differently categorized by different authorities.

**Unprotected Birds** Two introduced species, the European Starling and the House Sparrow, have become so numerous and widespread that they are not protected in the United States or Canada. A few other species, including the Rock Dove and members of the blackbird family, may damage crops or other birds and are therefore not fully protected in some areas.

**Game Birds** These may be hunted during an open season regulated by the various states and provinces. Information on limitations, licenses, and so forth can be secured from local agencies.

**Threatened or Endangered Birds** The populations of the following birds are threatened or endangered. Birders should take care not to disturb these birds or their nests or to damage their environment.

Brown Pelican, *Pelecanus occidentalis*
Wood Stork, *Mycteria americana*
Snail Kite, *Rostrhamus sociabilis*
Bald Eagle, *Haliaeetus leucocephalus*
Crested Caracara, *Caracara plancus*
Peregrine Falcon, *Falco peregrinus*
Whooping Crane, *Grus americana*
Piping Plover, *Charadrius melodus*
Eskimo Curlew, *Numenius borealis*
Least Tern, *Sternum antillarum*
Red-cockaded Woodpecker, *Picoides borealis*
Scrub Jay (in Florida), *Aphelocoma coerulescens*
Black-capped Vireo, *Vireo atricapillus*
Bachman's Warbler, *Vermivora bachmanii*
Golden-cheeked Warbler, *Dendroica chrysoparia*
Kirtland's Warbler, *Dendroica kirtlandii*

## PICTURE CREDITS

The numbers in parentheses are plate numbers. Some photographers have pictures under agency names, which appear in boldface. Photographers hold copyrights to their works.

Robert P. Abrams (78, 81, 82)

Ron Austing (72, 115, 116, 142, 144, 288, 292, 293, 306, 308, 362, 367, 369, 410, 440, 455, 456, 472, 496, 536, 553, 558, 571, 577, 582)

Robert A. Behrstock (301, 361)

Steve Bentsen (284, 337, 389, 398, 492, 546, 586, 591)

Nick Bergkessel (438)

Fred Bruemmer (37, 39, 42, 89, 101, 203, 278)

Gay Bumgarner (298, 463, 474, 545, 548, 592, 613)

Robert Campbell (310)

Priscilla Connell (480)

**Cornell Laboratory of Ornithology**
Lang Elliott (359)
Keith Walton (458)
J. Wiessinger (572)

Sharon Cummings (24, 77, 127, 263, 304, 384, 535, 598, 634)

Rob Curtis/The Early Birder (53, 63, 71, 153, 193, 219, 222, 223, 331, 352, 353, 358, 379, 382, 400, 405, 408, 419, 437, 466, 476, 489, 524, 533, 542, 544, 573, 575, 576, 643)

Mike Danzenbaker (35, 76, 140, 148, 215, 249, 264, 402, 414, 428, 443, 494, 502, 525, 526)

Richard Day (280, 283, 623)

Susan Day (479)

**Dembinsky Photo Associates**
Dan Demspter (580)
Barbara Gerlach (209, 425)
John Gerlach (98, 99, 239, 411)

Doug Locke (617, 621)
Gary Meszaros (43)
Skip Moody (305)
Ted Nelson (363)
Rod Planck (258, 432, 499)
Carl R. Sams (345, 628)
George E. Stewart (611)

Jack Dermid (165, 226, 262, 268, 368, 381)

Larry R. Ditto (9, 164, 172, 346, 372, 401, 433, 599)

Jon Farrar (13, 25, 327, 434)

Todd Fink/Daybreak Imagery (566)

Jeff Foott (7, 10, 134, 137, 143, 155, 170, 271, 275, 299, 344, 465)

Michael H. Francis (605, 630)

Joe Fuhrman (248)

Chuck Gordon (32, 110, 131, 151, 156, 159, 182, 191, 197, 198, 199, 206, 246, 251, 289, 518)

John Heidecker/Nature Photos (22, 108, 149, 174, 371, 601)

John Hendrickson (328, 338)

Greg R. Homel/Natural Elements, Inc. (2, 67, 88, 186, 218, 250, 267, 579)

Isidor Jeklin (449, 519)

Kevin T. Karlson (50, 91, 92, 107, 154, 184, 192, 207, 448, 561, 563, 567, 600, 618)

Robert Y. Kaufman/Yogi, Inc. (95, 102, 130, 175, 309)

Steven C. Kaufman (93, 273)

G.C. Kelley (97, 114, 133, 173, 177, 233, 282, 302, 442, 475)

Ted Kinchloe (404)

Wayne Lankinen (1, 178, 190, 200, 276, 307, 364, 481, 482, 487, 608, 615)

Harold Lindstrom (28, 36, 61, 86, 120, 125, 228, 245, 247, 254, 257, 300, 387, 396, 420, 439, 445, 470, 506, 511, 512, 513, 515, 520, 521, 530)

Kathy Lindstrom (123, 568)

Bates Littlehales (11, 17, 21, 26, 66, 124, 126, 188, 213, 260, 290, 348, 392, 413, 436, 505, 523, 531, 549, 604)

John Martin (640)

Barry W. Mansell (285, 366)

Joe McDonald (431, 552, 642)

Charles W. Melton (118, 145, 150, 162, 168, 196, 227, 240, 427, 570)

Steffan Mittelhauser (297, 503)

C. Allan Morgan (54, 56, 65, 69, 80, 83, 84, 87, 94, 187, 291, 296, 336, 365, 488, 541, 627)

Arthur & Elaine Morris/ Birds As Art (5, 8, 12, 14, 18, 19, 29, 38, 40, 41, 49, 51, 52, 57, 59, 60, 62, 64, 96, 104, 112, 117, 135, 141, 157, 160, 167, 169, 179, 181, 183, 185, 195, 201, 212, 214, 221, 230, 235, 237, 244, 253, 255, 256, 303, 385, 390, 393, 399, 406, 412, 459, 471, 490, 498, 509, 543, 551, 559, 574, 607, 614, 633)

James F. Parnell (3, 58, 236, 238, 277, 403, 417, 461, 468, 560)

**PHOTO/NATS, INC.**
Cortez C. Austin, Jr. (6, 176, 231)
Priscilla Connell (161, 612)
Sam Fried (16, 370, 483, 644)
Dr. Charles Steinmenz, Jr. (631)
David M. Stone (225)
Ed Thurston (386)

Rod Planck (31, 48, 73, 128, 171, 229, 378, 394, 450, 473, 501, 626, 641, 646)

Jean Pollock (295)

Betty Randall (70, 100, 136, 383, 457, 493, 564, 581, 637)

Barbara Reed/John Williams (15)

J.H. Robinson (30, 446, 540, 556, 597)

**ROOT RESOURCES**
Jim Flynn (111, 132, 138)
Ben Goldstein (265)
Anthony Mercieca (360, 397)
Alan G. Nelson (269)
C. Postmus (391, 620)

Johann Schumacher Design (234, 441, 477, 517, 635)

Gregory K. Scott (557)

Ervio Sian (426, 622)

Robert C. Simpson (4, 20, 146, 266, 274, 377, 416, 435, 460, 478, 504, 528, 538, 547, 569)

Robert C. & Melissa Simpson (68, 407, 467)

Arnold Small (90)

Brian E. Small (85, 189, 243, 294, 347, 418, 491, 507, 522, 578, 610, 619, 629, 639)

Hugh P. Smith, Jr. (163, 202, 329, 334, 351, 451, 469, 606, 625)

Mitchell D. Smith (339)

Charles G. Summers, Jr. (241, 341)

Frank S. Todd (55, 350)

Tom J. Ulrich (23, 79,

105, 109, 122, 166, 194, 272, 281, 286, 287, 332, 342, 343, 355, 373, 374, 375, 376, 395, 444, 453, 454, 464, 495, 529, 539, 550, 555, 562, 584, 590, 593, 602, 603, 609, 616, 624, 632)

**VIREO**
Nick and Nora Bowers (565)
R.K. Bowers (424)
R.J. Chandler (208)
Helen Cruickshank (204)
Harry Darrow (44)
T.H. Davis (46)
J.H. Dick (508)
J. Dunning (500)
V. Hasselblad (421)
B. Lasley (534)
R.L. Pitman (74, 75)
R. Ridgely (588)
D. Roby (139)
D. Roby/K. Brink (103)
P.W. Sykes, Jr. (113)
Brian Wheeler (335)
K. Zimmer (447)

Tom Vezo (47, 259, 587)

Mark F. Wallner (129, 152, 210, 211, 217, 242, 354, 415, 422, 430, 452, 510, 516, 532, 537)

Larry West (27, 205, 330, 380, 485, 596, 645)

Gregory J. Winston (279)

Dale & Marian Zimmerman (33, 147, 216, 220, 333, 409, 554, 594, 595, 638)

Paul Zimmerman (340, 349)

Tim Zurowski (34, 45, 106, 119, 121, 158, 180, 224, 232, 252, 261, 270, 356, 357, 388, 423, 429, 462, 484, 486, 497, 514, 527, 583, 585, 589, 636)

# INDEX

Numbers in boldface type refer to plate numbers. Numbers in italic refer to page numbers.

## A

## Y



## Z

## STAFF

Prepared and produced by
Chanticleer Press.

Founding Publisher: Paul Steiner
Publisher: Andrew Stewart
Managing Editor: Edie Locke
Production Manager: Deirdre Duggan Ventry
Art Director: Amanda Wilson
Publishing Assistant: Kelly Beekman
Text Editor: Patricia Fogarty
Consultant: Wayne R. Petersen
Copyeditor: Kathryn Clark
Editorial Assistant: Peggy Grohskopf
Photography Editor: Lori J. Hogan
Drawings and Silhouettes: Paul Singer, Douglas Pratt
Range Maps and Map of North America: Paul Singer
Original series design by
Massimo Vignelli.

Address all editorial inquiries to:
Chanticleer Press
568 Broadway, Suite #1005A
New York, NY 10012
(212) 941-1522

To purchase this book or other National Audubon Society illustrated nature books, please contact:
Alfred A. Knopf, Inc.
201 East 50th Street
New York, NY 10022
(800) 733-3000

NATIONAL AUDUBON SOCIETY
FIELD GUIDE SERIES

Also available in this unique all-color, all-photographic format:

Birds (*Western Region*)

Butterflies

Fishes, Whales, and Dolphins

Fossils

Insects and Spiders

Mammals

Mushrooms

Night Sky

Reptiles and Amphibians

Rocks and Minerals

Seashells

Seashore Creatures

Trees (*Eastern Region*)

Trees (*Western Region*)

Weather

Wildflowers (*Eastern Region*)

Wildflowers (*Western Region*)